BRITISH A
NORMANDY

The popular perception of the performance of British armour in the Normandy campaign in 1944 is one of failure and frustration. Despite overwhelming superiority in numbers, Montgomery's repeated efforts to employ his armour in an offensive manner ended in disappointing stalemate. Indeed, just a week after the D-Day landings in June, the Germans claimed to have halted an entire British armoured division with one Tiger tank. Most famously of all, in July, despite a heavy preparatory bombardment, three British armoured divisions were repulsed, by much weaker German forces, to the east of Caen, suffering the loss of over 400 tanks in the process. Explanation of these and other humiliating failures has centred predominantly on the shortcomings of the tanks employed by British formations. An orthodoxy has emerged that the roots of failure lay in the comparative weakness of Allied equipment, and to a lesser extent in training and doctrine.

This new study by John Buckley challenges this standard view by analysing the reality and level of the supposed failure, and the causes behind it. By studying the role of the armoured brigades as well as the divisions, a more complete and balanced analysis is offered in which it is clear that while some technologically based difficulties were encountered, British armoured forces achieved a good deal when employed appropriately. Such difficulties as did occur resulted from British operational techniques, methods of command and leadership, and the operating environment in which armour was employed. In addition, the tactics and doctrine employed by both British and German armoured forces resulted in heavy casualties when on the offensive. Ultimately, the experience of the crews and the effects of the fighting on their morale is studied to provide a complete picture of the campaign.

This groundbreaking new study of the Normandy campaign will be an essential reading for all military historians and general readers with an informed interest in the subject.

CASS SERIES: MILITARY HISTORY AND POLICY
Series Editors: John Gooch and Brian Holden Reid
ISSN: 1465–8488

This series will publish studies on historical and contemporary aspects of land power, spanning the period from the eighteenth century to the present day, and will include national, international and comparative studies. From time to time, the series will publish edited collections of essays and 'classics'.

BRITISH ARMOUR IN THE NORMANDY CAMPAIGN 1944

John Buckley

Routledge
Taylor & Francis Group

LONDON AND NEW YORK

First published 2004
by Frank Cass, an imprint of Taylor & Francis
2 Park Square, Milton Park, Abingdon, Oxon, OX14 4RN

Simultaneously published in the USA and Canada
by Routledge
711 Third Avenue, New York, NY 10017, USA

Routledge is an imprint of the Taylor & Francis Group, an informa business

©2004 John Buckley

Typeset in Garamond by
Integra Software Services Pvt. Ltd, Pondicherry, India

British Library Cataloguing in Publication Data
A catalogue record for this book is available from the British Library

Library of Congress Cataloging in Publication Data
Buckley, John (John D.)
British armour in the Normandy campaign, 1944 / John Buckley.
p. cm. — (Cass series—military history and policy, ISSN 1465–8488; 15)
Includes bibliographical references and index.
ISBN 0–7146–5323–3
1. World War, 1939–1945—Campaigns—France—Normandy.   2. Great
Britain. Army—Armored troops.   3. World War, 1939–1945—Tank
warfare.   I. Title.   II. Cass series—military history and policy; no. 15.

D756.5.N6B83 2004
940.54'2142—dc22
2004001402

ISBN10: 0-7146-5323-3 (hbk)
ISBN10: 0-4154-0773-7 (pbk)

ISBN13: 978-0-7146-5323-5 (hbk)
ISBN13: 978-0-4154-0773-1 (pbk)

CONTENTS

SERIES EDITOR'S PREFACE

Campaigns are the building blocks of war, and none of the campaigns fought during the Second World War surpasses the Normandy campaign in importance – or in controversy. Field Marshal Montgomery's personality and style provided ample grounds for dispute while the campaign was still under way, and the methods employed by him and by his commanders in Normandy during the months of June and July 1944 soon gave rise to criticisms which have provided the basis for decades of historical dispute. The critics, whose numbers include Chester Wilmot, Sir Basil Liddell Hart, Carlo d'Este, Sir Max Hastings and Sir John Keegan, are many and distinguished and the multiple grounds on which they have found fault with the campaign have included almost every aspect of its conduct. Among the plethora of issues which have been raised in this debate, none is more fundamental than that of the fighting power of the British Army, apparently condemned to a place in the military league table far below that of the German Army despite the fact that it was victorious in Normandy.

Condemned from start to finish – indeed from before its start – Normandy can all too easily become a litany of failures. Sent across the Channel to fight in inferior tanks as a result of a policy of tank procurement which had been going wrong ever since 1940, British tankers justifiably developed 'Tiger-phobia' as they came to grips with the enemy's Tiger and Panther tanks, greatly superior to their own Shermans, Churchills and Cromwells in both armour protection and gun power. Worn down by months of combat before they arrived in France, crack units such as 7th Armoured Division performed badly, while new formations lacked the 'do and die' attitude to combat displayed by their enemy because, as senior British commanders privately confided to one another, 'Tommy is no soldier'. Doctrinal confusions and battlefield flux were alike papered over by Montgomery's assertions that all was going according to plan. The result, exemplified in Operation GOODWOOD (18–20 July) when British armour was committed on a front only two thousands yards wide and some 400 tanks were lost in a failed breakthrough attempt, can be made to appear almost inevitable.

As John Buckley shows in the pages that follow, almost every one of these received truths is at the very least an over simplification and many are so misleading as to amount to misapprehensions. Mistakes were undoubtedly made: the successes that were hoped for and expected on the first day failed to materialise in part because planning took too little account of terrain and rested on over ambitious expectations about the ability of armoured forces to drive swiftly inland. The methods of fighting applied at the outset of the campaign were, however, logical; the high premium placed on movement reflected the desire to avoid being caught up in wasteful slogging matches and an acute awareness of a manpower problem which meant that human resources had to be carefully nurtured. Similarly, the weapons with which British armour entered the campaign made good sense: the fighting in the Western Desert had shown the anti-tank gun to be the prime enemy of the tank and had therefore demonstrated the importance of a 'dual use' tank gun which could fire both armour-piercing and high explosive ammunition. In Normandy, however, Tiger and Panther tanks and self-propelled artillery turned out to be the major threat and dealing with them required an HV gun and not a medium-velocity one.

Normandy turned out not to be quite what anyone expected. Criticisms based on lack of foresight can only justifiably go so far, and it is perhaps more important to understand how logical methods could have consequences no-one appreciated until they transpired. As John Buckley demonstrates, there was a defensible logic behind the design for combat which informed the minds of British commanders as they crossed the Channel on 6 June 1944. Unhappily, it was not one which fitted well with the defining features of the battle they were about to enter. Perhaps the most important finding of this book, however, is that the British Army demonstrated a high degree of adaptivity to the combat conditions it faced once it came to grips with the enemy in Normandy. The lack of a centrally imposed tactical doctrine uniformly followed by all, which Montgomery incorrectly claimed to have introduced, allowed the space for experimentation and adaptation as the inadequacies of the early methods of combat became evident. This led to such successful innovations as the brigade groups composed of mutually supporting infantry battalions and armoured regiments introduced by 11th Armoured Division and the Guards Armoured Division. On this count alone, the British Army in Normandy turns out to have had more 'fighting power' than some of its critics have allowed.

Revising the judgements of history, and of historians, both deepens our knowledge and sharpens our understanding of the past. Here, it takes us through critical issues of doctrine and method, design and planning, production and supply, morale and motivation as John Buckley's careful, thorough and illuminating research corrects many of our assumptions and conclusions about the Normandy campaign – and about the men who fought it. The campaign itself will doubtless remain a battleground for controversy, but in many respects we shall now be able to make wiser judgements because we are better informed about how and why British armour performed as it did in the *bocage* during the summer of 1944.

JOHN GOOCH
University of Leeds

ILLUSTRATIONS

Dempsey and Monty had attempted to have Adair
replaced prior to *Overlord*, but Adair performed well
enough in northwest Europe. (IWM B13027)

11. Monty with Bobby Erskine, GOC 7th Armoured Division.
Erskine was sacked in August during *Operation Bluecoat*,
along with many other officers in the division
and at corps level. (IWM H36006)

12. Pip Roberts, GOC 11th Armoured Division, considered
to be the best armoured divisional commander
in 21st Army Group. (IWM B9183)

13. Tiger. Heavily armoured and equipped with
an 88 mm gun, the Tiger was much feared by Allied
tank crews. Yet, only some 120 served in Normandy
and the tank was notoriously unreliable. (BOV 438/H3)

14. Stug III. Unsophisticated and workmanlike,
the increasing numbers of self-propelled weapons,
such as the Stug, nevertheless caused tactical
difficulties for the Allies in Normandy. (BOV 2175/D5)

15. A27M Cromwell. Fast and manoeuvrable, the Cromwell
was superior to the Sherman, but still lacked sufficient
firepower to tackle heavy German armour. (BOV 4751/E3)

16. Armour protection on most Allied tanks offered
little defence against German anti-tank weaponry
in Normandy. (BOV 2876/66)

All images reproduced courtesy of the Imperial War Museum, London and
RAC Tank Museum, Bovington, Dorset.

FIGURES, MAP AND TABLES

Figures

Map

Tables

ACKNOWLEDGEMENTS

I am indebted to many institutions, colleagues and friends who have supported the research and writing of this book. To the staffs of the Public Record Office, Kew, London; the Liddell Hart Centre for Military Archives, King's College London; the Imperial War Museum London; Churchill College Archive, Cambridge; the RAC Tank Museum Library and Archive, Bovington, Dorset; the US National Archives II, Maryland, USA; the Directorate of History, Canadian National Defence Headquarters, Ottawa; and the University of Wolverhampton Library, I owe thanks for their patience and professionalism. Research has also been aided by the support of friends and family, particularly JD and Viv McNeil, Maurice and Betty Keeler and my parents.

It is also my pleasure to thank colleagues and students who have contributed to the War Studies Department's annual battlefield tour of Normandy since 1997, notably Peter Caddick Adams, Peter Macdonald, Stephen Webley, Piers Brand and in particular Paul Ruewell and Toby McLeod. Many students have also interviewed veterans over the last few years, often in conjunction with the King's Shropshire Light Infantry Museum, Shrewsbury, and this has uncovered much valuable information. My colleagues at the University of Wolverhampton have offered help and advice throughout this research, and the Department of History and War Studies has generously provided financial support and time away from other duties. I am particularly grateful to Professor John Benson, Professor Mike Dennis, Dr Paul Henderson, Dr Dieter Steinert and Professor Malcolm Wanklyn. I have also greatly benefited from the work of two research assistants, David Burns and Andrew Reece, who have conducted archival work and assiduously transcribed interviews.

An early working paper on this topic was presented in 1998 to the British Commission for Military History and thanks are due to Dr Paul Harris and Professor Martin Alexander for their constructive comments. Professor Terry Copp kindly forwarded in 2002 a draft copy of *Fields of Fire*, for which I am very grateful, and delivered an excellent paper at the department's research seminar programme. Both were immensely useful. Tom Almond thoroughly read the whole manuscript, detecting many infelicities, and offered thoughtful comments and advice. My work has also benefited greatly from the comments and suggestions of Dr Paddy Griffith, Ian Daglish, Professor John Gooch, Charles Singleton, David Fletcher, Dave Hutchby and Dr Stephen Badsey. I am also thankful to Andrew Humphrys and the staff at Frank Cass for their considerable patience.

Finally, my greatest debt is to the veterans who agreed to give up their time and be interviewed. My thanks are due to: Captain Andrew Burn, Major Bill Close, Major Johnny Langdon, Major-General Roy Dixon, Captain Robin Lemon and Trooper Austin Baker.

ABBREVIATIONS

2TAF	2nd Tactical Air Force, RAF
21AG	21st Army Group
A22	Churchill tank
A27L	Centaur tank, liberty engine
A27M	Cromwell tank, meteor engine
A30	Challenger tank
A34	Comet tank
A41	Centurion
A42	Churchill tank Mark VII
ACIGS	Assistant Chief of the Imperial General Staff
ADAFV	Assistant Director of Armoured Fighting Vehicles
AFV	Armoured Fighting Vehicle
AGRA	Army Group, Royal Artillery
AORG	Army Operational Research Group
AP	Armour Piercing
APC	Armour Piercing Capped
APCBC	Armour Piercing, Capped, Ballistic Cap
APCR	Armour Piercing, Composite, Rigid
APDS	Armour Piercing, Discarding Sabot
AT	Anti-tank
ATI	Army Training Instruction
ATM	Army Training Memorandum
AVRE	Armoured Vehicle, Royal Engineers
AWOL	Absent without leave
BAOR	British Army of the Rhine
BEF	British Expeditionary Force
BGS	Brigadier General Staff
BLM	Montgomery Papers, Imperial War Museum
BOV	Bovington RAC Tank Museum Archive
CAB	Cabinet Office documents
CCA	Churchill College Archives, Cambridge

CCS	Combined Chiefs of Staff
CIGS	Chief of the Imperial General Staff
CinC	Commander-in-Chief
CLY	Country of London Yeomanry
CO	Commanding Officer
CoS	Chief of Staff
COSSAC	Chief of Staff to the Supreme Allied Commander
CRO	Current Reports from Overseas
DAFV	Director(ate) of Armoured Fighting Vehicles
DC (S)	Defence Committee (Supply), War Cabinet
DCIGS	Deputy Chief of the Imperial General Staff
DD	Duplex-Drive
DDAFV	Deputy Director of Armoured Fighting Vehicles
DGA	Director-General of Artillery
DMO	Director of Military Operations
DMP	Director of Manpower Planning
DMT	Director of Military Training
DRAC	Director, Royal Armoured Corps
DTD	Department of Tank Design
ENSA	Entertainments National Service Association
FAC	Forward Air Controller
FOO	Forward Observation Officer
FUSAG	First US Army Group
Gen	General
GHQ	General Headquarters
GOC	General Officer Commanding
GSO	General Staff Officer
HE	High Explosive
HMSO	His/Her Majesty's Stationery Office
hp	Horse-power
HQ	Headquarters
HV	High Velocity
IWM	Imperial War Museum
KSLI	King's Shropshire Light Infantry
LHCMA	Liddell Hart Centre for Military Archives, London
Lt-Col	Lieutenant-Colonel
Lt-Gen	Lieutenant-General
M3	Lee/Grant medium tank
M3/M5	Stuart (or Honey) light tank
M4	Sherman tank
M10	Tank destroyer with three-inch or 76 mm gun
M10 17-pdr	M10 tank destroyer with 17-pdr gun
M36	Tank destroyer with 90 mm gun
Maj-Gen	Major-General

MG	Machine gun
MTP	Military Training Pamphlet
MV	Medium Velocity
NAC	National Archives, Canada
NATO	North Atlantic Treaty Organisation
NCO	Non-Commissioned Officer
NTW	Notes from Theatres of War
ORS	Operational Research Section
PREM	Prime Minister's Papers, PRO
PRO	Public Record Office, Kew, London
RA	Royal Artillery
RAC	Royal Armoured Corps
RAF	Royal Air Force
RAMC	Royal Army Medical Corps
RE	Royal Engineers
RHA	Royal Horse Artillery
RHQ	Regimental Headquarters
RMO	Regimental medical officer
R/T	Radio Telephone
RTR	Royal Tank Regiment
SHAEF	Supreme Headquarters Allied Expeditionary Force
SP	Self-propelled
TEWT	Tactical Exercise Without Troops
US NAII	US National Archives II, Maryland
VCIGS	Vice Chief of the Imperial General Staff
WO	War Office
WTS, FF	Weapons Technical Staff, Field Force

1

INTRODUCTION

'The scandal of the European campaign was the inability of Western
democracies to produce armor and, perhaps doctrine, that was at least
on a par with that of their opponents.'

Roman Jarymowycz, *Tank Tactics:*
From Normandy to Lorraine, p. 110.

On 6 June 1944 Allied armies stormed ashore on the beaches of Normandy
to open the campaign that would for the Allies be the defining phase of the
Second World War. Months of careful preparation and planning came to fru-
ition during the crucial early hours of D-Day to ensure overall success and,
despite some reverses, by the end of the first day over 150,000 Allied troops
were firmly established in Normandy.[1] Behind the soldiers, as they waded and
fought their way on to mainland Europe, lay the vast armada assembled by
the Allied nations, consisting of 1,213 naval fighting ships supported by over
5,500 landing, ancillary and merchant vessels. Within 24 hours 6,000 vehicles
and 10,000 tons of stores had been put ashore.[2] Overhead the sky was filled
with aircraft of the RAF and USAAF, who dominated the western theatre
of operations to such an extent that they had achieved not just air superiority,
but total air supremacy. On D-Day the Allies could call upon in excess of
12,000 aircraft, while the *Luftwaffe* in northwest Europe could muster fewer
than 200 serviceable aeroplanes to contest the landings.[3]

Undoubtedly, *Operation Overlord* was an overwhelming achievement, quite
beyond the capabilities of any other individual or group of military powers.
Furthermore, any hope the Germans had of defeating the Allied invasion came
to nought within the next few days, and by late June the *Heer* and the SS were
desperately attempting to the stem the inland advance of the Allies. For a time
they appeared to be succeeding, but it was at a heavy price as their forces
haemorrhaged to destruction over the ensuing weeks. In contrast, the Allies
grew stronger, improving both qualitatively and quantitatively to such a degree
that in early August they delivered for the West a crushing victory, almost
entirely wiping out the German 7th Army and the 5th Panzer Army. In the wake

of the disastrous Mortain counter-offensive and the flight from the Falaise Pocket, out of seven armoured divisions, perhaps as few as 24 tanks and 1,300 men escaped across the Seine to fight on in defence of the Third Reich in September.[4]

The scale of the Allied victory was stunning. In less than 80 days the Allied humiliation of 1940 had been reversed and the *Wehrmacht*'s greatest achievement overturned. Indeed, in the pursuit from Normandy to Belgium in August and September 1944, the rate of the Allied armour spearheaded advance even outstripped that of the much-vaunted *blitzkrieg* to the English Channel in May 1940. More German troops and units may have been written off as a result of the Soviet *Bagration* offensive in the summer of 1944, but the loss of France was a much more important psychological blow to the Third Reich, and one from which it could not recover. Although the war was far from over by September 1944, its outcome was clear. The Western Allies' contribution to the defeat of Nazi Germany had been emphatically made and their influence on the post-war map of Europe assured.

However, in spite of the tremendous achievements in the summer of 1944, the Allied victory was not unqualified. The failure to close the neck of the Falaise Pocket as early as possible has been the source of some debate, with heavy criticism levelled at the Allies, particularly Montgomery and to a lesser degree Bradley, for not co-operating more effectively to bag as many German soldiers as possible. The stout defence of the German border later in 1944 was partly a result of this mistake, it is contended. The inability of the Allies to win as conclusively as they might in August may seem in retrospect to be churlish considering the overwhelming nature of the victory and the level of the achievement, but the censure of the Allied high command is not without substance.[5]

Unquestionably, this debate has in part fuelled the ongoing differences between British, Canadian and American analysts and historians of the campaign in the ensuing years. Correspondence in the respected *Journal of Military History* in 2002 illustrated some of the opinions clearly, when the British military historian Robin Neillands refuted what he saw as the persisting allegations from the United States of over-caution, timidity and excessive tea drinking on the part of the British forces in northwest Europe in 1944–45.[6] In his most recent popular work, *The Battle for Normandy 1944*, Neillands has worked hard to impress upon the critics of the British that there was little to choose between the battlefield effectiveness of the respective Allied armies, though he concedes that in tactical ability the Germans were superior.[7] Others however, continue to support the view that a hierarchy of operational and tactical effectiveness can be established with the Germans at the head followed, in order, by the Americans, the British and finally the Canadians.[8]

The view that the Allies won by massive application of resources and that this compensated for weak battlefield craft, particularly on the part of the Anglo-Canadians, has become the orthodoxy since 1945. John Ellis especially developed this argument in his work of 1990, *Brute Force: Allied Strategy and Tactics in the Second World War*.[9] More recently still, the eminent international and military historian, John Gooch, demonstrated how much this view has become common currency when he wrote that in comparison with the Germans, between 1944 and 1945, the British Army was 'found to be wanting in almost every respect' and was saved only by its artillery and supporting air power.[10] If one wanted to seek out the exponents of the high arts of operational technique in the Second World War, it seemed, it was the Germans one turned to. It was contended that against the odds they had won spectacular victories in 1940 and 1941 and had held off overwhelming numbers with great skill from 1943 onwards.

In the post-war era, as NATO military planners and analysts sought answers to the difficulties of preventing much larger Warsaw Pact forces from swarming into western Europe, they seemed to have a fair blueprint in the techniques of the Germans in the closing years of the Second World War. Despite being heavily outnumbered the Germans had stymied vast enemy armies for periods of time, both in the east and the west, supposedly by employing cunning and resourceful battlefield craft. Lt-Gen Giffard Le Quesne Martel claimed in 1951 that in order to stop the Russians the West would have to learn from the Germans and employ mobile armoured tactics. He stated that 'linear defence is fifteen years out of date for European warfare, and we must do the same as the Germans did with their mobile forces'. The Allies might have won the war, but their success was based upon sheer weight of numbers and resources, not operational and tactical acumen, it was claimed by senior officers. That the Germans had employed a static rather than a mobile defence in the summer of 1944 was carefully ignored, as was the obvious point that they had found little success in stopping either the Soviets or the Western armies no matter what tactics they had used.[11] Furthermore, as Terry Copp has argued, this interpretation also put aside the harsh and brutal methods the German army employed as a means of instilling fear of recrimination for retreat or failure, and focused instead purely on the tactical and operational methods utilised, especially against Allied and Soviet armour.[12]

This developing assessment by senior officers such as Martel was in part predicated upon the analysis of historians such as Basil Liddell Hart, intent on proving that the Germans had been influenced by his pre-war works and had developed their techniques from his ideas of dynamic, mobile armoured warfare.[13] The efficacy of this was demonstrated not only in the so-called *blitzkrieg* period but also in the manner in which the superior tactics of the Germans confounded the Allies in Normandy for so long, and against all the odds. Although the Allies held considerable resource advantages in artillery, air power and armour, they were unable to bring their tanks to bear as effectively as they should because they ignored the lessons they might have learnt from Liddell Hart or from the success of the Germans in the early phase of the war.[14]

This reading of the war's events compounded with predominating post-war American views that the root of German effectiveness against superior weight of numbers and equipment lay in the effective delegation of command

and decision-making to leaders at the frontline, not those miles behind. The over-control of a commander such as Montgomery and his desire to grip his subordinates resulted in the suffocation of commanders' initiative and squandered opportunities for exploitation on the battlefield. By embracing the mission tactics approach of the Germans, rather than the orders-based tactics employed by the Allies in the Second World War, it was posited that NATO forces would greatly enhance their likelihood of halting a Soviet invasion.[15] A German-style mission-based doctrine, or *auftragstaktik*, would free commanders to deal with the enemy in a flexible and dynamic manner, in contrast to the sluggish, predictable and ponderous *befehlstaktik*, or order-directed methods employed by the Allies in Normandy in 1944.[16] The criticism of the Allied approach, that they got stuck for two months when holding all the advantages, and their clear inability to conduct high-tempo armoured operations appeared to be supported by the events of 1944. It was a perception further reinforced in the post-war years when the British Army of the Rhine conducted tours of the Normandy battlefields, employing British, Canadian and German veterans, including members of the SS, to comment on the events. When serving officers were told the stories of such operations as *Totalise, Bluecoat* and most infamously of all *Goodwood*, it seemed perfectly clear and obvious that the Allies had performed poorly, whilst their wily opponents had demonstrated tactical superiority.[17] The *Goodwood* battle of 18–20 July encapsulated everything that was wrong with British armoured forces in the Second World War. Despite huge firepower support, including the use of the Allied strategic air fleet, three armoured divisions had been repulsed with heavy losses by much smaller enemy forces, and over 400 British tanks knocked out of action in just one battle. It seemed that little more needed to be said about the inefficiency of British and Canadian tank formations.

Historical criticism of Allied armour and its impact on the Normandy campaign has been obvious and overt. Liddell Hart may have been instrumental in the formulation of this orthodoxy in the 1950s, but the more recent historiography also supports the contention. In 1990, John Ellis was roundly critical of the armoured divisions in 21st Army Group, while in 1991 John English claimed: 'Without question, the tank arm remained the weakest link in the Anglo-Canadian order of battle.'[18] Russell Hart in 2001 even went so far as to state: 'British armour made little contribution to Allied victory in Normandy.'[19]

The supposed failure of the Anglo-Canadian armoured forces to stage a strategic breakout and exploitation prior to mid-August, and only then achieved because of the American successes in the west, has been attributed in post-war literature to three key factors. First, it has been asserted that the techniques employed by Montgomery and his senior staff were deeply flawed and reduced each operation to an attritional, slogging battle, in which the initiative was too often squandered. The stalemate was therefore self-imposed and could have been broken if alternative techniques had been employed. To a significant degree the weakness of Anglo-Canadian armour was a critical failing as, when hurled upon the German lines, it was palpably unable to break the deadlock and was repeatedly thrown back. In 1983, in his famous work *Decision in Normandy*, Carlo D'Este took the Allies, in particular Montgomery, to task for their overly deliberate and predictable tactics and operational techniques. More recently, Roman Jarymowycz has been critical of the Allied approach in Normandy, and he compared their style unfavourably with the capabilities of the Soviets' deep battle methods, used with great, if costly success against the Germans on the Eastern Front.[20] The campaign also supposedly exposed the tactical weakness of British armoured units. Liddell Hart was the most significant critic of the tactical techniques and methods employed by the armoured arm of 21st Army Group. He argued that the British had demonstrated a poor grasp of armoured doctrine in Normandy, a view supported by some senior veterans of the fighting, such as the future Field Marshal Michael Carver.[21]

However, the employment of armour in Normandy requires deeper analysis, and it is not enough merely to attribute Allied victory to the blunt employment of mass. Others had relied on superior numbers but failed, notably the French in 1940 and the Soviets in 1941. Greater numbers and resources do not guarantee success – strength and force have to be brought to bear effectively at critical points in a campaign and the battle in order to prevail, and to this end the Allies appear to have been successful. Overall casualties in Normandy were within predicted limits, and the approach adopted by Montgomery and 21st Army Group delivered an overwhelming victory against a highly experienced and recalcitrant foe. Stephen Hart has recently re-evaluated the operational techniques of 21st Army Group and found them to be much more effective and appropriate than previously believed. Moreover, he contends that Montgomery's curious and largely disagreeable personality has been allowed to confuse and cloud the issues.[22]

In addition, it is clear that the denigration of the armoured forces on a tactical level fails to acknowledge the context of the campaign, nor take account of the innovation and flexibility of British brigades and divisions, particularly obvious in the mid-to-later stages of the fighting. It is certainly the case that much criticism of the employment and conduct of armoured operations in Normandy is founded upon a misconception that the Allies should have fought a different style of campaign to the highly successful one they did prosecute. Consequently, the operational and tactical conduct of British armour in Normandy requires a fuller and more appropriate analysis, one in which the starting point is not that, because their techniques did not mirror those of the Germans, ergo they were misguided and flawed. Too much previous analysis has assumed failure on the part of Anglo-Canadian armour simply because it did not follow the pattern set by the Germans in 1939–42, the one so much admired, and arguably misunderstood, in the post-1945 world.

The second, and to many most important reason why Allied armoured forces failed to come to terms with the requirements of the campaign in Normandy was the inferior equipment with which they were forced to fight. The techno-logy-oriented explanation for the difficulties encountered by Allied armoured forces in Normandy focuses on the relative weakness of the Shermans and Cromwells fielded by the British, Canadians and Americans when compared with their German counterparts, the Tigers and Panthers. Famously, during the war and shortly afterwards, the MP for Ipswich, Richard Rapier Stokes, among others, repeatedly attempted to take the government to task over the deficiencies in British tanks. He was particularly critical in a secret session of the House of Commons on 24 March 1944, when he challenged James Grigg, Secretary of State for War, to a tank duel in which Stokes would command a Tiger and Grigg a Cromwell.[23] In a speech to the House in August 1944, Stokes claimed that he had been informed by a 'responsible general' that in tank design, 'Relatively speaking, to-day, we are just as far behind the Germans as we were in 1940.' Following a contradictory interruption, Stokes continued:

> If he [Rear-Admiral Beamish] took the trouble to read my speeches he would be aware that all along my criticisms have been based on irrefutable facts. [*laughter*] It is all very well for hon. Members to laugh, but these men are dying.[24]

Stokes certainly captured the sense of frustration felt by some tank crews and commanders in Normandy. He pointed out that in one unit, he was regarded as the patron saint of the regiment, for protesting against the inadequacies of British tanks. In 1945 he published *Some Amazing Tank Facts*, a pamphlet in which he outlined the 'scandal' and the crucial tank gap that had bedevilled the efforts of British armoured units in the Second World War, even in the closing phase from 6 June 1944 onwards. Emotively he stated:

> Thousands of the boys who went out to fight for us are not coming home again because our Ministry of Defence failed, through stupidity and weakness in the department of weapons.[25]

A simple comparison of the firepower and armour protection afforded to the respective British and German types of tanks seemed to demonstrate the main reason behind the inability of the Allied armoured formations to impose themselves on the campaign. In short, it was, and is, argued that Allied tanks were technically inferior and thus could not engage effectively with enemy armour.

Historians and writers such as Roman Jarymowycz, Peter Beale, Russell Hart, Kenneth Macksey and many others have all placed great emphasis on the fail-ings of the tanks themselves as an explanation for the poor showing of Allied armour in Normandy. Max Hastings in particular argued this case in 1984 in *Overlord*, in which he claimed that the most fundamental failing of the Allies in Normandy was their inability to deploy a tank to rival those of the Germans. In addition, one of the key factors behind this deficiency was the weakness of

British tank design and production in the years leading up to *Operation Overlord*. Jarymowycz argues that the British were simply unable to build a reliable and functional tank during the war and thus switched to the flawed but dependable Sherman, while Beale is vitriolic in his condemnation of the whole British design and procurement process.[26] Most recently of all Tim Ripley has claimed:

> The Villers Bocage, Goodwood and other battles showed up the tremendous technological superiority of German tanks over their Allied opponents. The Tiger I, Panther, and, to a lesser extent, Panzer IV all had far greater range, hitting power, and armored protection than the American Shermans or British Cromwells and Churchills.[27]

Technical explanations are easily quantifiable and lend themselves to popular history, such as heavily illustrated books and audio-visual sources, but they offer an incomplete and distorted view of the reasons behind the relative success and failure of Allied armour in Normandy. Although the Allied tanks were deficient in some ways to the Tigers and Panthers, they were the equal if not superior to most German models, such as the Panzer IVs and Stugs, and these were by far the majority, constituting some 70 per cent of the German armoured force. Moreover, it is not enough to rely on the argument that because a tank is technically inferior on paper, that this will then be reflected in operational failure on the battlefield. German armoured formations were equipped with inferior tanks in 1940 against the French and certainly in 1941 against the Soviets, yet prevailed. Furthermore, British tank design and production was far from being completely redundant in the Second World War. The A27M Cromwell of 1944 was superior to the M4 Sherman, while the A22/42 Churchill provided armour protection thicker than anything deployed by the Germans in Normandy, save a handful of Tiger IIs. Moreover, the 17-pdr gun was a more than an adequate weapon, especially when coupled with the new sabot ammunition. By late 1944 the A34 Comet, the Cromwell's successor, was arriving in service and was a fine tank, which rivalled the Panther, while the A41 Centurion introduced in 1945 seized the lead in tank design.

That British armoured formations in Normandy were to a degree handicapped by their Shermans, Cromwells and Churchills is not in doubt, particularly because of the weak anti-armour capabilities of the standard MV 75 mm gun, but German units also suffered badly from poorly designed and unreliable tanks, many of which were indifferent in terms of performance. It is therefore essential to establish accurately what the real deficiencies of Allied tanks were, and then to identify those factors which had a substantial impact on the conduct of the campaign. Furthermore, it is then necessary to examine why the British deployed the tanks they did in northwest Europe in 1944 and to what extent the design, production and supply process can be seen to have succeeded or failed. Ultimately, it is fundamental to any study of British armoured forces in Normandy to analyse the extent to which a technical explanation of the nature and experience of armoured warfare in Normandy is either sufficient or appropriate.

Finally, a third major reason posited for the deficiencies in British armoured forces in Normandy centres on the low determination and lack of aggression in Allied troops, certainly when compared with their German counterparts. Chester Wilmot, a contemporary journalist, commented in 1952 in his widely read account of the northwest European campaign that British troops lacked the desire and initiative for high-intensity fighting. He, like many others, deferred to the tenacity and resolve of the German soldier.[28] British commanders by 1944 were also of the opinion that their charges lacked the desire for close combat and suffered from weak determination, and that such considerations impacted on chosen operational techniques, to a degree dictating directly and indirectly the cautious and supposedly ponderous nature of Allied, particularly Anglo-Canadian, operations.[29] The timid approach obviously then shaped the conduct of armoured operations as the dash and aggression required for dynamic tank warfare did not exist. German commanders such as Kurt Meyer famously criticised British and Canadian tank crews for their tentativeness at crucial moments in battle, which resulted in great opportunities being squandered. Liddell Hart again supported this view, effectively implying that the lions led by donkeys epithet of the First World War could be easily reversed in the Second World War. Too often, he claimed in 1952, attacks petered out following trifling casualties, particularly amongst the armoured formations.[30]

However, any analysis of morale is replete with methodological difficulties and shortcomings, and the evidence on which many previous analyses are based is questionable.[31] German sources worked to a different agenda, either attempting to bolster morale during the war, or rationalise the ultimate defeat of the *Heer* and the SS after the event. Some senior Allied command sources even sought to explain away the criticism of their leadership of the campaign by claiming that their troops lacked drive, and that operational methods had to accommodate this in planning.[32] Much of the remaining evidence offered to support the thesis is anecdotal or at best circumstantial. The argument supporting the view that the morale and determination of Allied troops and armoured forces was wanting in northwest Europe therefore requires closer scrutiny and reinterpretation based upon available more reliable sources, as well as a considered and thoughtful use of those mentioned hitherto.

One further, and now orthodox view is that veteran units suffered from even poorer morale and lower determination during the campaign and that this was reflected in their weak battlefield performance. Perhaps the most famous example offered is the 7th Armoured Division, a unit badly mauled at Villers Bocage, wary of commitment during *Goodwood* and implicated in a series of high-level sackings following a sticky performance during *Operation Bluecoat*

8

in late July and early August. Yet even this view is open to question, as other veteran armoured units appeared to fight as effectively as inexperienced formations. To what extent, therefore, is this link between veteran status and lower morale tenable?

Finally, it is necessary to examine in some detail the experience of armoured warfare in Normandy to ascertain the crucial factors behind maintenance of morale in tank units. The extent to which tank warfare differed from the other arms and the nature of particular problems confronting tankcrews will therefore be a key aspect of the analysis of morale in the British armoured arm in Normandy.

Allied armoured units also encountered a series of problems and difficulties that shaped the nature of the campaign and affected the manner in which armour was used and has since been analysed. The Allies had intended that artillery and air power would play a pivotal role in Normandy, preparing the ground of any offensive by thoroughly undermining the German defences. However, although the Germans became rightly fearful of Allied firepower, artillery and air power could not influence the campaign to the level desired, particularly when the fighting bogged down in mid-June. Consequently, the close-combat arms, tanks and infantry, had to shoulder a much greater burden. Infantry casualties in Normandy were excessive, at times surpassing those of the worst battles of the First World War, and the infantry arm endured some 70 per cent of the total casualties suffered by 21st Army Group in Normandy, despite only constituting 15 per cent of the force structure.[33]

For the armour, there was no direct historical comparison, but the tanks clearly fought a difficult campaign in exceptionally trying circumstances. Most obviously and importantly, it was a campaign somewhat different from that expected or trained for. The armoured arm played the role expected in storming ashore, but the drive inland stalled and the Allies found themselves fighting for a long and unexpected period in the close terrain of Normandy, most famously of all in the *bocage*, with very high and steeply banked hedges surrounding raised fields, often no more than 100 yards across. In addition, the countryside was sprinkled with orchards, woods and small but stout stone farmhouses and out-buildings, often nestling in rising and dipping valleys and ravines, cut by small but troublesome rivers. This was exceptionally difficult tank country, but the armour was forced to adapt and play as full a role as it could in providing close fire support.

Of course the greatest obstacle to overcome was the burden of offence. By 1944 the operating environment was radically different to that of 1940, not only in the physical sense of Normandy and its terrain, but on a tactical and operational level. The conditions greatly favoured defence, but it was the Anglo-Canadians in particular who had to drive on against German defensive lines, the strength and depth of which had yet to be encountered in the Second World War. And all of this had to be attempted with largely inexperienced formations tasting battle for the first time. Consequently, the performance of British armour in Normandy must be viewed in the context of the campaign as it actually existed in 1944, not in an idealised world of *blitzkrieg*.[34] The Allies fought a very different war in northwest Europe, one that maximised their advantages, one based on resources and strength in depth, which sought to minimise risk and deliver a victory to the West, tolerable in terms of casualties.

It is into such a context that this book will attempt to place the British armoured forces in Normandy in 1944, exploring the realities of their various roles, analysing the factors that shaped the conduct and nature of tank warfare in the campaign, and one which will seek to offer a more complete view of their contribution to Allied victory.

2

FIGHTING THE CAMPAIGN

On 6 June 1944 the first Anglo-Canadian armoured units forced their way ashore on the Normandy beaches and began a long, arduous and at times frustrating campaign against the *Heer* and Waffen SS, though one that ultimately resulted in a tremendous victory. Yet despite this success and that of subsequent operations, the Allied tank forces are widely considered to have failed substantially in their efforts throughout most of the campaign, and have been variously described as doctrinally naïve, inflexible, poorly prepared and ill-equipped. Indeed, it is considered by some that Allied armour signally failed to come to terms with the operating environment of Normandy. In contrast, German armoured units and commanders are viewed as a flexible, intuitive, and highly effective force more than capable of outperforming their Allied counterparts, even in the face of great adversity. Critics of British armour point to the disasters at Villers Bocage (13 June) and *Operation Goodwood* (18 July), the offensive frailties displayed in and around Hill 112 and Caen in June and July, and during the drive towards Mont Pinçon in August. Even when German resistance was crumbling in August, Anglo-Canadian armour struggled to make progress during *Operations Totalise* and *Tractable*. It has even been suggested that British armour did little to bring about the Allied victory throughout the campaign.[1]

However, this is an incomplete and distorted view of the contribution of British armoured forces to the conduct of the campaign. Anglo-Canadian armour did adapt, and to a tactical and operational environment for which it had not been prepared, and did display organisational flexibility. Moreover, a great deal has been made of the supremacy of German armoured technique and equipment and its capabilities, when in reality *Heer* and Waffen SS armour also suffered, especially on the offensive. Indeed, it is possible to argue that the Germans failed to mould their operating doctrine to the necessities of the Normandy campaign as much if not more so than the much-maligned Allies. This chapter will therefore examine the realities and the extent of the supposed ineffectiveness of British armour in Normandy. By analysing the formations and their battlefield roles, the employment of armour throughout the campaign, and the difficulties encountered in Normandy, a more complete picture

11

of the effectiveness or otherwise of Anglo-Canadian armoured forces can be established.

Formations, units and organisations

Twenty-First Army Group fought the northwest European campaign with a significant body of armour. Six divisions would be inserted during the summer of 1944, four British, one Canadian and one Polish. In addition, eight independent brigades were deployed, one of which was Canadian, to support more closely the efforts of the infantry divisions. In total, armoured personnel constituted some 7 per cent of the fighting force of British 2nd Army, numbering approximately 43,000.[2]

Most historical writing and attention, however, has been devoted to only one part of the force, the armoured divisions. The glamorous and dashing nature of the exploitation phase of Montgomery's set-piece battles has resulted in excessive focus on the most active elements of this operational method. Consequently, Britain's three mainstream armoured divisions, 7th, 11th and Guards have received greatest attention in the historiography of the campaign.[3] Indeed, Russell Hart's recent *Clash of Arms: How the Allies Won in Normandy* mentions only on one occasion a British armoured formation other than the three divisions in the chapter devoted to the Normandy campaign, yet supposedly offers a balanced analysis of the effectiveness of armour.[4]

This has distorted our view of the effectiveness of British armour in the fighting in France, for by focusing on the exploitation phase, historians have

---

Divisions

79th Armoured Division *(Maj-Gen Percy Hobart)*
7th Armoured Division *(Maj-Gen Bobby Erskine/ Maj-Gen Gerald Verney)*
11th Armoured Division *(Maj-Gen Pip Roberts)*
Guards Armoured Division *(Maj-Gen Allan Adair)*
4th Canadian Armoured Division *(Maj-Gen George Kitching)*
1st Polish Armoured Division *(Maj-Gen Stanislaw Maczek)*

Independent brigades

8th Armoured Brigade
2nd Canadian Armoured Brigade
27th Armoured Brigade *(disbanded 29 July 1944)*
4th Armoured Brigade
31st Tank Brigade
6th Guards Tank Brigade
33rd Armoured Brigade
34th Tank Brigade

Figure 1. Armoured formations in 21st Army Group, Normandy, 1944

in fact concentrated on the weakest link in 21st Army Group's operational technique. The methods employed by the Anglo-Canadians often hindered armoured exploitation (see Chapter 3) and thus the historiography, which has placed greatest attention on the armoured divisions and the breakthrough and exploitation phase, has in consequence, emphasised the supposed failure of armour. Consequently, the effectiveness or otherwise of the other armoured units, the independent brigades in particular, has too often been overlooked or marginalised.

In fact, the skewing effects of the emphasis on the armoured divisions has exacerbated matters further, for the operational technique of 21st Army Group may have been less effective in break-through actions and mobile exploitation, but it did support break-in assaults quite well, and reacted in excellent fashion to ensuing enemy counter-attacks. In this role, the independent armoured and tank brigades were relatively successful and became increasingly so as the campaign progressed. Therefore, the view hitherto of British armour in Normandy has emphasised the negative aspects at the expense of the positive.

Moreover, in the assault phase of *Overlord*, and then in specialised supporting actions throughout the campaign, elements of 79th Armoured Division proved highly effective in getting infantry on to objectives. German forces were particularly intimidated by flame-throwing Churchill Crocodile tanks, and American forces were also suitably impressed when they were employed in support of their troops.[5] The value of the amphibious Sherman DD (Duplex-Drive) tanks on D-Day was considerable, and on landing beaches where they foundered, or on the US beaches where the support of 79th Armoured Division's supporting equipment was eschewed, difficulties were encountered, difficulties overcome elsewhere.[6] Yet general studies of the campaign have often marginalised the contribution of these specialised armoured units. Awkward to analyse and unconventional, they were nevertheless effective. However, again they were primarily used during the break-in phase of operations and thus suffered from the limelight being cast over the dynamic role of armour, the divisional exploitation, so often eulogised by post-war analysts.[7] In truth, 21st Army Group's most sizeable group of armoured formations was not the divisions, but the independent brigades. In Normandy, the Anglo-Canadians deployed five armoured divisions in total (not including the 79th, which never acted as a division), though only three saw action before August, whilst there were eight independent armoured and tank brigades in action during the campaign.[8]

The divisions were intended for fast-moving exploitation once a penetration had been created in the German defences, and thus were supposed to be held back until a break-through was imminent. In practice, however, 21st Army Group often employed them in an assault role for which they were neither designed nor trained, with serious consequences, particularly in *Operation Goodwood*.[9]

The independent brigades, according to the War Office's official doctrine, were intended to provide close support for infantry formations, particularly

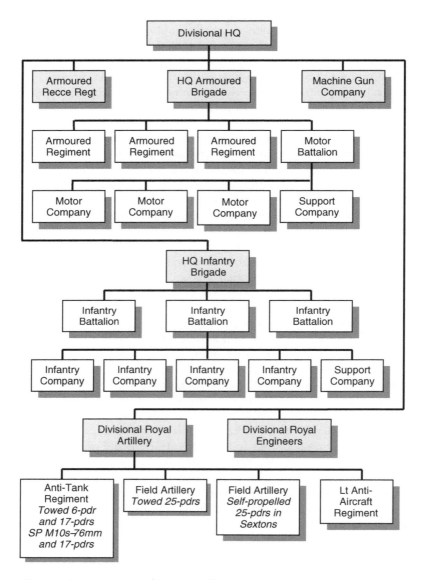

Figure 2. British armoured division, 1944

during the assault phase, often at divisional level. Montgomery, 21st Army Group's CinC, saw little need for different approaches for divisions and brigades and argued for all formations to be similarly equipped and trained, to enhance flexibility.[10] This dichotomy in doctrine was to be a clear source of disagreement, and units deployed for action having largely prepared for specific types of operation, either largely centred on infantry–armour co-operation, or on exploitation. The structure of these two separate types of formations made their intended battlefield role clear.

Although the armoured divisions suffered apparent repeated failure in Normandy, once employed in their intended role of rapid exploitation, they performed more than adequately. Arguably, many of their earlier difficulties resulted not from their own inadequacies but from premature and inappropriate employment.[11] Indeed, when in open country the divisions raced deep and hard into enemy territory, maintaining the initiative in a manner not too removed from the heady days of *blitzkrieg*. In advancing from the Seine to Brussels over a period of 12 days, British 2nd Army tanks averaged 26 miles per day.[12] Even in 1940, German armour only managed 21 miles per day between crossing the Meuse and reaching the English Channel.[13] Nevertheless, during the slow-moving phase of the Normandy campaign, the armoured divisions were forced to reorganise to facilitate closer tank–infantry co-operation. Maj-Gen Pip Roberts, GOC 11th Armoured Division, with Lt-Gen Richard O'Connor's (GOC, VIII Corps) full acknowledgement and support, deployed his two brigades in a mixed fashion from *Operation Bluecoat* onwards.[14] Instead of keeping the armoured brigade regiments effectively separate from the battalions of the infantry brigade, as War Office doctrine and training dictated, the GOC of 11th Armoured Division balanced one tank regiment with an infantry battalion to provide improved co-ordination.[15] In the close terrain of Normandy, mutual support was essential. The Guards Armoured Division followed suit, as did the Polish 1st Armoured Division.[16]

Percy Hobart's 79th Armoured Division was constructed very differently. The division had been redesignated as a specialised assault formation in April 1943 with three armoured brigades (1st Tank Brigade, 30th Armoured Brigade and 1st Assault Brigade) as opposed to the usual single brigade in other armoured divisions. Units of 79th Armoured Division provided the specialised elements designed to aid the initial assault on D-Day. 'Hobo's Funnies', as they were colloquially known, provided mine-clearing flail tanks (Crabs), bridging tanks, bulldozers, petard tanks, carpet layers and a variety of others, the majority of which were successful in supporting the assault phase of D-Day.[17] Indeed, the level of specialisation in planning and engineering was in stark contrast to the ad hoc approach of the Germans, and arguably quite beyond them in 1944. Subsequently, 79th Armoured Division provided specialised support for break-in and assault operations and played a significant part in II Canadian Corps' searchlight-directed *Operation Totalise* in August.[18]

The independent armoured and tank brigades were intended to provide close support for infantry divisions during the assault phase of operations, but a major squabble had broken out in 21st Army Group over their use in northwest Europe. War Office doctrine argued that the Independent Tank Brigades, equipped with the heavily armoured Churchill infantry support tank, were best suited to close assault operations, but Montgomery and his ex-8th

Army staff believed in the concept of a single 'capital tank' design capable of both mobile and close support duties.[19] They argued that the American designed M4 Sherman was the closest approximation to the dual-purpose tank and thus were unconvinced over the need for the slow-moving Churchill.[20] They claimed that in a rapid pursuit and exploitation, the Churchill's top speed of 12 mph would be a liability, though in practice the Churchill would more than hold its own in this respect.[21] Moreover, they were resistant to any doctrinal distinction between armoured brigades largely equipped with Shermans, and tank brigades equipped with Churchills. The War Office demurred in the light of evidence from Italy that the Sherman was too vulnerable and should not be deployed in the same manner as the Churchill.[22] It had been the War Office's original hope that all independent brigades be equipped with Churchills, but production of these tanks was insufficient for the eight brigades pencilled in for *Overlord*.[23] Consequently, the Sherman was pressed into service, creating the distinction between tank and armoured brigades.[24] Attempts within 21st Army Group, prior to Montgomery's arrival, to develop specific tactics for Shermans to be used in the infantry support role, as they would so function in the independent armoured brigades, were effectively blocked.[25] However, whatever the theoretical differences in doctrine, Montgomery as the new commander imposed his operational view on the employment and use of all the independent brigades. Interestingly, Patton and the Americans came to the same conclusion as the War Office, and called for a heavily armoured tank to be produced for infantry support duties.[26]

Nevertheless, the three independent tank brigades, 31st, 34th, and 6th Guards, principally equipped with Churchills, and the five armoured brigades, 4th, 8th, 27th, 33rd and 2nd Canadian, largely equipped with Shermans, were supposed to fight in a similar manner. As will be seen in Chapter 4, however, loose interpretation of doctrine was endemic and in practice units developed their own methods, often only guided by high-level views.

The prevalent armoured fighting body in Normandy was the brigade, either within a division, or independently deployed in support of infantry. Armoured brigades consisted of three armoured regiments usually with a single supporting motor battalion of infantry, which throughout the campaign too often proved to be inadequate. Each regiment subdivided into three squadrons, and each squadron into four troops of tanks. Each troop consisted, generally of four tanks when equipped with Shermans or Cromwells, or three tanks if Churchills.

Most armoured brigades of divisional or independent variety were equipped with Shermans as the standard troop tank, with one in each troop designated a Firefly and fitted with a harder-hitting 17-pdr gun, as opposed to the more usual MV dual-purpose 75mm gun.[27] Each armoured division also had an armoured reconnaissance regiment, equipped with the Cromwell cruiser tank, although 7th Armoured Division's regiments were all so equipped. These tanks were also fitted with 75 mm guns and, as the 17-pdr could not

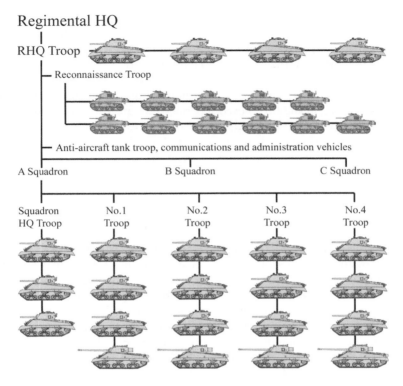

Regimental HQ

RHQ Troop

Reconnaissance Troop

Anti-aircraft tank troop, communications and administration vehicles

A Squadron   B Squadron   C Squadron

Squadron HQ Troop	No.1 Troop	No.2 Troop	No.3 Troop	No.4 Troop

A small proportion of cruisers were designated close support tanks and were fitted with weapons such as the 95mm gun/howitzer.
Armoured Reconnaissance Regiments were equipped with A27 Cromwells in place of 75mm gun Shermans, and fielded more Honeys.
Independent Tank Brigades replaced Shermans with Churchills, and each troop had three, rather than four tanks.

Figure 3. British armoured regiment, 1944

be squeezed into the Cromwell, regiments were strengthened with Sherman Fireflies at the rate of one per troop. In late July, the Fireflies in Cromwell regiments began to be replaced by a new equipment, the Challenger, essentially an elongated Cromwell with a 17-pdr gun, though such tanks were not a resounding success. A number of Cromwells were equipped with 95 mm short-barrel close-support weapons. All regiments were also supplied with American-designed Stuart (or known in the British Army as Honey) light tanks for reconnaissance purposes and these were deployed and utilised at regimental level. Self-propelled anti-tank guns in the form of American M10s, fitted with 76 mm or 17-pdr guns, were also deployed by the Royal Artillery to stiffen the mobile anti-armour firepower of British and Canadian formations.

Tank regiments equipped with Churchills were supposedly not intended to duel with enemy armour too often and thus did not receive 17-pdr Shermans, which were considered too weak in armour to function in the close support role. The Churchill, like the Cromwell, could not carry the 17-pdr gun, and in order to boost anti-tank capability a troop of M10 tank destroyers was on occasion attached to a regiment or squadron of Churchills. Some Churchills retained the 6-pdr gun and this proved superior in the anti-tank role. However, the latest versions of the Churchill were clad in excess of 150 mm of frontal armour, even more than the famous German Tiger I tank, and it had been hoped that such protection would defeat most enemy anti-tank equipment. Yet by 1944, with HV 75 mm and 88 mm guns in widespread use, even the Churchill was vulnerable.

Armour in the campaign

The assault phase of *Operation Overlord* witnessed the use of a variety of elements of 79th Armoured Division, most notably crabs (mine-clearing flail tanks), AVREs (Armoured Vehicle, Royal Engineers) and armoured bulldozers. Units of 2nd County of London Yeomanry (Westminster Dragoons) supported 50th Division's assault and the 22nd Dragoons aided 3rd Canadian and 3rd British Infantry Divisions. In addition, DD tanks of a variety of regiments swam ashore to provide immediate armoured support to the landings, while self-propelled close-fire support was added by Centaur tanks (under-powered Cromwells with 95 mm howitzers) of the Royal Marines armoured support regiments and batteries.[28]

The task of clearing paths through the German defences and minefields was partially successful. Although many tanks bogged down or were knocked out by remaining German anti-tank guns, seven out of 12 planned paths were cleared ahead of XXX Corps' drive out from *Gold* beach.[29] The 3rd Canadian Division was aided by the clearing of 12 paths, and in all cases the dual capabilities of the 79th Armoured Division's tanks allowed them to provide fire-support when the DD tanks suffered in the awkward weather conditions and failed to press ashore in the numbers hoped for. Nevertheless, in contrast with the 90 per cent DD tank failure rate on *Omaha* beach, a factor in the near disaster suffered there, the Anglo-Canadians were more successful in beaching their amphibious armour, and in any case were able to supplement their supporting firepower with the 79th Armoured vehicles. Notably, 13th/18th Hussars, of 27th Armoured Brigade, managed to get 33 out of 40 DD tanks ashore on *Sword* beach. In total, the 79th Armoured Division's losses included 12 out of 50 Crabs and 22 out of 120 AVRE equipments.[30]

Nevertheless, although the assault armour aided the landings considerably, there were problems. Despite meticulous planning and preparation, and although the path clearing achieved its objectives ultimately, it took longer than expected. Undoubtedly, the traffic jams in the first few hours were a major contributory factor to the sluggish drive inland achieved on the first day. It took some hours to clear enough pathways through the beach obstacles to facilitate the inland push, and on *Juno* beach, the Canadians were not able to clear a route until late morning.[31] Indeed, within an hour of the assault, the mine-clearing flail tanks had been reduced to just one per lane by enemy anti-tank fire, difficult ground and mines.[32] The congestion on the beaches was attributable in large part to the weather, which resulted in there being only 10 metres of hard sand between the sea-wall and the water by mid-morning. This undoubtedly added greatly to the congestion and confusion, and prevented crucial equipment and armour getting forward to where it was urgently required.[33]

The inability of the landing forces to clear pathways off the beaches quickly was to be a contributory factor in the failure of Allied armour on the first day to support the bold drives inland called for by Montgomery. He had envisaged a series of powerful armoured thrusts on 6 June, at almost any risk, to develop depth in the bridgehead.[34] His assault Corps Commander, Lt-Gen John Crocker, was also well aware of the need for bold armoured operations to expand the lodgement.[35]

Caen was a crucial objective for D-Day, as this city and the open country to the south was viewed as the linchpin of the eastern sector, and it would be on this point that, according to Montgomery's plan, the whole Allied front would pivot during the breakout phase. Although it was considered ambitious to attempt to seize the city within the first 24 hours, it was a clear and greatly desired intention. Crocker's I Corps was to take Caen and the high ground to the immediate south of the city, with 3rd Infantry Division supported by 27th Armoured Brigade. The right flank was to be covered by 3rd Canadian Infantry Division supported by 2nd Canadian Armoured Brigade, who were to seize the Putot-en-Bessin to Carpiquet area, most notably the airfield.[36] It was deemed critical that the armour of 27th Brigade in particular be ready to support the dash to Caen by mid-morning at the latest. The infantry of the 2nd King's Shropshire Light Infantry (2KSLI), part of 185th Brigade (3rd Division), was supposed to ride on the back of the tanks of the Staffordshire Yeomanry of 27th Armoured Brigade to facilitate a more rapid advance.[37] This was admittedly a compromise as the troops would be exposed to mortar, artillery and small-arms fire, but speed was considered essential.

However, the drive on Caen failed to materialise in the manner hoped for. The Staffordshire Yeomanry tanks became fouled up on the beaches in the morning, with their tanks at one stage remaining stationary for over an hour.[38] By early afternoon, the regiment had still not extricated itself from the congestion, a fate which also befell the 7th Field Regiment Royal Artillery, and the decision was taken for 2KSLI to proceed on foot, with the armour catching up when it could.[39] Thus, as McKee famously stated, 'The lightning punch at Caen had been reduced to a few hundred plodding riflemen.'[40] To complicate matters further, two squadrons of the Staffordshire Yeomanry became embroiled in supporting infantry units as they attempted to winkle the Germans out of the *Hillman* bunker, a defensive complex that threatened the advance inland. The expected armoured drive to Caen ultimately fizzled out into a bold dash by 2KSLI, latterly supported by one squadron of the Staffordshire Yeomanry. Despite their efforts resistance hardened around Caen, and the British troops were forced to fall back.[41]

However, although 27th Armoured Brigade and 3rd Division have been criticised over their efforts to advance on Caen on 6 June, they were hindered by three critical factors. The first was obviously the confusion and hold-ups on the beaches. The log jam, however, was always a possibility, and despite the success of 79th Armoured Division's specialised units, delays off the beaches were always likely to occur. The weather contributed significantly to the congestion, but the likelihood of being formed up and ready to advance on Caen within a few hours of landing was based on a near-flawless landing phase. The second crucial factor was the terrain immediately inland of the beaches. Much of this consisted of built-up areas to a depth of some 500 metres, behind which lay zones of flooded marshland. Beyond that lay the Périers Ridge which rises to some 50 metres above sea level at its highest point. The rapid advance or even movement of armoured vehicles through such terrain was always going to be difficult, especially if opposition was unsuppressed.[42] The third factor was the level of resistance encountered by the assaulting forces. The British units expected less opposition than that which confronted them on the morning of 6 June. Brig. K. Pearce Smith, commanding 185th Brigade, claimed that he had been briefed to expect resistance from the German 716th Division, but that with the support of 27th Brigade armour, this should not be an insurmountable obstacle.[43] However, intelligence reports in May had alerted 2nd British Army to the deployment of 21st Panzer Division in the area, though it was supposedly dispersed all around Caen.[44] Nevertheless, the possibility of elements of the division being to the north of the city was acknowledged, and indeed, the British advance on Caen encountered 21st Panzers, and importantly its anti-tank artillery on Périers Ridge, just south of the channel coast. This contact sealed the fate of any plan to seize Caen on the first day, for with such opposition, however disorganised the response of the German panzers may have been, any hope of pushing one battalion of infantry and one squadron of tanks forward into Caen with any possibility of being able to hold it, was dashed. In defence however, the Staffordshire Yeomanry proved more than a match for 21st Panzers, while the foresight of Lt-Col J. A. Eadie emphasised the capabilities of British armoured commanders.[45] The effective disposition of Eadie's 17-pdr-equipped Shermans was commented upon by his opposite number, Lt-Gen Edgar Feuchtinger, and 21st Panzer's counter-attacks on 6 June were thrown back with significant losses.[46]

Undoubtedly, there had been a breakdown in the communication, or realisation of intelligence, as the SHAEF intelligence report indicating the potential for 21st Panzers to be ensconced in and around Caen had not obviously shaped or influenced Crocker's I Corps plans. With such opposition, the likelihood of a successful assault by British forces on Caen receded dramatically, and with potential problems likely to be encountered in and around the beaches, the possibility of success was low. However, the failure was not one founded on the inadequacy of British armoured forces or its equipment. The opposition encountered fielded at best Panzer Mark IVs, a type at least matched by the Sherman, and in defence the Staffordshire Yeomanry had acquitted itself well. In addition, the 6th Regiment of the Canadian 2nd Armoured Brigade had driven some way inland, reaching their final objective, the Caen–Bayeux road. However, without adequate infantry support, they had been forced to pull back.[47]

Allied armour had achieved a good deal on D-Day, predominantly in supporting the assault itself. The inability of the British to launch a successful strike on Caen was a result of poor weather, optimistic planning that took too little attention of the terrain and any potential friction, and over-expectation about the ability of armour to drive inland, especially when confronted by greater levels of opposition than imagined. Nevertheless, in the post-war period Miles Dempsey, GOC 2nd British Army, remained convinced that the capture of Caen had been possible, and that the D-Day plan should in fact have been more ambitious rather than less. He conceded: 'The spearheads may have in fact been checked in their advance inland...[but] this was no argument against aiming at ambitious objectives and giving the troops plenty to go for.'[48]

However, by 1944 the British Army had been trained and indoctrinated with the need to plan, prepare and conduct set-piece battles, certainly since the elevation and subsequent success of Montgomery. Therefore, the likelihood of commanders on the spot being able to throw off such thinking and demonstrate tremendous flexibility in the face of particular difficulties and against unexpected levels of opposition was remote. The consequences of the failure of the armoured groups in and around Caen on the first day, nevertheless, had serious effects on subsequent operations.

The armoured brigades were involved in a series of further actions in the days following the invasion, actions which demonstrated emerging difficulties. Eighth Armoured Brigade, which had landed on *Gold* Beach as part of XXX Corps, was soon deployed in an attempted drive inland, with the ultimate objective being Villers Bocage. The push south, however, was continually held up in confusion and frustration. Tank crews, especially commanders, became wary of snipers, and enemy infantry armed with the *panzerfaust*, a throw-away short-range hollow-charge weapon more than capable of knocking out a Sherman, also emerged as a threat.[49] The brigade continued to be involved in a series of difficult actions, in particular at Tessel Wood and Fontenay, before being held in reserve prior to the launching of *Operation Epsom*. Notably, the British troops, like the Germans, proved more adept in defence than in attack, and a number of enemy armour attacks were beaten off by Allied tanks and troops.

In the eastern sector 27th Armoured Brigade, like many other armoured formations, began to recognise the need for improved levels of infantry–armour

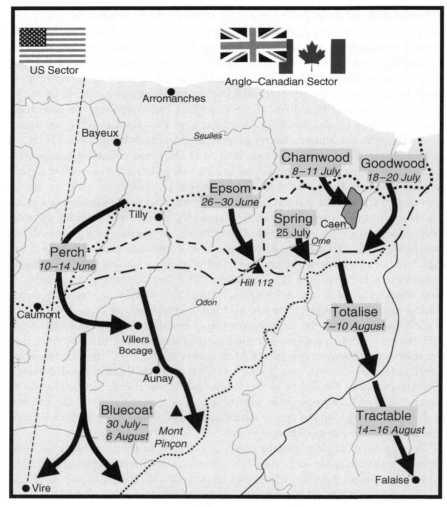

US Sector

Anglo–Canadian Sector

Arromanches

Bayeux

Seulles

Charnwood
8–11 July

Goodwood
18–20 July

Epsom
26–30 June

Tilly

Spring
25 July

Caen

Orne

Perch
10–14 June

Hill 112

Odon

Caumont

Totalise
7–10 August

Villers
Bocage

Aunay

Bluecoat
*30 July–
6 August*

Mont
Pinçon

Tractable
14–16 August

Vire

Falaise

•••••••• Captured by c. 18 June

– – – – Captured by c. 1 July

— · — · Captured by c. 30 July

·············· Captured by c. 6 August

——— Captured by c. 13 August

Map 1. Principal operations in Normandy, June–August 1944

co-operation. Early encounters demonstrated that commanders and troops were using a variety of different methods of working with infantry, as well as having to adapt tactics to the new situation and terrain.[50] Infantry commanders complained that no two armoured units applied the same techniques and that consistency was required. It was also a problem that armoured brigades and regiments tended to be moved around between divisions, with the consequence that the units would be separated just as an understanding between commanders and troops was emerging. This was to be a problem for the independent brigades throughout the campaign.[51]

This experience was similar to that of the Canadian 2nd Armoured Brigade. After having made good progress on the first day, the Canadians then encountered more serious opposition on 9 June. The 6th Canadian Armoured Regiment collided with German Panthers, but although heavy fighting ensued, the Sherman acquitted itself well according to Canadian tankcrew. In defence especially, the Firefly's 17-pdr gun was lethal, and from a flanking ambush position Lt G. Henry accounted for six Panthers from seven shots.[52]

Villers Bocage and *Operation Perch* (10–14 June)

Two operations have defined the modern view of British armour in Normandy more than any others – *Operation Goodwood* in July, and *Operation Perch*, which resulted in the Villers Bocage action of 13 June. The latter, because of its timing so early in the campaign, and because it coincided with growing alarm throughout 21st Army Group about the capabilities and deficiencies of Allied tanks, has come to epitomise the failings of British armour in the final stages of the war. Yet the Battle of Villers Bocage was just one action, and although much has been written about the defeat suffered there by 7th Armoured Division, a good deal of the commentary and analysis has suffered from hyperbole and propaganda. In particular the role of Michael Wittmann has been widely publicised and his impressive achievements exaggerated and eulogised to the extent that accounts have often implied that one Tiger tank stopped an entire armoured division.[53] One historian recently claimed that the 7th Armoured Division's spearhead was 'all but annihilated by the lone Tiger tank of Lt. Michael Wittmann'.[54] The reality, although highlighting errors and failings on the part of 7th Armoured Division, is quite different.

With the failure to seize Caen on 6 June, Montgomery and Lt-Gen Miles Dempsey were presented with alternatives regarding further actions to remove the German presence from that pivotal city. Dempsey had always been aware that the immediate seizure of Caen might prove unsuccessful, and deliberation had been given to other options.[55] *Operation Perch* had been considered in planning prior to the invasion as a measure open to 2nd Army in the days following D-Day. It had originally called for a drive to the west of Caen by XXX Corps, spearheaded by 7th Armoured Division and 8th Armoured Brigade to Tilly-sur-Seulles, and ultimately on to Mount Pinçon. However, this operation had ground to a halt as Panzer *Lehr* battled hard to hold Tilly. Dempsey and his staff had also been planning a more audacious operation, codenamed *Wild Oats* that called for a dashing drive by armoured forces to the west of Caen, supposed ultimately to meet up with 1st Airborne Division, which was to be dropped to the south of the city. A further effort to the east of Caen would see 51st Highland Division, supported by armour, break out from the bridgehead and also join up with 1st Airborne. *Wild Oats* was to occupy the planning staff of 2nd Army in the immediate aftermath of the invasion, but foundered on the opposition of Air Marshal Trafford Leigh-Mallory, the Allied air commander, and the unfolding situation. A key component was to be the effort of 7th Armoured Division in precipitating the western breakout, but in order to co-ordinate the whole effort and to have the appropriate level of logistical support, *Wild Oats* was delayed. By the time Erskine's armour was released on 10 June to begin the attack, valuable time had been lost. Moreover, the prospects for *Wild Oats* were poor and were to fade rapidly with the stalled progress of both 7th Armoured and 51st Highland Divisions.[56]

With the front congealing, as Dempsey put it, it was imperative that 7th Armoured be deployed more forcefully. Following discussions between Dempsey and Bucknall, GOC XXX Corps, and Erskine, GOC 7th Armoured Division, on 12 June *Operation Perch* was altered. Erskine's brief was now to leave most of his divisional infantry, the 131st Queen's Brigade, along with 8th Armoured Brigade and 50th Infantry Division in the line opposite Tilly, and release 22nd Armoured Brigade, supplemented by elements of the Queen's, commanded by Brig. Robert 'Loony' Hinde, on a western flanking manoeuvre. A gap had developed in the German lines between Panzer *Lehr* to the east and 352nd Infantry Division to the west, and Hinde's armour was to drive through this opening, seize Villers Bocage and then advance behind and into the flank of Panzer *Lehr*.

Speed and impetus were critical, but time had already been lost over the *Wild Oats* plan, and Dempsey recorded that he had to go to XXX Corps HQ and instil some greater action into Bucknall's team on 11 June. By this time, Erskine was becoming frustrated by the inactivity. He believed that *Perch* could have been initiated some 24 hours before it was and that valuable time had been frittered away in spurious planning.[57] Erskine's problem now was to make up for lost time by pushing on as quickly as possible. The 4th County of London Yeomanry (4CLY) Armoured Regiment was tasked with spearheading the assault with elements of the 1st Battalion Rifle Brigade in support, along with reconnaissance and anti-tanks units and elements of the Queen's Brigade.

The flanking advance began on 12 June at 16:00 hours but was held up at Livry, and by the late evening Hinde had decided to hold his position for fear of displaying his intentions to the Germans.[58] Early on 13 June the advance continued, though this time without the regimental reconnaissance elements ahead of 4CLY. The leading units reached Villers Bocage around 08:00, and

Hinde persuaded a reluctant Lt-Col Arthur Cranley (commanding 4CLY) to push on to Point 213, the vital high ground to the east of Villers.[59] Cranley saw the need for further reconnaissance but was effectively overruled. With two squadrons, the regimental HQ elements and attending supports stretched out through Villers and up to Point 213, the British force was assaulted by five Tiger tanks of 101st Heavy Tank Battalion. Four Tigers, later supported by anti-tanks guns and Panzer Mark IVs, pummelled the exposed leading elements of 4CLY on the road up to Point 213, whilst Obersturmführer Michael Wittmann, a very experienced and highly decorated tank commander, broke into the 4CLY position and proceeded to advance down through the town, brewing up a variety of light and HQ tanks, artillery observation vehicles, and an array of infantry transports. He was eventually driven out by the prospect of further duelling with a Sherman Firefly (equipped with a 17-pdr gun). As it exited Villers eastwards, Wittmann's Tiger was disabled at point-blank range by a 6-pdr anti-tank gun. The units of 4CLY trapped on the road up to Point 213 were whittled away as the morning went on and were captured by early afternoon. British reinforcements entered the town from the west throughout the morning, and in the afternoon became embroiled in fighting with Ralf Mobius' 1st Company of 101st Heavy Battalion, supported by infantry and tanks of Panzer *Lehr*. Losses were sustained on both sides in the fighting in Villers Bocage, but the likelihood of a sweeping penetration up to Mount Pinçon was now minuscule and Erskine withdrew, with the consent of Bucknall, later to be criticised heavily by Dempsey for so doing. However, Erskine still saw opportunities on the following day if he could be reinforced quickly, especially with infantry. Bucknall arguably misread the position and merely attempted to push from the north to reach Villers with 50th Division and supporting elements.[60] The opportunity, if it truly existed, was missed but the Germans suffered their own defeat on the night of 13 June when a two-battalion attack supported by perhaps 30 tanks was beaten off by the elements of 7th Armoured Division still in position to the northwest of Villers Bocage. Notably, the Germans, attacking across small high-banked fields encountered all the problems confronting the Allies, while the troops of the 7th Armoured for once enjoyed the advantages conferred by the terrain. Nevertheless, little more could be achieved and Erskine's division was withdrawn north on 14 June.[61]

The debacle was a humiliating reverse for 7th Armoured Division, which had arrived in Normandy with a fine reputation built on campaigning in the Mediterranean. Indeed, a frustrated Dempsey described the prosecution of the whole operation as a disgrace.[62] Clear errors in judgement were made, arguably at all levels, but the delayed timing and the unduly ambitious nature of the operation unhinged it from the start. Moreover, the notion that a reduced armoured brigade (22nd Armoured Brigade had left one of its three regiments with the divisional infantry brigade), with only limited mobile infantry and artillery support, could achieve a decisive penetration in the face of hardening opposition was optimistic. In addition, the level of support required to pursue the operation effectively was not forthcoming. Brig. Hinde also pointed to difficulties of operating in close country and the density and quality of the enemy forces. He further complained about the inadequacies of British tanks, arguing that Shermans and Cromwells were no match for Tigers and Panthers.[63] It should be noted, however, that the weakness of British tanks played little part in precipitating the set back at Villers Bocage. Indeed, although British losses were heavy, with some 40- plus vehicles being written off, German losses were also significant, with six or so very valuable Tigers being lost, along with other forces. In addition, the assault by 2nd Panzer Division's reconnaissance units on 7th Armoured's defensive position on the evening of 13 June had also suffered heavy casualties before being driven off.[64]

Many factors have been offered as reasons for the Allied setback during *Operation Perch*. Max Hastings blames poor co-ordination of infantry and armour, insufficient infantry support and the inadequacies of British tanks as the key reasons for British failure, while Carlo D'Este is more critical of British commanders, most notably Bucknall, XXX Corps commander. Michael Reynolds widens the net and is critical of British command generally.[65] All imply that the achievements of a single Tiger tank and its crew, Wittmann in particular, were critical.

However, although Wittmann displayed great bravery and daring in leading his attack, the roots of the failure at Villers Bocage are broader and deeper. This was a failure on the part of the British rather than a demonstration of superior German armour. Indeed, when German tanks went on to the offensive in Villers later on 13 June they too displayed poor armour–infantry co-operation.[66] The inadequacies of British tanks, in particular the new Cromwell, were real, but the fighting in Villers Bocage did little to expose them. The heavily armed and armoured Tiger tanks effectively ambushed the leading elements of 4CLY in and around Point 213, and Wittmann's destructive raid into the town itself encountered half-track transports, light reconnaissance tanks, regimental HQ tanks with their crews stood down, and artillery observation tanks, one of which had a dummy wooden gun. When Wittmann was fired upon by a Firefly, he prudently withdrew.[67]

The lack of infantry support was used as a factor in explaining the British defeat, as Villers Bocage supposedly could not be held in strength on the night of 13 June, but more infantry was available just a few miles away and elements of the 131st Queen's Brigade were fed into the fighting in Villers Bocage throughout 13 June. In addition 151st Infantry Brigade, in Corps reserve, was also capable of being deployed. Therefore, infantry was available, but was not as fully engaged as it should have been. The arrival of 2nd Panzers in and around 7th Armoured's position has also been cited as a reason for the British withdrawal, but Bucknall had begun the retreat before 2nd Panzers arrived in any real strength.[68] Moreover, Erskine certainly believed that more could have been achieved, if adequate support had been forthcoming, in spite of a scare-mongering report that 40 Tigers were approaching Villers Bocage.[69]

The most crucial factors in the defeat undoubtedly resided at command level, and in two particular cases. First, operational command demanded and expected great dash and boldness from 7th Armoured and methods of fighting supposedly akin to *blitzkrieg*. In essence, once 22nd Armoured Brigade was through the gap in the German lines the whole operation appeared to be an archetypal armoured exploitation. The commanders of 7th Armoured also viewed the task as one of 'going swanning' rather than heavy fighting. In reality, the penetration was weak, and the unwillingness of Bucknall in particular to support the attack when problems developed undermined the whole operation. However, the second and perhaps most pertinent factor in the failure was an inadequate linking of force structure to circumstance. More than any other armoured division in the British Army, the 7th was prepared for mobile operations in exploitation of opportunities and breakthroughs, yet the events of 12 June indicated not a break-through so much as an evasion of heavy combat. Stalled in front of Tilly by Panzer *Lehr*, 7th Armoured attempted to replace direct assault with manoeuvre, not in itself an inappropriate stratagem, but one which required forceful and determined leadership, along with closely co-ordinated combined arms tactics. The more independent 'swanning' approach of 7th Armoured may have been suitable for open country operations in the desert, but it certainly was not for the congested and close terrain of north-west Europe, which required intimate co-operation of infantry, artillery and reconnaissance units with the armour. The division's approach to operations had been exposed as flawed, and as the commanders and troops attempted to adapt, reputations began to crumble.

Operation Epsom, 26–30 June

Over the next two weeks or so Anglo-Canadian armour aided the expansion of the bridgehead still further, but 21st Army Group was planning a much more ambitious use of the growing strength of 2nd British Army. After the debacle of *Operation Perch*, Montgomery reverted to his preferred methods of employing large-scale, properly prepared set-piece battles to achieve his object-ives. Consequently, a three-corps attack was planned in the Odon Valley, spearheaded by the newly arrived VIII Corps commanded by the highly respected Lt-Gen Richard O'Connor. XXX Corps was to support on the right flank by seizing the Rauray Ridge which overlooked the axis of advance to be taken by VIII Corps. On the left, I Corps was to occupy Carpiquet, which also offered an observation point over the battlefield, before pushing on to Caen itself.

The main thrust by VIII Corps, however, was to come from two infantry divisions (15th Scottish and 43rd Wessex), an armoured division (11th), an armoured brigade (4th) and a tank brigade (31st), totalling over 600 tanks. Artillery support from some 700 guns would be available and a significant level of air support was to be provided. The objectives were to cross the River

Odon, take the high ground beyond, most notably Hills 112 and 113, and thrust into the Orne Valley, thus cutting Caen off from the south and forcing the Germans to give up the city. The armour was to be used in the classic manner, with the heavy infantry Churchill tanks of 31st Tank Brigade closely supporting the 15th Scottish in the initial assault, to be supported by the 43rd Wessex with the Sherman-equipped 4th Armoured Brigade under command. Ultimately, when the moment was ripe, 11th Armoured Division would be released to exploit the penetration and burst into the Orne Valley.[70]

However, various factors militated against the success of *Epsom*, and although the operation has been described as 'the best executed British assault in Normandy' in reality, on a tactical level, it proved to be a muddled, confused and frustrating mess, though one in which a good deal was learned about fighting in northwest Europe.[71] Of critical importance once again were the difficult terrain, consisting of high corn fields, *bocage*, the thickly wooded Odon Valley and finally the rising high ground of Hill 112, and the poor weather, rain and low cloud, which hindered the use of air support.

Operation Martlet, XXX Corps' attempt to drive the Germans away from high ground overlooking the main thrust of *Epsom* with 49th (West Riding) Infantry Division supported by 8th Armoured Brigade failed, and consequently, VIII Corps' advance had to contend with exposed flanks.[72] German artillery observers were thus able to direct very accurate shelling and mortaring on to the British positions as they drove forward. Still further, the terrain was dense and undulating, limiting the rate of advance and creating great difficulties for the attackers. Finally, the quality of the German defence was rapidly supplemented by quantity as units were fed into the line in a desperate attempt to prevent a British breakout.

The Churchill tanks of 31st Tank Brigade were the first of VIII Corps' armoured units into action on the morning of 26 June. In close support of 15th Scottish they advanced on a two-mile front, making fair progress, but the inexperience of the two formations, which had never worked together before, soon told. With the assault slowing by the hour, and with the Odon crossings still some two miles off, O'Connor took the decision to launch the 11th Armoured Division prematurely. The division should have been unleashed *after* the Odon crossings had been seized, but O'Connor reckoned that without an immediate boost the British might not reach the Odon at all. Consequently, the largely inexperienced armoured division, commanded by Maj-Gen Pip Roberts, was ordered to attack. A further curious decision followed when the division's reconnaissance regiment, the Northants Yeomanry, equipped with the lighter Cromwell, was used to spearhead the assault. Roberts himself stated that 'I never thought much of their luck if they had to make a fight of it', though in the circumstances this was clearly what they were expected to do.[73] When their advance had predictably petered out, Roberts pushed the division's armoured brigade into the attack, passing through the 15th Scottish Division, but 26 June ended with the British still a mile short of the

Odon. On the following day, further progress was made and on 28 June Hill 112 was seized and held for a time by 11th Armoured Division, whose officers also believed that further progress could be made.[74] However, with the opposition ahead of VIII Corps hardening, and as the available intelligence provided by *Ultra* underpinned this view, Dempsey and O'Connor called a halt to the operation on 30 June.

Epsom had failed in its main aim of breaking though to the Orne Valley, though it had undermined the German ability to prepare a major counter-attack in the area, as arriving reinforcements had to be fed piecemeal into the battle to block British progress. Moreover, when the Germans had once again gone on to the counter-offensive, as they did on 27 June and again on Hill 112 on 1 July, they were repulsed with heavy losses.[75] The British had amply demonstrated that the key to wearing down the Germans in Normandy was to draw them into counter-attacking where they would suffer irreplaceable losses. However, the battle had demonstrated the British armoured forces' inexperience and questionable infantry–tank co-operation capabilities in a number of ways. O'Connor believed Roberts had not developed the knack of utilising his armoured and infantry brigades in a mutually supporting manner, and Roberts was critical of the level of infantry–tank co-operation he witnessed in 7th and 9th Royal Tank Regiments of 31st Tank Brigade.[76] More importantly for the armoured forces, the battle had illustrated the misuse of tanks and a lack of appreciation of the force structure of the armoured division by the senior leadership, both at corps and army level. There is no doubt that O'Connor intended his activation of 11th Armoured on the afternoon of 26 June to force a breakthrough where 15th Scottish and 31st Tank Brigade had failed. He even claimed that this use of 11th Armoured was 'according to plan'.[77] Yet the armoured division was designed for exploitation, not penetration, and Roberts had deep misgivings over his armour being used in this manner.[78]

Therefore, during *Epsom* 11th Armoured had been misused and yet, though demonstrating its inexperience, had still performed well. The Churchills of 31st Tank Brigade had displayed poor co-ordination with the infantry they were designed and trained to support, though this can be partly mitigated by the units not having worked together prior to 26 June. Finally, 4th Armoured Brigade, an experienced unit, had also struggled when called into action to support a drive towards Hill 113. The command structure of the brigade was hit with the death of its CO, Brig. John Currie, who was replaced by Michael Carver, and as the battle progressed the inadequacies of other senior officers resulted in the replacement of four key commanders during the brigade's first action in Normandy.[79]

Operation Windsor, 4 July

One of the key components of *Epsom* had been the drive by I Corps, on the left flank of O'Connor's force, to seize Carpiquet and in particular its airfield, but this had failed to materialise and was postponed until 4 July.[80] The operation, codenamed *Windsor* was to prepare the ground for a much larger effort to dislodge the Germans from Caen, pencilled in for 8 July. Nevertheless, *Windsor* was to employ 8th Infantry Brigade (from 3rd Canadian Division) supported by a regiment of tanks, 10th Armoured Regiment (Fort Garry Horse) from 2nd Canadian Armoured Brigade. In addition, 79th Armoured was to provide three squadrons of close support armour, in particular a squadron of flame-throwing Churchill Crocodiles.

The assault struggled to make headway against determined opposition, but the village of Carpiquet was seized, though the airfield remained stubbornly out of reach. During an attack from Marcelet by the Royal Winnipeg Rifles, the supporting armour stood off and attempted to shoot the infantry on to target from static positions, but failed to provide adequate close support. It was not until early afternoon that armour advanced to aid the offensive.[81] Even so, the attack faltered and the Canadians were driven back later that afternoon, with armour duels between Allied tanks and Panthers and Mark IVs being a key feature. The Allies came off worst, with one Panther commander claiming six Shermans in the firefight, and it may well be the case that no German tank was irretrievably lost.[82] Nevertheless, 12th SS suffered the loss of some 155 men, mostly in the counter-attacks of 5 July, while the Canadians endured 377 casualties.[83]

Operation Windsor was considered a disappointment. Once again, although some progress had been made, an infantry brigade and two armoured regiments, amply supported by artillery, naval and air power, had been stymied by a much smaller force of less than one battalion, a company of tanks and six 88 mm guns. The failure prompted John Crocker, I Corps commander, to attempt to have 3rd Canadian's GOC, Maj-Gen Keller removed, claiming that poor leadership had been the key factor in the limited achievements of *Windsor*.[84] However, the operation had also again demonstrated a degree of weakness in armour–infantry doctrine, the capabilities of the experienced German troops in defending Norman terrain, and the problems the belligerents, both the Allies and the Germans encountered when on the offensive.

Operation Charnwood, 8–11 July

Montgomery and Dempsey now sought to remove the German presence from Caen by means of a fully fledged set piece assault. Attempts to flank the city to the west and east had failed, but the pressing need to seize Caen remained. Montgomery had now secured the support of the strategic air forces for this new operation, codenamed *Charnwood*, and 21st Army Group was again to deploy Crocker's I Corps in the key role, with three infantry divisions, two armoured brigades and units of 79th Armoured Division in support. The armoured brigades employed were to be 2nd Canadian and 27th Armoured. The action was to be on a much broader front than previous actions in order to increase the pressure on the German defensive lines and disperse their defensive fire, a lesson gleaned from *Windsor*.[85]

The preliminary air raid on the evening of 7 July achieved very little, unfortunately, despite the use of over 450 Lancasters and Halifaxes. The RAF had been concerned about friendly fire casualties and thus unloaded their bombs some 6,000 yards ahead of the British lines, but this overshot most of the German troops and equipment and merely wrecked Caen, hindering later use of the road network by Allied armour and vehicles. The German casualties were slight, with 12th SS claiming to have lost only two Mark IV tanks and less than 20 troops.[86] Moreover, I Corps troops failed to follow up the aerial bombardment immediately, inactivity that perplexed the Germans.[87]

Progress by the Allied troops was costly on 8 July, but heavy fighting forced the stubborn German defenders back across the Orne and into new defensive positions in the south of the city on the following day. Once again during this operation, Anglo-Canadian tanks often stood off and shot their infantry on to objectives rather than supporting them closely, and this was noted as one of the causes of the infantry's heavy casualty rates.[88] Nevertheless, armoured losses were also significant with some 80 Allied tanks being written off.[89] German losses during the fighting were not slight, and the repeated Anglo-Canadian assaults were slowly whittling away the higher-quality German units. The 12th SS Panzer Division's infantry was reduced to the equivalent of one battalion, and armour and anti-tank gun losses were considerable, with around ten Panthers and 22 Mark IVs being destroyed.[90] Many of these were once again lost in localised counter-attacks, during which German tanks became as vulnerable as their Allied counterparts.[91] During one action around Buron, Royal Artillery M10 17-pdrs proved the vulnerability of German armour when on the offensive, and in one brief action alone some 13 panzers were destroyed.[92]

Allied troops and armour again had made progress but at heavy cost to the infantry, and in the minds of the enemy the Anglo-Canadians had lacked the ability or desire to press home advantages. Kurt Meyer, GOC 12th SS Panzers, recorded that continued pressure by the Allies on the night of 8 July may well have broken his division completely.[93] However, Allied losses were already heavy and the cost of further intensive assaults would have been prohibitive. Progress had been made and the first use of massed heavy air power had indicated what might be possible if technique and co-ordination could be improved. By the time *Charnwood* had ground to a halt, the Germans, despite having been forced to surrender part of Caen, were dug-in in strength on the south side of the River Orne and the open country to the south was still denied to 21st Army Group.

Operation Jupiter, 10–11 July

A complementary operation to *Charnwood* was conducted by VIII Corps to the west of Caen on 10 July, with the aim of exploiting the expected German retreat from the city forced by *Operation Charnwood*. Once again the objective was to seize Hill 112 and Maltot and then unleash armoured forces into the Orne Valley. Codenamed *Jupiter*, VIII Corps deployed 43rd Wessex Division, under the command of the fearsome Gen Thomas, and 46th Highland Brigade, with 31st Tank Brigade in support. The exploitation role was to be undertaken by 4th Armoured Brigade, commanded by Michael Carver.

The initial advance towards the summit of Hill 112 began in the early hours of 10 July and was conducted by 4th Somerset Light Infantry supported by the heavily armoured Churchill infantry tanks of 7th Royal Tank Regiment (7RTR). Despite the infantry losing three of their four company commanders, they fought their way to the crest but were stopped by anti-tank guns and recently arrived Tigers of 102nd SS Heavy Tank Battalion deployed on the reverse slope.[94] The 7RTR Churchills suffered heavily and fell back to hull down positions, thus removing close support for the infantry as they attempted to clear the area on the southern slope of Hill 112 prior to 4th Armoured Brigade's thrust to the Orne.[95] Carver was well aware of the inadequate situation and point-blank refused to release his armour until the position was secure, much to the fury of Thomas.[96] The demise of the Churchills when they had skylined on the crest would seem to support his decision. A further attack by 5th Duke of Cornwall's Light Infantry supported by 14 Churchills of 7RTR enjoyed more success, but bitter fighting continued both on Hill 112 and around Maltot and Eterville, both of which were ultimately held by the Germans. The day's fighting saw 31st Tank Brigade lose 39 tanks, approximately a quarter of its fighting strength.[97] Further losses were sustained on 11 July in a renewed effort on Hill 112 but the operation was called off by Thomas later that day when it became perfectly clear that little would be gained by further action.

Despite considerable superiority in tanks, infantry and firepower the Allies had failed to drive the dwindling troops of I and II SS Panzer Corps from the route to the Orne. The Allied armour had been forced to make frontal and at times inadequately supported attacks on strong defensive positions, and with German anti-tanks guns and Tigers in particular taking up strong reverse slope positions, the capture of Hill 112 was always going to be difficult. To the east, in and around Maltot and Eterville, a series of to-and-fro engagements had yielded little, but had further reinforced the view that even the Germans, when provoked into localised counter-attacks, suffered heavy casualties, especially from Allied artillery and anti-tank guns. *Jupiter* also further exposed the problem of congestion for Allied armour, an issue already noted at *Epsom*, and one that would continue to plague tank commanders in Normandy.[98] The constricted space over which Allied offensives were being prosecuted, other than *Charnwood*, was also hindering the speed with which supplies, replacements and reinforcements could be brought into the line.[99] In addition, the operation also proved that at the ranges actions were taking place in the enclosed Norman countryside, even the Churchill's 150 mm-plus frontal armour was no protection against the anti-tank weaponry – infantry portable hollow-charge weapons as well as 75 mm and 88 mm guns – with which the Germans were equipped. In contrast, the 75 mm guns of the Allied tanks were struggling to cope with the heavier frontal armour of the Panther and the Tiger's all-round defence. In one action, at a range of just 800 yards, a tank of the Royal Scots Greys hit a Panther four times with its 75 mm gun only to see the shells bounce off harmlessly.[100]

Nevertheless, despite difficulties, British armour had supported a series of infantry assaults and, like previous operations, facilitated limited initial advances. Yet further progress, or indeed in *Jupiter* the ability to hold gains, proved unattainable through a combination of the Allies' unwillingness to endure heavy losses and vigorous but costly German counter-actions. The Allied approach was sustainable and logical, largely because the German method was not. Carver's refusal to throw his Shermans against a still heavily defended German position was perfectly understandable and demonstrated the limited grasp of armour capabilities of an infantry commander such as Thomas. However, such clarity of understanding in how armour could and should be used was not to be displayed a few days later to the east of Caen.

Operation Goodwood, 18–20 July

The employment of massed armour to the east of Caen on 18 July in what appeared to be a bold and imaginative plan of breakout by 21st Army Group, and its subsequent dismal failure in front of the Bourguébus Ridge later that day, has become synonymous with the shortcomings of Allied armour in Normandy. Criticism has been heaped on British armour tactics, command, and on the Allied tanks, which were outgunned and under-armoured for such an assault. Whilst much of the furore over the failure of *Goodwood* centres on the political and high-level command pressures and squabbles involving Montgomery, Eisenhower and Tedder, there is little doubt that a good deal of controversy surrounds the operation itself and in explaining why it did not achieve all that it might. It is therefore instructive and useful to analyse the role and employment of armour in the operation.

Goodwood was 2nd British Army commander Lt-Gen Miles Dempsey's plan. With the Americans bogged down and preparing for their next breakout attempt, to be *Cobra*, Dempsey persuaded Montgomery to back an ambitious all-armoured corps operation to the east of Caen. It would place all three of the British armoured divisions (7th and 11th were now supplemented by the newly arrived Guards Armoured Division) under the command of O'Connor's VIII Corps, which would be thrust from the Allied bridgehead to the east of the Orne, south towards the Bourguébus Ridge, which commanded the road to Falaise. If successful, penetration further south towards Falaise was a possibility, or so Dempsey believed, and he positioned himself for the battle close to O'Connor's tactical HQ so that he would be on hand to command an exploitation phase should it arise.[101] Dempsey was also conscious of the need to limit infantry casualties in 21st Army Group, and considered that employment of the armoured divisions, little used since the invasion, would ease the burden on the rifleman.[102] Equipment could be replaced, whereas personnel could not.

Dempsey's plan called for VIII Corps, with the three armoured divisions, to move across the Orne and the Caen Canal and drive south, spearheaded by a massive aerial and artillery bombardment. The Bourguébus Ridge was the first objective and from that point further exploitation could hopefully be developed. The recently established II Canadian Corps, commanded by Lt-Gen Guy Simonds, would provide support by clearing the rest of Caen in *Operation Atlantic,* while Crocker's I Corps and Ritchie's XII Corps would cover the flanks of the advance. Montgomery initially approved the plan at a meeting with Dempsey on 12 July, only to clip its wings a little on 15 July, when he met with O'Connor and Dempsey.[103] The prospect of real exploitation beyond the Bourguébus Ridge was downplayed to reconnaissance by armoured cars which would 'spread alarm and despondency and... discover "the form"'.[104] Only if the situation developed much in VIII Corps' favour would there be the option to 'crack about' as Montgomery put it.[105] It is clear that although Dempsey's optimism had been dampened a little by his immediate commander, and that the expectation was not for a breakout but a writing down of German strength, the 2nd Army commander still harboured hopes for a decisive penetration of the German defences. At the very least, *Goodwood* was to be a major multi-corps operation involving the use of massed strategic bombers and political expectations were therefore high.

However, *Goodwood* was a flawed plan, poorly executed and with little chance of success when it was launched on the morning of 18 July. Most importantly, it demonstrated an inadequate appreciation of the role and capabilities of armoured divisions. They were not constructed to act as battering rams to lead a penetration and their force structure was accordingly ill-suited to an operation such as *Goodwood,* where the armour was to lead the attack. In some ways *Goodwood* mirrored *Epsom* in that the armoured division was to be used to breakthrough, not exploit an opportunity, the role actually envisaged for them in pre-D-Day planning and training.

However, *Goodwood* went much further in flouting the basic principles of armoured warfare as they pertained in 1944. Montgomery had for some time argued strongly against the employment of an all-armoured corps, largely because of difficult experiences in the Mediterranean campaign.[106] Indeed, he had stated quite clearly at a 21st Army Group staff conference in January that he would never employ an all-armoured corps.[107] Yet because of the broader strategic picture, and the situation in and around Caen in mid-July 1944, Dempsey persuaded a reluctant Montgomery to unleash such a formation into a heavily defended German zone. The major difficulty facing an armoured division acting independently centred on the low levels of infantry support available, there being just one motor battalion in the whole armoured brigade of an armoured division in 1944. Moreover, the speed with which O'Connor's armoured units were to dash towards the Bourguébus Ridge, to the southeast of Caen, minimised the likelihood of the lorried infantry in the armoured division's infantry brigade keeping pace. O'Connor later claimed that, in recognition of this weakness, he attempted to persuade Dempsey to allow the conversion of self-propelled artillery equipment into crude armoured personnel carriers.[108] Dempsey, however, was unconvinced and blocked the measure.[109] The problem of maintaining appropriate infantry support was compounded by O'Connor himself, however, when he instructed Roberts to use his division's infantry brigade to seize Cuverville and Demouville well to the north of the Bourguébus Ridge. Roberts argued that this would denude his armour of any realistic hope of retaining adequate infantry support for the middle-to-latter stages of the first day's operations, arguably just at the moment they would need it most, when the paralysing effects of the aerial and artillery bombardment on the German positions would have faded. Moreover, to Roberts' chagrin and dismay, his division was also ordered to take the fortified village of Cagny en route to the first stage objective. Roberts pointed out the pitfalls to O'Connor twice, once in writing, arguing that 51st Highland Division could take Cuverville and Demouville, thus releasing 11th Armoured's infantry for forward operations.[110] O'Connor demurred and threatened to remove 11th Armoured from the vanguard of the attack, but he did allow Roberts merely to 'mask' Cagny, leaving it for Guards Armoured Division to capture.[111] This proved to be an error, however, for by not taking Cagny, the left flank of 11th Armoured's advance was exposed to the German 88 mm guns positioned in the village, as well as to Becker's self-propelled guns, which constantly sniped at the British flank and then repeatedly and astutely relocated.[112] As a result some 16 tanks were lost to the forces in Cagny alone. Roberts remained bitter about the plans to retain his infantry in a cautious and defensive posture, even after he discovered later that *Goodwood*'s aims had been downgraded by Montgomery on 15 July, something that had curiously not cascaded down to the divisional commanders, who remained overly sanguine about the operation's chances.[113] Nevertheless, the repercussions were significant, and as predicted a shortage in infantry was a major factor in preventing the tanks of 11th Armoured Division from seizing Hubert-Folie and Bras on the Bourguébus Ridge in the early afternoon of 18 July.

Operation Goodwood also suffered unduly from poor all-arms co-ordination, partly a product of the nature of the plan, but which impacted severely on the armoured regiments. Already denuded of adequate levels of infantry support for the critical stages of the battle, the armour was to be left without effective fire support by the late morning and thus quite helpless when confronted by alerted and determined German opposition, in particular on the Bourguébus Ridge. The speed and distance over which the Allied armour had advanced outpaced artillery support, the mobile elements of which were still struggling to get across the congested bridges over the River Orne and the Caen Canal.[114] Indeed, the priority in planning was for the armour and the motor battalions to cross first, but even they encountered great difficulties throughout 18 July, leading to considerable slowing of progress.[115] Consequently, artillery support for the leading armoured units dwindled as the day went on. Moreover, air support also faded, despite the tremendous effects of the initial heavy bombardment. In part this was due to the great depth of the German defences defeating the bombing plans of the Allied air forces, but also because the forward air controller (FAC) assigned to the 29th Armoured Brigade was badly wounded in sight of the Bourguébus Ridge and knocked out of the battle.[116] Tactical air support from then on became sporadic and patchy, just at the crucial moment when it was most required. There is certainly a degree of misfortune over this incident, but the fact that only one FAC was allotted to the leading brigade of this major operation was a major error in judgement and planning.

The *Goodwood* plan also demonstrated a poor understanding of the employment of armour in terms of manoeuvring space. Attempting to push three armoured divisions across six bridges in the space of a few hours, partly in darkness, was ambitious enough, but the frontage of the assault was to be just 2,000 yards, initially along narrow lanes cleared through minefields and then across bomb-cratered terrain. Whatever the advantages of a narrow-front assault, the problems it created for armour were nowhere better exposed than *Operation Goodwood*. It was unsurprising that Erskine, GOC 7th Armoured, was highly critical of the employment of armour on 18 July.[117] With the British armour charging a recovered and reinforced German defensive line while backed by inadequate artillery, infantry and air support, and with only limited manoeuvring space, it was little wonder the assault failed.

Attempts by Dempsey and O'Connor to revive the flagging operation on 19 and 20 July fizzled out as the weather deteriorated, German defences hardened still further, and attention swung to the American sector and the impending *Operation Cobra*. Although the wider impact of *Goodwood* may have been to absorb German resources and ease the task facing Bradley's forces in the west, it came at no small cost to 21st Army Group with over 6,000 casualties, some 14 per cent of the total suffered by the Anglo-Canadian forces since D-Day.[118] Although many were later recovered, the British had lost well over 400 tanks, in excess of a third of their total frontline strength during *Goodwood*.[119] Although there is little evidence that fighting units suffered as a result of equipment shortages caused by *Goodwood*, an impact on morale and confidence was apparent.[120]

The failure of *Goodwood* is all too often viewed as a failure of armour, but the circumstances dictated that a much more co-ordinated and sophisticated plan was required to defeat the depth and strength of German defences confronting VIII Corps on 18 July. Indeed, when on 19 July 11th and Guards Armoured Divisions were properly constituted with appropriate levels of support, they made good progress against a prepared and determined German defence along the Bourguébus Ridge, though by this time hopes for a decisive breakthrough had evaporated.

Perhaps *Goodwood's* greatest failing was that it was too ambitious for its own good. Previous operations had made effective use of defensive positions and firepower to defeat German counter-attacks and inflict heavy casualties, as part of the overarching policy of writing down the enemy. Dempsey arguably deviated from this concept by overreaching on 18 July and exposing his leading elements as they attempted to seize Bourguébus Ridge. A more defensive posture using available terrain may have limited British losses while still provoking the Germans into costly counter-attack.

Moreover, the tactical considerations for British armour in *Goodwood* were considerable and quite alarming. Maj. Tony Sargeaunt, the tank expert attached to No. 2 Operational Research Section at 21st Army Group, was shocked when he first viewed the *Goodwood* plan. The final stages would be fought across a flat and open area of some 4,000 yards, which would offer the static anti-tank gunnery of the Germans a huge advantage whilst denying British armour any cover or hull-down firing positions. Allied tank guns attempting to knock out camouflaged enemy anti-tank guns needed to be at a range of some 800 yards or less to have a fair chance of rapid success. At ranges of some 2,000 yards, however, it would take Shermans and Cromwells some 15 rounds of high explosive (HE) to eliminate the target. Even with multiple tanks engaging the enemy, it was probable that four or five Allied tanks would be knocked out in the process. Consequently, in the later stages of *Goodwood*, in the final push to the Bourguébus Ridge, Allied tanks would be at their most vulnerable just at the time when the effects of artillery and air support were likely to be diminishing. It made little sense to push on towards the ridge across open ground until adequate firepower support could be guaranteed to suppress the enemy guns, but this was precisely what Dempsey's plan implicitly called for.[121]

German losses over the period of the operation were still considerable, however, and this played a role in aiding *Cobra*. Nevertheless, whatever the strategic consequences of the operation, *Goodwood* was, as Dempsey put it, 'not a very good operation of war tactically'.[122]

Operation Spring, 25 July

In order to support the US breakout attempt in the west and because the Anglo-Canadians were under growing political pressure from SHAEF, Montgomery planned a sizeable action to the south of Caen, employing four divisions and supporting forces. The main objective was to tie down high-quality German forces in the east, maintain Anglo-Canadian pressure and perhaps push into the Falaise Plain in an expanded multi-corps endgame.[123] Codenamed *Spring*, and planned for 25 July, the operation was to be the first major effort of the campaign for II Canadian Corps, commanded by the highly thought of

Lt-Gen Guy Simonds. Two British armoured divisions were allocated to II Canadian Corps, 7th and Guards, and Simonds also had 2nd Canadian Armoured Brigade in support of 2nd and 3rd Canadian Infantry Divisions.

However, any expanded follow-up to *Spring* was effectively doomed from the start. Simonds' troops were to be launched against the strongest sector of the German defensive lines, which included the highest density of SS troops yet encountered. Indeed, if II Canadian Corps had been successful they may have locked horns with 1st, 9th and 12th SS and 2nd and 21st Panzers. Nevertheless, *Spring* was conceived as a holding operation first and foremost and the Guards Armoured Division were under clear instructions not to take too many risks, while Erskine at 7th Armoured had already indicated that he saw little benefit in charging Cromwells and Shermans at heavily defended German positions.[124] However, it is arguable as to whether Simonds was afforded the support necessary to prosecute *Spring* effectively, even with limited objectives in mind. Moreover, criticism can be levelled at Montgomery for allowing II Canadian Corps to be committed to an action where progress was doubtful, was therefore unlikely to tie down German forces, and consequently would fail to pin German resources, let alone offer hope of a more decisive penetration.[125] As it was, *Spring* achieved little, even as a holding operation, for that was a role to be carried out more successfully in *Operation Bluecoat* a few days later.

The level of firepower support for *Spring* was less than that expected by the Germans, to such an extent that they remained sceptical as to whether this was a serious operation. Nevertheless, although the heavy bomber fleets were assigned to *Cobra*, *Spring* enjoyed medium bomber and substantial artillery support. However, the ground assaults were much too weak, with the armour of 2nd Canadian Armoured Brigade too dispersed to make considerable progress, despite the valiant efforts of the troops. The Royal Hamilton Light Infantry's seizure of Verrières was certainly noteworthy, but 22nd Armoured Brigade (of 7th Armoured Division) advanced cautiously under the direction of Erskine, now showing even clearer signs of a loss of nerve, or perhaps at best a lack of faith in the ability of armoured forces to engage German defences successfully.[126] Elsewhere, Canadian troops suffered heavy casualties, especially when a concerted German counter-attack hit the North Nova Scotias. Co-ordination of that regiment with its attached tank support, provided by a squadron of Fort Garry Horse Shermans, was poor, with the infantry becoming separated and the tanks being held back by Panthers mingling with the advancing troops. The Shermans lost 11 of 16 tanks, whilst the battalion suffered 139 casualties.[127]

Operation Spring fizzled out fairly quickly late on 25 July and further actions in support were cancelled. There is little doubt that the operation was a disappointment on many levels and had signally failed in its primary objectives. Allied armour had been too thinly dispersed, though this mirrored the whole approach to the operation, and arguably 22nd Armoured Brigade had yet again displayed the scars of Villers Bocage.

Operation Bluecoat, 30 July–6 August

That *Spring* failed as a holding operation is not in doubt, but 21st Army Group's subsequent action to support the breakthrough achieved by the Americans in *Cobra* was highly effective in tying down German forces, preventing them from hindering Bradley's progress in the west. This series of multi-corps actions conducted by Dempsey's 2nd Army, codenamed *Bluecoat*, also demonstrated, despite heavy casualties, a growing tactical flexibility in some armoured units and a willingness, at times, to exploit openings with dash. It also exemplified the advantages of close armour–infantry co-operation, and that flexible and adaptable units and commanders could cope with even a hastily mounted operation such as *Bluecoat*. Indeed, Dempsey was not issued with the directive to strike south in support of Bradley until 27 July, just three days before the launch of the assault.[128] Planning was necessarily rushed and units only became aware of their objectives on 29 July. Indeed, when VIII Corps' leading units engaged the enemy on the morning of 30 July, supporting units were still east of the Orne. Bucknall's XXX Corps, including 7th Armoured Division, was to drive south towards Mount Pinçon, while O'Connor's VIII Corps, including 11th and Guards Armoured Divisions as well as 6th Guards Tank Brigade, was to seize Le Beny Bocage and Vire and force the crumbling German 7th Army to withdraw.[129]

Erskine's 7th Armoured Division as part of XXX Corps made only sluggish progress, at one stage exposing the flanks of the more successful 11th Armoured Division and causing O'Connor to slow his advance. After two days 7th Armoured was still five miles short of its objective, Aunay-sur-Odon. Despite being prompted by Dempsey, Bucknall's corps failed to pick up the pace, and he, along with Erskine, Hinde and around 100 other officers of the Desert Rats, were replaced in a cull to pep up the division.[130] XXX Corps chief of staff (CoS), Harold 'Peter' Pyman, considered the replacement of both Bucknall and Erskine as entirely justified as neither had shown enough drive in the opening stages of *Bluecoat*.[131] However, the terrain of the *Bluecoat* operation, particularly around Mount Pinçon was hardly conducive to rapid offensive actions, and it is almost certain that Erskine, Hinde and Bucknall all paid more for previous failures than those demonstrated during late July and early August.

In sharp contrast, O'Connor's VIII Corps made good progress. The newly arrived 6th Guards Tank Brigade, commanded by Brig. Gerald Verney, won many plaudits for its closely co-ordinated work with the now battle-hardened 15th Scottish Infantry Division.[132] Their capture of Hill 309 and the ground before Caumont on 30 July demonstrated the value of good training (it was the tank brigade's first action in Normandy), the advantages of having co-operated and trained with 15th Scottish in Britain, and the excellent cross-country performance of the Churchill tank.[133] Indeed, Verney's reputation was such that following Erskine's dismissal he was appointed to command 7th Armoured Division.

39

VIII Corps' superior performance was also a consequence of the growing realisation amongst its armoured commanders of the need to reorganise the armoured divisions to facilitate superior infantry–armour co-operation, especially as during *Bluecoat* they were to operate in the heart of the close *bocage* countryside. Both Roberts (11th Armoured) and Adair (Guards) divided their divisions into two brigade groups, each with infantry battalions and armoured regiments in mutually supporting combinations. Such a restructuring proved highly successful. Adair modified the structure later in August and retained it throughout the rest of the campaign, while Roberts employed it more flexibly, but settled with it following the capture of Antwerp. Indeed, Adair claimed that 'adopting this organisation was the best thing I ever did', while Roberts argued that it was only from *Bluecoat* onwards that the appropriate divisional structure was employed.[134] O'Connor was well pleased with his armoured commanders in *Bluecoat*, praising the often maligned Adair as well as Verney and Roberts for their determination and dash at critical moments in the battle.[135] The 11th Armoured Division's determination in exploiting the unexpected seizure of a small bridge over the Souleuvre River was particularly noteworthy.[136]

However, desperate and determined German counter-attacks and defence held the front together, and the unevenness of the British assault prevented the more decisive penetration, hoped for by Dempsey. Casualties throughout *Bluecoat* were high, but progress was made and the first objective of pinning and writing down German troops in the British sector, in the most difficult circumstances of the campaign, was largely achieved. Moreover, British armoured forces were in some cases demonstrating that lessons were being absorbed and applied to the battlefield.

Operation Totalise, 7–10 August

With terrific American progress in the west following the *Cobra*-led breakout, 21st Army Group endeavoured to make its contribution to the looming envelopment of the German armies in France. With Dempsey's 2nd British Army pressing on the western flank, Montgomery decided upon a major assault from Caen towards Falaise, to be conducted by Crerar's recently constituted 1st Canadian Army. The operation was to be spearheaded by Simonds' II Canadian Corps, with a heavy contingent of armour in the van, comprising two newly arrived armoured divisions, 4th Canadian and 1st Polish, with 2nd Canadian Armoured Brigade and 33rd British Armoured Brigade in support. *Totalise*, as it was to be codenamed, included many innovations, intended by Simonds to rectify the operational difficulties thus far encountered by the Anglo-Canadian forces.

First, Simonds was keen to effect surprise and thus prevent the Germans being able to stymie the attempted break-through by their being aware too soon of the nature and intentions of 21st Army Group assaults. To this end Simonds decided to launch a carefully planned and strictly timetabled night-time operation, with heavy artillery support only kicking in when the offensive was under way. Ample use of air power was factored in to compensate for this, and to offer firepower support to the leading echelons when they had outpaced the less mobile artillery.

Second, *Totalise* was to retain momentum and not get bogged down. Simonds realised that a number of 21st Army Group's operations had effected break-ins, but had been unable to maintain the advance. His plan addressed this concern in three ways. First, air power would play a more complete and integrated role by providing firepower support deep into German-held territory, just at the moment when the effectiveness of Allied artillery would be waning. Second, the depth of German defences had continually confounded Allied efforts, and therefore *Totalise* was to be a two-stage plan, with the second phase, particularly a second aerial bombardment, intended to breach the main German defensive line. Finally, II Canadian Corps' leading forces would not suffer from inadequate levels of infantry support, as Simonds had ordered the conversion of surplus self-propelled artillery equipment into armoured personnel carriers, codenamed Kangaroos. Such vehicles would keep pace with the armour cross-country and would sustain the tempo of Allied operations. With these factors in place, Simonds hoped to achieve a break-through, at which point his two armoured divisions would be unleashed in the exploitation role.

In view of the weakness of the German forces holding the sector, and the overwhelming strength of the Allied units to be hurled at them, prospects looked good for *Totalise*. However, the plan was undone because of its own flaws and the rapidity of the German response. Indeed, although the plan was innovative in many ways, Simonds still retained tight control of his forces and employed a narrow-front attack to maintain this. Unfortunately, this greatly hindered the effective use of armour, which was severely bunched and unable to manoeuvre effectively. Both armoured divisional commanders, Maczek and Kitching, requested more frontage than the 2,000 yards across which both divisions were expected to deploy, but Simonds refused.[137] When German counter-attacks came in on 8 August, Allied armour was too constricted to deploy to make advantages in numbers tell. However, the initial advance still largely succeeded and by the morning of 8 August, II Canadian Corps had in effect breached the German lines. This, however, raised the second failing and that was the plan's rigidity. A second phase bombardment was unnecessary, for the German defences, stretched to their breaking point by the demands of continuous action for over two months, were in no position to offer resistance in depth. Yet the bombing raid had been ordered precisely to overcome this and Simonds and Crerar were unwilling to cancel it, even if they had been in a position to do so easily. A six-hour delay ensued, buying time for I SS Corps commander Sepp Dietrich to rush troops to plug the gap created by the Anglo-Canadians. However, II Canadian Corps also required time to reorganise and set itself for a further offensive. Momentum may have been lost but further progress would have been costly and contrary to the tenets of Simonds' operational technique. Nevertheless, Simonds became increasingly frustrated, particularly with the Poles, and attempted to direct the battle directly by radio.[138] To compound matters, once darkness fell, the armoured forces leaguered in accordance with standard doctrine and just at the time when Simonds wanted dash.[139] The inexperience of the two armoured divisions, now supposedly spearheading the second phase of *Totalise*, also militated against success. Despite some progress on 9–10 August, setbacks were suffered, the most famous of all being the loss of Worthington force. The inability of the Poles and Canadians to co-ordinate attacks and exploit opportunities effectively saw the end of *Totalise* on 11 August.

Totalise, despite innovative measures and an impressive advance of eight miles, had still fallen short of expectations and hopes, though once again these were perhaps unrealistic. Moreover, the rigidity of Simonds' plan certainly hindered a more dynamic employment of Polish–Canadian armour. He did not see it this way and browbeat his commanders, the armoured leaders in particular, for their lack of drive, determination and tactical flexibility. He accused them of being unwilling to get amongst the enemy and for sticking too rigidly to roads when the open country was available. This was distinctly unfair, for the north–south road network in the *Totalise* area is limited to say the least, even today. Moreover, Simonds clearly had no concept of the realities of armoured warfare as it existed in 1944, for implicit in his critique was the view that Shermans and Cromwells could survive against German anti-tank gun batteries if the armoured commanders were bold enough.[140] To a degree, Simonds, like Dempsey before him at *Goodwood*, demonstrated unwavering faith in the dominance of the tank on the Second World War battlefield, on one that simply did not exist.

However, there had been positive outcomes and lessons. The Kangaroos had certainly proved their worth, and they would be squabbled over by Allied commanders in ensuing weeks as they each sought to deploy them. In addition, once again, Allied armour had proved itself more than capable of dealing with German armour in a defensive capacity. More than anything, Simonds' plan, though not without shortcomings, had demonstrated considerable innovation on the part of the Allies, and a willingness to adapt and learn from previous errors. O'Connor positively enthused about Simonds' new ideas in *Totalise* and wholeheartedly recommended them to Montgomery.[141] In addition, the Germans had suffered yet further loss, most notably the crippling of 12th SS.[142]

Operation Tractable and the closing of the Falaise Pocket, 14–22 August

Nevertheless, Montgomery, desperate for 21st Army Group to play a full part in sealing the Falaise Pocket that was now developing to the south, issued another directive to Crerar to push on to Falaise and beyond as soon as possible. Simonds therefore devised *Operation Tractable*, effectively a follow-up to *Totalise*. The II Canadian Corps commander built on the experiences of *Totalise* and re-employed the successful aspects of that operation. Although in *Tractable* Simonds attacked in daylight, he did so under the cover of a thick smoke screen and employed mixed combined-arms groups for the break-in, with armoured brigades working in close tandem with mechanised infantry, closely followed by lorried infantry brigades. A complicated fireplan was devised that called for the use of flanking smokescreens, aerial bombardment and artillery barrages.[143] However, even with German defences crumbling *Tractable* almost came badly unstuck as elements of the leading units, unused to smoke, became lost and dispersed.[144] The River Laison then proved more of an obstacle than had been envisaged by engineers and the advance slowed, though the level of fire support prevented the Germans from unduly interfering with the crossing.[145] Once across the river the leading elements of II Canadian Corps ran into opposition from 85th Infantry Division and elements of I SS Panzer Corps and *Tractable* appeared on the verge of stalling completely.

However, although the Germans were still offering resistance, their flanks were open and Simonds unleashed 4th Canadian and 1st Polish Armoured Divisions to the east and ultimately to close the Falaise Pocket at Trun and Chambois. Maczek's Poles demonstrated considerable flexibility in this role, reorganising into four battlegroups akin to the model adopted by Roberts and Adair for *Bluecoat*. Moreover, 1st Polish Armoured Division displayed dash in seizing commanding positions on Mount Ormel overlooking the route being taken by the fleeing German forces. Despite repeated German attempts to shift them, the Poles held firm until relieved.[146]

The success of *Tractable* and the apparent flexibility of the armoured divisions employed should not be overstated, however, as the opposition encountered in getting to Trun and then St Lambert and Chambois bore little resemblance to that stymieing previous Allied advances. Indeed, even in the increasingly advantageous operating environment 4th Canadian Armoured remained sticky and Simonds sacked its GOC, Kitching, on 21 August for not doing enough to reach the beleaguered Poles.[147] Nevertheless, Simonds had spotted the chance to exploit the situation and the Poles in particular had seized the opportunity when presented.

Tractable was the last major operation of the Normandy campaign for 21st Army Group, and the armoured divisions were subsequently unleashed in hot pursuit of the fleeing German forces, following the Falaise Pocket battles. Within days leading elements were in Belgium, and 11th Armoured had captured Antwerp intact. In contrast with the difficulties and exigencies of the previous fighting, this was a pursuit *par excellence* that even exceeded the efforts of Rommel and Guderian in 1940.

Conclusions

Twenty-First Army Group achieved its ultimate objective in *Overlord* of dislodging the Germans from Normandy and driving them back out of France. By September the progress of the campaign was way ahead of schedule and Hitler's armies had suffered a decisive and crippling defeat. Yet question marks remain against the effectiveness of the Allied armies. Their apparently sluggish advance during the first two months of the fighting, from early June until the collapse of German resistance in August, has been the focus of considerable criticism for some decades. It is alleged that Montgomery's forces struggled to assert themselves when they enjoyed overwhelming material superiority, and in particular, that Allied armour proved to be a miserable disappointment.

Yet, as this chapter has demonstrated, armour did play a major role in the defeat of German forces in northwest Europe in 1944 and did contribute significantly to the unfolding campaign particularly in supporting initial advances and break-ins. There is also evidence of doctrinal flexibility and many units innovated and adapted to the prevailing circumstances. Despite shifting operational technique and the flawed employment of armour on a number of occasions, the capabilities and effectiveness of Anglo-Canadian armour generally improved as the campaign progressed. Moreover, these achievements were made in the face of determined and skilful opposition, in unhelpful terrain, and largely with crews of limited initial experience often utilising equipment that demonstrated some obvious shortcomings.

That there was a variety of problems is not in question (to be explored throughout this book), but the emphasis on explaining perceived failure has undoubtedly been skewed by excessive focus on the inability of the Allies to achieve operational level breakout with armoured divisions and mechanised infantry. The need for this so-called strategic breakout has too often been overly emphasised by those who wished to see the Allies fight a quite different style of campaign than that which they needed to. As Montgomery realised, a low-risk campaign heavily reliant on the Allies' materiel superiority was preferable to a hazardous and less controllable series of battles of manoeuvre. Consequently, the Allies constantly drove forward with a chain of set-piece operations, heavily supported and reliant on armour, as well as the other arms, intended to win ground and provoke the Germans into costly counter-attacks, tactics which ultimately delivered to the Allies an overwhelming victory.

3

OPERATIONAL TECHNIQUE

The perception of the operational effectiveness of armour in shaping the 1944 Normandy campaign is one of disappointment and failure. In the 1950s, Basil Liddell Hart recorded his belief that British armour had 'done badly' in Normandy, while John English, in his critique of 1st Canadian Army, and most recently Russell Hart in *Clash of Arms* have variously claimed that Allied armour performed disappointingly or added little to the Allied effort.[1] In comparison with artillery and air power, armour is considered not to have lived up to expectations, and that as a consequence, particular operational difficulties ensued. It is further contended that much of 21st Army Group's inability to exploit advantageous situations was related to the ineffectiveness of British and Canadian armoured forces, particularly the armoured divisions.[2] Even during well-prepared set-piece engagements, 21st Army Group's armoured forces often failed to achieve operational objectives quickly, if at all. On the first day of the campaign, the tanks of the Staffordshire Yeomanry, of 27th Armoured Brigade, proved unable to support the drive towards Caen effectively, and Montgomery's much-vaunted armoured thrusts deep inland failed to materialise.[3] When during *Operation Perch* British armour was unleashed, the 4th County of London Yeomanry, of the famed 7th Armoured Division, suffered a considerable mauling at Villers Bocage.[4] Most famously of all *Operation Goodwood*, the three armoured divisional thrust to the east of Caen on 18 July, resulted in heavy loss for only limited gains.[5]

The explanation of such failure has usually centred on technical inferiority and tactical difficulties during the fighting in Normandy, and indeed these aspects were undoubtedly significant.[6] However, the argument that focuses largely on the tactical application of armour and difficulties encountered therein presupposes that the operational art of 21st Army Group and its planning structures were supportive of, and appropriate to, the employment of armoured formations, and that those expectations were both realistic and achievable. In order to ascertain the relative success or failure of Anglo-Canadian armoured forces it must first be established that the structure of, and doctrine employed by, 21st Army Group did indeed effectively support the available armoured forces as they existed in June 1944.

Much has been written concerning the operational methods employed by Gen Bernard Montgomery, his army commanders, Lt-Gen Miles Dempsey (2nd British Army) and Lt-Gen Harry Crerar (1st Canadian Army), and their respective corps commanders during the Normandy campaign. Ellis' anodyne official history aside, much of this literature has been critical, highlighting the lack of drive, weak and fragile morale, an unwillingness to engage in determined assault, and importantly for the employment of armour, an inability to exploit opportunities provided by the ebb and flow of battle.[7] More recently, however, David French and Stephen Hart have gone some way to rehabilitating Montgomery and 21st Army Group's approach to confronting the German armed forces in northwest Europe in 1944–45.[8] In particular they have argued that the operational techniques employed in northwest Europe may have resulted in certain characteristics on the battlefield, but they were a logical and appropriate response to the situation the Anglo-Canadian forces found themselves facing in 1944.

However, as will be seen, Montgomery and his staff's approach to operational art in 1944–45 may in many ways have served the general needs of the British Army and supported the political requirements of the government, but it also created certain difficulties for the employment of armour, particularly in the exploitation role. Moreover, this approach compounded with poor appreciation of the true capabilities of British armour in 1944 and resulted on occasion in the development of plans with unrealistic objectives. The adoption of a doctrine to serve broader requirements was not necessarily unjustified or indeed inappropriate, though it had shortcomings, but it has had repercussions on our appreciation of the role armour was expected to, and could realistically play, in Normandy in 1944. It is therefore necessary to analyse the cornerstones of British doctrine in 1944, examine their impact on the employment of armoured forces, and appreciate the extent to which the consequences of these choices were understood and incorporated into planning prior to and during the Normandy campaign.

Operational methods in 21st Army Group

The operational doctrine employed by Montgomery's forces in Normandy was theoretically founded upon three key principles, consequences of the politico-strategic situation in which the British Army was operating by 1944 – the manpower crisis, the fragile nature of the British Army and the materiel superiority of the Allies.

The first and most pressing concern, and one that had been developing as the war had progressed, was the manpower shortage.[9] British pre-war strategy was predicated upon a heavy investment in air and maritime forces to support the French army, and the defeat of France and Britain's change in strategy in 1940 had further emphasised the expansion and support of such forces, placing a still greater burden on available manpower. Additionally, the mobilisation of the British economy to support the war effort proved a further drain on available pools of personnel, with the consequence that by 1943 the British Army was forced into evaluating its operational technique in line with a dwindling reserve of personnel. By 1942 wastage rates within the army exceeded recruitment, and in the Mediterranean theatre, Gen. Harold Alexander had already been forced to break up two divisions in December 1942 to replace losses in other formations.[10] In addition, miscalculations in 1943 resulted in the War Office being forced into sending drafts from six Lower Establishment Home Defence divisions to support 21st Army Group's build-up.[11] In the light of the manpower crisis being 'very serious indeed', Montgomery even requested that Brooke start combing out the training schools for more personnel, though this was rejected.[12] It was clear that the maximum establishment of the British Army had been reached and would, as a result of wastage in Normandy, become a shrinking force from the summer of 1944 onwards.

Planning for *Operation Overlord* was markedly influenced by the awareness of the manpower shortage and in March 1944 Montgomery confided to Lt-Gen Ronald Weeks, DCIGS, that the invasion of Europe had to be accomplished 'with the smallest possible casualties'.[13] Montgomery informed Chester Wilmot in 1946 that by 1944 'the British Army was a wasting asset' and that the War Office had made it clear to him that replacements would only be available for the first month of operations in Normandy.[14]

An obvious and important method of conserving manpower was to emphasise methods of achieving operational and tactical objectives that utilised firepower and equipment to shoulder the burden, rather than the fighting man, in particular the infantry. By Normandy, the British and Canadian armies were backed by larger allocations of artillery and armour, and less so by infantry than hitherto, for it was correctly perceived that it was the basic rifleman who suffered the heaviest casualties on the European battlefield. This decision was to have serious consequences when the campaign did not unfold as Montgomery

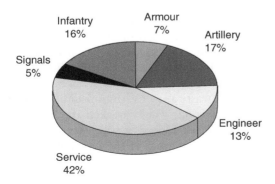

Figure 4. Second British Army composition, June 1944
Source: CAB 106/112, 30 June 1944

had expected, and the limited infantry arm was called upon to endure heavy fighting and consequent casualties, to a degree weakening the whole concept.[15]

There is also evidence that 21st Army Group and Montgomery in particular were influenced by pressing political concerns. Because 21st Army Group was a wasting asset by the summer of 1944, Montgomery had to ensure that it did not diminish to such an extent that the British effort in the final fighting for Germany was undermined by the necessity of adopting a lesser role due to personnel shortages. It would have been unwise, Montgomery later claimed, to have won in a military sense, if Britain's power base had been so severely compromised by the weakened state of 21st Army Group at the war's conclusion that Britain could not support its war aims with armed force.[16] Thus, the planning and conduct of operations in Europe was to be shaped by manpower concerns both in terms of the manner in which Britain's forces would fight, and the need to preserve the capablities of 21st Army Group.

The second key concern facing Montgomery and his staff in 1944 was their perception of the British and Canadian army's ability to take on the German forces and defeat them without being compromised structurally or in terms of morale. Concerns over the nature of the British soldier had developed in the interwar era and permeated the command levels of the British Army in the Second World War. Gen Archibald Wavell confided to Brooke in 1942 that 'we are nothing like as tough as we were in the last war and ... British and Australian troops will not ... stand up to the same punishment and casualties as they did in the last war'.[17] Brooke replied, concurring with Wavell's estimations, 'our one idea is to look after our comforts and avoid being hurt in any way'.[18] Montgomery commented after Alamein: 'The trouble with our British lads is that they are not killers by nature.'[19] Even in Italy it seemed that British troops needed to be 'taught the desire to kill'.[20] Whilst it is, and probably always will be a trait of ageing army officers to inflate the memory of their own youthful abilities and *elan*, concern over their charges' lack of drive was nevertheless a further pressure working upon senior commanders during the planning of *Overlord*.

In preparation for D-Day, Montgomery worked hard to build and sustain morale, for he believed that if this was lacking, any operation, however good the plan or the preparation, was doomed to failure.[21] He was determined to avoid the heavy price in life that had been paid in the First World War and the burden that this had placed on the soldier's personal morale.[22] First, clearly such profligacy with life would waste away the diminishing manpower available to 21st Army Group and, second, would weaken the supposedly fragile morale of the Anglo-Canadian forces. Indeed, it was perceived that the soldier of the 1940s was a different being to that of the Great War era and could and should not be expected to suffer as he had 25 years previously.[23] Nevertheless, according to Brig. James Hargest, a New Zealand army observer attached to XXX Corps in Normandy, and in keeping with more general views on the nature of the citizen soldier in the twentieth century, the British soldier 'will accept losses without losing morale provided that he sees some results'.[24]

Twenty-First Army Group, therefore, worked to support the fragile morale of the fighting man, particularly the infantry, by providing the most amount of firepower support possible. Montgomery was also determined to keep the campaign moving and avoid at all costs allowing his forces to become caught up in slow-moving or static attritional slogging matches.[25] In both cases the role planned for armour was to be critical.

The third cornerstone of 21st Army Group's thinking was founded upon the materiel superiority enjoyed by the Allies in 1944. Because of strategic choices made in 1940–42, Britain had adopted a policy of building a small but well-equipped army to conduct future operations against the German ground forces in Europe, a policy which built on interwar doctrine, and one that focused on the use of equipment rather than manpower to win battles. Twenty-First Army Group's chief intelligence officer, Brig. Edgar Williams recorded that the doctrine 'Let metal do it rather than flesh' rested at the heart of the British Army's philosophy.[26] By 1944 the British Army was replete with artillery and armour at the expense of infantry, as it was to be equipment and ultimately firepower that was to win 21st Army Group's battles.[27] In seeking reasons for their defeat, German forces emphasised their view that Allied forces lacked drive and determination in the latter stages of the Second World War, and compensated with an overwhelming weight of materiel. The German interpretation, therefore, was not that they were outfought by the British, far from it, but they were merely outproduced. The British Army's reliance on material advantage was, however, entirely understandable. Many criticised Montgomery for his caution and lack of drive in chasing Rommel back to Tunisia in 1942, the US official history, for example, likening his progress to that of a pachyderm, and German accounts very often criticised the Allies for their sluggishness.[28] However, it was not necessary for the British Army to take risks and be overly bold, because their overwhelming superiority in equipment and supplies made it unnecessary. They could afford to utilise their vast resources of artillery, air power and mechanised support forces to defeat the more experienced German ground forces. The notion of using technology and equipment to spearhead battles and military operations was one that took root in the Western industrial world in the nineteenth century and fused with the more individualistic approach to life in the capitalist liberal democracies of the West. By the latter stages of the Second World War, it made logical sense for the Allies to employ their most obvious advantage of materiel superiority to defeat the Germans and thus win with technology and equipment. This resulted in a growing reliance on artillery, air power and armour by 1944.

The three precepts of 21st Army Group's doctrine were therefore to shape and influence the operational approach employed by Montgomery and his army and corps commanders. It was necessary to avoid heavy casualties, sustain fragile morale and combat efficiency, and employ Allied materiel advantage to its utmost. The manner in which 21st Army Group translated these underlying concerns on to the battlefield remains a hotly contested debate. It has recently been argued that much of the historiography of the subject has been skewed by overemphasis on Montgomery's singular personality and by German criticism of the Allied armies' cautious and ponderous style.[29] However, by examining closely the methods employed by Montgomery and his staff, a more complete picture can be formed of the role armour was to play in supporting 21st Army Group doctrine.

The most famous description of the technique employed by the British and Canadian forces came from Montgomery himself. He argued that 21st Army Group concentrated 'great strength at some selected place and hit the Germans a colossal crack'.[30] Moreover, a clear statement on the operational policy to be employed by 21st Army Group in Normandy was contained in a directive on operational policy issued by Lt-Gen Guy Simonds, the new and highly thought of commander of II Canadian Corps. Conscious of the inexperience of some of his subordinates, Simonds set out the technique, derived from his experience in the Mediterranean, that he intended to employ to defeat the Germans. It conformed completely with Montgomery's opinions and those of Lt-Gen Miles Dempsey, GOC 2nd British Army. There is little doubt that 21st Army Group had a collective operational view, based on success in North Africa and Italy, which was to dictate the conduct of the Normandy campaign.[31]

It was an operational technique that emphasised highly focused concentrations of force, most notably artillery and air-based firepower, at a given point in the frontline to inflict heavy punishment upon the Germans, prior to a well-prepared and organised armour-supported attack.[32] When the moment was deemed appropriate an exploitation phase would follow in which mobile armoured forces would develop the position still further. If, however, it seemed that the attack's impetus was petering out or degenerating into an attritional slog, then the operation would be closed down and the centre of gravity shifted to another part of the line. Great emphasis was placed on firepower, firm central control of operations and attack in depth to maintain pressure, limit casualties on individual formations, and exploit opportunities thrown up by the unfolding battle.[33] Such a method of battle would fulfil many of the requirements imposed on 21st Army Group. Reliance on firepower would diminish the fighting strength of the experienced German forces without having to outfight them in close combat, whilst simultaneously emphasising Allied superiority in artillery, air power and armour. Firm control of operations and retention of initiative would ensure that the Allies would be able to bring their materiel superiority to bear and prevent the Germans from throwing them off balance. Deep and narrow attacks rather than wide front operations would allow 21st Army Group to interpenetrate new and battle-weary formations, thus dispersing casualties and sustaining morale.[34] It would also facilitate greater support from concentrated firepower to spearhead attacks and suppress or destroy enemy defensive lines. A major benefit of this approach would also be the provocation of German counter-attacks, a response which would expose the enemy to much higher levels of attrition. Finally, the doctrine would allow the Allies to exploit their superiority in mobility and manoeuvre, initially by choosing the location of attack, thus retaining the initiative and keeping the enemy in a reactive posture, and ultimately in exploiting the breakthrough, once achieved, by pushing armoured forces into the open country beyond.[35]

However, although operational technique appeared to conform to 21st Army Group's perceptions of the army as a whole regarding manpower, morale and materiel superiority, it was to have noticeable consequences for the employment of British armour. The impact of the choices made by Montgomery and his staff were to fall into two groups – those that were unfortunate but necessary by-products of the adopted doctrine, which may or may not have been foreseen, and those that worked against the employed doctrine, at times undermining the whole process. In order to consider these implications further, it is necessary to analyse more closely a number of the principles that determined Montgomery's approach to operations in Normandy and their impact on armoured operations.

Firepower

There is little doubt that 21st Army Group sought to open offensives by applying concentrated and decisive firepower in a manner that reflected experiences in North Africa and Italy.[36] In Normandy, the level of artillery support was impressive with huge concentrations at corps and even army group level, concentrations that made German commanders blanch.[37] It appeared to some that the Allies were waging a war without any regard to expense.[38] Land-based firepower was supplemented by aerial bombardment, from both tactical and strategic air forces, with sometimes stunning and overwhelming effects. This application was not always successful, and in the case of massed strategic bomber raids, techniques had to be developed and fine-tuned as the campaign progressed.[39] Nevertheless, the Anglo-Canadian armies could call upon up to 4,500 guns in Normandy, and in specific cases some 700 guns were used to support *Operation Epsom* and, 760 to support *Operation Windsor*, while *Goodwood* was aided by 720 guns and over 1,000 heavy and medium bombers.[40] Montgomery employed heavy firepower concentrations to prepare the ground properly for infantry and armour assaults in an effort to minimise casualties, and Stephen Hart has argued that this approach 'enabled Allied troops to get on to their objectives with tolerable casualties'.[41] The importance of artillery support, even to armoured divisions was clear. Indeed, 11th Armoured's integral field artillery (13th Royal Horse and 151st Field Regiments) fired ten times the number of rounds than the armoured regiments' tanks during the northwest

European campaign.[42] It was impressed upon armoured commanders in the months leading up to *Overlord* that suppressive artillery support would be crucial to allowing armour to get forward with acceptable casualties, as the tanks themselves would have little resisting power to German anti-tank gunnery.[43] However, there were shortcomings with the firepower-based approach of 21st Army Group, shortcomings that impacted significantly on the employment of armour.

As the war progressed, Allied troops had come to respect, be grateful for and ultimately be reliant upon artillery bombardments to such an extent that it was viewed as a panacea. Commanders came to rely on the aid provided by artillery to such an extent that unit advances were governed by the level of artillery support provided. Indeed, training imbued such thinking into infantry commanders, though it should be noted that reliance on artillery was in part due to the relative ineffectiveness of battalion level close-support weapons such as the two-inch and three-inch mortar.[44] Nevertheless, as early as June 1944 a report had been compiled that indicated that officers were calling upon artillery in increasing amounts to deal with minor targets.[45] In northwest Europe, rates of infantry advances could sometimes be so sluggish that enemy formations were able to hinder Allied attacks or fall back in good order and be in a position to defeat or thwart follow-up forces.[46] Consequently, advances slowed and hopes of mobile armoured exploitation receded. Indeed, although 15th Scottish Infantry Division is regarded as having done an excellent job in the circumstances, its inability to seize crossings over the Odon on the first day of *Epsom* (26 June 1944) resulted in 11th Armoured Division being launched prematurely by O'Connor.[47]

It was not only the slow rates of break-in forces such as infantry that were governed by the degree of firepower support, for armour often held back and called upon the artillery to deal with problems.[48] Moreover, on occasion armour took to fighting in a self-propelled artillery role, offering static fire support. This arose partly as a consequence of receiving tanks equipped with the dual-purpose 75 mm gun, capable of providing decent HE fire support to infantry, but also because it appeared to certain units that such tactics fulfilled the requirements of infantry support most effectively.[49] In Normandy, 1st East Riding Yeomanry, part of 27th Armoured Brigade, which came ashore on D-Day itself to support 3rd Infantry Division, operated in the static fire support role in support of 2nd Royal Ulster Rifles' attack on Cambes on 9 June.[50] A month later they repeated their actions during *Operation Charnwood* and carried out a similar static firepower support role in support of 59th Division's attacks on Galmanche, St Contest and Malon.[51] Their experience was by no means standard tactical doctrine in British armoured units, nor indeed necessarily inappropriate, but it demonstrated the expectations placed on firepower by advancing infantry. It was also another indication of the reliance placed on firepower support and its potential consequences, as such tactics were not always conducive to maintaining forward momentum in armoured actions.

During *Operation Totalise*, for example, German defences had crumbled to such an extent that an Allied breakthrough and exploitation was possible, but did not occur due to 21st Army Group's at times inflexible doctrine that massed firepower preparation must precede set-piece attacks. Lt-Gen Simonds had planned a second aerial bombardment to blast II Canadian Corps through what he believed to be the rest of the German defensive line, but this may well have been unnecessary and contributed to a hiatus in the operation, used gainfully by the Germans.[52] Kurt Meyer, commander of 12th SS Panzer Division, claimed that this was a tremendous opportunity frittered away by the Anglo-Canadian forces, though II Canadian Corps may well have required time to reorganise in any case, making further immediate progress unlikely.[53] Moreover, reliance on aerial bombardment and artillery support, even in *Totalise*, was not necessarily wrong in concept, but it does begin to explain why armoured forces were employed in the manner they were and why they appeared cautious both to opponents such as Meyer and post-war historians.

Paradoxically, the *elan* of armoured units in the early to middle stages of the war had been considered misplaced because it too often resulted in excessively zealous charges against enemy anti-tank guns, unsuppressed by supporting artillery. Yet by the time artillery and air-based firepower support was effective enough to facilitate thrusting armoured manoeuvres, the operational approach of the British Army in effect worked against such methods.

Twenty-First Army Group's reliance on massed firepower hindered armoured units still further by working against manoeuvre and mobility in a physical sense, particularly by disrupting or destroying road networks or churning up the terrain over which Allied forces had to advance. Because assaults tended to be concentrated over narrow fronts, partly to focus heavy applications of firepower, so the areas over which follow-up forces advanced remained small. Within such small areas only limited communication and transport networks existed and these were pummelled by artillery and air strikes in the early phases of an attack. The benefits of such heavy bombardments were often crucial, but for mechanised and motorised forces hoping to exploit penetrations or support initial break-ins, the damage and disruption caused hindered progress, slowed advances and allowed the Germans to plug gaps and improvise effective defences.[54] The problems were exacerbated because 21st Army Group was largely a mechanised body reliant on good road networks to get forward when progress seemed likely. Moreover, dependence on artillery support prompted the desire to push artillery, either towed or self-propelled, into positions to support forward units. Consequently, pressure on a small number of nodal points in the road network often created chokepoints, with armoured exploitation forces struggling through supporting motorised units, redeploying artillery, retiring battle casualties and logistical support for frontline units. Indeed, during *Operation Goodwood*, 3RTR ran short of ammunition because resupply was hindered by the churned-up ground and the pressure placed on the north–south road network.[55] When the ground over which all such forces were moving was broken up or cratered from bombardment, progress slowed and the conditions for the application of armour worsened.

Operation Epsom was conducted over a particularly narrow frontage of some two miles, though it had originally been intended to be twice this width, and the village of Cheux was to become the bottleneck through which supporting forces would have to advance. However, considerable damage was inflicted on the village and its road network, making progress for the follow-on forces of 11th Armoured Division and 4th Armoured Brigade difficult.[56] In addition, bad weather resulted in the roads being churned up still further.[57] During *Operation Bluecoat*, Lt-Gen Bucknall's XXX Corps advance was based on a single track, unsuitable for tanks, and one road shared with O'Connor's VIII Corps. The ground and network, such as it was, had been damaged by the artillery and aerial bombardment, compounding the wear and tear caused by so many vehicles attempting to use the same inadequate links. It was little wonder, Bucknall later complained to Dempsey, that progress was slow.[58] The classic example, however, remains *Goodwood* where the heavy aerial bombardment in particular caused considerable cratering, hindered progress and forced advancing armoured formations to become dispersed and disorganised. Lt-Gen Richard O'Connor, corps commander for the operation, was appalled by the damage done to the terrain by the heavy bombers, and tank crews had to manoeuvre and make detours to avoid becoming bogged down.[59] Third Royal Tank Regiment, which spearheaded 11th Armoured's advance at *Goodwood*, recorded the necessity of slowing down to a crawl to negotiate the craters.[60] Cratering was still noted as a hindrance to manoeuvre during *Bluecoat*, with the consequence that by *Totalise* careful consideration was given to the type of ordnance utilised and the areas in which it should be deployed in order not to impede Allied mobility.[61]

However, although armoured progress in such operations was hindered by heavy bombardment, arguably the most serious deficiency of the firepower policy was that it did not deliver all that had been hoped for. Quite simply, although great reliance was placed on artillery and aerial fire support, it could not fulfil all expectations. The most obvious concern and problem centred on the deficiencies of the artillery equipment and the limitations such weaknesses placed on the use of artillery as an operational battering ram. The standard British field artillery piece in the Second World War was the 25-pdr gun/howitzer, a design introduced in 1937.[62] The specification had called for a weapon that could fire at least 12,000 yards and thus outrange similar contemporary German equipment. It was also to be a light and mobile artillery piece, and it was this thinking that undermined its contribution and created difficulties in Normandy. The method of achieving extra range and mobility was to sacrifice shell weight, and while the British gun could unloose a 25 pound shell some 7–8 miles, the German 105 mm field gun fired a considerably heavier 32 lb shell.[63]

Moreover, the explosive content of the 25-pdr shell was only some 7 per cent of total weight and by 1942 was often of lower-grade explosive material.[64] In action, whilst the 25-pdr gun could deal effectively with troops in the open, a shell had to fall within 3 feet 6 inches of a slit trench to have any significant impact on dug-in German soldiers and only a direct hit would cause casualties.[65] To exacerbate the problem, only some 3 per cent of 25-pdr shells actually fell into trenches and earthworks.[66] By 1944, the standard medium artillery piece in the British Army was the 5.5-inch gun/howitzer. This weapon fired a 90 lb shell some 16,000 yards, though this was often too short for effective counter-battery work. The lethal range of its shell was greater than the 25-pdr, but not markedly so and again only direct hits were likely to cause serious damage or casualties.[67] Although British artillery demonstrated great flexibility and speed of fire concentrations during the Normandy campaign, the actual physical damage it could deliver was limited.[68] Great firepower density was required for even modest destructive rewards.[69]

Consequently, some of the significant effects of artillery in Normandy were to be psychological, and artillery officers were well aware of this, employing what French has described as 'pepper-pot' tactics.[70] It was clear that it was the quantity of guns firing rather than weight of shell that was important in sapping and ultimately undermining morale.[71] Thus, 21st Army Group's artillery commanders endeavoured to fire as many weapons as possible on to a target to achieve the desired results. The need to focus firepower in this manner narrowed the scope of offensive operations, as even in Allied armies of 1944 there was only so much available artillery. Indeed, horse-trading between senior officers at army and corps level for artillery allocations immediately followed the announcement of each new operation. Artillery doctrine, therefore, focused on suppression and undermining enemy morale and the key was in getting Allied forces forward quickly enough to exploit such paralysis. Unfortunately, the nature of achieving the suppression at times worked against such exploitation by hindering rapid manoeuvre.

Heavy aerial bombardment could deliver greater destructive and psychologically devastating power, destroying even 54-ton Tiger tanks and causing troops to go temporarily insane, but it could also be an imprecise and clumsy weapon. Co-ordination between ground forces and non-tactical air forces was very limited, and during *Operation Totalise*, II Canadian Corps was unable at the last moment to redirect a heavy bomber raid in response to new intelligence reports and the shifting nature of the battle.[72] Moreover, the Allied bomber barons were always loathe to be drawn from their preferred role of strategic bombardment. Indeed, it is more than likely that Montgomery had to overplay the possibilities and intentions of *Goodwood* in order to secure the support of Tedder and Eisenhower in accessing the firepower of the strategic air forces.[73]

Tactical air power played an important role in Normandy, but it was best suited to battlefield air interdiction rather than close air support. Locating concealed enemy forces from the air was all but hopeless until they had exposed themselves by firing upon advancing Allied units or were in the act of counter-attacking. Even then, the effects of tactical air power were often suppressive as the ability to destroy heavily armoured vehicles and dug-in troops was strictly limited.[74]

The difficulty was in conducting and maintaining such a degree of firepower in such a way as to allow advancing troops to get forward. The 'stun' effects of artillery and aerial bombardment were often short lived and advancing armour often found its way blocked by anti-tanks guns and, more frequently than campaigns prior to Normandy, by self-propelled guns which it had been hoped would be neutralised by firepower.

The use of artillery and air forces to blast infantry and armour on to targets was flawed in other ways. Allied artillery fireplans had to adapt and develop as the Normandy campaign progressed because the Germans had developed new methods for dealing with heavy artillery concentrations, methods nurtured with some success on the Eastern Front. German forces were usually deployed in much greater depth than hitherto with the foremost areas only being held by small forces designed to disrupt and hinder Allied troops as they advanced. The bulk of German strength lay further behind and counter-attacking forces back still further. Consequently, early Allied fireplans were too shallow and merely devastated areas over which a sprinkling of German troops were deployed. Allied advances therefore trundled forward a limited distance and then encountered the largely intact main German defensive line.[75]

For Allied armour this was doubly troublesome and frustrating as early actions exposed poor co-ordination with supporting infantry and resulted in the armour moving too far ahead and being surprised by concealed, largely undamaged enemy assault guns, tanks, anti-tank guns, or, as a further unpleasant innovation, German infantry equipped increasingly with hand-held anti-tank weaponry, such as the *panzerfaust*. Although *Operation Goodwood* saw the deepest and probably most flexible German defences in Normandy, the Allied fireplan shot O'Connor's forces some six miles into the German defences before falling foul of the main German defensive position on Bourguébus Ridge.[76] The Allies did learn, however, and by *Operation Bluecoat* air assets were being used to support advancing troops more effectively in suppressing the deep-lying German defensive forces.[77] Second Canadian Corps went further during *Operation Totalise* by pre-planning a secondary fireplan to blast through the main German line.[78] However, it was not until the Rhine crossings that 21st Army Group had in place a truly flexible firepower doctrine.

Clearly, there were marked problems in utilising firepower effectively to get troops and armour forward. All too often attacks bogged down because of the limits of artillery and air power and the inexactitude of fireplans. Moreover, the shortcomings of artillery and air power compounded with the difficulties created by the terrain and resulted in a much greater burden than had been expected being placed on the close-combat arms of 21st Army Group – infantry and armour. The assumption that firepower could blast troops on to target with sustainable casualties proved a qualified success and infantry losses were excessive even on such set-piece operations as *Epsom*. During *Epsom*, 15th Scottish Division suffered 2,331 casualties, which constituted over 50 per cent of its Rifle Company strength.[79] Moreover, 2nd Battalion Glasgow Highlanders suffered a 34 per cent loss in just one day in the fighting for Cheux.[80] Overall casualties suffered by 21st Army Group in Normandy were still tolerable, but were unduly focused on the infantry partly because artillery and air power were unable to contribute as fully as hoped. Armour nevertheless played a full role in supporting the infantry, but the employment of massed firepower at times added to the problems already confronting the use of tanks in the close terrain of Normandy in the summer of 1944.

Command and over-control in Normandy

With due reason Montgomery and his commanders pursued a policy in Normandy of close control of subordinates throughout the campaign. This approach mirrored Montgomery's cautious nature, his lack of faith in the abilities of many of his commanders and his confidence in his own, and his desire to retain firm control of operations to minimise the chances of the astute Germans scoring a morale-sapping success over 21st Army Group. Montgomery, his army commanders and his corps commanders had developed a method of operating in the Mediterranean theatre based on close and tight control to minimise errors and to emphasise the Allies' advantages of materiel strength. This policy was supported by Montgomery's belief that the British Army and its commanders were limited in their capabilities and could and should not be expected to fulfil complicated and sophisticated tasks.[81] Opportunities to destroy Rommel's Afrika Corps following Alamein may have been frittered away in 1942, but more importantly for Montgomery, he had given his opponent no chance to retrieve the situation for the Axis forces. Considering the question marks that had been placed against British armoured command and leadership in the North African campaign in 1942, this was entirely understandable, but the manner of 8th Army's success began to be accepted without deeper analysis.[82] The operational methods of the Anglo-Canadian forces were shaped by Montgomery's perceptions and in turn they closely constrained the employment of armoured forces, most notably in the exploitation phase of an operation. The impact of the desire to retain tight control on operations manifested itself in a number of ways.

First, a primary concern for Montgomery was maintaining firm control of unfolding battles and this required subordinates to do only that for which he had briefed them. The concept of the set-piece battle and the rigid predetermined plan was designed to ensure that little could go wrong. However, in order to ensure that such control was maintained it was necessary for commanders to retain tight control over subordinates to keep the plan on track.[83] Although Montgomery also claimed that it was the initiative of field commanders that was vital to success, in reality he rarely allowed his subordinates too much room for manoeuvre.[84] Partly this was due to a lack of faith as well as greater confidence in his own capabilities. Montgomery knew that Dempsey, though a good learner, was inexperienced at army command level and would have to be watched and helped when necessary.[85] His confidence in Harry Crerar (1st Canadian Army) was very low indeed. He had not been first choice to lead the Canadians and although Montgomery liked him personally he did not believe Crerar up to army command.[86] At corps level, faith in Gerald Bucknall (XXX Corps) drained within a week of D-Day; Neil Ritchie (XII Corps) had much to live down after failure in North Africa; Brian Horrocks (Bucknall's replacement in early August) although popular, was still sickly; and Richard O'Connor (VIII Corps) was thought perhaps too old and out of touch for corps command after two years in a POW camp in Italy. Montgomery also probably saw O'Connor as a potential rival and this may also have fuelled a whispering campaign against him.[87] Of Guy Simonds (II Canadian Corps) Montgomery had a very high opinion, though he was still inexperienced, but he fell under Crerar's command.[88] Of his armoured division generals, Montgomery had already tried to get Allan Adair (Guards Armoured Division) replaced, Bobby Erskine (7th Armoured Division) fell with Bucknall; George Kitching (4th Canadian Armoured Division) was sacked in August; and disappointment was expressed over Maj-Gen Stanislaw Maczek following his 1st Polish Armoured Division's initially sluggish progress during *Totalise*.[89] Only Pip Roberts (11th Armoured Division) enjoyed strong support and in June he was, by his own admission, still inexperienced at divisional leadership and liable to err.[90] With such doubts it is perhaps understandable why Montgomery was unwilling to allow fluid and expansive operations with rapid exploitation at their heart. This lack of faith and confidence filtered down the chain of command and other commanders monitored their subordinates very closely also. Dempsey was involved in the attempt to get Adair sacked, was almost waiting for an opportunity to replace Bucknall and Erskine after the bungling of *Operation Perch* and the dismal setback at Villers Bocage, and restricted Crocker's (I Corps) options on the deployment of his armour in June.[91] O'Connor recognised Robert's lack of experience at *Epsom* (as did Roberts himself)[92] as well as his own rustiness, and Simonds was determined to keep a close eye on his divisional commanders, Maj-Gens Keller and Foulkes, after they had demonstrated a lack of tactical ability.[93]

Consequently, Montgomery felt the necessity to watch over his commanders and ensure that they did not blunder too often or too grievously. It was, therefore, essential that a firm plan was established and that all commanders understood their role and not deviate from it. Montgomery explained this approach when he lectured his army, corps and divisional commanders in January 1944, and this was further emphasised in a supporting pamphlet.[94] During the campaign itself, Montgomery exercised close control through a group of liaison officers who sat in on daily divisional planning meetings and reported back to 21st Army Group HQ on aims and objectives for the following day, thus keeping Montgomery apprised of the picture and surreptitiously letting the divisional commanders know that they were under scrutiny at all times.[95] Dempsey also employed two to three liaison officers and found them invaluable for keeping a tight grip on events.[96] Moreover, developments in the use of radio networks allowed HQs further up the chain of command to monitor divisional traffic and build a clear picture of unfolding events. This was not in itself a problem, and indeed it was a technique that mirrored German doctrine, but in the 21st Army Group it allowed a still tighter rein to be maintained on subordinate commanders.[97]

Nevertheless, 21st Army Group's senior commanders noted the positive aspects of the control offered by Montgomery's all seeing eye. Almost all considered him a sharp and intelligent individual, even if some favoured the man-management skills of leaders such as Dick O'Connor or Brian Horrocks.[98] Pip Roberts, GOC 11th Armoured Division, much preferred Montgomery's clear and disciplined approach to previous experiences with intricate codenames, map traces and complex, 'laborious staff work' generated alternative objectives, whilst O'Connor referred to a 'sense of assurance' with Montgomery's plans with their clear statement of aims and objectives.[99]

However, this tightly structured style of command, despite engendering stolid confidence, also required limitations being placed on lower-level initiative and for all commanders to adhere to a carefully organised set-piece plan. Moreover, for Montgomery's concept of the structured and focused battlefield operation to be sustained, great care had to be placed on preparation, planning and the scope of operations. Twenty-First Army Group eschewed operations that had not been as fully prepared as they might or did not have the level of logistical support required to make the Allies' materiel superiority tell sufficiently. Indeed, *Epsom* was postponed because of the channel storm and its impact on the build up of supplies and munitions.[100]

This desire to prepare as fully as possible fused with Montgomery's concerns over the flexibility of his forces, their tactical acumen and their ability to improvise and cope with open and fluid situations. Consequently, 21st Army Group plans were in practice tight and prescribed affairs to allow full use of concentrated artillery to prepare and support operations, with considerable care given to protecting flanks and lines of supply and communications.

Much debate since 1944 has focused on the true aims and objectives of operations such as *Goodwood*, but it is clear that the level of concern in many set-piece battles over flank protection for 21st Army Group assaults limited the degree of risk accepted in attempting to attain distant objectives. Brig. Hinde, commanding 22nd Armoured Brigade during *Operation Perch*, noted that exposed flanks were part and parcel of armoured thrusts, yet claimed his troops had proved deficient in reacting to such difficulties.[101] In addition, *Operation Epsom* was partly compromised by XXX Corps' inability to take Rauray on the western flank of the attack, and by the failure of I Corps' 3rd

Canadian Division to seize Carpiquet. Thus, when O'Connor's VIII Corps made a four-mile penetration to Hill 112, there was constant pressure on the flanks and determined German counter-attacks were only beaten off by artillery and doughty defence. Ultimately, despite 11th Armoured's perception that further progress could have been made from Hill 112, growing concern over the threat to the flanks of the penetration, as well as intelligence reports, brought an end to *Epsom*.[102] Planning for *Goodwood* was also governed by protecting flanks and ensuring that the Germans could not get into a position to launch potentially irksome counter-attacks.[103] Indeed, instructions given to O'Connor placed mutually opposing pressures on the corps commander. Although the armour was to be given the ability to dash forward, they also had to ensure that their efforts did not unbalance the whole eastern flank of 21st Army Group's position.[104] In August, moreover, in order to minimise risks Montgomery was unwilling to consider launching *Operation Kitten*, a rapid eastward exploitation to the Seine, until German resistance had crumbled, and thus the operation was not launched until the 16th.[105] *Operation Bluecoat* also saw concerns over flanks hindering progress in what was already a difficult and at times tortuous assault. O'Connor's troops again led the way, but the ponderous progress of XXX Corps forced VIII Corps to shore up their eastern flank with the excellent 15th Scottish Infantry Division.[106] O'Connor also then held back 11th Armoured's progress on 3 August as he required still more infantry to secure the flanks of the armoured penetration. Chester Wilmot, present at the moment of this decision, considered this a mistake.[107]

Almost certainly, greater caution was imbued following the failure of 22nd Armoured Brigade's attempt at 'swanning' about in the flank and rear of Panzer *Lehr* a week after D-Day.[108] Other factors were certainly as important, if not more so, in accounting for this defeat, but by *Operation Epsom* two weeks later, the set-piece prescribed battleplan was enshrined in 21st Army Group thinking.

However, the ability of Anglo-Canadian troops to improvise and show tactical daring leading to operational success was demonstrated in Normandy. During *Operation Bluecoat*, an error in deployment and delineation of zones of responsibility by the German 3rd Parachute and 326th Infantry Divisions, presented an opportunity in the Forêt L'Evêque to 11th Armoured Division, which they successfully exploited. The whole mood of the operation changed, and 2nd Army and VIII Corps demonstrated flexibility in being able to shift the gravity of the operation away from the slogging match being endured by XXX Corps further to the east.[109] Moreover, II Canadian Corps demonstrated considerable operational flair in *Operation Totalise*.[110]

Nevertheless, the operational technique of 21st Army Group placed great emphasis on firm control, careful planning and organised assaults. Once an attack had become disorderly, Montgomery and his subordinates slowed the pace of operations to facilitate reorganisation, resupply and to maintain the balance of the forces.[111] Thus, the approach of the Anglo-Canadians was unlikely to precipitate dynamic armoured thrusts. Opportunities were in any case few and far between against canny opponents such as the Germans and armoured forces had many further difficulties centred on terrain, the nature of anti-tank defence, and the supposed technical inferiority endured by Allied tanks in Normandy. The strategic situation and the operating environment in which the tank existed in 1944 were quite different to the halcyon days of *blitzkrieg*, and Montgomery and his team saw that those types of operations were simply unworkable by 1944 without enduring excessive casualties, and that they were unwilling to countenance. Whatever the consequences of tight control for Montgomery's armoured forces, it is not a statement on the validity or otherwise of 21st Army Group doctrine, merely another factor in understanding why the performance of British armour has been viewed so negatively since 1945.

Narrow fronts and limited manoeuvring space

A further aspect of 21st Army Group's operational approach was the desire to concentrate attacks on narrow frontages. Operations *Perch, Epsom, Jupiter, Goodwood, Totalise* and *Tractable* were the major examples of this policy. All were conducted across a frontage much narrower than German or even US operations, save *Cobra*. *Epsom* was launched over an area some two miles in width, though the intention was for flank corps to offer further support, whilst *Goodwood* began across an area of just 2,000 yards.[112] This compares with the British Army's approach in the First World War, when in August and September 1918 assaults were launched over 11,000–15,000 yards.[113] The advantages of the narrow approach were clear and suited the operating doctrine of 21st Army Group. Most obviously, a narrow concentrated assault facilitated the focused use of firepower to blast a hole through the opposing forces. Concentration of firepower was essential to overcoming the German defenders, and by attacking over a limited frontage, available artillery and air power could be utilised in great strength to spearhead the attack. Second, narrow fronts allowed formations to deploy in depth, often with one or two brigades up and one back. Indeed, Montgomery had declared this to be desirable in January 1944.[114] Brigades in turn deployed with strength to the rear, with two battalions or regiments up, one behind, and supporting forces following on. To ensure even greater depth of force, corps often passed divisions or independent brigades through each other with the aim of exploiting or widening openings or breaches in the line, and to maintain pressure and momentum. Again this was the intention at *Epsom, Jupiter* and *Goodwood*.[115]

Montgomery also believed that by attacking in depth, frontline units could be quickly supported and fresh troops interpenetrated to prevent excessive wear and tear on break-in units. He compared his approach favourably with the US doctrine of wider but shallower front attacks.[116]Although US operations generally put more pressure on the German lines, it simultaneously increased stress on American troops and formations, pressure that Montgomery saw as unnecessary. Moreover, it limited the amount of artillery support that could be offered to US assaults, anathema to the Anglo-Canadians.

However, although advantages were gained from narrow-front assaults problems were also encountered, problems that hindered the employment of armour. The practice of passing formations through each other caused difficulty when added to the consequences of bombardment, damage to road networks, cratering and the exposed flanks of penetrations. Moreover, the inexperience of units in conducting the difficult task of passing through, hindered operations, though where formations had trained together problems were lessened. Fifteenth Scottish Infantry Division and 6th Guards Tank Brigade had co-operated closely in Britain and this showed during *Bluecoat*.[117] The same infantry formation had also worked with 11th Armoured Division prior to D-Day and encountered fewer problems in interpenetrating during *Epsom*, despite the inexperience of many troops.[118] However, 15th Scottish Division ran into difficulties when working with 31st Independent Tank Brigade during the same operation, and in many cases the shock and impact on morale of advancing troops passing through areas with wrecked friendly vehicles and littered with corpses and casualties was significant. Quite often troops gained the impression that even when formations had successfully interpenetrated, in the opinion of higher command, the whole battlefield was still chaotic, jumbled and unhelpful to rapid progress.[119] This added to the caution of 21st Army Group commanders, whose desire to retain firm control resulted in them viewing the disorderly interpenetrations of formations as a reason to halt and reorganise.

Additionally, a significant problem created by narrow penetrations was the exposed nature of the troops passing through the salient. Concerns over flanks were often understandable when German troops could observe Allied units advancing along corridors and were able to pick them off with short-range small arms fire as well as long-range gunnery.[120] The failure of XXX Corps to seize Rauray as a preliminary to the launching of *Operation Epsom* allowed German 88 mm guns to snipe at and hinder the progress of elements of 11th Armoured Division as they advanced and dashed for Hill 112.[121] A key concern during the *Goodwood* offensive was the enfilading fire of German units to the east of the thrust and those still ensconced in the eastern suburbs of Caen. During *Operation Bluecoat*, the failure to occupy high ground on the flanks at Amaye hindered progress.[122] Allied advances were all too often in the sights of unsuppressed German guns on the flanks that were in perfect positions to observe, inflict damage and retard progress. When one considers the vulnerability of Allied tanks to HV German anti-tank gunnery, the risk of exposing even more vulnerable flanks was great and units understandably halted to deal with such threats.

To compound the problem still further for armoured forces, the lack of width inherent in 21st Army Group assaults, constrained manoeuvre and mobility.

One of the obvious key advantages of mechanised armoured forces is mobility, and a requirement of operations is the space to employ this potential. Fourth County of London Yeomanry, badly mauled at Villers Bocage, complained that their freedom of movement was curtailed by the requirement of keeping to a limited area of penetration, thus exposing their flanks to counter-attack on the morning of 13 June.[123] During *Operation Jupiter* (10–11 July) tank commanders complained about too much armour in too little space.[124] Still further, although *Operation Goodwood* was supposed to be a two-divisional-wide attack (11th Armoured and Guards), because of the constraints of space, it was in reality led by one armoured brigade of 11th Armoured Division. When Guards Armoured Division and the rest of 11th eventually managed to get forward, though in some disorder, Brig. Hinde, commanding 7th Armoured Division's 22nd Brigade, which was following on in support, decided that there was simply too much armour milling about in such a confined area and deferred his advance until more space had been secured.[125] Indeed, Bobby Erskine, GOC 7th Armoured, was highly critical of the employment of armour in this operation.[126] During *Operation Totalise*, both George Kitching (GOC 4th Canadian Armoured Division) and Stanislaw Maczek (GOC 1st Polish Armoured Division) requested more space over which to employ their armour, but were refused by Simonds.[127] There were clear difficulties in employing armour in such confined areas, and during operations to the west and south of Caen such manoeuvring difficulties were compounded by the dense and claustrophobic terrain.

However, armoured forces faced even more difficulties should they be able to advance, for the limited width and scope of Anglo-Canadian operations served to allow the Germans time to deploy reserves, improvise defences and halt or hinder potential penetrations. Despite initial progress on 26 June, *Epsom* was blocked by the Germans, who quickly directed units into the area. Even small determined forces were able to hold the British advance long enough for reserves to arrive, and although subsequent counter-attacks towards Cheux by II SS Panzer Corps (9th SS and 10th SS Panzer Divisions) were driven off with crippling losses, they were enough, in conjunction with *Ultra* intelligence, to persuade Dempsey to close down the operation.[128] *Operation Jupiter*, a further attempt to seize Hill 112, also suffered from the Germans being able to move reserves quickly into the line to hold back the attack by 15th Scottish and 43rd Wessex Infantry Divisions, supported by 4th Armoured Brigade and 31st Tank Brigade.[129] However, *Bluecoat* was fought over a much wider area and did not encounter the same level of problems, and though the fighting was intense and casualties heavy, significant progress was made.

The narrow front operational technique employed by 21st Army Group therefore created some difficulties in developing battles once initial break-ins had been achieved, and arguably the most significant impact fell upon the armoured units, especially those intended to advance in support or to exploit opportunities. There is little doubt that the problems of interpenetration and consequent disorganisation, vulnerability of flanks, lack of manoeuvring space and the limited area over which German forces were required to concentrate to close penetrations all served to hinder the progress of Anglo-Canadian mechanised forces. Despite the advantages of narrow-front assault, problems ensued and added further to the difficulties confronting armoured forces in Normandy in 1944.

Planning and expectations

The operational technique developed and employed by 21st Army Group was not always strictly adhered to, but in the main it formed the basis of how the Anglo-Canadian forces fought in northwest Europe in 1944–45. For British armoured forces the adoption of such techniques had particular implications, however. Moreover, the logic and rationality of Montgomery's Colossal Crack operational technique in part rests on the assumption that the disadvantages were clearly understood by the planners and commanders, and that forces were employed according to a basic understanding of their capabilities and how they supported the adopted doctrine. The development of, and emphasis placed upon, firepower was clearly appreciated, as was the reasoning that 21st Army Group was reliant on materiel superiority and operating with diminishing reserves of manpower.

However, the manner in which planners and commanders aimed to employ armour raises more questions. If Colossal Cracks and its deficiencies were clearly appreciated and battles fought within these parameters, then the impact of this technique should be reflected in the planning process and in the expectations placed upon armoured forces. Indeed, if 21st Army Group commanders were fully aware that, in conjunction with other major tactical and operational factors, firepower reliance, narrow-front assaults and close control would hinder the ambitious use of armour, their plans and expectations would mirror this.

This, however, was not always the case, particularly in pre-*Overlord* planning and during the early stages of the campaign. The plan for *Neptune*, the assault phase of the invasion, demonstrated that 21st Army Group had a muddled appreciation of what armour could or could not achieve in northwest Europe in 1944. Moreover, early errors in judgement were to be repeated until it became clearer that the operating environment did not support the kind of actions envisaged for Anglo-Canadian armoured forces. Early expectations were high and armour had a particular role to play, one that did not always sit comfortably with the caution and firepower reliance at the heart of Montgomery's and 21st Army Group's operational technique. Moreover, the historical perception that armour failed in Normandy rests largely upon these stated expectations and has shaped understanding of the effectiveness, or lack of, since 1945.

Concerns about the manner in which armour could be used on the offensive had been growing since the Mediterranean campaigns. Maj-Gen W. E. Clutterbuck, commanding 1st Division in Tunisia, believed that the mine and the heavy anti-tank gun had 'seen off' the tank as the key supporting weapon to the infantry.[130] Moreover, in the close-country fighting of Italy, the dense terrain and the methods employed by the Germans made it clear that the tank was no longer able to take the kind of bold dashing action supposedly employed by panzer divisions and desired by the Royal Armoured Corps.[131]

Nevertheless, 21st Army Group planners envisaged just such bold dashing penetrations, particularly in the early stages of *Overlord*. During the meetings and briefings at St Paul's School, London, Montgomery made it perfectly clear that he intended his armoured forces to drive inland as quickly as possible on D-Day and thereafter secure a deep as well as broad lodgement area. In his notes, *Some Army Problems* (20 March 1944), he wrote concerning the static defence points likely to be encountered by Allied troops: 'We must not let these areas hold up our rapid penetration inland. We have to gain the tactical advantages quickly, and to push ahead and seize our own pivots – using armoured and mobile forces.'[132] The depth of the bridgehead would be crucial. In mid-April Montgomery again expressed the importance of armour to the *Neptune* plan: 'The best way to interfere with the enemy concentrations and counter-measures will be to push forward fairly powerful armoured force thrusts on the afternoon of D-Day.'[133] His plan called for two armoured brigade groups to drive inland as rapidly and as aggressively as possible on D-Day:

> The result of such tactics will be the establishment of firm bases well in advance of our main bodies ... I am prepared to accept almost any risk in order to carry out these tactics. I would risk even the total loss of the armoured brigade groups.[134]

The importance of the need for drive and dash was clearly noted by subordinates, such as I Corps Commander, Lt-Gen John Crocker: 'As soon as the beach defences have been penetrated, not a moment must be lost in beginning the advance inland. Armour should be used boldly from the start.'[135]

Maj-Gen David Belchem, head of 21st Army Group's planning and operations staff, later claimed that, although the stated plans called for such dash and *elan*, it was as much to placate air force commanders, who were concerned over the capture of sites appropriate to the establishment of forward air fields. It was never a realistic expectation that mobile forces would penetrate to Caen or beyond, so Belchem claimed.[136] It was also the case that Montgomery had been concerned during *Exercise Thunderclap*, a thorough examination and testing of the *Overlord* plan in April 1944, that his assault commanders had hung back somewhat, and that he wanted to stamp this out.[137] However, this equally implies that Montgomery expected such aggression and dash and was determined to instil it into his troops. It is certainly the case that, although his wider plan called for the Anglo-Canadians to act as a pivot for the main Allied drive to the Seine, they were not merely to hold. In order to be effective, they had to push inland as quickly as possible and crucially secure Caen. Post-war claims by Montgomery and his supporters, who argued that it was never the intention to push towards the south of Caen and reach the Orne valley, are symptomatic of the general observation that 21st Army Group often exaggerated its intentions for purposes of securing resources, morale and politics. Even if this were so, and it is unlikely in the case of the *Neptune* plan, it is apparent that Montgomery and his commanders hoped for impressive results from the rapid deployment and aggressive use of armoured columns, particularly on D-Day.[138]

Yet these were the same troops and lower-ranking commanders who had been imbued with the Monty method of fighting, having previously experienced and enjoyed the weight of firepower support, and who were used to cautious and careful progress. General Alexander had already commented upon the lack of initiative and thrust on the part of subordinate commanders as early as 1942, and German opponents still noted similar traits throughout the Normandy campaign.[139] Gen Diestel, GOC 346th Infantry Division, who arrived in Normandy on 8 June, recorded a lack of originality on the part of the British, who always followed set patterns of attack and lacked imagination and drive.[140]

On 6 June, the armour, expected by 21st Army Group planners to thrust purposefully inland, ground to a halt, for a variety of reasons. Levels of German opposition were greater than expected and the bad weather also played a critical role in hindering the drive inland, but these factors compounded with a degree of hesitancy on the part of the forces. Unused to operating in circumstances that required rapid decision-making and initiative, commanders vacillated. Concerned about lack of organisation, minimal fire support and the risks of by-passing dug-in German defensive points, British troops stalled before Caen, and the long slog to take the city had begun.[141] It should not be viewed as the pivotal factor in the failure to capture Caen in the first days of *Overlord*, but Montgomery and Dempsey clearly hoped for the type of drive and dash from their armoured spearheads that was distinctly unlikely to be displayed once initial difficulties were encountered. It was entirely correct that commanders aimed high in their planning and estimations, and indeed Dempsey in 1968 rejected the notion that the objectives for D-Day were too ambitious, rather they were not ambitious enough. Nevertheless, in spite of the remarkable achievements of D-Day, there was a clear mismatch between what was likely to be achieved with the forces available and the *Overlord* plan.[142]

The inappropriateness of planning was again demonstrated shortly after D-Day during *Operation Perch*. This bold venture called for 7th Armoured Division to burst through an opening in the German lines and drive on to Villers Bocage, thus turning the flank of Panzer *Lehr* and beginning an encirclement of Caen from the east. This was to be the precursor to *Operation*

Wild Oats, whereby 7th Armoured would link with a western encirclement of Caen by 51st Highland Division, meeting in the Orne Valley, where British 1st Airborne Division was to be dropped to complete the effective capture of the city. Progress by 7th Armoured was slow and the division demonstrated sluggishness in attempting this manoeuvre, before being ambushed by elements of Panzer *Lehr* and 101st SS Heavy Tank Battalion in and around Villers Bocage. That the operation was botched and that Hinde, Erskine and Bucknall demonstrated lack of flair is not in question, but Dempsey's stinging criticism of them and his view that much more could have been achieved illustrated the poor appreciation of the realities of armoured operations by 1944 and of the capabilities of British armoured force structures. A very narrow, largely unsupported penetration deep into enemy territory, with resistance hardening in the shape of 2nd Panzer Division and 101st SS Heavy Tank Battalion as well as elements of Panzer *Lehr* was hardly likely to succeed. The nature of the operation was bold, but the force structure of British armoured divisions, the 7th in particular, was inappropriate for such actions, the leadership was unprepared for the methods of fighting in northwest Europe, and the techniques employed by 21st Army Group were inconsistent with these deep penetrations. Yet Montgomery and Dempsey employed these methods, arguably demonstrating a blurred appreciation of what armoured forces were capable of against determined and capable opposition in the terrain of Normandy.

Even in subsequent set-piece operations, the hopes of employing armoured forces in bold and ambitious exploitations were evident. *Epsom* called for 11th Armoured Division to dash for the Orne Valley through the gap created by 15th Scottish and 31st Tank Brigade. Again the expectation of armour was optimistic and somewhat unrealistic. The 11th Armoured may have progressed beyond Hill 112, but would have been exceptionally vulnerable, a product of the narrow front operational techniques of 21st Army Group. The true aims and expectations of *Goodwood* may never be satisfactorily appreciated, but Dempsey was hopeful of much more than a 'writing down' operation, as claimed by Montgomery.[143] The notion that an armoured-only thrust of the nature of *Goodwood* being able to breach the six miles or so of heavily defended German lines was quite unrealistic, but again demonstrated on the part of a very senior British commander unrealistic expectations of armoured formations. Although it is probably the case that the British commanders did not expect to reach Falaise, they did aim to seize the Bourguébus Ridge, but even this was denied to them. Poor planning, partly born out of inappropriate understanding of armoured warfare, and largely a result of the operational techniques employed by 21st Army Group, again undermined the whole operation.

It is clear that early expectations placed on British armoured forces were quite at odds with the realities of warfare in 1944 and demonstrated an unrealistic view of the capabilities of armour. Moreover, the balancing of 21st

Army Group's operational techniques with the employment of armour did not always take place effectively. The consequences of firepower reliance, narrow front attacks, and close control and its impact on the use of armour were not fully appreciated by British planning and operations staff. The impact of this was that at times commanders and planning staff called upon armour to fight in a quite unsuitable manner in northwest Europe in 1944, and this has provided the yardstick by which British armour has come to be measured. On D-Day it failed to drive inland to Caen, received a humiliating setback at Villers Bocage, twice got stuck on Hill 112 and was repulsed with heavy losses at the Bourguébus Ridge. In these cases planning expectations were unrealistic and the appreciation of armoured warfare at odds with the actuality, and yet it is by these unrealised aims and objectives that British armour is perceived to have failed.

Conclusions

Any assessment of the employment and effectiveness of British armour during the Normandy campaign must be viewed in the light of 21st Army Group's operational technique. The adopted processes by which Montgomery's forces attempted to defeat the *Heer* and the SS had serious and crucial implications for armoured formations, implications which were not always fully appreciated by planners and commanders. It was to be expected that 21st Army Group would use methods that would reflect Allied strengths, while simultaneously masking and minimising their weaknesses. Consequently, the adoption of firepower reliance, narrow front attacks and firm and cautious control was both rational and logical. The technique allowed 21st Army Group to deploy its superior capabilities and fight to its strengths, but consequences flowed from the adoption of such fighting methods. First, the operational techniques employed by Anglo-Canadian formations often worked against the effective use of armour, particularly in the exploitation phase of any action. Heavy reliance on firepower and narrow front attacks may have aided the conduct of operations for 21st Army Group generally by reducing casualties, but they were often antithetical to the employment of armour. Second, this was not fully appreciated by 21st Army Group commanders and planners who failed to match the force structure of armoured units, the divisions in particular, to the techniques with which Montgomery's armies endeavoured to defeat the Germans in Normandy. The most obvious consequence of this was the inappropriate use of armour, as commanders attempted to use tanks in an ambitious manner to achieve objectives, when the wider operational methods of the Anglo-Canadian forces largely worked against this by emphasising firepower, constricting manoeuvring space and eschewing fluid and expansive operations. Ultimately this dichotomy has resulted in historians viewing the non-achievement of operational objectives by 21st Army Group's armour as 'failure'. In reality, it represented the consequences of adopting particular operational techniques, the tactical environment prevailing in northwest Europe by 1944, the terrain and the failure of Anglo-Canadian commanders and planners to employ armour more appropriately within the overarching doctrinal framework.

4

FIGHTING THE BATTLE

The Normandy campaign, though conforming generally to the overarching plan envisaged by Montgomery and his staff, deviated from the patterns of battle imagined in Allied command and planning prior to the invasion. Indeed, although the strategic vision largely remained intact, the methods and nature of combat were such that criticism began then, and has continued ever since, of the battlefield craft displayed by the Allied forces, and 21st Army Group in particular. The supposedly crude tactics of mass employed by the Allies served to demonstrate their lack of acumen and guile, while simultaneously illustrating the tactical superiority of German troops. On an operational level it is contended that battlefield opportunities and possibilities were eschewed and that commanders and troops failed to exploit advantages when offered. Consequently, the campaign dragged on when drive, dash and opportunism might have expedited victory. Two of the three tenets upon which this view is founded – inadequate operational art and questionable morale – are discussed in other chapters, but a third measure of failure, the lack of tactical ability and dynamism, remains. Moreover, such criticism has cast a shadow over the achievement of the Allies in the summer of 1944 and resulted in the prevailing view that victory was achieved through artillery, air power and overwhelming logistical support.

Armoured forces in 21st Army Group have not been spared this harsh analysis. While views on morale in armoured units have been more favourable when compared to the infantry, this has not been the case with tactical comparisons. Liddell Hart castigated the Allied armoured units in Normandy for lacking drive and for too often refusing tactical openings. He cited the weak and inadequate grasp of armoured tactics displayed by commanders in Normandy as the principal reason for the frustrating and sluggish performances of armoured units during the campaign.[1] Those who had witnessed the actions of armour in 1944 also raised particular questions. No less an authority than Field Marshal Lord Carver, who commanded 4th Armoured Brigade in Normandy, criticised the manner in which armour fought its battles in the summer of 1944. He argued that poor battlefield tactics resulted in armour being too often employed inappropriately, and that when opportunities for dash presented themselves, tank commanders had such little faith that a co-ordinated attack could be mounted effectively that they shied away from seizing the initiative. Too often early in the fighting, tankcrews had demonstrated spirit and *elan* only to see their attacks peter out in poorly supported actions. Consequently, they adopted more cautious tactics as the campaign progressed.[2]

Perhaps the most cited contemporary critic of the tactical ability of Allied forces in Normandy was Brig. James Hargest, the New Zealand observer with XXX Corps. In mid-June he recorded:

> Our tanks are badly led and fought. Only our superior numbers and our magnificent artillery support keeps them in the field at all. They violate most of the elementary principles of war. They bunch up – they are the reverse of aggressive – they are not possessed of the will to attack the enemy...[3]

He described examples of poor, and indeed near non-existent co-ordination between infantry and armour, even within an armoured division, and cast aspersions on the structure of British armoured units, claiming that giving tanks to cavalry regiments had been a profound error, as cavalrymen, or 'donkey wallopers' as they were also known, had no affinity for tanks.

This testimony requires closer consideration, however. There is no actual evidence that ex-cavalry units in Normandy performed noticeably any differently to other armoured or tank regiments. Indeed, 6th Guards Tank Brigade, drawn from traditional units outside of the RAC demonstrated great dash, determination and tactical ability in its first action during *Operation Bluecoat*, while 31st Independent Tank Brigade (RAC regiments) had a disappointing and frustrating combat initiation at *Epsom*.[4] In addition, Hargest also had only limited experience of the fighting prior to being killed in July, and thus he did not witness the later improvement in the co-ordination of armour and infantry. Moreover, his criticism of 7th Armoured's lack of infantry–armour co-operation ignored the fact that they employed a mixed group as early as 11 June, having quickly identified the need for close infantry–armour co-operation in the Norman countryside.[5]

Nevertheless, though some reservations can be placed against the observations offered, it is the case that controversy persists over the tactical ability of Allied armour in the Normandy campaign. This raises issues over the nature of doctrine and training in 21st Army Group and provokes investigation into how Allied tank units translated the requirement to secure battlefield objectives in preparation, planning and prosecution of combat. Consequently, this chapter will examine the development and implementation of tactical doctrine both in training for and during the fighting in Normandy. A number of key themes will be closely examined. First, the extent to which armour co-operated effectively with infantry during the summer of 1944 and how closely this related to the training and experience garnered prior to D-Day requires analysis.

71

Second, the effectiveness of Allied armoured doctrine and tactics in coping with the increased threat of enemy tanks and self-propelled guns in Normandy, and the tactical problems thrown up by the defensive density of German anti-armour opposition, demands attention. Finally, the impact of the tactical environment on the conduct of armoured warfare requires scrutiny, not least the shaping of the campaign by the terrain through which it was fought. Ultimately, this will facilitate a clearer analysis of the effectiveness of Allied armour on a tactical level during the Normandy campaign.

Doctrine: the employment of tanks in battle

Historians have highlighted a number of key issues centred on armoured doctrine from the Normandy campaign. Distinct problems concerning the use of armoured divisions, the precise role of independent brigades and the effectiveness of infantry–armour co-operation have been identified. As has been previously discussed, the operational technique and methods developed and utilised by Montgomery and his staff, while understandable and successful in a wider sense, often served to act against the use of armoured divisions in their intended role of exploitation and manoeuvre. During actions such as *Goodwood* and *Epsom* they were too readily used as battering rams, a role for which they were unprepared and ill equipped. In addition, the independent armoured and tank brigades found themselves caught in a doctrinal squabble between Montgomery and his staff on one side and the War Office on the other. While the brigades were essentially equipped with two distinct types of tank – the heavy infantry support Churchill, and the pseudo-cruiser, the M4 Sherman – doctrine theoretically remained constant, thus not reflecting the differing capabilities and intended roles for each vehicle. In addition, the degree of infantry and armour co-operation throughout 21st Army Group was initially somewhat inconsistent, resulting in some inappropriately and occasionally poorly co-ordinated actions in which minor problems, requiring integrated attacks, could not be overcome effectively. These issues were, to greater or lesser degrees, shaped by the development of armoured doctrine in Britain in the years and months leading up to *Overlord*.

The place of the armoured division in battle was a matter of considerable debate and discussion in the period between Dunkirk and D-Day, shaped by the development of War Office doctrine, itself informed to varying degrees by new equipment and experience gleaned from the Mediterranean campaign. Unfortunately by the summer of 1944, the doctrine underpinning the employment of armoured divisions had been disseminated too casually, issued too late and was in essence too vague and imprecise to alleviate the problems generated by three years of soul searching. The impact of this would have been disastrous if the British had relied heavily upon or enforced doctrine in the manner the Soviet, and to a lesser degree the German, army did. As will be seen, however, the looser and more flexible approach to doctrine enshrined in the British Army served 21st Army Group quite well, and importantly allowed them to adapt to the situation in Normandy and find their own workable answers.

In the aftermath of the German army's spectacular successes in France in 1940, the British Army sought solace in a major reappraisal of the structure of modern armies.[6] Unfortunately, the principal lesson of armoured warfare derived from the defeat centred on the primacy of the panzer rather than of the panzer division. Consequently, the development of the British armoured arm was predicated on a flawed understanding of the innovative methods employed by the German panzer divisions in May and June 1940. Thus, the British strove long and hard to raise six new armoured divisions from the autumn of 1940 without due consideration as to how they might be best structured, or indeed employed in battle. The armoured division of 1940–42 was intended to eschew direct assault on heavily defended enemy positions and was instead to seek and destroy enemy armour in tank versus tank combat.[7] The force structure of British armoured divisions of this period mirrored this doctrine, being constructed around two armoured brigades. The absence of a substantial infantry presence beyond the motor battalion attached to each armoured brigade implied a great deal about the role for which the armoured division was intended.[8]

However, the experience of the Western Desert forced a major reappraisal of the structure of armoured divisions in mid-1942. Theatre lessons demonstrated that the tank's primary activity in the Mediterranean was centred on dealing with non-armoured opposition.[9] Indeed, the Germans in Libya frequently won control of the battlefield by neutralising British armour with dug-in anti-tank guns when the British advanced seeking tank versus tank combat against German armoured forces.[10] British armour was thus forced to seek methods of engaging the enemy's infantry and anti-tank guns, and the low level of infantry support available to British armoured divisions in 1940–42 proved wholly inadequate, while the tanks themselves were largely equipped with 2-pdr guns, incapable of delivering a formidable degree of HE firepower. Consequently, in the restructuring of British armoured divisions the number of armoured brigades was cut to one, while an infantry brigade was added.[11]

However, the issue of how infantry could be suitably integrated into the workings of the armoured division remained to be resolved. While an infantry brigade had been included in each armoured division, War Office doctrine still dictated that armour and infantry be kept separate, as they did not want to see the armoured force's mobility constrained by accommodating slower moving and less mobile infantry. In essence, the infantry brigade was to provide a shield around which the thrusting armour could be deployed.[12] In addition, the motor battalion attached to a British armoured division's armoured brigade, theoretically to provide organic infantry support, was until 1944 simply not mobile enough and thus had great difficulty operating with armour. This was to a degree ameliorated by the introduction of M3/5 half-tracks in the months leading up to *Overlord*, which provided greater manoeuvrability. Some discussion also took place regarding the use of tank-riders, whereby infantry would be carried forward into battle on the tanks themselves, debussing directly into action, rather than prior to it. The increased vulnerability of such infantry to artillery and small arms fire, and other operating difficulties, fused with negative reports from North Africa and resulted in the War Office dismissing such tactics, other than in exceptional circumstances.[13] Nevertheless, in order to expedite the initial push on Caen on 6 June, and during the fighting in the *bocage* in Normandy, tank riders were pressed into service, despite the supposed disadvantages.[14]

However, more fundamentally, the crucial problem centred on doctrine, especially for the motorised infantry, which was always intended to be deployed only when armour encountered a situation that it could not easily handle, such as dug-in infantry and anti-tank guns. In such circumstances, the motorised infantry would be deployed forward to deal with the difficulty, thus freeing up the armour. War Office doctrine has espoused this view in 1941, but it took until the following year for units training in the UK to accept this, as they had hitherto relied upon armoured charges to overwhelm all enemy targets. However, although this new doctrine was closer to the ideal of armour–infantry co-operation, in 1942 armoured regiments only mounted 2-pdr or occasionally 6-pdr guns in the UK, and were thus incapable of providing enough HE firepower to defeat any but the most trifling of non-armoured opposition. Thus they would have had to call upon the motor battalion in a great many circumstances, making excessive and acutely attritional use of these troops. Moreover, motor battalions took far too long to get forward and shield the armour until the advent of armoured half-tracks and the like in 1944. Fortunately, by the time of *Overlord* armoured units carried sufficient HE capability, following the introduction of the 75 mm dual-purpose gun, to share the burden with the infantry of dealing with targets hostile to armour.

To undermine the value of supporting infantry still further, throughout the 1941–44 period, the motor battalion was always intended to operate to the rear of armoured formations and not provide immediate close support. Consequently, armoured thrusts could be brought to a standstill and valuable time lost while infantry was called up to combat any threat uncovered by an advance. Still further, with the bulk of a British armoured division's infantry brigaded together separately from the armour, there was never enough infantry to deal with emerging problems on the battlefield. Indeed, each armoured regiment could effectively call upon only one company (attached from the motor battalion) to provide infantry support. In contrast, in German panzer divisions, experience dictated a much closer and integrated approach to the use of infantry directly with the armour, to facilitate a more flexible and immediate response in action. Clearly, the British armoured divisional structure was to store up problems of infantry–armour support that the Normandy campaign would initially expose.

The extra burden envisaged for motorised infantry until 1943 was to a degree born out of the inadequate HE firepower of British tanks prior to the introduction of the dual-purpose 75 mm gun from 1942 onwards. As Timothy Harrison Place has argued, the War Office attempted to deal with this difficulty by adapting official doctrine to suit the available armour, but alas there was a persistent mismatch between doctrine and equipment between 1941 and 1944, leading to some confusion in training in Britain.

Meanwhile, in the Mediterranean, formations developed a self-taught doctrine that adapted official policy to the particular demands of fighting in the Western Desert. Such tactics, while appropriate to the operational and equipment situation in North Africa, did not for obvious reasons take sufficient account of the wider context, notably future enemy developments in armour and the likely operating environment of Allied tanks in northwest Europe.

The armoured division in North Africa continued to operate separately from its infantry for much of the campaign and persistently dabbled with armoured charging tactics, leaving the infantry and artillery in defensive boxes. Tactics slowly shifted following contact with the Afrika Corps, but the inadequacy of British HE firepower caused headaches and problems that were not resolved until the introduction of dual-purpose 75 mm guns, first in the M3 Grant and then in 1942 in the M4 Sherman. Armour had to rely heavily on field artillery to neutralise enemy anti-tank guns and this required a sophisticated level of co-ordination too often lacking in British formations in North Africa. The situation became worse when the 2-pdr began to prove inadequate against the latest German tanks and the 25-pdr was pressed into service as a supplementary anti-tank gun, thus drawing it away from its principal task of indirect fire support. This highlighted the inadequacy of British tanks' capabilities against soft targets, which varied between close-range engagements with machine guns or literally driving over or at such targets. Neither was ideal and casualties were often heavy. The relief in British armoured forces when the 75 mm gun appeared was considerable and led to an inflated opinion of the true worth of the weapon, with resulting impact on equipment policy well into 1943.[15] Indeed, the Grants and Shermans now available to the Mediterranean armoured forces allowed the effective implementation of the War Office's 1941 doctrine, which called upon tanks to provide a degree of HE fire support for themselves. Until 1942, however, no tank in service had been capable of this. However, the 75 mm gun provided armoured regiments with enough HE firepower support to prevail in the open operating environment of North Africa, in the manner imagined by the War Office, and allowed the separate armour and infantry brigade notion to persist into 1944 when the conditions did not particularly suit it.[16]

In Britain the development of doctrine and training for those armoured units preparing for the invasion of France was shaped by the War Office's attempts to adapt to the lessons of North Africa, to the new equipment being introduced and by experienced commanders returning from the Mediterranean.

In 1942 armoured brigade training had moved to attempting to fulfil the requirements of War Office doctrine, that is, using armoured firepower to support advancing tanks in an integrated and mutually supporting fashion. Originally this was hoped to be provided by the advancing tanks themselves, but reservations over firing on the move began to grow and the superiority of static fire support was noted.[17] By 1943 both Guards and 11th Armoured Divisions were employing static firing as the standard.

Nevertheless, the drive towards fulfilling the combined approach evinced by the War Office in 1941 seemed to be bearing fruit as infantry and integrated fire support from tanks emerged more obviously in the training of armoured regiments in 11th and Guards Armoured Divisions. The most significant drawback to this combined arms approach was the insufficient HE firepower delivered by 2-pdr- and 6-pdr-equipped tanks, which consequently increased the pressure on the motorised infantry to deal with enemy positions unsuited to armoured assault. By 1943 however, salvation appeared to be at hand in the form of the 75 mm-gun-equipped tank.

Paradoxically, just at the moment when the British began to take delivery of tanks capable of fulfilling the 1941 doctrine, the War Office changed tack in an effort to plug the gap in their armoured warfare thinking exposed by the weak HE firepower of British tanks to that point in the war.[18] The three-volume MTP No. 41 issued in 1943 covered the armoured regiment (Part 2, February 1943), the motor battalion (Part 3, June 1943) and the armoured division as a whole (Part 1, July 1943). The separated infantry and armoured brigade approach was reaffirmed, but Part 2 argued that massed HE fire support was required to suppress, if not eliminate targets preparatory to assault. This doctrine appeared to take little account of the introduction of dual-purpose 75 mm guns more than capable of providing high-quality fire support, without the need to mass tanks together in the manner of self-propelled artillery. Units therefore began to employ one squadron in three to provide concerted fire support to the other two squadrons in each regiment as they advanced on, and at times charged at, the enemy.

Two problems resulted from this new approach. First, it often took valuable time to prepare such set-piece attacks, time which allowed the enemy to react or prepare stronger defences.[19] Thus, the momentum of the armoured division's advance would be lost, while the overarching doctrine still called for constant movement and probing to exploit potential battlefield opportunities. Second, opportunities would also be squandered through the lack of troop level fire and movement tactics. Regiments would deal with developing battlefield problems at squadron level, whereas a flexible troop level response would be more appropriate in dealing with difficulties quickly. Perversely, troop level fire support tactics were less appropriate prior to the introduction of 75 mm-gun-equipped tanks, but by 1943 were consistent with available armoured equipment, yet the new War Office doctrine undid this prospective harmony.

Crews enthusiastically took to using the M4 Sherman in the massed fire support role where the 75 mm gun appeared to do a splendid job, putting right the obvious failings of the 2-pdr and 6-pdr guns employed hitherto. The advantages of the new tank and dual-purpose gun were such that regiments regressed in some ways back to charging targets once the ground had been prepared by a squadron level 'shoot'.[20] The Guards had never really abandoned such tactics entirely, but now even 11th Armoured began to pick up such habits.

Following Maj-Gen Pip Roberts' appointment as GOC 11th Armoured Division in late 1943, some measures were taken to eliminate the bad behaviour acquired over 1943. Roberts argued that the set-piece battle, the basis of the squadron level fire support tactic, was fundamentally flawed, as it worked against the basic tenet of armoured warfare, which was mobility. He endeavoured to eradicate the idea that a high concentration of HE fire support was required from a squadron to shoot other armoured formations on to their targets. A much more flexible approach was preferable, one that maintained mobility and manoeuvre on the battlefield, the true role of the armoured division. This was to be achieved by utilising artillery as the major source of covering fire support, not the tank, which would be freed to act in small groups, providing immediate and necessary fire support to release other tanks to advance, all conducted in a mutually supporting manner.[21] The importance of experienced and competent leadership was evident in the appointment of Roberts in December 1943 and his influence was marked throughout the campaign in Normandy.[22]

The War Office debated the issue further over the latter half of 1943 and the opening months of 1944, but the squadron level fire support tactic was not abandoned, though the importance of fire and movement tactics was to be emphasised further in later War Office doctrine. However, this was not issued until just prior to D-Day, much too late to have any significant impact on the manner in which armoured divisions initially fought in Normandy.[23] Consequently, official armour doctrine was still in a state of flux on the eve of D-Day.

Although there was some debate over the manner in which armoured brigades within divisions would carry out their battlefield role in Normandy, the place of the independent armoured or tank brigade was shrouded in yet more controversy. Although the War Office had established a series of independent armoured and tank brigades with the intention of employing heavily armoured infantry support tanks to provide mobile firepower for infantry divisions, by the autumn of 1943 there was still little harmony over this approach. A key factor influencing the doctrine in infantry support brigades was the available equipment. By the autumn of 1943 it was becoming clear that the War Office could only provide three brigades of heavily armoured Churchills, well short of the requirement for eight such brigades. Maj-Gen Norrie, the RAC advisor at the War Office, maintained that the other independent brigades, now to be equipped with M4 Shermans, were unsuited to fulfilling a similar role. However, Lt-Gen William Morgan, 21st Army Group CoS prior to Montgomery's arrival, disagreed and insisted that available doctrine be altered to allow the Sherman to function in a close support role.[24] Montgomery rejected this.[25] He cited his experience in the Mediterranean campaign and argued that all armoured brigades should be interchangeable and capable of armoured and infantry support operations irrespective of their equipment. He made no distinction between formations armed with Churchills (tank brigades) or Shermans (armoured brigades), despite the latter's shortcomings in the close support role.[26] Thus by the time of *Overlord* Montgomery intended to employ his armoured and tank brigades as he saw fit and not necessarily as they had been established and devised by the War Office.[27]

To complicate matters still further, Montgomery also attempted to impose the 8th Army's view on how infantry support operations should be conducted at a tactical level, further confusing and muddying matters in 21st Army Group. This exacerbated ongoing doctrinal difficulties in the British Army regarding infantry–armour co-operation, problems that have been much cited as a key factor in explaining the supposedly weak performance of Allied armour in the Normandy campaign. It is certainly the case that by the summer of 1944 there was little uniformity and discipline over the manner in which armoured and infantry units would co-operate together on the battlefield and that consequently some problems ensued.[28]

The roots of this problem date back to the development of doctrine in the independent armoured and tank formations in the years leading up to *Overlord* and the manner and effectiveness with which overseas experience was simultaneously embedded into the tactical training of units. Doctrine disseminated just prior to the outbreak of war, MTP (Military Training Pamphlet) No. 22, *Tactical Handling of Army Tank Battalions*, had outlined an approach based upon heavily armoured tanks advancing independently of infantry up to 1,000 yards into the enemy's rear to suppress strongpoints. More tanks would follow, leading the infantry on to the enemy's positions, while a final echelon of mixed troops would consolidate the position.[29] For such an approach to work the infantry support armour needed to be capable of surviving on the battlefield when devoid of infantry protection, and in 1940 this seemed to be possible. The enemy, Arras apart, appeared to be devoid of the heavy anti-tank guns required to stop the Matilda II, and against such opposition British armour enjoyed considerable success, notably as evidenced by actions in North Africa against the Italians. Supported by such successes, the War Office underpinned its avowed doctrine in ATI (Army Training Instruction) No. 2, *The Employment of Army Tanks in Co-operation with Infantry* (March 1941).[30]

The basics were still in place from the 1939 pamphlet, though the independent role of the leading tanks was further emphasised. The belief that tanks alone, following a rolling artillery barrage could advance some 1,000 yards into enemy positions with endurable losses, and thus prepare the ground for the following echelons of tanks and infantry, persisted as long as the Matilda's invulnerability was assured. By the spring of 1941 it was not.

The example of Arras indicated what the Germans, equipped with 88 mm anti-tanks guns, might do against such tactics, but it took until the painful experience of *Operation Battleaxe* in the summer of 1941 for it to become apparent that the Matilda's survivability in the face of German heavy anti-tank guns was low. Consequently, the notion of leading armour–infantry assaults on prepared positions with tanks alone began to be questioned, though still further evidence from *Operation Crusader* was required to underline the lesson.[31]

First British Army's experiences in Tunisia in the winter of 1942–43 also raised questions about the 1941 doctrine.[32] The units employed in this campaign had trained in the UK according to the tenets of ATI No. 2 (March 1941), though it was somewhat modified in that a so-called 'sandwich' formation was employed. In this method the leading tanks would be followed by an echelon of infantry, with a further echelon of armour following on providing flexible support, applying it as and when required.[33] However, although a refined version of the official doctrine, based upon training experience, the sandwich method as employed in Tunisia was found wanting. Too often the leading echelon of tanks stalled when confronted by difficult terrain, anti-tank guns and, most often, mines. Consequently, the rolling artillery barrage intended to precede the tanks on to their objective and suppress enemy forces, moved on leaving the tanks floundering and exposed in its wake. Reconnaissance elements simply could not provide enough intelligence on enemy dispositions and the locations of the increasingly troublesome minefields. Experience demonstrated that infantry was best suited to leading the advance with armour following on behind, advancing from one defensive position to another, providing fire support. Infantrymen were not overly impressed by this turn of events and the belief began to develop that the tank was virtually redundant in the face of the mine and heavy anti-tank gun.[34] Tankcrew responded that the armour could best provide support for the infantry with firepower, and the comforting sight of armour close by infantry on the battlefield served little practical purpose. By being too closely tied to the infantry, mobility, a key strength of the tank, was rendered worthless. Thus, doctrine should employ the tank in its most appropriate role, that of providing fire support from hull-down positions, rather than advancing when exposed. Ultimately, the tank could provide no support at all if it was reduced to a burning wreck by enemy anti-tank guns.[35]

Although the War Office is open to criticism for allowing the obviously flawed doctrine of 1941 to persist into 1943, in May of that year a new ATI No. 2, *The Co-operation of Infantry and Tanks* (May 1943) was published to guide armour–infantry co-operation.[36] This was a more flexible approach and one that took on board the lessons from the Mediterranean as well as training programmes in Britain. The new doctrine envisaged a three-phase battle – initial penetration, development and exploitation. In each phase operations would be conducted by armour and infantry divided into two echelons – assault and support. There were no hard and fast rules concerning the constitution of the echelons, but guidance was given as to when mixes of units might be more appropriate. The instructions certainly emphasised that tanks would be of little use in the assault echelon during the initial penetration phase, and that even in the development phase, when units would be striking forward decisively against targets in the enemy's territory, tanks and infantry should co-operate closely together in a mutually supporting manner. ATI No. 2 (May 1943) appeared to have accepted that the tank was highly vulnerable unless adequately supported and that a flexible doctrine was required. However, the impact of this approach was less than might have been expected for a number of reasons.

By the autumn of 1943, 21st Army Group was preparing for action the following year and the formulation of appropriate doctrine was naturally part of this process. In November, under the tutelage of Brig. Harold 'Peter' Pyman, *The Co-operation of Tanks with Infantry Divisions in Offensive Operations* was issued.[37] This work built on ATI No. 2 (May 1943), but also acknowledged that some of the eight independent armoured brigades being prepared for *Overlord* were going to be equipped with the M4 Sherman and not the heavily armoured A22 Churchill, now only going to be supplied to three of the eight brigades. The Sherman was considered unsuited to the same type of close-support role originally envisaged for the independent brigades, and consequently Pyman and his team issued a set of supplementary tactical notes for the use of Shermans in a close-support role. Essentially, this centred on using the Sherman in a largely self-propelled artillery role, shooting advancing infantry on to target with 75 mm HE gunfire, rather than advancing in close support. Pyman's team considered that this would best suit the more lightly armoured M4, whereas the Churchill would be able to provide much closer support, the later versions having in excess of 150 mm frontal armour. In either case, the old doctrine of leading with tanks was discouraged, other than in exceptional circumstances.

Despite being issued formally by 21st Army Group in December 1943, the revised doctrine was never to be firmly embedded, however.[38] With Montgomery's arrival at 21st Army Group HQ matters were to become somewhat confused. The new CinC disagreed with the November pamphlet on a number of levels. First, he saw no distinction between any armoured brigade in his new command, as they should all be equally capable of fulfilling any given battlefield role. Second, Sherman and Churchill units should conform to the same doctrine, thus underpinning Montgomery's belief that a single capital tank was all the British Army needed. Third, issued doctrine should be simple and straightforward and he regarded Pyman's team's pamphlet as overly complex in certain areas and likely to engender confusion. Fourth, and perhaps most pertinently for infantry–armour co-operation, he rejected the contention that formations should not generally lead with armour.[39] He concluded that Paget, the 21st Army Group GOC he was to replace, had been 'gravely misled by someone' and he wanted to know from Lt-Gen Archie Nye, VCIGS, who was behind the pamphlet.[40] Nye was somewhat vexed by

Montgomery's tone and countered that the officers behind the pamphlet, Brig. Pyman, Lt-Gen John Crocker (later to command I Corps in Normandy) and Maj-Gen Raymond Briggs, DRAC, all had experience from North Africa.[41] Regarding the distinction between Shermans and Churchills, Nye commented to Alan Brooke: 'Are Sherman equipped regiments handled when supporting infantry in exactly the same way as infantry tank battalions? General Montgomery says they are, and everyone else says they are not.'[42]

However, in Montgomery's view the 8th Army had developed its own doctrine, one somewhere between the sandwich method and the approach of ATI No. 2 (May 1943). In this it was accepted that in the initial penetration phase of battle, infanttry and engineers should lead supported by tank firepower where possible, but diverged from ATI No. 2 (May 1943) and 21st Army Group policy by then reverting to the sandwich method, with tanks leading the advance from the channels developed in the enemy's minefields.[43] Such views were issued to 21st Army Group in February, notes which argued for tanks alone to lead an advance, ahead of infantry, once any necessary penetration of enemy minefields and defences had been achieved.[44] Thus, the more flexible mixed infantry–armour assault echelon doctrine, and that of shooting the infantry on to target from hull-down positions, was supposedly jettisoned in the spring of 1944, largely at the behest of Montgomery.

Timothy Harrison Place is especially critical of Montgomery for his arrogant imposition of a flawed doctrine, one that ran contrary to the experience of many prior to 1944.[45] However, of greater importance in determining the manner in which infantry–armour co-operation was conducted in Normandy was the lack of enforcement of any standardised doctrine, flawed or otherwise. Many commanders interpreted official doctrine as they saw fit and thus the approach of units varied. It was axiomatic that when infantry and armour combined on the battlefield they did so according to a common doctrine, especially when such units may not have worked together before. In Normandy, however, although the basics of the various doctrines circulated in the year leading up to *Overlord* can be detected in armour–infantry actions, there was little uniformity. The enforcement of official doctrine was always patchy in the British Army, even after the arrival of the 'great commander' from the Mediterranean, and it was because of this general attitude to doctrine in the British Army that 21st Army Group was able to adapt relatively quickly in Normandy, once some original concepts had been found wanting. Consequently, the arrival of Montgomery and his tactical views, though confusing matters, did not have the disastrous impact they might otherwise have had in a more rigid doctrinal environment.

Training

The ability to transfer doctrine into practice depended heavily upon worth-while and efficient training to inculcate the right habits and drills into units.

Armoured units differed from others in that training was in essence divided into two – technical and tactical. For a tank formation to work effectively, the degree of tactical knowledge required was involved and substantial, but was principally required of tank commanders rather than whole crews. Therefore, unlike infantry, crews other than commanders, did not need a firm grasp of how the tank would interact within a troop or a troop within a squadron.[46] However, the other technical tasks, such as maintenance, gunnery, driving and radio operation, did require a high level of drill efficiency.

In training armoured units the British Army did the technical well, but the tactical less so. Training supported the development of the technical skills very effectively, and tank commanders in Normandy were usually impressed by the ease with which a replacement could fit into a crew due to his sound technical training.[47] Unfortunately, the development of tactical skills proved more problematical, certainly at the level of the squadron and above, and it was here that doctrine and battlefield craft had to be implanted in order to facilitate operational effectiveness.

Following standard army training – square bashing and the like – all tankcrew undertook a basic training programme centred on the essentials of armoured warfare, before moving on to field units where crews would learn how to operate together efficiently and respond to direction without hesitation. Basic armour training took as little as four weeks but was enhanced in the units eventually deployed in Normandy either by extended periods of training in Britain, or most effectively by the experience of armoured warfare in the Mediterranean. Even during the North African campaign, units would take time to hone technical skills, and when in reserve would fine-tune tactical skills, though this was usually conducted at the troop and rarely at squadron level.[48] Although battle experience could not be matched by training, the tactical skills developed in the operating environment of North Africa were not always as relevant to northwest Europe as the battle-hardened veterans who fought in 21st Army Group hoped. The experience of 7th Armoured Division is a clear example of where skills appropriate to one theatre proved to be of lesser value in another.

Nevertheless, the armoured tactical training in Britain also encountered problems. Officers were given rigorous training to supplement their basic grounding in armoured warfare, and courses at Sandhurst would last months, covering all the key aspects of tank tactics as well gunnery, maintenance, organisation and so forth. The practical application of armoured command theory was valuable, but limited. Although four weeks was given over to tactical training on the areas around Sandhurst, only so much could be achieved in the confined space. Troop level manoeuvres could be conducted but little beyond that and this was an obvious limitation, for it was particularly at the squadron level and above that greatest difficulties were likely to be encountered in interpreting doctrine.[49] Nevertheless, the quality of what was taught appears to have been high and many sources attest to the validity of the programme.

Higher-level tactical training was of course critical to building an effective tank arm capable of conducting operational level manoeuvres, but obstacles existed to hinder such development. Space was strictly limited and armoured formations were not in a position to rampage across the British countryside at will, despite the desire of the Guards to charge about in cavalier fashion. In fact, units were under orders to avoid agricultural areas and stick to roads when possible for fear of damaging home-grown food supplies.[50] Despite the expansion of training areas for armoured formations to test their skills and tactics, tank units would be lucky if they spent more than three to four weeks in any given year on a major exercise range equipped with a variety of terrains, obstacles and targets.

Armoured training was also hindered by the supply of appropriate equipment. It has already been noted that doctrine was shaped by the capabilities or otherwise of tanks to mount effective HE-firing guns. Until the advent of a plentiful supply of 75 mm guns for training purposes in 1943, units had to practise with 2- and 6-pdr guns, unlikely to provide the appropriate conditions for the fire support tactics being suggested by the War Office. In addition, units were forced to train on low-quality tanks, such as the disastrous and hopelessly unreliable A13 Covenanter. Troops training in Britain mirrored their contemporaries in North Africa by having to learn how to maintain their tanks and cope with their vicissitudes rather than develop battlefield skills. Only by mid-1943 were units in Britain being supplied with the Shermans, Cromwells and Churchills they would employ in Normandy. Still further, the Firefly, sporting a 17-pdr anti-tank gun, arrived only in the late spring of 1944, thus allowing very little time to train and develop new tactics to incorporate them as successfully as possible. There were many debates as to how the Firefly should be incorporated into troops and squadrons and whether troops should have three or four tanks.[51] Crews and units were eventually forced to learn in harness with little if any practical experience.[52]

As new tanks and especially new weaponry were introduced into training in the UK further problems emerged. Previous armament, most often the 2-pdr gun, had both a limited effective range and no substantial HE content. Thus, when engaged at long range by enemy anti-tank guns, tanks could themselves do little other than rely on artillery support. The introduction of the 75 mm gun into home units, particularly in 1943, altered this relationship as tanks were now able to deal with soft targets at long range, with the consequence that training had to be expanded and designed to accommodate this. Moreover, the ranges over which anti-tank exchanges were likely to take place also increased both with the introduction of the 75 mm gun and the 6-pdr. Tankcrews and commanders had to train in tactics applicable across the ranges from point-blank to over a mile. This entailed incorporating co-operation with infantry and artillery at a variety of distances as well as developing skills in single and multiple tank tactics for action at ranges usually up to 1,200 yards, but also up to maximum likely distances of engagement.[53]

Troops training and building experience in the Mediterranean campaign also had to integrate new equipment into tactical thinking. In North Africa battle ranges were often much higher than they were to be in Normandy and emphasis was placed on long-range gunnery, especially the ability to combat dug-in anti-tank guns with HE gunfire. The addition of the 75 mm-equipped gun further underpinned this doctrine.[54] Consequently, armoured forces training in Britain developed better skills and drill in short-range combat, while those in the Mediterranean proved more adept at long-range engagements and gunnery. Although in the confines of Norman terrain combat ranges tended to the short, thus rendering the experience of the Mediterranean of limited value, the troops who trained in the UK also suffered, largely from the inherent problems of developing skills which were useful only for short-range combat. This was doubly so in the case of mobile armoured formations, sup-posedly intended for the exploitation role. Infantry support armoured tactics could to a greater degree be integrated into artillery fireplans and infantry operations, but fast-moving troops could not be so constrained. Testing the techniques and skill levels of mobile armoured formations, and their ability to combine with flexible artillery and air support proved particularly problematical.

Conversely, the level of planning and tactical training for specific assault duties and operations, especially on D-Day itself, proved highly effective. The amphibious swimming tanks, the DD Shermans, posed a considerable tactical and training problem, but one that was overcome, as were those of employing 'Hobart's Funnies' of the 79th Armoured Division. These were complex issues, requiring specialised training and tactical preparation, and the fair success of the armoured forces in assaulting the Normandy beaches is evidence of the quality of such training. There was a price to be paid, however, as those units trained in assault tactics had less time devoted to preparation for conventional armoured operations and as a consequence possibly suffered when in Normandy.[55]

Thus, by 1944 British armour, although well prepared in many ways, had an uneven and questionable development of battle doctrine both in the armoured divisions and the independent brigades. The divisional force structure was intended to support fast, mobile actions in which the divisions would exploit weaknesses in the enemy's defences and provide operational manoeuvre. It was a doctrine best suited to open country and to employment against an enemy already reeling from offensives led by artillery, air power and infantry, supported by independently brigaded tanks and armour. It was never intended for such units to spearhead attacks or to get bogged down in attritional infantry-based operations, though of course this was precisely what happened. The independent brigades were better suited to the style of operations imposed by the unfolding Normandy campaign, but suffered to a degree because their initial tactical methods were at times found wanting. To compound matters, experienced units returned from the Mediterranean had for the most part built their practical knowledge of combat in an environment quite alien to that of northwest Europe, thus rendering their prior learning of less value than was imagined or hoped. Moreover, the training of units in Britain suffered on a tactical level due to constraints on both space and time.

New tactical problems in Normandy

The essence of the Normandy plan as outlined and discussed by Montgomery and his staff in April and May 1944 was for deep armoured thrusts inland as soon as practicable following the D-Day landings. In the Anglo-Canadian sector, this required armoured columns to strike south on 6 June to capture Caen and the commanding high ground beyond, and secure it by 10 June. Once established in this beachhead, Allied forces could then develop, preparatory to further advances.[56] Carlo D'Este has made much of the controversy about where Montgomery intended the British to be positioned shortly after D-Day, once this initial drive inland had been accomplished. He has argued that when they failed to reach the ground south of Caen, Montgomery glossed over this shortfall, later claiming that Caen itself had always been the hinge or pivot in Allied strategy.[57] This debate is of crucial concern because the area over which British armour was intended to be fighting in the days and weeks following D-Day is fundamental to any assessment of planning, training and force structure. The plan for *Overlord* undoubtedly envisaged deep armoured thrusts by the Anglo-Canadians to seize ground from which further operations and set-piece attacks could be developed, but the terrain over which such operations would be conducted was supposed to be that beyond Caen, especially to the southeast, which was more open and conducive to mobile operations.[58]

Such considerations are important in understanding the tactical problems that confronted British armoured units in the weeks following 6 June. Planning notes distributed in preparation for D-Day considered the terrain to the south and southeast of Caen markedly superior to that to the west, southwest and north of the city for large-scale operations based on manoeuvre and mobility. The *bocage*-type countryside that was a feature of the terrain to the west of Caen was noted as being a severe hindrance to cross-country movement. It consisted of seemingly sunken roads with a patchwork of small fields, around 300 feet across, edged by steep-banked hedges, sometimes over 12 feet high. Such terrain threatened to aid enemy troops in defence and to undermine the advantages of equipment and manoeuvre held by the Allies. The lie of the land to the west of Caen was also deeply unhelpful, for the topography ran across the likely axes of advance open to Allied armies endeavouring to strike south. They would have to cross the River Odon in particular. The terrain to the east of Caen in the River Dives area was also likely to be unsuitable for offensive actions, being water-logged and flanked by high ground, often wooded. Once again, however, such terrain was likely to be ideal for defence.[59]

It therefore made perfect sense for the Allies to attempt to strike south as quickly as possible to ensure that they did not get ensnared in this problematical terrain. Indeed, 21st Army Group planners worked on the assumption that they would be beyond Caen fairly quickly, and in the more open country of the Falaise plain they would be able to employ their armour in the classic manner. Montgomery and his team also presumed that Rommel, after failing to defeat the invasion on the beaches in the first hours of the campaign, would deploy an elastic defensive cordon around the Allied lodgement in Normandy. This, it was considered, would be based in the eastern sector on the high ground to the east of the River Dives, and to the south occupying the high ground between Falaise and St Lô, particularly the so-called *Suisse Normande*, as this would allow Rommel to hold the Allies with infantry and try and mass his armour for a counter-attack in good tank country, beyond the range of Allied naval gunfire. It also made more military sense for the Germans to fall back in good order rather than dig-in and launch localised, but unco-ordinated and sporadic counter-attacks, which would undoubtedly drain their dwindling resources.[60]

However, the Allies' failure to capture Caen in the first days of *Overlord* and Hitler's no retreat philosophy forced Rommel and Rundstedt to adopt precisely those tactics dismissed by the Allies of digging in around Caen and fighting it out. The advantages conferred on the Germans by the terrain around the city were balanced by the necessity of operating within range of Allied naval guns and of having to fight in a largely ad hoc and improvised manner. In fact, the failure to take Caen may well have proved beneficial for the Allies for it lent the city a symbolic status that lured Hitler into defending it at all costs, even though it prevented Rommel, Rundstedt and Geyr von Schweppenburg from fighting in the manner they desired. Ultimately, the battles in and around Caen proved ruinously costly for the Germans, as the units they fed into the area haemorrhaged to destruction without ever being able to pose a serious offensive threat to the beach-head, nor being in a position to stymie American activity in the West.[61]

Nevertheless, when Caen did not fall in the first hours of *Overlord*, British armour was then forced to fight a campaign through terrain for which it had little prepared, with various consequences. First, the likelihood of rapid exploitation by an armoured division in the manner outlined in established tactical doctrine became distinctly unrealisable. The close terrain to the west and southwest of Caen through which the Anglo-Canadians would now have to bludgeon a path was most unsuitable for such armour, particularly as the tanks in British and Canadian armoured divisions were less well versed in close co-operation with infantry, fundamental to success in dense terrain and *bocage* countryside. That to the east of the city was flooded and too narrow, lying between the suburbs of Caen itself and the high ground of the Ranville Ridge and areas of woods. Second, as has been noted previously, infantry–armour co-operation was in a state of some confusion when the Allies landed in Normandy, and the tactics necessary for successful close co-operation had yet to be firmly embedded within unit doctrine. Paradoxically, because doc-trinal indiscipline was commonplace in British tank and armoured units, they were more amenable to new ideas and proved suitably flexible once they experienced battle in Normandy. Nevertheless, however successfully doctrine adapted and developed after 6 June, British armour, whether independently brigaded or within armoured divisions, found itself fighting in close terrain for much longer than had been anticipated in pre-*Overlord* planning. Indeed, consideration had been given to closer infantry–armour training prior to *Overlord* but had been rejected because Montgomery expected to be fighting beyond the *bocage* fairly quickly.[62]

A third tactical factor confronting British armour as a result of the extended fighting in the terrain was the enhancement provided to the German defenders. The *bocage* countryside, and that of small but stout farmholdings dotted with woods and orchards stretching across rising and dipping valleys and ravines, lent itself admirably to canny and resourceful defence, a skill previously honed by many of the German troops now in Normandy when previously in action against the Soviets. Indeed, Stephen Badsey has argued that the terrain in Normandy, particularly the *bocage*, was the principal factor behind the length of time taken by the Allies in pushing inland in the summer of 1944.[63] Certainly German tankcrews recognised the necessity of camouflage in Normandy, the benefits of which were less relevant, though still important to advancing Allied tanks.[64] British tankcrews and infantry ruefully noted the ability of small numbers of German troops, equipped with well-sited and concealed anti-tank guns, *panzerfausts* and on occasion Stugs and tanks, to stall an Allied advance with relative ease.[65] Allied tanks were particularly vulnerable to short, almost point-blank-range attack, and began to rely heavily on infantry support. Infantry also suffered heavy casualties because of the nature of the terrain, and they often had to operate ahead of the Allied tanks in order to locate enemy anti-tank elements, prior to bringing up the British armour to provide close-fire support against enemy infantry. British forces quickly realised that a radical tactical rethink was required to winkle out the Germans. Roy Dixon, then a junior commander in 7th Armoured Division noted:

> When we first landed we were in these tiny, little fields with these great big banks, and it was very difficult just physically getting from one field to another...Everything was at very close range...You were creeping around rather than rushing, and people were discouraged by that...We spent our time trying to think of ways to deal with that.[66]

Maj. Bill Close, a highly experienced tank commander with 11th Armoured Division recorded:

> *Bocage* was quite different entirely; it's not good tank country. We found it most difficult to operate in the *bocage*...very small fields

with big hedgerows mounted on top of banks. [It was] difficult for the tank driver, and the enemy tanks, anti-tanks guns and *panzerfausts* could operate in these small fields and hedges much more easily against a tank than we could against them. So when we first went into the *bocage* we did have great problems.[67]

Gen Fritz Bayerlein, GOC Panzer *Lehr*, also considered Normandy to be poor tank country, pointing out after the war to Liddell Hart the tactical difficulties created for both German and Allied armour by the *bocage*.[68]

To compound matters, in Normandy British armour was confronted not only with problematic terrain, but much greater density of opposition than hitherto encountered. The geography of the desert campaign had contributed to fluid and relatively thin defensive lines, other than on rare occasions. In northwest Europe however, the depth of German defensive positions came as a rude shock to British troops and planners. On a number of occasions, operational plans were based on the assumption of being through German defensive positions after some 3–4 miles penetration, only to come unstuck against much deeper defensive positions. Artillery and air bombardment plans were initially much too shallow and were later forced to adapt and expand their area of operations. By *Operation Totalise* a two-stage air bombardment supported by a highly sophisticated artillery fireplan was in place to defeat the expected level and importantly depth of German resistance. In contrast in *Operation Goodwood*, while the density of the air bombardment was impressive, its timing was insufficient to prevent the Germans blocking the Allied attack. Advancing British armoured forces, particularly when in the role of break-through and exploitation, were repeatedly confounded by the depth of German defences. Leading armoured troops, believing they were at the point of breaking through the enemy's lines, would receive a nasty shock when further fierce resistance was uncovered, opposition often untouched by the too shallow Allied artillery and air fireplans. Indeed, the Germans became acutely aware of how the Allies operated and attempted to defeat them by deploying deep defences where and when possible.[69]

In addition to the depth of resistance, in Normandy British forces began to encounter high concentrations of elite German units, and as Hitler and his staff identified Caen as the linchpin of the eastern sector, many of these units congregated around that much-disputed city. Montgomery made much of this in his memoirs as a defence against the claim that the Anglo-Canadians had stalled while the Americans had made better progress during the campaign.[70] For example, by 25 July the British and Canadians faced five SS and three *Wehrmacht* panzer divisions, supported by three heavy Tiger battalions (the only such formations in Normandy), while the US forces confronted only two panzer divisions. For the British and Canadian armoured units this represented a major problem, for artillery and air power could not do enough to eliminate or suppress such doughty and determined units. It was advancing

Allied armour that suffered as a consequence, and it was they who had to deal with the heavy concentrations of panzers and Stugs and suffer the casualties.

In addition to the problems posed by the terrain and the depth and quality of opposition, British armour also had to contend with the tactical difficulties posed by new types and levels of German equipment. The *panzerfaust*, a short-range disposable, hollow-charge infantry-wielded anti-tank weapon, was encountered in large numbers for the first time in Normandy. It was fired by one man and was easily capable of penetrating the armour of Allied tanks. Generally, its major disadvantage was its short range though new versions could theoretically engage enemy armour at some 200 feet.[71] However, in the close terrain of Normandy the lack of range was much less of a shortcoming, and in the *bocage* where engagements regularly took place at considerably less than 300 feet, the *panzerfaust* became a viable weapon. Nevertheless, although a further disincentive for Allied tankcrews to close on enemy positions, *panzerfausts* did not account for a high proportion of British tank casualties in Normandy, perhaps around 6 per cent only, and some British commanders and analysts were critical of German tactics with the new weapon.[72]

Of more importance was the shift towards self-propelled artillery and assault guns in the German inventory by 1944.[73] This move had been identified by the RAC as early as 1942 and the potential implications noted for the tactical employment of armour in the following two years.[74] The tank's major opponent in the Second World War had been the towed anti-tank gun, a weapon easily concealed and highly potent in defence. By the middle point of the war however, the anti-tank gun was becoming more vulnerable. Opposing armour was now less likely to charge around the battlefield exposing itself to carefully concealed guns, while the anti-tank gun itself was becoming increasingly exposed to heavy artillery bombardment, particularly when as ferocious as the types employed by the Soviets, but also increasingly by the Western Allies. Moreover, as tanks became more heavily armoured as the war progressed, anti-tank guns had to respond by increasing in calibre and consequently size, thus rendering them more difficult to conceal and camouflage. Larger guns could also take much longer to deploy and dig in, as noted by the Royal Artillery when they replaced the 6-pdr with the much larger 17-pdr gun.[75]

The concept of using anti-tank guns to halt an armoured assault was not invalid by 1944, but the method of employing them successfully required revision. To limit the vulnerability of the anti-tank gun and to increase its mobility, armies began deploying them as self-propelled equipment, sometimes quite heavily armoured, though often in thinly protected open-topped vehicles, which nevertheless offered fair protection against artillery, unless hit directly. Furthermore, such vehicles allowed rapid deployment of heavy anti-tank guns to areas of crisis. The self-propelled equipment was not without weaknesses, however, as it offered a much larger target than corresponding towed guns, increased pressures on vehicle maintenance and logistical support, and often provided confined spaces within which the gun crew could operate.[76]

Nevertheless, German production programmes for 1945 emphasised self-propelled guns such as the Stug and medium tanks at the expense of heavy tanks.[77]

In Normandy, however, the increased use of self-propelled guns created tactical difficulties for Allied armour. First shot from a steady and well-sited platform was critical in armoured warfare, and defending units were often afforded this considerable advantage. Once their position was given away and they had been located, however, a more even engagement could follow. Yet self-propelled anti-tank guns were able to loose off a few rounds, often causing casualties, before relocating to repeat the scenario elsewhere. Of course normal tanks were likely to do this, but the self-propelled guns employed by the Germans enhanced their capability to use such tactics by increasing the numbers of mobile gun platforms available.[78] *Operation Goodwood* illustrated the point when Becker's hotchpotch of self-propelled guns, often mounted on old vehicles which otherwise would have been written off, caused great difficulties for 11th Armoured Division as they charged towards the Bourguébus Ridge on 18 July.[79]

In addition, many self-propelled guns were encased in fair amounts of armour protection, such as the Sturmgeschütz III and IV. Such weapons made particular demands of British armour, for, not only did the advancing tankcrew have to spot the self-propelled gun, they also had to be able to disable it, and with the low armour penetrating firepower of most Allied tanks, this could be a problem. With some self-propelled guns, such as the Jagdpanzers, sporting armour of considerable resisting power, British tankcrews had to deal with an enemy to whom a steady first shot was available, who had the ability to relocate quickly, and who carried reasonable armour protection against the MV 75 mm gun.

Even without heavy armour protection, German self-propelled guns afforded fair protection to their crews against artillery fire, a considerable advantage over towed gun teams. This was doubly so in Normandy where the Allies expected to limit the levels of anti-tank gun resistance to their own armoured assaults by suppression with heavy artillery bombardments. This was not worthless against self-propelled guns, but it offered much less of a solution than had been imagined or planned. Consequently, the great conundrum of the desert war, how to eliminate the enemy's anti-tank guns and thus allow your armour to dominate the field, solved by effective employment of artillery, no longer pertained to the same extent. The tactical environment in Normandy was such that British and Canadian tanks would have to deal with enemy anti-tank firepower with direct-fire engagements.[80] As Allied armour-piercing (AP) firepower was relatively weak, and with the Germans holding the advantages of first shot, potential concealment and camouflage, the possibility of relocation and resistant armour protection, the increased numbers of self-propelled anti-tank guns presented a considerable tactical difficulty to British armour.[81]

The Germans also expanded their use of heavily armoured tanks in Normandy, most obviously the Tiger and the Panther. The British had known about the existence of both types since 1942, though clearer data on the Panther did not become available until later in 1943. Senior commanders and planners were certainly aware of the difficulties that might emerge from the increasing employment of heavy tanks by the Germans, though it is unclear as to how widely known this was at frontline level. Moreover, planning took only limited account of heavy German armour, for a number of reasons. First, 21st Army Group staff expected to be fighting a mobile war in northern France, south of Caen, in terrain unlikely to offer clear advantages to heavily armoured vehicles. The slow-moving Tigers would be forced to manoeuvre excessively, something for which they were ill-suited, and would lead to them being overwhelmed.[82] Second, British intelligence had a fairly low opinion of the Tiger anyway, considering it to be unreliable, cumbersome and sufficiently vulnerable to new Allied anti-tank weaponry to render it no more than a minor problem.[83] Finally, intelligence sources reported that there would be few Tigers in Normandy as it was unsuited to mass production and absorbed too many resources. Indeed, pre-invasion estimates of the numbers of Tigers likely to be encountered proved fairly accurate for the campaign, despite the vast number of sightings reported by Allied troops.[84]

In contrast, the Panther was something of an unknown quantity, certainly to British tankcrews, who were extremely unlikely to have encountered them prior to *Overlord*. Nevertheless, it was the Panther that proved more of a problem in Normandy, in spite of the publicity surrounding the Tiger. British tankcrews quickly recognised that the fast-moving and manoeuvrable Panther was a formidable opponent in all circumstances and situations, whereas the Tiger's reputation grew because of the close nature of the fighting.[85] Both created difficulties, however, particularly the Tiger when the fighting bogged down. The heavier all-round armour protection of the Tiger proved to be the closest disposition to the idealised homogenous armour distribution described by the No. 2 Operational Research Section (ORS), 21st Army Group.[86] Front heavy armour, such as that carried by the Panther, was of less value in Normandy because of the nature of the short-range engagements, which often allowed flanking shots.[87] As the Panther's armour was relatively thin on the sides, it could be outmanoeuvred and dealt with, assuming of course it did not manoeuvre or reposition. In contrast, the Tiger was often able to withstand flanking shots even at close range, and was thus well suited to the tactical environment in Normandy. However, the ORS went on to argue that increasing armour protection on Allied tanks in close terrain such as Normandy was a waste of resources, as they would still be vulnerable to heavy anti-tank guns. In contrast, for the Germans, facing the lower-velocity weapons of the Allies, the Tiger's armour provided reasonable all-round protection.

Once again German heavy armour only became an issue when the Allies became stuck for weeks in terrain they expected to have pushed through within a few days of 6 June. The nature of the tactical difficulty presented by heavy German armour has been much exaggerated, and indeed it could be argued that the Panther's and Tiger's superiority in long-range gunnery was only fully realised in open terrain, such as that fought over in *Goodwood* and *Totalise*. Nevertheless, coping with heavy German armour was a further problem and one much resented by Allied tankers. They were particularly vexed by claims from Montgomery that Allied tanks could deal with German armour without difficulty, when they and he knew that to be patently untrue. On a tactical level, the importance of Tiger-phobia was much more psychological than real. It was the growing insecurity of Allied tankcrews, as they believed that behind every hedge was a Tiger, perceived to be quite invulnerable to the 75 mm guns of the Allies, that served to damp down the enthusiasm of British armour.[88]

The tactical consequences of the Anglo-Canadians becoming bogged down around Caen were critical, and they serve to explain many of the problems confronting Allied armour during the campaign. When the British stalled to the north of Caen in early June, it threw the entire tactical approach of the armoured forces into question, and required them to adapt to a slow-moving attritional style of war for which they were largely unprepared. In addition, they were then confronted with a depth and quality of opposition able to exploit the tactical advantages of the terrain to the full. To make matters worse, the armoured units in 21st Army Group had to come to terms with the diminishing effectiveness of Allied artillery in suppressing anti-tank opposition, and the potency of even limited quantities of enemy heavy armour in close terrain. Armoured doctrine had to be adapted quickly and tactics revised to meet this new operating environment, and both the tanks of the armoured divisions and the independent brigades soon discovered that the doctrinal underpinnings of the training conducted in Britain, and the experience of desert warfare, were of limited value in Normandy.

From 6 June onwards, therefore, British armoured units applied their tactical training and experience to the task of advancing the Allied cause in Normandy, in a difficult and changing operational environment. They were certainly unprepared for aspects of the campaign, as has been discussed, and were forced to adapt and redefine methods and approaches to cope with the problems thrust upon them. Nevertheless, the most important factor defining the tactical environment, and the employment of armour therein, was the burden of the offence. To the Allies went the mantle of the initiators of the campaign, and it was axiomatic that if they wished to defeat the Axis forces both in Normandy and in western Europe, they needed to be aggressive, remain on the offensive and take the battle to the *Heer* and the SS. In essence, it was up to the Allies to attack, using whatever methods were appropriate, and dislodge the Germans from their defensive positions in Normandy.

When the campaign became more static than had been planned, and artillery and air power proved less able to blast a path through the intransigent Germans than had been expected, it fell upon the close-combat arms – the infantry and the tanks – to maintain the offensive, despite the many problems now confronting them. It should be noted that although the fighting in Normandy threw up a variety of new issues to contend with, by 1944 there was a general trend in warfare towards the defensive. The dynamism of 1940 had been replaced with a much more attritional style of operations, as evidenced both in the eastern and western theatres from 1943 onwards.[89] In part this was a result of the increasing sophistication of defensive modes of combat and of the experience, capabilities and firepower of those defending – both Axis and Allied. On a tactical level this resulted in combined arms teams finding it increasingly difficult and costly to mount and prosecute an attack, because those resisting them were well versed and prepared in hindering or stopping them, or at the very least exacting a heavy price.

It should be borne in mind throughout the following discussion, that both Allied and German forces encountered great difficulty in forcing their enemy to fall back and then to hold the ground seized, without suffering heavy casualties. A much-repeated sequence of events in Normandy was for an Allied attack to drive the Germans back a short distance, before being met by a localised counter-attack. In both cases, the attackers and counter-attackers suffered the heaviest casualties rather than those defending. German tactical philosophy insisted on an immediate counter-attack where possible to prevent the enemy from establishing themselves on a new position.[90] Once dug in, it was believed, it would be much more difficult to dislodge them. This doctrine was not invalidated by the experience of Normandy, but the cost of prosecuting even a limited counter-attack in the immediate aftermath of an Allied push now proved inordinately costly in lives and equipment. The most significant lesson drawn from the Normandy campaign by the *Heer*, and to a lesser degree the SS, was that the Allies were more than capable of defending gains flexibly with air power, artillery and mobile anti-tank gunfire.[91]

For armour on both sides the problems of advancing in a hostile and unhelpful tactical environment were considerable. For British tank units, less effectively supported by artillery and air power than had been envisaged, the difficulties were greater still, as they were forced to mount offensives for longer and more often than their German counterparts. Moreover, they were required to assault well-prepared and deeply defended areas, as well as having to cope with all the inherent problems of employing armour in the Normandy terrain. Conversely, when German armour counter-attacked it was more often against hastily prepared defences, though even then the Axis tanks were repeatedly driven back with heavy losses.[92]

The development of tactics in Normandy

Ultimately, following spotty doctrinal preparation, British armoured units were forced to adapt tactical methods to an unhelpful operating environment while simultaneously shouldering the increasing burden of maintaining the offensive. In spite of this, the tactical approaches developed by the Allies demonstrated considerable flexibility, more so than the Germans who persisted with the immediate counter-attack, even when evidence clearly indicated that in the circumstances such methods resulted in heavier losses than the Axis were capable of sustaining, and for no discernible benefit. It should also be noted that Allied tank casualties remained within pre-invasion estimates even during the harshest fighting in Normandy, though tank commander losses on reconnaissance patrols did become a concern.[93]

British armour employed two distinct tactical approaches to provoking combat. First, in an advance to contact or in pursuit, armour would be used to probe an enemy's position to ascertain their strength and to apply pressure. Firepower support would be employed as and when necessary to suppress enemy strongpoints and areas of resistance. Second, in a prepared offensive against a known enemy line of resistance, armour, along with infantry, would integrate with a predetermined air and artillery fireplan to overwhelm the enemy. Often a suppressive rolling artillery barrage would lead with the close-combat elements following on as quickly as possible behind.

Advances would often be on two or more axes with the British employing the principle of 'two up, one in support'. This entailed each squadron leading with two troops, with one or sometimes two in support, while the regiment would often advance with two squadrons leading on two lines of attack. Again, the third squadron would trail in support. Other elements such as self-propelled artillery would provide follow-on forces to be deployed forward when required. The brigade would again lead with two regiments, with one in support. When a position was seized, it was considered essential to bring up self-propelled anti-tank artillery, followed by towed anti-tank guns to stiffen the resistance to likely German responses. British armour would be withdrawn into reserve to provide a counter-attacking force should the Germans threaten any given position. Leaving tanks in forward defensive positions, especially at night, despite the morale boost offered to infantry, was eschewed.[94]

In the case of the advance to contact scenario, the initial lead would often be taken by elements of the reconnaissance troop, equipped with Honey light tanks.[95] Their role was strictly to force the enemy to show their hand, and once under fire to fall back into flanking positions to provide localised support. The Honey's main armament was only a feeble 37 mm gun, and in some formations the turret was even removed to provide a lower profile.[96] In effect they acted as simple reconnaissance vehicles, and in mixed formations of infantry and armour this role was often undertaken by the reconnaissance platoon's universal or bren gun carriers.[97]

On a larger scale, divisional or corps level armoured and scout cars would be used in the probing role, screening friendly troops and seeking out the enemy and suppressing their reconnaissance elements. British armoured divisions were also equipped with an armoured reconnaissance regiment to fulfil this role in even greater strength. In both cases, however, once under sustained attack and increasing pressure, the reconnaissance units were supposed to fall back, allowing the main body to advance, supported by artillery. The armoured reconnaissance regiment was equipped with A27 Cromwell cruisers in British and Polish armoured divisions, but even this fast tank was considered too noisy and large to fulfil the requirements of a reconnaissance vehicle, and when the armoured divisions were restructured in July, such formations were recast simply as a fourth armoured regiment.[98]

The tactical formations employed by British armoured units were soon shaped and determined by the nature of the terrain over which the campaign was being fought, presenting problems to desert veteran and novice alike. For experienced commanders, the terrain in northwest Europe provided new difficulties and was considerably different to that of North Africa. Maj. Bill Close, 'A' Squadron commander in 3RTR claimed:

> We had to treat things quite differently. We had to travel on roads, for instance, instead of being able simply to deploy and open up your squadron or regiment. In fact, many times we operated on the divisional centre line and squadrons were put out on parallel roads, perhaps two to three miles to the right or left flanks, and travel on in the same direction.[99]

In open country, tactical manuals and experience from the desert campaigns offered a variety of formations, such as 'arrowhead' and 'diamond', with a troop of tanks spread out over perhaps a 300-yard frontage. In Normandy, such tactics were rarely appropriate as, due to the confining terrain, tanks were often restricted to operating along roads. If necessary, they would deploy into fields or go cross-country, but compared with using the road network this was time consuming and slow, and often the high-banked *bocage* fields prevented such movement.[100]

Tank units rapidly developed special tactics for operating along roads in close country, known to some as a snake patrol. In this, tanks would follow the route of a road with the leading tank halting when reaching a bend, at which point it would wait for the second tank to come alongside to provide a static overlooking firing position. The first tank would then carry on to the next bend and repeat the whole process.[101] The heavy Churchill tank was considered unsuitable to take the lead in a snake patrol, because if it was knocked out it was difficult to prevent it from blocking the road for following vehicles.[102] Troops of tanks within a regiment would employ such tactics along more than one roughly parallel route when possible. Snake patrol was particularly apt when advancing to contact or pursuing a retreating enemy, and was especially useful in very close country, becoming widely utilised in *Bluecoat*. Moreover, although teaching called for the troop's senior NCO to command the leading tank, officers often led by example and commanded from the front. This was considered better for morale and helped to maintain the pace of advances.[103]

Close co-operation with infantry was considered essential, with a suitable ratio of one troop of tanks to one company of infantry.[104] In the later stages of the campaign, tank units also took to carrying infantry with them, often as tank riders, so that they could deploy quickly into action and deal with dug-in enemy infantry. In larger-scale operations infantry began to be deployed in fully tracked Kangaroo armoured personnel carriers to debus them straight into action and to keep up with armour when travelling cross-country. The necessity of keeping infantry with armour was crucial and the advantages of even half-tracked armoured transports were recognised over the lorry in armoured divisions. As the Germans would often use small infantry–armour teams to delay an Allied advance, the deployment of mixed British armour and infantry forces in an advance was entirely appropriate and was mirrored in US Army tactics.[105]

Even when open ground was available, operational level commanders preferred to keep Allied armour bunched together to keep control of it and support it with artillery and air fireplans. During the opening phase of *Goodwood*, and again in *Totalise*, Anglo-Canadian tankcrews complained about the narrow frontages over which they were supposed to advance, which usually ran contrary to the tactical instruction they had received in Britain. In *Goodwood*, rather than deploying over a front measured in hundreds of yards, 3RTR, which led the assault of 11th Armoured Division, was squashed into a dense formation and was for most of the advance unable to deploy into the tactical groups desired in doctrinal teachings.[106]

It is of note that the type of tactics laid down in training in Britain was in need of considerable revision in Normandy. The Guards' charge was entirely inappropriate and unworkable, but even the tactics brought back from the desert by Roberts were also found wanting in the confined spaces of Normandy. The kind of manoeuvre-based fire and support troop level tactics he championed could create problems. The Roberts methods required medium to open countryside to be effective, but too often 11th Armoured found itself fighting in *bocage* or other types of difficult terrain. Moreover, the numbers of tanks in troops in armoured regiments and divisions had been increased from three to four in the weeks leading up to D-Day, following the arrival of the 17-pdr-equipped Firefly.[107] Many troop commanders had little time to develop new methods of directing an extra tank and found this an added burden in Normandy when tactical methods were already under scrutiny and revision.[108] In such circumstances, inexperienced crews and commanders had to improvise and it was to take some early setbacks before revised tactics were employed.

German forces employed tactics to exploit the terrain to the full in defence, camouflaging vehicles and digging in where possible.[109] This provided protection against Allied firepower, particularly roving fighter-bombers, and also made the job of advancing Allied troops that much more difficult. Until the enemy opened fire at close range, lead elements of British armour and supporting infantry would generally be unaware of their existence. German troops would not often be fooled by speculative machine gun fire from the Allied tanks, laid down in an effort to provoke a response and to give away concealed positions. British tankcrews claimed that first shot was not necessarily the key advantage, but that the enemy was static whilst Allied tanks would be moving, creating an unstable firing and observation platform, was critical.[110] However, location of the enemy once under fire was most crucial and provided all sorts of difficulties. German tankcrews were well versed in camouflage techniques, while the ammunition for their tanks' main armament tended to use low-flash powder, but the greatest problem was the inherent lack of situation awareness of tankcrews when on the move. In response, and despite the increased likelihood of commanders falling foul of shrapnel or small arms fire, all tank commanders in Normandy directed their vehicles with their hatches open. Some even used only one radio telephone (R/T) earphone to allow them to hear the battle around them, such that they could sense where an attack was coming from and react to it quickly.[111] Nevertheless, the first response of tank commanders when coming under direct fire attack was to head for cover. Once safe, they would then begin the process of pinpointing the enemy, which could take some time and some risk. Supporting infantry would be invaluable, as they had much greater capacity for observing enemy fire.

Enemy anti-tank guns were more difficult to locate as they were easily camouflaged, but once pinpointed they were vulnerable to direct HE fire. Operational research reports indicated that a troop of tanks firing 75 mm HE would have a good chance of eliminating an anti-tank gun if it was engaged at 800 yards or less, but once the range was up to 2,000 yards the tanks could well lose four or five vehicles prior to eliminating the enemy gun.[112] If an enemy tank or Stug was identified, one tank would fix them with fire, frequently relocating, whilst the others would attempt to move into flanking positions. Any such flanking moves in close country had to be screened with infantry, even though this was unpopular with the foot soldiers.[113] While moving, tanks in close country, especially *bocage*, were effectively blind and highly vulnerable to anti-tank guns and weaponry. Supporting infantry would therefore move ahead, securing positions or locating enemy guns before bringing up the tanks to provide firepower support against dug-in enemy infantry.[114]

Heavy German armour had to be dealt with by fixing the Tiger or Panther with the Firefly or self-propelled anti-tank gun, preferably a 17-pdr, whilst manoeuvring the other tanks into flanking positions.[115] Often the Tiger or Panther would be supported by a well-camouflaged Stug or Panzer IV, which could suddenly open up on British tanks attempting to reach a flanking position.[116] British commanders would often bring down artillery 'stonks' on to the target, not necessarily to destroy it, but to suppress it while the Allied tanks manoeuvred. Often, an artillery bombardment or even smoke would persuade an enemy tank, even a Tiger, to fall back, manoeuvre, or even be abandoned. It was also noted by experienced British armoured units that the quality of German tankcrews was declining, certainly when compared to those encountered in North Africa. Some crews could be panicked into flight or abandoning their tank merely by use of smoke, while ORS reports also later noted an increase in the number of discarded, yet still functioning German tanks, when subjected to heavy, though non-destructive firepower.[117]

It was clear that the campaign in Normandy placed a high premium on infantry and tank co-operation, both in the armoured divisions and the independent brigades. Initially, British armoured formations struggled to adapt to the tactical environment and co-operation with infantry was found wanting. Early errors occurred due to inappropriate doctrinal teaching in Britain, unsuitable tactics developed from North Africa, and the time necessary for regimental and battalion commanders to adapt to the conditions pertaining in Normandy.

Nevertheless, heavy criticism has been levelled at the poor nature of infantry–armour co-operation demonstrated by the British and Canadians in Normandy. It is not in doubt that errors were made, and some were particularly serious, such as the decision to charge armoured regiments with little infantry support at the Bourguébus Ridge on 18 July. Yet innovation, flexibility and adaptability were all evident as the campaign progressed, and the armoured divisions soon reorganised themselves to meet the needs of particular kinds of operations, while the brigades were employing a variety of approaches suitable for distinct types of actions. In most cases, the largely inexperienced British armoured units proved themselves capable of adapting and meeting the challenge of redefining the way they fought, whilst simultaneously coping with the excessive difficulties of conducting armoured operations in Normandy.

In the armoured divisions the employment of infantry in close harmony with the armour became self-evident following early encounters. Following early difficulties, 7th Armoured quickly acknowledged the need for closer infantry–armour co-operation: 'The need for more infantry was felt at once and the country, particularly in front of 5RTR, was unquestionably one for infantry supported by a few tanks and not for tanks with a small supporting component of infantry.'[118]

Maj-Gen Pip Roberts, GOC 11th Armoured, likewise recognised that he had to integrate his infantry and armour more closely following problems in *Epsom*, and Allan Adair, his counterpart in Guards Armoured, came to the same conclusion. Indeed, elements of the Guards, recognising that they might indeed have to fight in the *bocage*, began some limited training with integrated armour–infantry groups soon after landing in Normandy, partly to make up for the low level of such training in Britain.[119] Both Roberts and Adair were further influenced by the difficulties encountered in *Goodwood*, the former in particular when his armoured brigade had had to operate without the support of the infantry brigade, despite the opposition of Roberts. By *Bluecoat*, following discussion with VIII Corps commander Richard O'Connor, Guards and 11th Armoured were operating mixed brigade groups with each regiment of tanks co-operating closely with one battalion of infantry. An obvious difficulty was the problem of transporting the infantry with the tanks. For the motor companies this was less of a difficulty as they had half-tracks and carriers, but for the battalions of the infantry brigades there were only trucks, quite unsuitable for delivering troops into action. The issue was partly relieved by carrying the infantry as tank riders, despite the concerns about such tactics dating back to training in Britain. Infantry were then immediately available to debus into action and provide support to the armour, rather than having to stop and wait for the infantry to be brought up. Infantry commanders would ride on the armoured troop commander's tank in order to co-ordinate operations.[120] The ultimate solution, and one identified by Simonds, O'Connor and Patton, was for a dedicated fully tracked armoured personnel carrier to be introduced.[121] The half-track was not the answer as it could not maintain the pace of the tank when travelling cross-country, and a closed top vehicle was in any case preferable to limit losses to artillery and small arms fire. Indeed, one of the key lessons from the latter half of the war for the Germans was that during offensive actions panzer grenadiers suffered heavy losses to artillery, and that half-tracks offered only limited protection. The Canadians had demonstrated the possibilities of a tracked personnel carrier with their Kangaroos during *Totalise*, but more work was needed to develop fully mechanised infantry to deliver troops directly into the battlezone with minimal casualties.

Adair, Roberts and O'Connor in particular were all pleased with the mixed brigade group structure, and the armoured commanders considered this to be the most appropriate method of facilitating the tactics necessary for success in the close terrain of Normandy.[122] Roberts's 11th Armoured appeared to have employed the new tactics most effectively, but there is little doubt that the Guards also had some success with the new structure during the closing stages of the Normandy campaign.[123] Seventh Armoured Division continued to move individual battalions between brigades, and elements of the Queen's (131st) Infantry Brigade and 22nd Armoured Brigade co-operated at times very closely, though it appears not to have been as intimate as the levels developed in 11th Armoured.[124]

To illustrate further the contention that organisation and doctrine were often left to formation commanders to determine in the British Army, each of the three standard British armoured divisions employed separate and mixed brigade structures at different stages of the northwest European campaign. Seventh Armoured switched between the two, but actually employed a mixed group certainly as early as 11 June; 11th Armoured moved from separate to mixed by *Bluecoat*, back to separate for the pursuit to Antwerp, and then back to mixed from that point on; while Guards switched to mixed for *Bluecoat* and remained with that structure for the remainder of the war.[125] This was hardly a measure of a tactically inflexible and antediluvian force. Indeed, despite limited opportunities for battle, within weeks of arriving in Normandy the armoured divisions had begun to re-evaluate their tactics and force structure to suit the conditions in Normandy, and by *Bluecoat*, when they were pressed into action in quite the worst terrain for armour, they were able to achieve considerable success.

The armoured divisions, therefore, adapted themselves to the tactical conditions in Normandy by developing much closer infantry–armour co-operation. The independent armoured and tank brigades also had to mould their view on doctrine to the situation thrust upon them, sometimes when under the command of a divisional infantry commander who had little concept of armoured warfare.[126] The prevailing doctrine within the armoured formations dedicated to infantry support was, as has been noted above, in a state of some confusion by the beginning of *Overlord*. Again, the benefit of non-rigorous doctrine enforcement was proven when the tactical concepts championed by Montgomery prior to the invasion proved problematical in the close terrain of Normandy. It could be argued that the 8th Army method may have been better suited to open-country fighting, and merely fell victim to the German strategy of fighting it out in the close countryside of Normandy. However, there is little evidence that the 'tanks ahead of infantry' approach, once through enemy minefields, was at all appropriate for the nature of assault operations in northwest Europe. In any case, it mattered less than might have been imagined, for units demonstrated their tactical flexibility and soon developed their own methods for achieving more harmonious infantry–armour actions.

Units attempted to employ the techniques set down for them in training or gleaned from previous experience until they were proved wrong. Hence, when units were first in action, tanks often led assaults with infantry and then more tanks following on behind in the classic sandwich/8th Army method. However, this was found wanting, as the enemy would allow the leading tanks to pass by, suppress the following infantry, forcing it to withdraw, and then tackle the now exposed and near-blind tanks to attack from the flanks or rear.[127] Early actions involving 27th Armoured Brigade demonstrated the points well. In a first attempt to seize Cristot on 10–11 June, as part of XXX Corps' push south, Shermans of the 4th/7th Royal Dragoon Guards supported 6th Green Howards and soon found their tactics of leading with tanks, followed by infantry, and then by more tanks, wanting. German troops let the tanks pass by, then shot up the following infantry with machine guns, leaving the unsupported leading tanks to be taken out subsequently. Of nine tanks only two withdrew to safety.[128] Troops viewed the action as a dismal failure.[129] On 16 June a further attack was launched on the Cristot–Boets area, this time in support of units of the newly arrived 49th Infantry Division. The infantry and armour co-operated more closely, offering mutual support, and the attack was successful with no tank losses and only 27 casualties. Moreover, although B and C Squadrons of the 4th/7th Royal Dragoon Guards lost eight tanks, they claimed at least four Tigers, though these were almost certainly in fact Mark IVs.[130] It became apparent that leading with tanks in the dense terrain of Normandy only worked when the enemy was weak or caught by surprise, such as the assault on Hill 309 by 6th Guards Tank Brigade during *Bluecoat*.[131] A similar re-evaluation of the 8th Army method was also taking place in Italy by the spring and summer of 1944, as it was realised that tanks could not lead in close country where they were often confined to roads.[132]

In units equipped with Shermans there was a greater tendency to stand off and shoot the advancing infantry on to their target in the manner of self-propelled artillery, before moving up to provide support. This had been considered more appropriate in Brig. Harold 'Peter' Pyman's pamphlet because of the weakness of the M4's armour, but it is more likely that this method was a throwback to the tactics of the squadron-level shoot from the days before the 75 mm gun was introduced. Again the tactic was not completely devoid of merit, but risked the armour being too far behind the infantry to provide immediate and close-fire support against uncovered enemy positions likely to inflict casualties on the infantry. Infantry often felt vulnerable without the comforting presence of tanks and though the self-propelled (SP) artillery-style tactics arguably reduced armour losses, it placed still greater strain on the already overworked infantry. Moreover, if the target became shrouded in smoke or mist, the tanks might not be to provide support at all.[133] It was essential that tanks move up to support the infantry once objectives had been achieved, most importantly to provide anti-tank firepower. It took too long for towed anti-tank guns to get into position, and the employment of M10s and tanks to get forward and prevent immediate armour-spearheaded German counter-attacks from retaking the objective was essential. As in Italy, it took some early setbacks for this to be appreciated.[134]

The most sophisticated tactical approach was for infantry to operate in close harmony with the armour, sometimes intermingling, and sometimes in very close terrain, such as *bocage*, with the tanks screened by infantry. Tank troops could employ fire and move tactics, with armour advancing from one hull-down position to another while being overwatched by other tanks. Infantry would interact, providing the eyes of the team and directing tank firepower at potential and identified targets. In assaults against all but the heaviest concentrations of German defenders, these integrated tactics were relatively successful and most closely followed the doctrine that was becoming established in 21st Army Group prior to Montgomery's arrival.

However, the integrated tactics still presented problems. They were certainly best suited to heavily armoured tanks such as the Churchill, for Shermans could resist little in the way of German anti-tank weaponry at close range. This prompted occasional reversion in Sherman units to static fire support roles, with tank troops sticking to hull-down positions rather than then advancing in support of infantry. The tactics also demanded a good deal of infantry–armour communication capabilities, and this was wanting. The tank telephone was effective so long as it operated, but too often they were knocked out of action, being rather exposed to shell or mortar fire.[135] The 38-radio set was technically acceptable for infantry-to-armour command liaison, but infantry officers could or would not remain netted in throughout an engagement, as in addition they had to direct their own units. The system was workable but required a high level of training, often not present.[136] Methods for armour and infantry to signal to each other were developed in theatre, and this was often effected in Normandy by the use of Verey lights. However, it was argued that a more sophisticated system of target identification be established, perhaps employing marking flares or incendiary ammunition. Such problems could be partially resolved if tank regiments and brigades worked together over a period of days and weeks, but too often formations were moved around and individual armour commanders rarely co-operated with the same infantry leader on successive operations. This hindered the development of mutually understandable and recognisable working practices. It was a clear weakness of the non-rigid enforcement of doctrine that different tank units interpreted their role of infantry support quite differently to another, thus causing tactical misunderstandings when they attempted to work with a new unit for the first time. One report argued that at least two days' working up time was required between infantry and armour units attempting to co-operate for the first time.[137] The movement of supporting formations from one brigade to another was much resented by junior commanders, who saw great benefit in being linked to the same unit for a longer period.[138]

Nevertheless, both independent brigades and armoured divisional brigade groups had developed workable tactics for infantry–armour co-operation by the midpoint of the campaign, and the doctrinal difficulties partly created by pre-*Overlord* training and more importantly by the nature and terrain of Normandy were brought under control. On a number of occasions when appropriate tactics were employed and adequate firepower support was provided, British armour was more than able to integrate with infantry in the seizure of objectives. Although most attention on *Goodwood* focuses on the difficulties of 18 July, on subsequent days elements of the 11th Armoured Division were able to carry out a highly effective combined arms action to capture the Bourguébus Ridge, in particular Bras and Hubert-Folie. During *Bluecoat* 15th Scottish Infantry Division and 6th Guards Tank Brigade co-operated admirably, and subsequent actions during the drive southeast demonstrated that considerable progress in tactical integration had been made. It is apparent that the level of infantry–armour co-operation within 21st Army Group developed and improved considerably throughout the campaign, adapting quite effectively to the combat environment and circumstances thrust upon them.

Conclusion

The orthodox view of the tactical capabilities of British armour formations in Normandy is predominantly negative. A simple comparison with the dynamic achievements of the *Heer*'s panzer divisions in the 1939–42 period appears to emphasise the outdated, overly cautious and unimaginative tactical armoured doctrine of the British and indeed Canadian armies in 1944. Despite overwhelming advantages in numbers, firepower and resources, British armour failed to achieve the desired break-through without a long and tortuous period of attritional struggle. Much of this criticism is grounded in the perception that 21st Army Group did not employ its armour in the manner in which it should, that is, in following the trail blazed by the Germans in the so-called *blitzkrieg*.[139]

As has been noted in this chapter, however, this is a flawed and incomplete analysis and requires considerable revision. The British and Canadians did not employ the same kinds of tactics used by the Germans, nor indeed the Soviets, because they were entirely inappropriate to the political and military circumstances as pertained in Normandy. First and foremost, the terrain over which 21st Army Group operations were conducted in the summer of 1944 was largely inappropriate for the dashing, fluid and expansive armoured tactics desired by historians from Basil Liddell Hart through to Roman Jarymowycz. Moreover, the opposition confronting British and Canadian armour in the summer of 1944 was desperate, brutalised and quite capable of offering determined and stiff resistance, particularly when coupled with the advantages conferred by the close terrain. Furthermore, senior Allied commanders were acutely aware of their own position. Their citizen soldiery was less experienced in the brutalities of war than their counterparts and, in the case of the Anglo-Canadians especially, both unable and unwilling to accept heavy losses. It made perfect and obvious sense for the British to employ tactics and methods that exploited the inherent advantages and strengths of their own forces. This naturally emphasised firepower and logistical support in an effort to minimise casualties.

In this environment, particularly when the Germans employed a static forward defence, much to the surprise of Montgomery and his staff, the armoured tactics of mass and force employed by the Germans and Soviets would only have been practical if the British and Canadians had been willing to accept grievous losses. Quite rightly they were not. Soviet officers may well have examined the *Totalise* plan many years later and stated they would have shot any commander who could not have got his forces into Falaise by midnight on 8 August, but at what cost would this have been achieved?[140] It is self-evident that a big butcher's bill is no evidence of good tactics.

The greatest achievement of British armoured forces in Normandy was that they managed, in just a few weeks, to develop a suitable and workable doctrine appropriate to the new operating conditions thrust upon them. They achieved this in spite of patchy training and preparation, flaws in operational technique emphasised by the nature of the campaign, and their general inexperience. They demonstrated considerable tactical flexibility and adaptability, more so than their much admired and esteemed counterparts, the Germans, who continued to employ a doctrine of immediate counter-attack much longer than they should, that merely hastened their defeat by playing to the strengths of the Allies. British armoured tactics were not without fault, and the divisions and brigades were initially wrong-footed by the German response, the terrain and the flaws in their training, but they adapted and prevailed, and succeeded in playing a vital and crucial role in Allied victory in Normandy.

5

THE TANK GAP

Perhaps the most common explanation of the failure of Allied armour to impose itself more forcefully on the Normandy campaign is that centred upon technological inferiority. The prevailing view remains that the Allies had to persevere throughout the fighting in 1944 with obsolete and inadequate armour, against the much superior German Tigers and Panthers. Those with even just a passing interest in the history of the Second World War are likely to know that the M4 Sherman was hopelessly outclassed by the formidable Tiger tank with its deadly 88 mm gun and almost invulnerable armour plating. Moreover, such views are becoming reinforced by the plethora of satellite and cable television history channels that focus all too often on technological explanations of battlefield performance and effectiveness. Indeed, film footage and sophisticated computer graphics of armoured vehicles carry far greater appeal than involved discussion and debate over doctrine, planning and strategy. Consequently, technologically driven explanations of complex issues are more popular than ever.

Historians also put considerable emphasis on the relative capabilities of tanks in seeking to explain the apparent failings of Allied armour in action. Hastings in particular places great importance on the inadequacies of Allied equipment, armour especially, in explaining weak battlefield performance, even suggesting that the failings of the Sherman and Cromwell tanks were responsible for the failure of *Operation Goodwood*.[1] He also contends that 'no single Allied failure had more important consequences on the European battlefield than the lack of tanks with adequate punch and protection'.[2] More recently, Jarymowycz has argued that the Allies' inability to field a survivable main battle tank 'resulted in horrendous casualties to both its armored forces and the accompanying infantry',[3] while Russell Hart claims that 'the absence of a quality battle tank capable of engaging enemy armor on equal terms... brought heavy British tank losses'.[4] Still further, David French in *Raising Churchill's Army* has written that 'the RAC's tanks remained under-gunned and under-armoured compared to their German counterparts in the last two years of the war', implying that this was universally the case.[5]

Historians have therefore linked the technological shortcomings of Allied tanks to poor battlefield performance, arguing that because Allied equipment was inferior to German armour then heavy losses were incurred. Such arguments reflect, to a degree, the views of Allied tank crews and commanders during the war and since. In particular Tiger-phobia, the fear of the formidable German Tiger tank, became a cause of some concern in Allied high command, as tank crews quickly became convinced of the failings of their own equipment and the overwhelming superiority of all German armour.[6] That the Panzer Mark IV H resembled the Tiger did not help matters and Allied crews often reported being tackled by the latter when in fact it was the more commonplace, but much less fearsome former.[7] Moreover, Allied frontline troops were caught somewhat off guard by the appearance in larger numbers of the Panther, a mobile, heavily frontally armoured and powerfully gunned 45-ton medium tank. An oft-quoted account by an inquisitive British tank officer, newly arrived in Normandy, gives some indication of the problems crews were encountering.

> What do the Germans have most of?
> Panthers. Panthers can slice through a Churchill like butter from a mile away.
> And how does a Churchill get a Panther?
> It creeps up on it. When it reaches close quarters the gunner tries to bounce a shot off the underside of the Panther's gun mantlet. If he's lucky, it goes through a thin piece of armour above the driver's head.
> Has anybody ever done it?
> Yes. Davis in C Squadron. He's back with headquarters now, trying to recover his nerve.
> How does a Churchill get a Tiger?
> It's supposed to get within two hundred yards and put a shot through the periscope.
> Has anyone ever done it?
> No.[8]

Clearly problems had emerged in the minds of the crews and commanders of 21st Army Group, particularly when it came to tackling Panthers and Tigers. On one occasion on 12 June, it was noted that a single Tiger had held up an advance for an hour, sniping throughout, and had then driven off 'unmolested' by Allied tanks which had gone to ground.[9] During *Operation Epsom* (26–30 June), Kurt Meyer of 12th SS recorded that a single Tiger of 101st Heavy Battalion had blocked an Allied advance on Tourmauville at a critical moment in the first 24 hours of the assault.[10] On 16 June a report was even filed at SHAEF pointing out that Panzer Mark IVs were being disguised as Tigers to create trepidation in Allied tank crews. However, it was countered that this was simply the spaced skirts of armour fitted to Mark IVs to defeat hollow-charge weapons that were making the tank resemble the much larger Tiger.[11] Ad hoc in-theatre tests by crews appeared to reveal that the standard 75 mm gun carried by most Allied tanks was incapable of penetrating the frontal armour of the big cats of the German forces.[12] Troops of the 3RTR, as well as many others, considered that their tanks were hopelessly outclassed by their German opponents, and of particular concern was the vulnerability of the Allied tanks to HV German guns.[13] The mismatch was considerable and the worries of the frontline crews were apparently underpinned by later findings that it took 1.63 hits from German gunnery to knock out a Sherman, while the Allies required 2.55 hits to deal with a Panther and 4.2 to disable a Tiger.[14] One report also claimed that a Sherman or Cromwell's survival chances, once under fire from an enemy gun at a range of 500 yards or less, halved every six seconds.[15]

Concern rapidly spread to the higher echelons of command, with senior leaders becoming increasingly aware of the problem. After just two weeks of fighting Lt-Gen Miles Dempsey, GOC 2nd British Army, recorded in a 21st Army Group combat report that 'at the present time our armour is fighting under a considerable handicap'.[16] However, the greatest source of the panic that began to filter out to Britain was XXX Corps HQ. Undoubtedly still in shock after the reversal at Villers Bocage, Brig. Harold 'Peter' Pyman wrote to Maj-Gen Bobby Erskine, GOC 7th Armoured Division, copied to 2nd Army HQ, on 16 June 1944, claiming that recent operations had revealed 'that Tiger and Panther tanks now form a high proportion of the equipment of the German Armoured Regiments'. Moreover, it was clear to Pyman that such equipment was superior to the Sherman and the Cromwell:

> The result is that while 75 mm shot [of the Allies] has been failing to penetrate the front face of the Tigers and Panthers at ranges down to 30 yards, they can knock Shermans and Cromwells out at ranges up to 1500 yards with ease.[17]

Erskine, whose division had been at the receiving end of the Tiger's capabilities, enthusiastically endorsed the XXX Corps paper, and went further in claiming that the Tiger and Panther were 'infinitely superior' to Allied armour. Moreover, he argued that, 'our 75 mm gun or 17-pdr will not touch the German Panther or Tiger whereas the German tanks...will knock out our tanks, Cromwells or Shermans, from any angle'.[18] He went on to decry the fact that the British were having to fight with inadequate equipment: '...it cannot be stressed too strongly that at the present time we are fighting at as great a disadvantage... as we did in 1942 when we fought with the Crusader 2-pdr against the Mark IV.'[19] Both agreed that only the close terrain was aiding the Allies, for if battle were taking place at longer ranges, the advantages held by the Germans would only be exacerbated.

Both the paper circulated by Pyman on 16 June and Erskine's comments on the following day contained some scaremongering inaccuracies. Tigers and Panthers did not make up a high proportion of German armour in Normandy in the first ten days or so of the campaign, nor at any time, and the 17-pdr gun, either towed or carried in Sherman Fireflies and in modified M10 tank destroyers, could certainly deal with the Tiger or Panther at standard battle ranges (up to 1,000 yards). For Erskine to place it alongside the much weaker 75 mm gun was disingenuous indeed and perhaps highlighted his deteriorating confidence. It is notable that both Pyman and Erskine had had worrying experiences at Gazala in North Africa and this may have tainted their views of early difficulties encountered in Normandy.

Nevertheless, XXX Corps' GSO1 (Liaison), Lt-Col J. R. Bowring, used the Pyman and Erskine papers to construct a pessimistic report assessing the relative capabilities of Allied and German armour.[20] The paper leaked out beyond the confines of XXX Corps and 2nd Army, possibly direct to the War Office, and within a few days reactions began to appear.[21] Most vociferous, was the response from Maj-Gen George Richards, RAC, 21st Army Group HQ, who countered many of the more excessive and alarmist statements made by the XXX Corps staff. He argued that the 17-pdr was a weapon capable of dealing with Tigers and Panthers at 'any reasonable' range, and that even the 75 mm had on occasion eliminated Panthers, though he did not delve into the ranges and angle of attacks. More importantly, he pointed out that there were no more Panthers and Tigers in Normandy than had been expected and further, that a pamphlet had been circulated in April of 1944 outlining the failings of Allied weaponry against the heavily armoured German tanks. He went on: '...therefore nobody should have been surprised when they found out that what had been said in theory was proved correct in practice.'[22]

Whilst some of the issues raised by Bowring may have had some validity, the manner in which he circulated the paper infuriated Montgomery. He described Bowring to Brooke as an 'unbalanced officer and his views are of little value'.[23] He issued directives to Dempsey on 25 June that, 'GSO1s (Liaison) will write no more reports for the present. You will issue orders that further reports are forbidden until I give permission.'[24] Montgomery was clearly concerned that freely circulated downbeat reports could undermine morale, and insisted that all such information be relayed back to 21st Army Group HQ for appropriate vetting. If considered worthwhile, and presumably unlikely to weaken resolve or spread alarm, the information could then be disseminated throughout the army group. Montgomery wanted views, information and reports to be fed up the chain of command but was determined that it should be strictly controlled. He further confided to Brooke that he had had to stamp very heavily on reports of an alarmist nature about Allied equipment, particularly armour.[25]

To assuage general fears he issued a public letter to Sir James Grigg, Secretary of State for War, on 25 June, claiming that all was well:

> ... we have had no difficulty in dealing with German armour, once we had grasped the problem. In this connection British armour has played a notable part.
>
> We have nothing to fear from the Panther or Tiger tanks; they are unreliable mechanically, and the Panther is very vulnerable from the flanks. Our 17-pdr gun will go right through them. Provided our tactics are good we can defeat them without difficulty.[26]

Montgomery also issued Memo No. 506 on British Armour on 6 July, which carried much of the content of his letter to Grigg but also included comments on future policy.[27]

However, the issue would not go away. According to Grigg, William Anstruther-Gray MP, an officer in the Guards Armoured Division, may well have leaked information on the growing alarm over Allied tanks, and Richard Stokes MP raised the topic of the poor quality of Allied tanks in the House of Commons. He had previously done so to highlight the failings of British design and industry, but in July and August his questions asked for assurances from Grigg that Allied tanks were up to the task of dealing with the Tiger and the Panther. He was met with evasion and inaccuracy.[28]

Montgomery's dismissal of the growing concerns over the failings of Allied armour was for the most part intended to allay fears and bolster morale, but like Richards' comments, the defence was overstated. The claim that the 17-pdr would go right through the Tiger or the Panther was carefully worded, for the weapon struggled at longer ranges unless firing the new sabot or APDS (armour-piercing discarding sabot) ammunition, not introduced in significant numbers until the later stages of the campaign. He failed to discuss the problem that Sherman Fireflies (equipped with 17-pdr guns) were in short supply in Normandy, and that most Allied tanks carried the 75 mm gun, a weapon quite unsuited to duelling with Tigers and Panthers. To Brooke and Dempsey he argued that 21st Army Group required many more 17-pdr-equipped weapons as quickly as possible, and that the new sabot ammunition was well liked.[29] Clearly, Montgomery was well aware of the problem, but was concerned about openly admitting as much. Moreover, it was also obvious that the inadequacy of Allied armour was just one issue among many confronting 21st Army Group in Normandy.

Despite Montgomery's efforts and the eventual success of 21st Army Group in defeating the Germans in Normandy, the question of the extent and impact of the tank gap remains. The degree to which Allied armour was disadvantaged by technical shortcomings requires closer scrutiny, while the consequences of these deficiencies for the conduct of operations likewise necessitates investigation. What therefore were the realities of the gap between Allied and German tanks and anti-tank weaponry in Normandy and how important was it to the successful prosecution of operations?

Allied armour

M4 Sherman and Firefly

The most numerous tank employed by 21st Army Group in Normandy was the M4 Sherman, an American medium design dating back in concept to 1941. The M4 was in effect an improved and redesigned M3 Grant/Lee, and the lower hull of the tank closely resembled its predecessor, while the upper hull was reshaped to take a single large turret capable of carrying the MV

M4 Sherman
Crew: 5 **Weight:** 30 tons **Speed:** 24mph
Armour: front 50 to 80mm; side 45mm
Main Armament: medium velocity 75mm
L: 19ft 10in **H:** 9ft **W:** 8ft 7in

M4 Sherman Firefly
Crew: 4 **Weight:** 30 tons **Speed:** 24mph
Armour: front 50 to 80mm; side 45mm
Main Armament: 17-pdr
L: 19ft 10in **H:** 9ft **W:** 8ft 9in

A27M Cromwell
Crew: 5 **Weight:** 30 tons **Speed:** 35mph
Armour: front 63 to 76mm - maximum later
increased to 101mm; side 32 to 63mm
Main Armament: medium velocity 75mm
L: 20ft 10in **H:** 8ft 2in **W:** 10ft

A42 Churchill
Crew: 5 **Weight:** 40 tons **Speed:** 12mph
Armour: front 140 to 152mm; side 95mm
Main Armament: medium velocity 75mm,
6-pdr or close support weapons
L: 24ft 5in **H:** 9ft **W:** 10ft 1in

M3/5 Stuart or Honey
Crew: 4 **Weight:** 15 tons **Speed:** 40mph
Armour: front 40mm; side 25mm
Main Armament: 37mm
L: 15ft 10in **H:** 7ft 10in **W:** 7ft 6inn

Figure 5. Principal Allied armour types in Normandy

dual-purpose M3 75 mm gun. Those supplied to the British as part of the lend-lease programme were by the mid-to-later stages of the war for the most part the M4A4 model, which had a slightly longer hull than other versions and was powered by the Chrysler A57 multi-bank engine. This complex and less easily maintained engine and its slightly lower power output than other Sherman engine designs, resulted in the US army rejecting the M4A4 for overseas duties, but the British found the tank little different from the other variants of the M4.[30] As well as equipping the independent armoured brigades and three out of the four armoured regiments in all but one of the armoured divisions, the ubiquitous Sherman was employed in a whole host of supporting roles, from artillery observation to mine clearance. Armour protection was modest by 1944 standards and offered little defence against even the older 75 mm guns employed by the Germans at standard battle ranges (up to 1,000 yards). Moreover, ever since its introduction into the 8th Army in 1942, the Sherman had carried a reputation for exploding into flames when hit, and those crews brought up on British diesel-fuelled tanks were suspicious of the Sherman's petrol engines.[31] At a little over 30 tons and with a top speed of around 24 mph it was no high-performance vehicle either, and indeed, the much heavier Panther (45 tons) was faster and had superior cross-country capability.[32]

Yet the Sherman remained popular with British crews, perhaps because prior to the arrival of the later marks of the Cromwell in 1944, all other home-designed cruisers had been both mechanically unreliable and outperformed by upgraded Panzer IIIs and IVs. When the Sherman was first introduced in 1942 British crews were enthusiastic and the Germans impressed, but by 1944 it was obsolescent, most obviously because its 75 mm gun was inadequate against the Tigers and Panthers now being employed in increasing, though still limited numbers by the Germans.[33]

In order to rectify this problem a number of Shermans, codenamed Fireflies, had been refitted in the period leading up to D-Day with the 17-pdr anti-tank gun, a weapon capable of dealing with the heavier German tanks. However, these conversions were in limited supply during the Normandy campaign and still, of course, suffered from weak armour protection. By Normandy one Sherman in each troop of four had been converted to carry a 17-pdr gun.[34] The Firefly was not entirely successful, with the turret being particularly cramped and the gun causing excessive flash and smoke, which all too easily gave the tank's position away and hindered subsequent shots at the same target.[35] Moreover, the significantly larger 17-pdr gun and the armoured radio box on the rear of the turret made the Firefly an easy and obvious target for the Germans to single out, and there were even attempts to camouflage the much larger 17-pdr gun.[36] It was also considered prudent and appropriate in Normandy for troop leaders not to command from the Firefly, as these tanks would probably be the first target selected by German gunners.[37]

Nevertheless, crews were heartened by the arrival of the Firefly and believed they now had a weapon that would allow them to deal with German armour on a reasonably equal footing for the first time since 1940.[38] Still further, the Sherman held other minor advantages, with a high rate of fire and a powered turret traverse that bettered the German tanks of the period.[39] In addition, its much-maligned high profile was considered beneficial by opposing German crews in the hedged and high-banked terrain of the *bocage*, though in more open terrain this advantage melted away.[40] Therefore, the Sherman in 1944 retained a reputation for reliability and ease of maintenance, but also for being under-gunned (save the Firefly), under-armoured and prone to combustibility.

A27M Cromwell and A30 Challenger

Britain's long-running cruiser tank programme had by the summer of 1944 precipitated the Cromwell, the first truly reliable model and the first cruiser to carry the dual-purpose MV 75 mm gun, though it had originally sported the 6-pdr. The Cromwell was allocated to the armoured reconnaissance regiment in each British armoured division, and to all four regiments in the 7th Armoured Division, even though there was some opposition to this, as the Desert Rats had become well acquainted with the Sherman.[41] Design work had begun back in 1941 and the tank benefited from the lessons learned from the earlier cruiser tank programmes. The mechanical failings that had done for the Crusader and its predecessors, however, did not ultimately afflict the Cromwell, which, despite a patchy start, gained a reputation for excellent reliability and ease of maintenance.[42] In late August 1944, Maj-Gen Gerald L. Verney, the then GOC 7th Armoured Division, enthused about the Cromwell during the race to Belgium. He stated, 'the advance at one period was 250 miles in six days, with practically no casualties from mechanical failure'.[43] Fritz Bayerlein, GOC Panzer *Lehr*, was also impressed with the performance of the Cromwell in Normandy, while German intelligence reports praised the Cromwell's mobility in the *bocage* ahead of German models.[44]

However, although it was fast and manoeuvrable, topping 30 mph cross-country in dry conditions, the Cromwell suffered from similar deficiencies to the Sherman in terms of armour protection and firepower. It had been hoped at one stage that the Cromwell would carry the Vickers-designed HV 75 mm gun, later renamed the 77 mm gun to avoid confusion and fitted to the Comet, but the turret ring diameter was too small and the Cromwell was initially fitted with the 6-pdr.[45] By 1944, however, it carried a similar performance MV 75 mm gun as the Sherman and was thus similarly disadvantaged against the heavy German tanks, whilst its armour protection offered crews little comfort. Certain problems emerged in action, such as the weakness of the Cromwell against mines and the unnerving ability of the tank's exhaust system to gas its crew when static for any length of time. This latter problem was, however, quickly rectified in theatre.[46]

Significantly, the Cromwell was intended to act as a reconnaissance tank in the British armoured divisions, but was considered too noisy and large for the task. This, coupled with the lack of hitting power of the MV 75 mm gun, resulted in Montgomery's assessment that the Cromwell would have to go.[47] He wanted more 17-pdr-equipped tanks and called for the A30 Challenger to replace the Cromwell. The Challenger, however, was not the panacea Montgomery imagined. The Challenger's development dated back to early 1942 when the advantage of having a tank capable of carrying the new 17-pdr gun was first recognised. However, the attempt to fit it to a slightly larger Cromwell hull with an enlarged turret, essentially what the Challenger amounted to, resulted in limited success and by the summer of 1944 it was viewed by the RAC merely as an interim model. The tank's higher profile, the reduced armour protection, the elongated hull that restricted the Challenger's manoeuvrability and its general lack of reliability all served to undermine confidence.[48] These deficiencies and others resulted in only 200 Challengers being produced, and indeed the first batch of 100 had to be withdrawn for essential modifications in September 1944. Few A30s saw action before they, along with the Cromwell, began to be phased out in the winter of 1944 in favour of the much superior A34 Comet, a tank with similar capabilities to the Panther.[49]

A22 Churchill

The last in the line of infantry support tanks employed by the British was the A22 Churchill, the roots of which dated back to 1940. It had undergone a considerable amount of development and enhancement since its early days, and had even survived the opprobrium of the army following severe mechanical difficulties when first introduced. Moreover, the Churchill at various times fielded all manner of weaponry, upgrading from the 2-pdr, through the 6-pdr, to the ubiquitous MV 75 mm gun, which was phasing out the 6-pdr by Normandy. The Churchill was also utilised in a variety of specialised roles, most notably as the feared Crocodile flame-throwing tanks of 79th Armoured Division. The Churchills used in Normandy were for the most part heavily armoured, either upgraded earlier models, or the new Heavy Churchill Mark VII (also coded the A42). These carried frontal armour of over 150 mm, thicker even than the notorious Tigers. Most carried the MV 75 mm gun, though some retained the 6-pdr, while those of the 79th Armoured Division deployed a whole host of armaments and equipment.

The Churchill was designed to offer close infantry support and the War Office and the RAC had hoped that it would be supplied to all the independent armoured brigades to fulfil this role.[50] However, Montgomery opposed the use of infantry support tanks, preferring the concept of the single capital or universal tank, in his mind the Sherman.[51] To confound the War Office and the RAC still further, production of the Churchill was never going to be sufficient to equip all eight independent brigades in Normandy, and thus only three, titled independent tank brigades fought in the campaign with Churchills. Indeed, aside from those employed in specialist roles, only some 350 Churchills were ever in frontline units at any one time.[52]

Despite Montgomery's reservations, the Churchill proved popular with crews, particularly the later heavily armoured versions, which could often survive hits from all but the most powerful of German guns.[53] Moreover, unlike the Sherman, the Churchill did not burst into flames when penetrated, giving crews a better chance of baling out.[54] In addition, the Churchill proved adept at traversing difficult terrain, and the high-banked *bocage* hedges in particular. While Shermans had to be fitted with metal prongs to cut through the constricting hedgerows that closed down much of the Normandy terrain, the Churchill could cope with them. During *Operation Bluecoat*, Churchills of the 6th Guards Tank Brigade caught the Germans by surprise by traversing terrain considered impassable to tracked vehicles.[55]

The Churchill, however, did suffer from certain shortcomings, aside from Montgomery's hostility. Because the tank was designed for infantry support operations, rapid movement was not considered necessary, and the Churchill's top speed was only some 12 mph. Consequently, it was unable to participate in exploitation operations and suffered criticism because of this from Montgomery and his staff.[56] Additionally, although the Churchill's armament had been continually upgraded throughout the war, the 75 mm gun, like those carried by the Sherman and the Cromwell, was inadequate by 1944 standards. Similarly to the Cromwell, the Churchill's turret ring was too small to take the 17-pdr, and although the 75 mm gun's HE capability was well regarded, troops of Churchills were generally unable to tackle heavy German tanks. Some units asked for the 6-pdr with the new sabot ammunition to be retained and distributed on the basis of one per troop, as this weapon offered superior anti-armour capability.[57] However, even this gun was of only limited value against the Tiger and the Panther.

Most disappointingly for Churchill crews, their enhanced armour protection, which provided considerable comfort against older German 75 mm guns at medium-to-long ranges, could not defeat the latest German 75 mm and 88 mm guns. The weaponry carried by Panthers, Tigers and the latest tank hunters as well as large anti-tank guns could cut through even the Churchill's frontal six-inch armour plate at ranges over 1,000 yards, and the flanks were susceptible up to 2,000 yards.[58] As most of the Churchill's actions took place at close range in the dense terrain of Normandy, thus exposing itself to flanking fire, its armour was of limited value. In addition, Churchill troops were not aided by 17-pdr-equipped tanks in the same manner as Sherman and Cromwell units, though on occasion M10 tank destroyers were deployed with them to strengthen their anti-tank capability.[59]

Useful as the Churchill was in the close support role, and it was clearly superior to the Sherman, it emphasised the emerging maxim that top-class guns were, by the mid-to-closing stages of the Second World War, always likely to defeat even the most heavily armoured vehicles. If the Churchill's six inches of armour could not survive the Panther's 75 mm gun at standard battle range, then superior armament was the key, not further protection.

M3/5 Stuart (Honey)

The British Army had long identified a need for a fast reconnaissance, or light tank, and in 1944 the requirement was fulfilled by the American M3/5, officially known as the Stuart, though it was nicknamed Honey by British crews enthusiastic about its smooth running and reliability. It was the first US tank introduced into action in the Second World War and saw widespread service in the desert where its mobility and speed gained it a positive reputation. However, the tank was flawed in many ways, the most obvious being the weakness of the main 37 mm armament, which by 1944 standards was nigh on useless. The gun's HE shell was ineffective and the AP capability was insufficient to inflict damage on opposing German tanks.[60] Moreover, the tank's weak armour and high profile made it particularly vulnerable in northwest Europe where manoeuvring space was at a premium.

The Honey was intended to provide reconnaissance elements for armoured and tank regiments and 11 were included in the order of battle of each. The divisional armoured reconnaissance regiments had a higher proportion of Honeys to work with the Cromwells. However, due to its inadequate protection and firepower the Honey was able to act as little more than a fully tracked scout vehicle, and a rather conspicuous one at that. Indeed, some units removed the turret in order to lower the profile, and in effect the stripped-down tank became a battlefield transport operating around the other tanks and providing machine gun flank support. There is little doubt that in the confined space and terrain of Normandy the light tank was unable to play a significant role, and by the closing stages of the campaign official US reports claimed that the M3/5 was inadequate and unable to assist tank units in typical conditions.[61]

M10 tank destroyers – 76 mm and 17-pdr

In the wake of Germany's successful 1939–41 campaigns, US armour doctrine had incorporated the idea of fast, lightly armoured vehicles carrying dedicated HV anti-tanks guns as being the most appropriate method of defeating heavily armoured tanks. Consequently, in order to fulfil the requirement American industry had produced the M10 tank destroyer. In essence it was little more than a modified M4 with reduced, though more obviously sloped, armour and an open-topped turret initially carrying a three-inch gun, though this was later phased out by a lighter 76 mm gun. Some 1,648 M10s were delivered to the British, where they were occasionally referred to as Wolverines and were deployed in Royal Artillery (RA) anti-tank units throughout the Normandy campaign. Most initially carried the three-inch gun, but the British began refitting their M10s with 17-pdrs. Such vehicles were supposedly titled Achilles, and sometimes rather confusingly Firefly, but as in the case of the nomenclature Wolverine, these names were not widely employed, M10 being the standard reference.[62]

The mobility of the tank destroyer was its greatest asset, for it was able to get forward and into supporting positions quickly, while towed guns such as the 17-pdr could take 12–15 hours to be properly dug into place and be ready for action. M10s were therefore used for rapid anti-tank support, whilst the towed guns were used in more defensive positions as a 'long stop'.[63] In defensive situations the M10 proved to be more valuable, but it was vulnerable when called upon to be aggressive. In such situations it could only act as a mobile anti-tank gun and was highly susceptible to long-range gunnery, indeed, just as were all Allied tanks, save perhaps the Churchill. The M10's high profile compounded matters as it presented a larger target than similar German SP anti-tank equipments.[64] Moreover, the M10's open-topped turret was a cause of much concern, exposing the commander, gunner and loader to small arms fire and shrapnel, which on occasion set off ammunition stored in the turret itself.[65] The vulnerability of this configuration was demonstrated in the dense terrain of Normandy, and in-theatre attempts were later made to fit the turrets with armoured tops, but these were often little more than lash-ups.[66]

The most obvious failing of the M10, however, centred on its lack of punch. Although the three-inch or 76 mm gun had superior AP capability to the 75 mm gun (by some 35–50 per cent), it was still insufficient to overcome the heavy armour of the latest German tanks, save at very close range. Moreover, the 76 mm gun lacked a good HE shell and was 24 per cent less efficient in this role than the 75 mm gun.[67] US forces labelled the M10 as inadequate and called for it to be replaced more rapidly by the M36, a very similar equipment excepting that it carried a 90 mm gun, though there were even reservations about this weapon.[68] The British had already begun equipping their M10s with 17-pdr guns, as it was considered that the three-inch gun was not powerful enough, but by Normandy they were only just appearing in anti-tank units in any quantity and not without supply problems.[69]

Therefore, the M10 tank destroyers employed by the British were, when equipped with the three-inch or 76 mm, under-gunned for the role envisaged. Even the M10 carrying the 17-pdr gun was an inferior vehicle to the more heavily armoured Firefly. Still further, the M10 was considered too vulnerable to offer close support to the leading elements of assault forces, precisely where they were needed to deal with heavy German armoured fighting vehicles (AFVs) counter-attacking or in dug-in positions. Overall, the tank destroyer concept was inappropriate for the type of operation being undertaken by 21st Army Group in Normandy.

German armour

Panzer IV

Although the most feared and infamous German tanks of the Normandy campaign were the Tiger and Panther, the most numerous vehicle opposing Allied armour was the ageing Panzer Mark IV. In service throughout the war, the Panzer IV had been continually upgraded and the versions fighting in Normandy carried a powerful 75 mm gun that outperformed the Allied 75 mm version in armour penetration by some 30 per cent. In contrast, the armour protection of the Sherman and Cromwell was moderately superior to that of the Panzer IV.[70] However, such differences mattered little for both tanks' main armament could defeat the other's armour at up to 1,200 yards, and little successful anti-tank fire took place at ranges beyond that. The Cromwell could easily outmanoeuvre the Panzer IV, though this was of limited value in Normandy where much of the fighting was constrained by the terrain and was effectively static for so long. In battle terms there was little to choose between the Panzer IV and its opponents, and it was confounded only by the Churchill's heavy armour and outperformed by 17-pdr-equipped tanks.

Panzer IV H/J
Crew: 5 **Weight:** 25 tons **Speed:** 24mph
Armour: front 50 to 80mm; side 30mm
Main Armament: 75mm L48
L: 19ft 4in **H:** 8ft 10in **W:** 10ft 8in

Panther
Crew: 5 **Weight:** 45 tons **Speed:** 28mph
Armour: front 80 to 120mm; side 50mm
Main Armament: 75mm KwK 42
L: 22ft 7in **H:** 9ft 10in **W:** 11ft 3in

Sturmgeschutz III
Crew: 4 **Weight:** 24 tons **Speed:** 24mph
Armour: front 80mm; side 30mm
Main Armament: 75mm Stik 40
L: 18ft 4in **H:** 7ft **W:** 9ft 9in

Tiger I
Crew: 5 **Weight:** 54 tons **Speed:** 18mph
Armour: front 100mm; side 80mm
Main Armament: 88mm KwK 36
L: 20ft 4in **H:** 9ft 5in **W:** 12ft 3in

Figure 6. Principal German armour types in Normandy

Panther

The Panzer IV's long-term replacement as the standard medium tank of the German armed forces was the Panther, a fast, manoeuvrable, well-armoured AFV, equipped with a powerful, HV 75 mm gun. At Kursk in 1943 it had proved disappointing due to its lack of mechanical reliability, but by Normandy many of these problems had been solved, though the Panther never matched Allied tanks for reliability. Nevertheless, the Panther's main armament could cut through any Allied armour protection at distances well in excess of standard battle range, and even the heavy Churchill was vulnerable at over 1,000 yards. Moreover, the Panther's frontal armour protection was distinctly superior to the Shermans and Cromwells, being effectively invulnerable to the Allied 75 mm except at point-blank range. Even the 17-pdr struggled against the Panther's front glacis armour, though sabot ammunition was usually up to the task.[71] Additionally, the Panther was faster and more manoeuvrable than the Sherman, despite being over ten tons heavier.[72]

However, the Panther's armour distribution was such that even the later versions were weak on the sides and Allied crews were able to knock them out with flanking shots. This made the tank vulnerable on the offensive, and more particularly at close range. German tactical notes distributed to troops emphasised that the Panther should be employed at long range to prevent then enemy from prosecuting flank attacks and that other tanks should be employed on mopping up operations or in supporting troops in close terrain or in built-up areas.[73] When operating in Normandy, the size of the Panther and its long over-hanging gun also caused problems, and some commanders and crews argued that the Panzer IVs were better suited to the *bocage*.[74] Moreover, although the Panther's armour protection was considerable, qualitatively it was weak. Allied assessment found that the armour could flake and splinter internally when hit, causing casualties among the crew.[75] In addition, the Panther also developed in some circles a reputation for bursting into flames when penetrated, in a similar though not as frequent vein to the Sherman.[76] Like the 17-pdr, the HV 75 mm gun produced such a muzzle blast that gunners could not observe the fall of their shot, and they had to rely on the commander to offer guidance.[77] Nevertheless, the Panther was a formidable weapon, feared and respected by Allied tank crews, more so than any other German tank.[78] Some 650 saw action in Normandy, influencing operations far more than the infamous and feared Tiger.

Tiger

The notorious Tiger shaped the Allied tanker's view of the campaign more than any other. Tigers were apparently everywhere, despite the fact that only some 120–30 were ever deployed in Normandy. Indeed, 2nd British Army intelligence summaries claimed that in the first ten days or so of the fighting, the Tiger was the most numerous enemy tank encountered.[79] The reality was that nervous crews were mistaking Panzer IVs for their much more fearsome stable mates. The Tiger was a major piece of machinery, weighing in at around 54 tons, close on twice that of a Cromwell. It carried the feared 88 mm gun and was clad in all-round armour of 80–100 mm, making it almost impervious to the Allied 75 mm gun. Even the 17-pdr did not guarantee a penetration at standard battle range, as Sgt Stan Lockwood discovered when he hit Michael Wittman's Tiger at close range in Villers Bocage on the morning of 13 June.[80] The Tiger was, however, slow, unmanoeuvrable, difficult to maintain and notoriously unreliable – Wittman even had to abandon his own Tiger at Villers Bocage when it broke down after moving just a few yards. Indeed, many more Tigers were lost to mechanical failure than Allied gunfire across Normandy. German crews were also being advised not to demand the impossible from their Tigers, for it was clear that by 1944 the tank was vulnerable. 'No longer can the Tiger prance around oblivious to the laws of tank tactics', one tactical aide-memoire advised.[81]

Despite its failings, the Tiger elicited fear and trepidation among opponents, and though few in number in Normandy, they played an important part in subduing aggression in Allied tank crews. An even more potent version of the Tiger also made a brief appearance later in the campaign, carrying yet more armour and an even more powerful gun.[82] Yet the Tiger II, or King or Royal Tiger as it was variously known, achieved very little. It absorbed huge amounts of resources and contributed nothing that was not already being achieved by the Panthers and Tigers already in service.

Sturmgeschütz III

Although little discussed, the third most numerous German AFV in Normandy was the Sturmgeschütz or Stug III, with some 550 being employed in fighting units. Stugs were distributed to infantry and panzer divisions as well as forming independent assault gun battalions, and thus were commonplace across the theatre. The Stug was essentially a Panzer III chassis with a static, armoured fighting compartment equipped with a limited traverse 75 mm gun equivalent to that on the Panzer IV. Originally intended as an infantry support and assault weapon, by 1944 the Stug was playing a major part in providing anti-tank support for infantry units, and as tank destroyers with the panzer divisions. Its armour protection was similar to the Panzer IV, but was aided by the Stug's very low profile, making detection somewhat more difficult. Although of limited value in attack and generally outperformed by Allied armour, the Stug was a useful weapon in defence and its size and relatively effective main armament made it ideal for Normandy.[83]

The Allies also encountered a variety of tank destroyers in Normandy that were similar in design and concept to the Stug. Some, such as the Jagdpanzer IV, were well armoured, while others such as the Marder and the hotchpotch of vehicles utilised by 21st Panzers were effectively little more than mobile, open-topped anti-tank guns with very limited armour protection. All, however, were equipped with 75 mm guns at least, and the rare Jagdpanther sported the latest 88 mm gun, only mounted elsewhere in western Europe in the Tiger II.

The armour mismatch?

It is certainly the case that the mismatch in armour capability was not so pronounced as has been implied in many commentaries on the Normandy campaign. Of some 2,500 German tanks available for action throughout the June–August period, only around 30 per cent could be classed as clearly superior to the standard Allied models. Moreover, approximately only 5 per cent were the notorious Tigers, despite Allied tank crews' claims to have knocked out or destroyed 57 such vehicles over the period 6–30 June, some 18 per cent of the entire total tanks claimed.[84]

The vast majority of German tanks encountered in Normandy were either inferior, or at best, merely equal to the Shermans, Cromwells and Churchills employed by the Allies. Those German tanks with superior capability were also those most likely to break down, and leading German commanders interviewed after the war claimed that mechanical failure accounted for around 15–30 per cent of total tanks lost in action.[85] In addition, across the theatre, the Allies still enjoyed well in excess of a three-to-one superiority in total tanks committed.

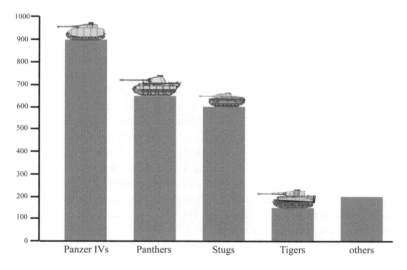

Figure 7. German armour committed to Normandy by type

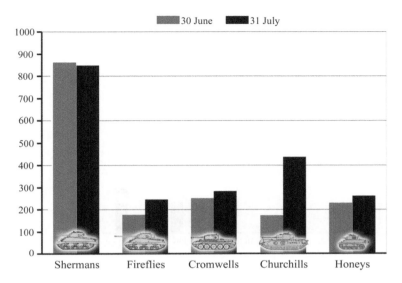

Figure 8. Frontline British armour strengths

Numbers relate to vehicles ready immediately or within 24 hours.
Figures do not include 79th Armoured Division, OP, AA or similar vehicles which
contributed some 1,000 extra AFVs in a great variety of types by early August.
4th Canadian and 1st Polish Armoured Divisions were added at the end of July and
early August but are not included in this chart.
27th Armoured Brigade was disbanded 29 July.

source: WO 205/637 Daily AFV states, June to July 1944.

However, this is not the entire picture, for 21st Army Group was far more likely to encounter stiff armoured opposition, comprising the superior elements of the *Panzerwaffe*, than US forces. Montgomery's strategy of drawing the best German armoured elements to the sector around Caen worked with varying degrees of success, but there is little doubt that at critical moments 21st Army Group hurled itself against some of the densest concentrations of high-quality opposition in the entire war. The importance of Caen as the fulcrum of events in Normandy was apparent to the German staff, and within days of the Allied landings, 21st Army Group was confronting 21st Panzers, 12th SS and Panzer *Lehr* around that disputed city. By the time of *Epsom* on 26 June, Dempsey's 2nd Army was facing the deepest and most hostile opposition across the theatre, and arguably anywhere in Europe.

Certainly, this was on a level never previously encountered by Montgomery and his staff, and during the ensuing weeks, British and Canadian tanks were often committed against heavy concentrations of German armour. Moreover, Montgomery's determination to attack on very narrow frontages exacerbated

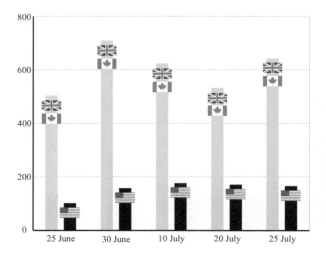

Figure 9. German armour confronting Allies by sector

this problem by allowing German resources to be focused where and when required. It was this density of firepower in defence, be it from tanks, self-propelled guns or towed anti-tank guns, that created the most severe problems for Allied armour. Moreover, as all but the Churchill tank was vulnerable to any German gun at standard battle ranges, the advantage of first fire from concealment was of more significance than whether the gun was mounted on a Panther or a Stug.

Nevertheless, approximately 30 per cent of German armour held certain qualitative advantages over Allied tanks, and during the critical defensive phases of operations such superiority could theoretically be brought to bear. Notably, available Tigers were employed as an emergency force to block penetrations, and although applied in a haphazard fashion, they often achieved their main objective. Such applications of scant resources, however, placed a heavy burden on the 'superior' element of German armour and the strength of this force haemorrhaged as the campaign progressed.

The destruction of Allied armour

To what extent, therefore, was the superior element of the *Panzerwaffe* responsible for the losses endured by Allied armour in Normandy? Ellis, in the official British history of the northwest European campaign, claimed that most tanks actually fell victim to 'long-range anti-tank guns, particularly 88s', but this is hardly a complete picture.[86] The sources are at times somewhat contradictory and derive findings from limited tests and evidence, but certain recurring factors can be detected.

Hollow-charge weapons such as the *panzerschreck* and the *panzerfaust* increased in importance as the northwest European campaign progressed, most obviously in 1945 once Allied armies had crossed the Rhine. The *panzerfaust* was particularly effective being a short-range, one-shot, disposable weapon that required little training to be used successfully. A new and more potent version had been introduced and detected by the Allies during Normandy, which increased the range to some 66 yards and enhanced armour penetration.[87] Allied summaries, however, criticised the use made by Germans of this weapon, even in terrain such as the *bocage*, which should have made it more of a problem than it was.[88] By late 1944, the proportion of Allied tank losses to hollow-charge weapons had increased to perhaps upwards of 25–30 per cent, though this was in part due to the decrease in available German anti-tank guns and armour.[89] During the Normandy campaign, however, hollow-charge weapons and other means of close-combat techniques probably accounted for no more than 15 per cent of Allied tank losses, depending on density of terrain. Indeed, hollow-charge weapons alone may have accounted for no more than 6 per cent of the total.[90]

Anti-tank mines played a more significant role during the static phases of the campaign and in set-piece battles, though the Germans did not employ them in the expected quantities during *Goodwood*. Three reports give figures of between 9 and 21 per cent of tanks being disabled by mines, though these findings are open to question as other sources state that more mines were being encountered by the Allies in northwest Europe than hitherto.[91]

While non-direct gunfire probably accounted for no more than 5 per cent of Allied tank casualties, direct gunfire was the most significant killer of Allied tanks in Normandy. Figures again vary but it seems that some two-thirds of 21st Army Group's tanks fell victim to German tank and anti-tank guns.[92] Disaggregating losses between anti-tank guns as opposed to tank fire is rather problematical, as the rounds fired by both were almost identical, though the propellant charges could be different. Thus, tanks disabled by 75 mm guns could just as easily have been hit by a towed Pak 40 75 mm anti-tank gun as by a KwK 40 weapon mounted on a Panzer IV.[93] Moreover, when a tank had 'brewed up', that is burst into flames after being penetrated, operational researchers found difficulty in distinguishing even between 75 mm and 88 mm penetrations. Relying on eye-witness accounts was also fraught with difficulty as tank crews often claimed to have been hit by an 88 mm gun when in fact it had been a 75 mm gun, whilst the reverse was never true.[94] However, the proportion of towed anti-tank guns to tanks and self-propelled weapons within the German forces in Normandy was roughly one to three, and German troops' claims of Allied tank kills ran at a not dissimilar rate, with anti-tank gun crews accounting for around one-third of the claims made.[95] Therefore, it would seem that as two-thirds of Allied tank losses were attributed to enemy gunfire, German tanks and assault guns may have accounted for around 50 per cent of all Allied tanks lost in Normandy.

Ultimately, therefore, the most significant problem facing Allied tank crews was enemy gunfire; tanks, SP guns and assault guns in particular. Enemy anti-tank guns were vulnerable to the heavy artillery barrages the Allies could bring to bear in Normandy, but armoured vehicles were much less so, and with increasing numbers of SP guns being deployed by the Germans in the summer of 1944, the difficulties were likely to intensify. The ability of 21st Army Group's tanks to deal with the problem was of paramount import- ance, and effective mobile firepower to eliminate enemy armour was the key. Both pre-*Overlord* planning and intelligence summaries, and Montgomery's memo in early July, placed primary emphasis on deploying as many 17-pdr- equipped vehicles as possible, and experience and evidence in Normandy proved that these assumptions had considerable validity.[96]

The failings of Allied armour

Discussion and comment, both during and since the war, on the inadequa- cies of Allied tanks deployed during the Normandy campaign have fallen broadly into three categories. Issues have centred upon: insufficient armour protection; the alarming tendency of the Sherman to 'brew up' when hit; and the lack of firepower. The importance and interrelationship of these three failings was obviously shaped by the relative values placed on protection and firepower in tank warfare by the latter half of the Second World War.

Armour protection

With the development and employment of ever more powerful guns and new types of ammunition, from the midpoint of the war onwards firepower dominated armour protection. By 1944, almost all armour could be defeated by the latest weaponry at standard battle ranges, that is, up to and around 1,000 yards. Beyond this no more than one-third of the total hits recorded was scored, while in Normandy this figure was lower still.[97] Nevertheless, in the minds of tank crews in the summer of 1944, the sight of their Shermans and Cromwells being torn apart by heavy German guns was enough to raise the issue of the inadequacy of Allied armour protection. Steel Brownlie, a troop commander with 2nd Fife and Forfar Yeomanry recorded:

> My crews got almost obsessive about not having a thick sloping glacis plate in front like the Panther. I recall deliberately backing into a firing position so as to have the protection of the engine. There was the added advantage that if you had to get out in a hurry you had all the forward gears.[98]

On occasion, other units mirrored the tactic of reversing into battle, previously employed in North Africa, in the belief that this enhanced protection, though there is no actual evidence that it did.[99] Steve and Tom Dyson, who served in 34th Tank Brigade, soon discovered the reality facing them:

> We also learned, to our dismay, of the devastating effects of the German 88 mm high velocity guns, mounted SPs, anti-tank guns, and Tiger tanks. The shells apparently went through our Shermans like a knife through butter.[100]

Crews took to adding track sections and sandbags to the front of their tanks in an effort to improve protection, though operational research reports proved that whatever morale-boosting effect this practice may have had, it had no actual physical value.[101] Moreover, the extra weight created excessive strain on the engines, increasing demands on maintenance procedures and shortening mechanical life expectancy.[102]

The most basic issue confronting Allied tank crews was that the armour of the Sherman and Cromwell could not withstand hits from any major German anti-tank weapon at distances close to standard battle range. Most anti-tank firing took place at less than 1,000 yards, especially in the close terrain covering much of Normandy, even with the improved long-range gunnery of 1944–45. Even to the south of Caen, Canadian after-action reports indicated that the mean range of anti-tank fire was still under 1,000 yards, while US figures for June–August showed that the average range of lethal engagement by anti-tank gunnery was less than 600 metres.[103] At such ranges Sherman and Cromwell armour offered no protection against German anti-tank guns of 75 mm calibre and above, or the weaponry carried by German tanks, assault and SP guns. At 500 yards it was difficult not to be hit by the enemy once engaged, and within a minute of being under fire the likelihood of not being penetrated was reduced to virtually nil. Indeed, it was contended that the survival chances of an Allied tank halved every six seconds in such circumstances.[104] Almost all 75 mm and 88 mm AP hits penetrated the Sherman's armour and in 62 per cent of cases knocked the tank out of action.[105] US 1st Army figures showed that 80 per cent of M4s disabled by gunfire had been penetrated.[106] Even the Churchill, despite its 150 mm-plus frontal armour, was still vulnerable to the latest versions of the 75 mm and the 88 mm gun.[107]

It should be noted, however, that German armour was similarly vulnerable at less than 1,000 yards to the best weapon available to the Allies, the 17-pdr, more emphatically so when it fired the new APDS round. Unfortunately, neither was in plentiful supply in Normandy, and when 75 mm shells bounced off Tigers, Panthers and the latest tank hunters, Allied crews naturally demanded to know why their tanks were not similarly protected. An operational research report by No. 2 ORS, 21st Army Group stated in 1945:

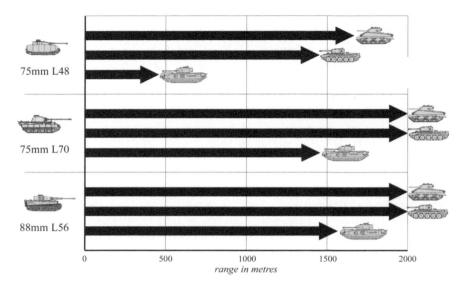

Figure 10. Vulnerability of Allied armour to principal German anti-armour guns

'It would seem that the tank crews expect protection from their armour and feel that they have been let down when they find by experience that it gives very little protection.'[108] The reality was that it would have made little difference. Number 2 ORS attached to 21st Army Group in 1944 recorded in Report no. 12, *Analysis of 75 mm Sherman Tank Casualties 6th June to 10th July*, that hits were roughly equally distributed between front and sides on the Sherman, and thus for up-armouring to be worthwhile a large area of the tank would have to be enhanced. Indeed, if the front were strengthened to resist 50 per cent of hits, penetrations would have been reduced by only some 15 per cent. In Normandy, all-round defence was considered best as the enemy was likely to wait until hits could be scored on the flanks and rear of advancing tanks. Such so-called homogenous defence was impractical in Allied tanks, and even the Panther was highly vulnerable when it adopted an aggressive posture and advanced on Allied positions, because it exposed its more thinly armoured flanks. The ORS team concluded that any increase in weight of Allied tanks should be used to increase firepower by carrying larger and more effective weaponry. Moreover, they argued that the supposed invulnerability of German armour was largely caused by the tactical situation pertaining in Normandy, where the enemy camouflaged its armour well, used low-smoke propellant, got in the first shot and more often than not deployed defensively.[109] Until better methods of spotting enemy tanks and anti-tanks guns were developed, the excessive vulnerability of Allied tanks to German direct gunfire would persist.

Combustibility

In addition to the perceived inadequacies of armour protection, Allied crews were also greatly concerned about the unnerving propensity of the Sherman to burst into flames, or 'brew up', when penetrated and disabled. With sardonic humour, crews christened their Shermans 'Ronsons' after the cigarette lighter, which, according to the advertising slogan, always lit first time. One commander noted that 'a hit almost inevitably meant a "brew-up" ... you were in a Ronson and if you were hit it was best to bale out p.d.q.'[110] Crews in one regiment even went into battle with the driver's and co-driver's hatches open to expedite baling out when hit.[111] A series of notes and memos was fed back to the RAC during the Normandy campaign, many claiming that the Sherman brewed up very quickly or that fires too frequently followed penetration, and that alarm and despondency was rising.[112] Even the Germans noted the Sherman's combustibility, referring to them as 'Tommy cookers'.

Evidence indicates that the Sherman deserved its reputation. A study of 45 Shermans knocked out between 6 June and 10 July uncovered that 37 of them had 'brewed up', 33 after being penetrated by AP shot.[113] Moreover, of 166 Shermans lost in 8th and 29th Armoured Brigades, on examination 94 were burnt out.[114] US reports indicated similar findings, with some 65 per cent of M4s burning after penetration by direct gunfire.[115] Reports on the Cromwell, the Honey and the Churchill were not so critical, often inferring that the chance of fire was considerably lower.[116] In contrast, Percy Hobart, GOC 79th Armoured Division, argued that there was little difference in the likelihood of Shermans and Churchills bursting into flames.[117]

Nevertheless, it was the Sherman that caused most consternation, and various theories were proffered to explain the problem. One frontline unit claimed that it was the wireless set in the tank that caused the vehicle to brew up, but this seems to have been dismissed.[118] Many believed that Shermans being fitted with petrol engines and fuel tanks, which were obviously highly inflammable, caused the problem.[119] Indeed, British crews, used to diesel-powered home-produced tanks such as the Matilda and Valentine, were initially distinctly wary of the petrol tanks on the Sherman. A few Shermans were equipped with diesel engines, but these were used as armoured recovery vehicles or in specialised roles, and the M10 was also diesel powered. Similar to their British comrades, American crews likewise subscribed to the theory that petrol Shermans were more likely to burn than diesel types.[120] However, operational research revealed that fuel-related fires and explosions, although not unknown, were not the major factors behind the Sherman's reputation. There were many examples of tanks that had burnt fiercely but in which the fuel was still intact. Moreover, many crews spoke of fierce, blinding jets of flame immediately after their tanks had been hit, inconsistent with petrol-related fires.[121] A much more likely cause was thought to be cordite flash. Such 'flash' occurred when the Sherman's ammunition cordite combusted following penetration of the tank, and in such circumstances crews had very limited time to bale out and avoid incineration. The reason why the ammunition in the Sherman should burn more often than in other tanks, however, was a cause of conjecture. Reports from the Mediterranean had already noted that cordite flash was the most likely cause of 'brew ups' and that armoured ammunition stowage bins should be introduced to prevent this occurrence. Indeed, stowage bins became a requirement in new tanks. Curiously, although most German tanks were equipped with similar stowage bins, they were dropped on the Panther, which could explain its reputation for bursting into flames when penetrated.[122] Further measures were undertaken to protect the ammunition bins in Shermans, most infamous being the addition of appliqué armour plating on the hull sides. This almost certainly made little if any difference and operational researchers noted: 'It should be recognised that in no recorded case in our sample has the extra appliqué armour resisted any hit.'[123] Another report concluded: 'There does not seem to be a very strong argument for these plates. It seems extremely doubtful whether the fitting of these plates is justified.'[124] Indeed, the extra armour might have worsened the situation as the plates may have acted as aiming points for German gunners, or served to deflect shells into the tank when they otherwise might have ricocheted away.[125] Consequently, although the stowage bins helped prevent internal fragments caused by penetration from igniting ammunition, perhaps reducing ammunition-created fires by some 30–40 per cent, they did little to hinder flash when an enemy shell penetrated directly into ammunition stowage bins.[126]

Loose ammunition stowed in the tank was also a continuing problem, as crews often carried extra rounds outside the bins to limit the need for battlefield replenishment. Experience in Italy had indicated that Allied methods of resupplying tanks in the field with 4×2 lorries were inadequate, and that copying the Germans, who utilised armoured half-tracks or obsolete tanks should be considered. Crews therefore had to balance the risks of carrying extra ammunition with the increased chance of incineration when penetrated.[127] Evidence suggested that units where the policy was not to carry extra ammunition suffered far fewer 'brew ups' than those that did.[128] Ultimately, later versions of the Sherman were equipped with 'wet' stowage bins whereby the ammunition was stored in water-jacketed containers, and this reduced the chance of cordite flash on penetration to around 15 per cent.[129]

The risk of fires, however, caused crews to abandon their Shermans when hit, sometimes allowing still fully functioning tanks to fall into enemy hands and be pressed into service against Allied units.[130] Nevertheless, although an ORS report in 1945 concluded that tank crews' perceived risk of burn casualties was 'out of proportion to the real danger', it was accepted that abandonment saved lives and that in the circumstances crews should not be criticised for it.[131]

Firepower

The most significant failing of Allied tank equipment in Normandy was undoubtedly its lack of effective anti-armour firepower. Crews complained bitterly about the inadequate capabilities of their tank armaments against a wide range of German AFVs, but most comments were focused upon the weakness of the MV 75 mm gun, fitted to the vast majority of Allied tanks. The weapon had largely been designed to engage soft targets with HE, and the advantage of a tank-mounted weapon capable of fulfilling this requirement effectively was underpinned by experiences in North Africa and Italy with 2- and 6-pdr guns, which for the most part could not. The 75 mm's efficiency as an anti-tank weapon was, however, by the prevailing standards of 1944, very limited.

Bill Close, a squadron commander with 3RTR, 11th Armoured Division, claimed: 'Our ordinary 75 mm gun could not knock out either a Tiger or a Panther except at about 500 yards range, and in the rear, and with a bit of luck in the flank.'[132] Sandy Saunders, a troop commander with 2nd Northants Yeomanry concurred: 'The 75 mm gun was only capable of knocking out German Mark IVs, and Panthers at point-blank range.' Simon Frazer 15/19th Hussars likened the mismatch to a David versus Goliath confrontation, with the 75 mm gun in the role of the 'sling'.[133] Steve Dyson, 107th Regiment RAC, 34th Tank Brigade, was informed by experienced crews that their 75 mm guns were 'about as much good against the Jerry tanks as a pea shooter'.[134]

The problem was clear enough. The most effective way of dealing with enemy tanks was by disabling them with AP ammunition, as 48 per cent of German armour was accounted for in this manner during the largely 'static' phase of the campaign (6 June–7 August).[135] However, the armour penetration performance of the great majority of Allied tank guns was lower than their contemporary German opponents. Most significantly, the MV 75 mm gun carried by most Shermans, Cromwells and Churchills, although an effective HE weapon, was by the standards of 1944 an obsolete anti-tank gun. Although soft targets, which required HE shells, continued to absorb most of a tank's firing activity in the summer of 1944, the Allied tank's greatest enemy was direct gunfire, which accounted for some two-thirds of all tank losses.[136] Around one-quarter of such gunfire resulted from towed anti-tank guns, and these were ideally dealt with by artillery or direct HE rounds. However, the greater proportion of direct gunfire was delivered by German AFVs, and thus the 75 mm gun's ability, or otherwise, to cope with such opponents, even when once located, became a significant issue.

Indeed, in basic technical terms the 75 mm gun firing APC (armour piercing capped) rounds was barely capable of dealing with Mark IVs and Stugs, let alone Panthers and Tigers.[137] A flood of reports hit 21st Army Group HQ, the War Office and RAC HQ from June 1944 onwards, with commanders and crews complaining that the 75 mm gun was hopelessly outclassed, particularly against Panthers and Tigers.[138] Indeed, the 6-pdr anti-tank gun, either towed or carried in the Churchill, was preferred for anti-armour actions, especially when equipped with the new APDS ammunition, which greatly enhanced armour penetration capabilities. Montgomery commented on the popularity of the 6-pdr with sabot ammunition in his memo no. 506 of 6 July, whilst simultaneously critcising the 75 mm gun.[139] However, the HE shell for the 6-pdr was inferior to the 75 mm version, and prior to the emergence of sabot ammunition in the early months of 1944, the 6-pdr had been largely phased out by the larger gun as a standard tank armament. Consequently, in Normandy most 6-pdr weapons were towed anti-tank guns used by infantry formations. The three-inch or 76 mm gun fitted to M10 tank destroyers was not the answer either. Although its AP performance was better than the 75 mm gun, it was still not sufficient to make much of an impact on the heaviest German tanks, and its HE capability was markedly inferior.[140] US forces had come to the same conclusion that the 76 mm was not an effective replacement for the 75 mm gun, and fumed at the necessity of having to accept them.[141] Montgomery was also informed by the RAC that despite its problems, the 76 mm would eventually appear in 21st Army Group, as the dwindling supply of 75 mm Shermans were being held back for conversion into Fireflies.[142]

The only truly popular anti-tank weapon available to 21st Army Group in Normandy was the 17-pdr gun. It appeared in towed versions, though it was considered cumbersome and of limited offensive value in this guise, and in Sherman Fireflies, M10s and, late in the campaign, in A30 Challengers. Because of the limited success of the M10 three-inch/76 mm version and of the weakness of the 75 mm-equipped Shermans, desperate cries for all 17-pdr-equipped AFVs grew in intensity as the static phase of the campaign became prolonged and confidence ebbed away.[143] Indeed, even prior to D-Day senior commanders, such as Lt-Gen Richard O'Connor, GOC VIII Corps, and Lt-Gen Miles Dempsey, GOC 2nd British Army, were fully aware that their anti-armour capability required enhancement, claiming that '17-pdrs in all forms and sabot ammunition are absolutely first in our priority for equipment'.[144] Crews were particularly impressed with the Firefly, one sergeant commenting: 'At last a gun which one could trust to get its teeth really deep into any German tank it met.'[145] After action 21st Army Group combat reports soon recorded that tank crews were suitably impressed by the Firefly and urged that the proportion of such tanks within squadrons be increased.[146] Montgomery reiterated this after the experience of a month's fighting, stating that 'the 17pdr tank is most popular', and US forces even lobbied for the introduction of the gun into their order of battle.[147]

There was no doubting that the 17-pdr rivalled the German long 75 mm and 88 mm guns for accuracy and armour penetration at standard battle ranges, though even it failed on occasion to defeat the Tiger's frontal armour or the Panther's sloping hull front. Moreover, like the 6-pdr, the 17-pdr's accuracy much beyond 1,000 yards was open to question.[148] The Firefly was the nearest the Allies had to a medium tank capable of duelling with any German armour, and when sabot ammunition became available in sufficient quantities from late July onwards, the 17-pdr could split open virtually any armour in the German inventory even at long range, assuming it could secure a hit. However, although the 17-pdr was the best the Allies had in Normandy, it was far from a panacea. The gun had been designed principally as an anti-tank weapon with high muzzle velocity to enhance armour penetration capability. This militated against its use as an infantry support weapon, however, for HE shells required lower velocity in order to be most effective. The means of solving this particular problem was a specifically designed reduced, lower muzzle velocity HE shell charge, but this was not available in Normandy, and nor could it be introduced *en masse* until the end of 1944 at the earliest. Until that time, even if there had been more Fireflies available, the decrease in infantry support capability would have weakened the case for their increased deployment beyond a certain level.

Moreover, the much-vaunted APDS ammunition, which was able to defeat any German armour then in use at standard battle ranges, was also not immediately available in June 1944.[149] Only in the closing stages of the campaign did it begin to arrive in sufficient quantities. Additionally, some concern emerged that the sabot round might be damaging the 17-pdr gun and shortening its effective life, particularly by fouling the muzzle brake.[150] It was also noted that even when available, the sabot round should only be used against very heavily armoured targets, for although its armour penetration capability was superior, it did less actual damage than a standard AP round. Still further, sabot ammunition was less accurate at ranges over 1,000 metres than other rounds, though for most of the Normandy campaign this was less of a disadvantage as anti-tank firing, more often than not, took place at under this range.[151] The 17-pdr gun, like other HV weapons, such as the German L/70 75 mm gun, also kicked up a large amount of dust in dry conditions, and emitted considerable levels of smoke when fired, and this not only gave the tank's position away, but more importantly it prevented the tank's gunner and commander from observing the fall and lie of shot.[152]

The most significant problems, however, centred on the prime carrier of the 17-pdr in Normandy, the Sherman Firefly tank. Although there was a clamour for more Fireflies, there were also concerns about the hybrid tank and how the 17-pdr gun fitted to it. Problems of German gun crews picking out the Firefly first have been alluded to (see above) but casualty rates for Fireflies were actually proportionally less than for 75 mm Shermans, principally because of their tactical employment.[153] Nevertheless, the conversions of Shermans into Fireflies had caused some difficulties. The optical equipment in the Sherman was not particularly suited to long-range firing, which of course the 17-pdr was theoretically more than capable of, and this compounded the difficulties

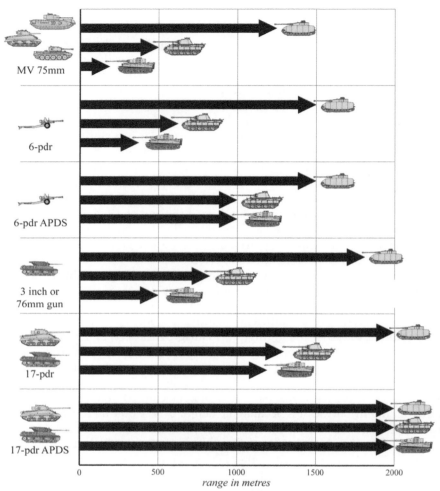

range in metres

Allied 6-pdr and 17-pdr guns became markedly less accurate at ranges
much beyond 1,200 metres, though armour penetration was still possible

Figure 11. Vulnerability of German armour to principal British anti-armour guns

created by excessive muzzle flash, a cramped turret and the limited amount of
time allowed to crews to familiarise themselves with the new tank.[154]

The 17-pdr-equipped tank, however, represented a major firepower advance
for the Allies and crews appreciated the potency of the new combination of
HV gun and reliable vehicle. The greatest hindrance to its having a major
impact on the campaign, however, was the shortage in numbers – only 84 on
11 June, 149 by the end of the month, and 235 by the end of July.[155] Ultimately,

it was the 75 mm tank gun that had to shoulder the burden of dealing with German armour, and although it was adequate in most cases, at critical points in set-piece operations, and in particular when on the offensive, the standard 75 mm-equipped Sherman or Cromwell had great difficulty in generating enough firepower to defeat defensively sited German AFVs. Twenty-First Army Group's ORS concluded as early as July that the most effective way Allied armour could be enhanced was to increase firepower and make enemy armour more vulnerable. Although technological inferiority was only one factor in explaining the limited success of Allied armour in Normandy, it was undoubtedly the inadequate firepower of 21st Army Group tanks that contributed most to this problem.

Conclusion

Historians' predilection for explaining the apparent failings of armour in Normandy in 1944 by means of a technological disparity is understandable in many ways. Primarily, it is a simple and easily measured comparison to contrast the technical capabilities of German and Allied vehicles, and by focusing upon the superiority of such tanks as the Tiger and the Panther, a clear and obvious explanation of Allied difficulties emerges. However, such a view is partial in two critical ways. First, the technical deficiencies were by no means so pronounced, as the majority of Allied tanks were roughly equal in performance to over two-thirds of the German vehicles they confronted. Second, even had the Allies been equipped with superior tanks, such as the A34 Comet or even a reliable Panther, it would have made little difference to battlefield performance and the outcome of set-piece operations. The prevailing tactical environment in Normandy and the doctrine and operational techniques adopted by 21st Army Group contributed far more to the difficulties encountered by Allied armoured units than technical weakness.

This is not to argue that technological inadequacy did not create problems, for it certainly did. The concern expressed in frontline reports and comments filtering back to 21st Army Group HQ and to Britain, in June especially, indicated the growing level of discomfort felt by crews and commanders. However, much of this was a result of the frustration felt by XXX Corps and 7th Armoured Division following *Operation Perch* and the debacle at Villers Bocage. Subsequent operations did indicate that problems existed but that they were not insurmountable and that other factors were at play in shaping the experiences of armoured forces in Normandy.

Nevertheless, technical failings did raise particular issues. Enhanced armour protection was unlikely to make any significant difference to the fighting, but the Sherman's reputation for 'brewing up' clearly did cause crews to abandon their tanks faster than they might otherwise have done. However, the most significant failing centred on the weakness of Allied tank armament, most obviously the 75 mm gun's lack of AP punch. Yet again, however, the real problems of operating tanks in Normandy came on the offensive, and the greatest difficulty centred on all-arms co-ordination and locating enemy armour. Improved weaponry would have alleviated this difficulty once the enemy had been pinned down, but its impact on solving the underlying problems of employing armour in Normandy in 1944 would have been limited. It should be noted that the tactical problems that befuddled the Allies were not easily solved by their opponents, and the SS and the *Heer* also suffered heavy armour losses when attempting counter-attacks, despite their supposedly superior tanks.

Ultimately, technical capability was only one cause of success or failure in the Second World War armoured operations. German tanks were inferior in many ways to Allied and Soviet armour in 1940 and 1941, yet they prevailed and achieved their battlefield objectives. A more complete explanation is required for German victories, and in a similar manner, technical deficiency, although an important factor in understanding the experiences and perceptions of Allied tank crews, is only one factor, and by no means the most important, in analysing the difficulties 21st Army Group faced in utilising its armour in 1944.

6

DESIGN AND PLANNING

'I feel the time has now come when we must certainly face the fact that British cruiser tank design and production has failed both in quality and in the time factor.'
Lt-Gen Sir John Fullerton Evetts, ACIGS, 11 September 1943[1]

Although the prevailing view that Allied tanks were overwhelmingly outclassed by their German counterparts in Normandy has been challenged elsewhere (see Chapter 5), there is little doubt that the armour available to 21st Army Group was not ideal. Shortcomings were apparent, most notably the weakness in Allied armoured firepower, and even though the reliable and dependable Shermans and Cromwells performed admirably in the exploitation phase from mid-August onwards, it was not until 1945 that truly competitive designs began to be introduced into frontline units. Ultimately, although the 'tank gap' was by no means as significant or as pronounced as claimed in some works, it remains the case that Allied tanks were deficient in a critical area, and any analysis of the employment of armour in Normandy requires this to be explained.

Indeed, it appears curious that while the Allies were able to seize notable technological leads in most areas of the war, they were palpably unable to achieve this for their armoured forces. When Allied tank crews looked into the skies during the summer of 1944 it would have become all too apparent that their comrades in the US 9th Air Force and the RAF's 2nd Tactical Air Force enjoyed technological superiority over the *Luftwaffe* as well as overwhelming numerical advantage. Indeed, whereas Spitfires, Mustangs and Thunderbolts dominated the skies over Europe, and had done so for many months prior to D-Day, it was not until the introduction of the A34 Comet and the A41 Centurion in the last months of the war, that British armoured units enjoyed the qualitative parity to complement their quantitative superiority.

Historians have offered many explanations for this. Ellis, in the official history of the northwest European campaign, indicates that the almost total equipment loss of 1940 was a key factor in the failure of British tank design in subsequent years, particularly 1940–42. For the British Army, in the dire post-Dunkirk era, any tank was better than none and with pressing need for armour in the Mediterranean theatre as well for home defence, output was boosted at the expense of design innovation and development, work which may have retarded production.[2] David Fletcher concurs to a degree but also questions the nature of British armour doctrine, as well as the whole apparatus for designing the tanks to support these requirements. He argues convincingly that because the British Army required separate tanks for distinct tasks, leading to cruisers, infantry support, light and even assault tanks, so the strain on the already weak design and production institutions was increased dramatically, further compounding the problem precipitated by the disaster of 1940.[3] The official history of the production of war materiel also argues that the shifting priorities of the General Staff, and the experience of war in the desert, skewed tank design and propelled it down a cul-de-sac.[4] Up to 1941–42 it had been believed that British tanks would principally engage enemy armour, but the experience of the fighting in North Africa led the General Staff to conclude that tanks needed to be able to deal with soft targets, such as infantry and anti-tanks guns as a priority. By the time of Normandy, when artillery was available in sufficient and appropriate quantity and mix, this emphasis placed on HE capability in Allied armoured forces was demonstrated to have been at the expense of anti-tank firepower. Alas, it was this inability of 21st Army Group tanks to deal with German armour that caused the most difficulty, for in 1944 it was the enemy's mechanised, armoured firepower that largely proved to be the undoing of Allied armour.[5]

A further concern that shaped tank development, and one that took priority over capability in the 1940–42 period, was mechanical soundness and reliability. Too many British tanks broke down before, during and after action and the faith of the crews in their equipment was severely dented by such lack of dependability. Consequently, efforts were put in hand to solve these problems ahead of enhancing armour protection and firepower. In the period of 1940–42 this consideration often took precedence over all others and it has been argued causing a delay in the development of more advanced models.

It has also been posited that British armour design and procurement was constricted by design dimensions which placed limitations on width and consequently weight of new vehicles. These restrictive design parameters were a consequence of the British railway transportation network, and resulted in smaller tanks unable to compete with the Tigers and Panthers that appeared from 1942 onwards.[6]

Ultimately, it could be argued that the whole design and development process failed British tank crews. In this vein, the most searing indictment has come from Peter Beale in *Death by Design*, wherein he is highly critical of the whole tank development structure. He catalogues a litany of failure dating back to the pre-war period and cites incompetence, intransigence and political and moral weakness as the key reasons behind the failure of British armour production and development.[7]

However, these explanations are not in themselves enough. Criticism of British tank design and development is due, but can only offer a partial insight. Indeed, the most numerous tank deployed by 21st Army Group in Normandy was the US-designed Sherman, by no means a product of British failings, though arguably the reliance on the M4 was a consequence of the shortcomings of British production (see next chapter). Better-quality British armour did emerge in the last year of the war, and the A34 Comet and A41 Centurion were the equal of, and possibly superior to, anything likely to be encountered in the German inventory. Indeed, the Comet was little more advanced in design principles than the Cromwell it replaced and could quite easily have been developed much earlier than it was. Moreover, the later versions of the Churchill infantry support tank also carried more armour than the infamous Tiger I, though its narrow turret ring prevented it from carrying a powerful gun. These factors imply that the design and development procedures were not in themselves inadequate but were perhaps mismanaged or misdirected.

Still further, a highly effective weapon in the 17-pdr gun was available from the midpoint of the war and the intention had always been to mount it on a tank. To supplement this, by 1944 innovation in ammunition design and ample supply of appropriate materials had delivered to the Allies a distinct advantage over the Germans, with the introduction of the APDS round.

Nevertheless, it is clear that certain issues did impede British tank design and contributed to the shortcomings inherent in the equipment deployed in Normandy. However, there has yet to be a convincing and complete explanation of why this came to be and it is surely not enough to highlight moral weakness.[8] Moreover, by focusing on inadequate firepower as being the most serious shortcoming of 21st Army Group's tanks, the consequences of the design and procurement process can be placed in context. As has been stated above, it is simply not enough to argue, as indeed some have, that because Anglo-Canadian armour was to a greater or lesser extent technologically inferior, such short-comings therefore had an obvious, immediate and deleterious impact on operational capability. The design process's failures were only relevant where they shaped the conduct of the campaign, and it was only in certain cases that they did so.

It should also be kept in mind throughout the following discussion that the British design process contributed only 25–30 per cent of the tanks deployed by 21st Army Group in the Normandy campaign, though Sherman Fireflies carried the British 17-pdr gun.[9] Despite the fact that it was, in part, the inability of British industry to provide reliable and effective armour in the first years of the war that prompted the greater use of US-designed equipment, it should still be noted that until the arrival of the M26 Pershing tank in the spring of 1945, American designs were no more advanced than British models available in Normandy the previous year. Indeed, it could be argued that denied the 17-pdr gun, US tank crews were in a worse position than their Anglo-Canadian colleagues, and it was fortunate that Allied strategy called upon 2nd British and 1st Canadian Armies, rather than Bradley's forces, to lock horns with the bulk of German armour in June, July and August 1944.

Policy, specification and design

British armour development in the Second World War was, in the pre-production stages, shaped by a variety of key influences, all of which played a significant role in determining the armour designs produced. Prior to production of a specified tank, four distinct factors can be detected as having come into play in moulding the developmental process: prevailing armoured doctrine, operational experience, intelligence on enemy armour and basic design principles and limitations.

Doctrine

The type and model of tank desired by the British Army during the Second World War was clearly and obviously driven by the manner in which such vehicles would and should be deployed and utilised. Unfortunately, there was a good deal of confusion among the General Staff as to how tanks ought to be used and what their precise battlefield role should be. This was still not resolved by the time of the Normandy campaign, and the ebb and flow of the various concepts of armoured doctrine prior to 1944 pushed design work in differing directions, often dissipating effort, placing a still greater strain on an already overburdened body of designers and manufacturers.

Prior to and during the opening phase of the war, British armoured doctrine called for the construction and deployment of three distinct types of tank to fulfil particular battlefield roles: the light tank, the cruiser and the infantry support tank. The light tank, armed with machine guns, was intended for reconnaissance and scouting duties and could be used in supporting roles as and when required.[10] In the early stages of the Second World War, the British Vickers Mark VI generally fulfilled this role, but by the time of Normandy 21st Army Group was employing American-built M3/5 Honeys. The light tank proved to be of limited value and as the war had progressed it became increasingly clear that it was being supplanted by fast cruiser tanks, and more notably by the emergence of better-quality armoured cars. As early as 1938, the long-term demise of the light tank was forecast, and throughout the war the General Staff passed up the opportunity to develop a new specification for the type, effectively allowing it to fade from the scene.[11] Nevertheless, in *The Armoured Division in Battle*, a pamphlet produced by 21st Army Group in December 1944, Montgomery still saw a role for the light tank, though this in fact equated to a vehicle capable of fulfilling such tasks as armed reconnaissance.[12] In 1944, some regiments even deployed the Honey without its turret and 37 mm gun, thus rendering it little more than a tracked, lightly armoured reconnaissance vehicle, a far cry from the original concept of the light tank.[13] Ultimately, although light tanks continued to play a minor role in Normandy, their overall numbers were small and the use of such tanks courted little controversy.

Of much greater significance was the doctrinal debate centred on the necessity or otherwise of maintaining two principal roles for armour during the Second World War. This disagreement between various elements within the design and development structure over the relative value of cruiser and infantry support tanks impacted on the types available, and employment of, armour in 1944. The debate on the employment of 21st Army Group tank formations in Normandy has been dealt with in detail elsewhere (see Chapters 3 and 4), but the controversy also shaped the manner in which design and development of tanks progressed in Britain prior to *Operation Overlord*.

In 1939 there was considerable confusion over the specific needs and requirements of armoured forces in the British Army. The debate over the variety of tank types required had been ongoing throughout much of the interwar period. In October 1936 four types were identified by the War Office: the light tank for the cavalry; a cruiser tank (in part derived from observations of Soviet armour); a medium tank for the hitting role alongside the cruisers in the tank brigades; and an infantry support tank for close co-operation with infantry formations.[14] However, difficulties had been encountered in the development of a true medium tank intended for shock action since escalating costs had caused suspension of such work in 1932. When in 1937 rearmament programmes began again in earnest, weakness in design expertise and the lack of an effective purpose-built power plant undermined the medium tank still further.[15] Consequently, the concept of the medium tank was subsumed by the development of the cruiser in the late 1930s, though the abandonment of the former was not a reflection of changing doctrinal attitudes but of an acceptance of inadequacies in design and production.

By the opening phase of the Second World War, therefore, the General Staff essentially saw a requirement for two principal types of tank, in addition to the light model.[16] An infantry support tank with heavy armour and machine gun/HE firepower was deemed necessary for close support of infantry actions, and a cruiser tank with anti-tank firepower coupled with greater speed bought at the expense of armour protection, was considered essential for the exploitation stage of operations. In July 1942, the Tank Board, the Ministry of Supply body co-ordinating and monitoring armour design and production, reiterated this division in the perceived role and types of armour required for operations, and planned accordingly.[17] This dichotomy, partly born out of the failure to develop a viable medium tank, therefore persisted well into the war and was to cause much friction from early 1943 onwards between Montgomery and the War Office, as the former saw little need for two distinct types and wanted a standardised 'capital' tank capable of fulfilling both infantry support and exploitation roles. By January 1943, Montgomery was sure that the M4 Sherman was the nearest the Allies had to such a tank, it being superior to anything British industry had thus far produced.[18] This thinking reflected his attitude to the employment of armour and his view that an armoured brigade should be flexible enough to fulfil either role on the battlefield. When he learned that the Churchill was still in full development, and that production was due to gather momentum, he complained that those responsible for AFV design in Britain were not listening to operational commanders.[19] The War Office in part demurred. In April 1943 they accepted that in the long term a single heavy cruiser tank was desirable but reiterated again in September that the requirements of the cruiser and the infantry tank were for the moment incompatible, both in an available design and production sense, but also at a doctrinal level.[20] Much of this hinged on the belief that a tank such as the Sherman was too vulnerable to enemy fire at close range to act successfully as a close-support infantry tank.[21] Consequently, a slow but heavily armoured tank such as the Churchill was deemed necessary to meet this latter need, a desire underpinned in September 1943 by the Organisation and Weapons Policy Committee in a statement on the General Staff's policy on tanks.[22] Churchill himself concurred with this, though from a political viewpoint, arguing:

> We shall, I am sure, be exposed to criticism if we are found with a great mass of thin-skinned tanks of medium size, none of which can stand up to the German guns of 1943, still less those of 1944.[23]

In Normandy, it could easily be argued that the Churchill tank proved itself when the fighting bogged down and that this supported the War Office's view. Many crews were more than grateful for the resisting power of the later Churchill's six inches plus armour protection.[24] Moreover, the Americans had also identified the necessity for a heavily armoured close-support tank to work with the infantry, rather than relying on the more thinly skinned existing types of M4s. The M4A3E2 Jumbo with frontal armour ranging from 102 mm to 178 mm was introduced in July 1944 as an interim compromise.[25] Montgomery, however, never one to admit an error or misjudgement, subsequently claimed that the Churchill's weaknesses were exposed in the pursuit to Belgium when the tank's lack of speed proved to be a considerable hindrance.[26]

However, although it is clear that doctrine played a key role in defining the type of tank required and then employed by the British Army in the Second World War, most obviously in the requirements for a cruiser and an infantry tank, the ongoing debate over whether a need existed for two distinct tank types played little part in shaping the tanks available to 21st Army Group in northwest Europe in 1944. The tanks employed in Normandy still fitted to the concepts of 1940 in that a cruiser (be it Sherman or Cromwell) and an infantry tank (Churchill) were deployed. This thinking persisted long enough into the war to define the tank models available for *Operation Overlord*, and despite Montgomery's efforts to evade the use of Churchills in Normandy, he was constrained by decisions made years before that an infantry tank was both required and would be deployed. However, it should of course be noted that Montgomery's views on doctrine certainly influenced the employment of available armour, even when this ran contrary to the developmental concepts underlying the equipment's design.

Operational experience

However, although the parameters had already been established over the desirability of separate cruiser and infantry tanks, and these would continue to drive development throughout the war, the influence of in-theatre experiences and field commanders' comments were also important factors in determining the nature of the tanks being developed. The relative value and desirable features of infantry and cruiser tanks were markedly shaped by operations and actions against the enemy, though the conclusions gleaned from such information were often conflicting, misleading and at variance with doctrine, particularly at the tactical level.

What did become clear from the experience of France in 1940 was that the proportion of cruisers to infantry tanks was likely to be askew in the foreseeable future, with too much emphasis hitherto having been placed on the latter. Britain's strategic position following the collapse of France dictated that a heavily armoured assault tank to aid any breaching of the Siegfried Line was now a low priority and the likely theatres of action were to be the Middle East and North Africa, where cruisers would be much more useful than their slower infantry tank cousins. Consequently, although doctrine and battle experience had only limited impact on the types of tanks to be produced in the UK, be they cruiser or infantry, they did begin to shape the desired proportions and essential features.[27] It was a matter of some regret to the RAC in late 1940, that in the near future there would be a considerable shortfall in the number of available cruisers, and that infantry types, already ordered and being produced, would have to be pressed into service in the armoured divisions, rather than operating solely with the tank brigades, these latter units being envisaged as support formations for the infantry divisions.[28] The inability of British industry to produce sufficient cruiser tanks, it being geared up more to infantry tank production, was a cause of some concern until 1942, when US types, particularly the M4 Sherman, began to arrive in quantity. With 8th Army experience influencing doctrine to the degree that by 1943 Montgomery saw no significant role or need for infantry tanks, the continuing production of such types, most notably the A22 Churchill, was to be a cause of some friction.[29]

Nevertheless, operational experience delivered a good many views on the weaknesses and failings of British tanks in action, and two key themes continually recurred. The first and most critical problem concerned reliability, while the second, an issue upon which views ebbed and flowed repeatedly, was firepower. The greatest contributing factor to operational British tank losses in France 1940 was not enemy action but mechanical failure, both among the cruisers and the infantry support tanks.[30] To a significant extent this was 'largely due to the refusal of manufacturers to produce spare parts [in sufficient quantities] with new productions of tanks', a difficulty only partly alleviated in the post-France environment by the crews' mechanical know-how.[31] However, the problem of mechanical reliability was to persist well into the period of the Mediterranean campaign, and on one occasion 100 Valentine tanks went into operation without any spare parts at all to back them up.[32] In May 1941 the Army Council deplored the high breakdown rates of British cruiser tanks in North Africa, and this problem continued to plague both Wavell's and Auchinleck's tenure of command in the Middle East.[33] When new models of tanks appeared, such as the Crusader and the Churchill, they also proved unreliable, further tarnishing the reputation of British-built tanks in the eyes of the frontline crews.[34] It was not until later versions of the Cromwell and Churchill were introduced from the end of 1943 onwards that tankers' faith in British produced equipment began to be re-established.

The reliability crisis in British tanks emerged fully in 1941, even to the extent of bypassing considerations over armour and firepower as the principal quality desired in a tank by the General Staff. Initially, the experience of 1940 and early campaigning against the Italians indicated that strong armour was the key factor in enhancing battlefield survivability, as evidenced by the success of the Matilda II infantry tank.[35] Yet unreliability became the predominant worry as the German 88 mm gun began to defeat the Matilda's armour protection, and thus attention was focused on the tank's tendency to break down in large numbers, before, during and after action. This was in turn seriously hampering training, as units became reluctant to use their tanks in anything but combat against the enemy.[36] Even so, 7RTR reported considerable loss of Matildas to mechanical breakdown within just three days of going into action against the Italians in December 1940.[37]

The demand for dependability intensified in 1941 as evidence began to mount that British armoured forces were now seriously compromised by mechanical unreliability. In May, emphasis had been placed on armour and armament ahead of reliability as desirable qualities in the design of future tanks, but in January 1942, Lt-Gen Ronald Weeks, Director-General of Army Equipment, informed the Tank Board that in the light of reports from the Middle East, mechanical soundness was now of pressing concern, ahead of sheer quantity.[38] By September this had been codified by the General Staff into a list of desirable qualities in tanks which placed reliability firmly at the head. Significantly, armour protection was now fifth on this list of six prioritised factors, and the greatest urgency focused on delivering reliable, high-quality vehicles.[39] It is a curious and telling statement that reliability was considered so crucial in a list of desirable qualities, for it is an obvious point that equipment should function as intended. Yet by 1942 the experience of war had demonstrated that the British tank industry had to solve a basic problem; quite pointedly, the British Army required tanks which did not persistently break down.

Yet by 1944 the problem had all but disappeared. The British tanks deployed from late 1943 onwards, predominantly Cromwells and Churchills, developed reputations for ease of maintenance, reliability and good logistical support.[40] Concern over the initial versions of these tanks had in effect dissipated by the time of *Operation Overlord* and crews, whilst critical of some facets of their tanks, rarely complained about reliability. In many ways the reliability issue was born of the pressing need to push any tank into service in 1940–42, and thus rushed programmes, and inadequate designs precipitated on to the battlefield equipment that was simply not up to the task, not only in terms of theoretical capability, but in mechanical reliability. By 1943, however, issues of technological capacity were re-emerging and it was these, rather than reliability concerns, that were to provoke much more concern in Normandy.

Firepower was the most significant issue to develop alongside dependability from the experience of the battlefield prior to the Normandy campaign. Views and opinions on the nature and primary capabilities of the armament to be fitted to British tanks varied and changed as experience of battle, largely in North Africa, developed and opinions crystallised. Although a straightforward desire emerged to equip tanks with ever larger guns, from the 2-pdr through the 6-pdr, ultimately to the 17-pdr, the most significant lessons gleaned from operational experience centred on the key role played by tank armament. Here there was a significant shift in emphasis between 1940 and 1942, and then a further reorientation between 1943 and 1944. The latter of these came too late to shape the Normandy campaign significantly, but its influence could be clearly seen in the crash programme to fit the 17-pdr gun to the Sherman, the pressure to introduce discarding sabot ammunition, and the squabble that developed over the failure of the Cromwell to take the new HV 75 mm gun designed by Vickers.

In 1940, the theoretical capabilities of Allied firepower were such that no significant problem was perceived either then or in the near future. The 2-pdr anti-tank gun had performed more than adequately in France and was easily able to defeat the armour of the German panzers then deployed against them. The 2-pdr was also superior to the German 37 mm anti-tank gun, being able to penetrate some 50 per cent more armour (approximately 40 mm) at 1,000 yards.[41] The British tanks had been undone by many factors, most obviously lack of numbers and mechanical breakdowns, but weak armour protection and inadequate firepower did not figure seriously in post-campaign thinking.[42]

Nevertheless, the RAC noted that the *Heer* were now obviously well aware of the inferior firepower of German tank and anti-tank guns and that in order to maintain their lead the British would have to focus on upgrading from the 2-pdr to the 6-pdr, and begin developing a new HV tank weapon, which ultimately became the 17-pdr.[43] However, the pressing need for numbers of tanks, and the perception that the 2-pdr was at least adequate informed decision-making, shaping the development of armoured firepower in the period following 1940. Emphasis was squarely placed on the immediate production of functional tanks, and in the summer of 1940 there was little reason to stall this in favour of enhancing armoured firepower. Ultimately, largely because of these decisions, it was to take until 1942 for the 2-pdr's replacement, the 6-pdr to appear in an operational tank.

The 6-pdr gun had been in development since 1938, and it had always been envisaged that it would be tank-mounted as well as being deployed in a towed version.[44] However, the General Staff showed little interest in the project until the outbreak of war and it was not until the spring of 1940 that the 6-pdr was adopted for future employment. It is worth noting that a stumbling block came in the autumn of 1939 when the General Staff pressed for a weapon capable of defeating 70 mm of armour at over 500 yards. The Ordnance Board reported that this would require a weapon of similar size and capability to the cumbersome 3.7-inch anti-aircraft gun, and the General Staff were forced to settle on the 6-pdr. Even then, however, it was found that the 6-pdr could not be fitted to the latest types of cruisers then in development.[45] Nevertheless, it should be noted that the General Staff were well aware that the adoption of the 6-pdr was desirable in 1940–41, but that to do so would require the considerable curtailment of 2-pdr production at a time when the British Army was desperately short of AFVs and anti-tank equipment.[46] Consequently, as the 2-pdr seemed competitive in 1940, the pressure to switch to the 6-pdr was by no means intense.

This decision was to hinder the development of tanks with superior hitting power for the next two years, but it was a second factor that served to create the armament shortfall of Normandy more than any other. The 2-pdr was certainly effective against the 1940–41 generation of panzers at medium-to-close range, but its shortcomings were ruthlessly exposed by the North African campaign and it was the experience of this that shaped the decisions made over tank armament in the period 1942–43. The critical factor centred on the lack of an effective HE shell for the 2-pdr. In the open terrain of North Africa, engagements took place at much longer ranges and the tactical advantage rested with the static anti-tank gun over the tank. Moreover, experience demonstrated that the tank's primary task in Egypt and Libya was firing at 'soft' targets, such as infantry, anti-tank guns and soft-skin vehicles, which naturally required HE capability, something lacking in the 2-pdr. This had a still further knock-on effect in requiring field artillery units of 25-pdrs to engage enemy soft targets, most notably anti-tank guns, as British tanks were incapable of so doing, short of running over them or using their machine guns. Unfortunately, the British found it particularly difficult to co-ordinate armour and artillery

144

closely enough, and when in 1941 new more heavily armoured versions of the Panzer III and Panzer IV began to arrive in Africa, the 2-pdr, already struggling to hit enemy tanks at long range, now struggled to penetrate them at all. Consequently, the task of stopping the panzers then fell on to the 25-pdrs in a direct fire role, taking them away from indirect fire support duties, most obviously against enemy anti-tank guns.[47] This exacerbated the problems facing Allied armour, as they were now more vulnerable than ever to German anti-tank guns against which they could still do little.

Experience of the desert war therefore indicated that tank armament needed to be dual purpose – capable of engaging enemy armour when required (though the Germans seemed to be able to knock out Allied armour predominantly with their anti-tank guns) but for much of the time to act against soft targets, again mirroring the Germans. However, when the 6-pdr arrived in service in 1942, it did not fit the bill. Although the gun's much superior anti-tank capability endeared it to the army, like the 2-pdr it also did not come with HE capability.[48] Consequently, the weapon of choice among British units became in 1942 the US designed dual-purpose MV 75 mm gun, an effective weapon for engaging soft targets, but one inferior to the 6-pdr in the anti-tank role and only barely capable of dealing with the latest Panzer IVs. Nevertheless, it came fitted to the M3 Grant tank and, by late 1942, to the even better M4 Sherman, both of which were reliable and superior to anything thus far developed by the British.

The influence of the MV 75 mm gun and its superior HE capability was significant. In mid-1942 General Staff policy posited that any future tank armament should be, as a top priority, a first-class anti-tank weapon. Its ability against soft targets was of secondary, though still crucial importance.[49] Indeed, the RAC regarded the diminution of armour protection as the likely consequence of further enhancement of anti-armour firepower, but that this was a price worth paying to maintain at least parity and hopefully regain superiority over German armoured firepower.[50] However, by the end of 1942, a revised policy was in place, one that was effectively to dictate the tank armament available to units in Normandy. The General Staff, influenced by reports from North Africa and Montgomery's views, shifted the emphasis towards armament that should be, as a first concern, an effective HE weapon, with its anti-armour capacity being capable of dealing only with 'enemy armour of the type so far encountered in this war'.[51] This did not readily allow for the possible enhancement of German armour protection, which of course is exactly what was to occur over the 18 months leading up to D-Day. The War Office ratified this change in policy and claimed that it would seek to facilitate the production of the US 75 mm gun in Britain as soon as possible.[52] It had already been accepted in November that the 75 mm was superior to the 6-pdr and should be adopted as the first-choice weapon.[53]

By February 1943 tank armament policy appeared to have been firmly established. The MV 75 mm gun was to equip 60 per cent of British employed tanks in 1944 with 30 per cent to be fitted with the most potent anti-armour weapon then available, meaning the 6-pdr in the short term, and possibly the new Vickers-designed HV 75 mm gun, the US 76 mm or even the much bigger 17-pdr in the long term. Finally, the remaining 10 per cent would carry the new 95 mm howitzer for specialised close-support duties.[54] There is little doubt that the faith placed in the dual-purpose MV 75 mm gun had emerged principally as a result of operational experience in the desert. To the 8th Army, enjoying great success in the autumn of 1942, the introduction of the M4 Sherman and its 75 mm gun had solved all its problems, and there seemed no reason why standardising on that tank did seem entirely logical. By February 1943 it had been established that the new A27 cruiser tank, Cromwell, could also carry the MV 75 mm gun and it later began to supersede the 6-pdr in that vehicle.[55] The Churchill infantry tank followed suit and it was clear that by the time of D-Day in 1944, the great majority of tanks in British units would be carrying the 75 mm gun. Nevertheless, as will be explored below, the debate was by no means over in the spring of 1943, though the operational experience of the North African campaign had played its role in driving policy in the direction of adopting the 75 mm as first-choice weapon.

However, although there was enthusiastic endorsement of the 75 mm gun, the RAC, the War Office and the Tank Board all recognised that there was a need to introduce superior firepower when possible to meet the requirement that 30 per cent of Allied tanks should have top-class anti-armour capability and two programmes were in hand to facilitate this. First, the 17-pdr was to be fitted to a new cruiser, A30 Challenger, and second, it was planned that the Cromwell would ultimately be equipped with the new Vickers-designed HV 75 mm gun, a weapon that would combine great hitting power with good HE capability. However, both plans failed, the latter completely (see Chapter 7), and when it became apparent in 1943 that the Germans were moving further ahead still in AFV armour protection and firepower, the shortcomings of the MV 75 mm gun began to ring alarm bells.

Intelligence

A third factor that shaped the development of British tanks was the knowledge or otherwise of what the enemy was or may be about to deploy against Allied armour, then or in the future. In particular, this was to cause great concern in 1943 when information began to dribble back to Britain about the new big German cats – Tiger and Panther. Hitherto, tank production policy in the UK had for much of 1940–42 been based upon replacing the heavy losses incurred in France as quickly as possible.[56] Moreover, intelligence and after action analyses had implied that some British tanks, reliability aside, were at least a match if not superior to those in the German inventory during the French campaign of 1940. Therefore, the assumption was made that the British would be given time to develop new equipment whilst relying on older, capable designs in the interim.

However, in 1941 it was becoming clear that the Germans had reacted quickly to make good their technical deficiencies exposed the previous summer, and the superiority enjoyed by some British tanks quickly began to ebb away. MI 10 reports issued to the War Office indicated as 1941 progressed that the Panzer III was now being equipped with the more potent 50 mm gun rather than the 37 mm, and that by the end of the year the Germans would begin introducing into service a range of new 75 mm guns. Most worryingly, in 1942 a new 75 mm gun began to be fitted to the Panzer IV, which, coupled with enhanced armour made it a most formidable tank.[57] This version of the Panzer IV, known to the Allies as the Mark IV Special, completely outclassed anything until the arrival of the M4 Sherman in the autumn of 1942.[58] The Panzer IV would be upgraded still further in 1943–44 when an improved 75 mm gun with enhanced hitting power was fitted and further armour protection added. These H and J models formed the backbone of the *Panzerwaffe* in Normandy and were similar in performance to the Shermans and Cromwells confronting them. Notably, both the Panzer III and IV were originally designed in the 1930s with only moderately stressed suspensions to emphasise speed. This allowed considerable increase in weight once operational experience had demonstrated that armour protection was inadequate. Moreover, the design principles of German tanks differed in that the turret rings were wide enough to allow substantial armament upgrades when once again battle proved that enhanced firepower was required.[59] In addition, German armament development took into account the requirement to fire HE shells, as it was clear from experience that dealing with soft targets was a high priority in modern armoured warfare.[60] In August 1942, the War Office argued that the Germans had learned a good deal from the Spanish Civil War and by operating throughout a variety of theatres from the onset of the Second World War. Somewhat grudgingly, they also conceded that German armour superiority was attained by 'good design and planning'.[61]

Matching and surpassing the capabilities of the Mark IV Special was therefore the priority confronting the Allies in the autumn of 1942, and the arrival of the M4 Sherman seemed to meet this need. In addition, British production, focused on the new A27 Cromwell cruiser, the A22 Churchill infantry tank, and the introduction of the 17-pdr and HV 75 mm guns sometime in 1943, seemed to support the future enhancement of Allied armour. However, the War Office and MI 10 also warned in August 1942 that the capacity of the Panzer IV to be further upgraded was now exhausted and 'that the time was near when a new [enemy] tank must come into the field'.[62]

A further innovation detected by the Allies in 1942 was the increasing use by the Germans of SP equipment.[63] This saw the mounting of heavier guns on obsolescent tank chassis in non-traversable armoured fighting compartments rather than orthodox turrets. Two versions of SP equipment were in place by the midpoint of the war – the assault gun or tank hurter, in which the vehicle was relatively well armoured and intended for close support against soft targets and/or long-range sniping at tanks, and the mounted anti-tank gun, a lightly armoured vehicle designed specifically for long-range engagement of enemy armour. In both cases the growing employment of these weapons by the Germans potentially weakened the value of Allied armour. Towed anti-tank guns, hitherto vulnerable to Allied artillery, were now much less so when mounted on vehicles and placed in even semi-armoured fighting compartments. Consequently the amount and value of heavy, yet mobile anti-tank firepower on the battlefield was significantly increased, and the future operating environment for Allied armour was therefore likely to be seriously compromised, especially in close terrain and in a restricted geographical area, both of which pertained to Normandy.[64]

The most famous of these SP guns, the Sturmgeschütz or Stug III, was produced in great quantities and provided close support for infantry units and effective anti-tank capability when necessary. Indeed, by 1944 Stugs were being used as tank destroyers in place of scarcer dedicated designs.[65] In a defensive posture, the Stug assault gun was ideal, though its limited traverse was an inconvenience, especially when advancing. The Germans had recognised that as firepower was the crucial factor in armoured warfare, and that they may well be defending previous gains, the Stug compromise was a cost-effective measure.[66] By late 1943 and 1944 it was apparent to the Allies that the latest types of 88 mm guns were being mounted on Panzer IV chassis, though the fighting compartment was open topped and lightly armoured (the Nashorn), and even on the new Panther.[67] This latter example, the Jagdpanther, saw the extremely potent Kwk 43 88 mm gun fitted into a sloped and heavily armoured fighting compartment.[68] However, worrying as these developments were to the Allies, they were manifestations of over-kill as Allied tanks were already vulnerable enough to the 75 mm gun, rendering the late 88 mm and the later Jagdtiger's 128 mm guns somewhat unnecessary.[69] In any case, such equipment was not encountered until it was too late to influence the development of Allied armour deployed in Normandy.

The next generation of German tanks, the Mark V Panther, first encountered by the Allies in 1943, and the Mark VI Tiger, met in Tunisia in late 1942, was a significant advance on previous types. The Tiger, although more orthodox in design, supposedly posed the greater threat, being heavily armoured all round to such a degree that the MV 75 mm gun could not defeat it at anything other than very close range. The Tiger also carried a powerful KwK 36 88 mm gun, based on the anti-aircraft weapon that had been pressed into an anti-armour role in 1940, and had subsequently dominated the battlefields of the western desert. It could destroy any Allied tank at any likely battle range. Although rumours dated back to 1941, the British first became aware of the Tiger's existence in the frontline in November 1942, and in December greater information on the tank's capabilities began to emerge.[70] Indeed, in that month the Germans initiated a propaganda campaign by publishing a photograph in *National Zeitung* of a Tiger in Tunis, and by

January 1943 the British had a fairly accurate idea of the Tiger's specifications.[71] A field report drawn up by two tank experts from the Weapons Technical Staff, Field Force (WTS, FF), indicated that in spite of the hyperbole, the 6-pdr could penetrate the frontal armour of the Tiger at up to 300 yards, and more importantly claimed that the flanks were particularly vulnerable.[72] On 21 April 1943, a Tiger was captured intact by the Allies. It was examined closely in Tunisia, by Winston Churchill and King George VI no less, along with the technical teams, but it took until October of that year for the tank to arrive back in Britain and be fully assessed by the School of Tank Technology at Chertsey.[73]

However, although in theory the emergence of the Tiger might have set alarm bells ringing, initial impressions of the Tiger in action were not such as to cause undue panic. An MI 10 report of 12 August 1943 indicated that though the Tiger was worthy in some ways, it was also a compromise, and an unimpressive one at that. The attempt to combine invulnerable heavy armour with armament superior to any opposing weaponry was not successful, the report claimed, principally because the Tiger would be vulnerable 'to anti-tank weapons now in the development stage', presumably meaning the 17-pdr and the new sabot anti-tank round.[74] Importantly, the report asserted that mass production of such a complicated piece of engineering was not feasible, certainly not alongside any significant medium tank programme.

However, the RAC took a slightly different view, one tinged with a serious note of caution. In a paper for the General Staff on tank policy, Maj-Gen Raymond Briggs, Director, Royal Armoured Corps (DRAC), argued with some prescience that the Tigers defeated in Tunisia had been used poorly by the Germans and that well handled in defence '... it may well prove a problem to which we have not yet the answer'. He also raised the spectre of the effect on the morale of Allied tanks crews if they had to confront an adversary against which they were close on impotent.[75] After some discussion it was agreed that amendments to tank policy should be proposed, including the development of a heavy tank to rival the Tiger and more importantly, a re-emphasis on HV weaponry.[76] The Organisation and Weapons Policy Committee therefore recommended that the new Vickers HV 75 mm gun be properly adopted, and that this be further supplemented by the 17-pdr. In addition, they pressed for the abandonment of the War Cabinet Defence Committee's policy that all current weapons programmes had to bear fruit by the end of 1944 in order to be of any use in the current war. It was contended that this policy was hindering the development of modern tank designs, especially those likely to provide equipment capable of defeating the new heavy German tanks. Almost certainly this was in part dictated by growing concern over the likely problems to be encountered in northwest Europe in 1944 if consideration were not given over to coping with the Tiger.[77]

The Panther, or Panzer Mark V, did not elicit the same kind of interest in Britain as the Tiger, even when more information began to become available.

First intelligence on the nature of the specification of the Panther had been uncovered in 1942, but it was June of the following year before more complete information was available.[78] The same sanguine MI 10 August 1943 report on the Tiger also discussed the Panther, but did so in much less detail. Nevertheless, it was stated that the Panther would carry significantly increased armour protection to the Mark IV, perhaps up to the level of the Tiger, would sport a HV weapon, and would emphasise speed and manoeuvrability.[79] A further report in October compared the Panther to the Soviet T-34 and implied that it would be a formidable opponent.[80] However, as late as June 1944 the RAC was still calling urgently for information on battle experience against the Panther, and it was only in that month that officials from the DTD were able to study a captured Panther in detail.[81]

It was clear by the late summer of 1943 that a new generation of German tanks was being phased in, a generation that on paper appeared to outclass anything the Allies currently fielded. Moreover, the emphasis placed on the MV 75 mm gun in late 1942 now began to look unsound. The reports and intelligence gathered on the Tiger and Panther indicated that superior armour penetration power would be required, though it was the RAC that began to realise this and push for further and faster development of 17-pdr and HV 75 mm-equipped AFVs and new sabot ammunition. Indeed, contrary to some views, the RAC was not caught out by the Normandy campaign and had been disseminating data and warnings relating to the difficulties likely to be encountered in northwest Europe for months leading up to D-Day. At a conference held at the War Office in April 1944 concerning AFV policy, a variety of 21st Army Group armoured formations commanders, such as Erskine (7th Armoured Division) and Roberts (11th Armoured Division), made it quite clear that they were aware of the difficulties ahead in Normandy.[82] The eventual and most effective response, and indeed the only realistic one in the limited time available, proved to be the M4 Sherman Firefly, for it was now too late to press anything else into service in time for *Operation Overlord*. However, this was not entirely down to decisions made in late 1942, for it was also to a significant degree due to the failure or weakness of other construction programmes, such as the A30 Challenger, and the inability to fit the HV 75 mm into the A27 Cromwell.

However, it is also evident that operational experience from the desert wrong footed the British in 1942 and early 1943, and by the time it became apparent that anti-armour punching power had been overly sacrificed in order to standardise on the MV 75 mm gun, too much time had been lost to make good the deficiency.

Design principles and limitations

A key argument posed by a number of writers seeking an explanation for the weakness of British tanks in the era of the Second World War has been that designers had to conform to a series of restrictive size and weight limitations, parameters essentially imposed by the British railway loading gauge. This was nothing to do with the distance between the rail tracks, but was governed by the narrow bridges and tunnels in Britain constructed in the early development of the rail network. Such dimensions restricted the size of British engines and rolling stock, and consequently impacted proportionally upon their ability to carry large vehicles, such as tanks, beyond a certain size.[83] However, because of the high levels of wear and tear imposed by road travel on tanks, the War Office insisted that all tanks should be rail transportable, without having to disassemble them.[84] Consequently, all British tanks designed prior to 1939 were restricted in width to eight feet nine inches, though this was subsequently eased to nine feet six inches allowing the Churchill to be developed. This restriction in turn had the effect of restricting length, and ultimately weight. The former was restricted as increases in the length of a tank have to be matched by proportional increases in width, otherwise the tank becomes difficult to steer; overly long caterpillar-track-driven vehicles would not be sufficiently manoeuvrable on the battlefield.

Obviously, this therefore impacted on the weight of the tank as only so much armour, engine and armament could be loaded on to a body less than ten feet wide and high. In theory, this therefore created a disadvantage for British tanks from the midpoint of the war onwards as continental railways could carry larger rolling stock (the continental express railway traffic width is ten feet six inches) and thus larger tanks, allowing the Germans to build vehicles with heavier armour and larger armament still capable of being transported by railway. It should be noted, however, that neither the Tiger nor the Panther conformed to the continental loading gauge, with special measures having to be taken to transport these heavier vehicles about Europe. British designs had to conform to the loading gauge until the War Office abandoned the restriction in March 1942, recognising that road transporters were the only obvious long-term solution to the problem. This decision was taken far too late to influence the designs available in Normandy, for both the A22 Churchill and the A27 Cromwell had been built to specifications laid down prior to the War Office's policy change. Indeed, although the original width allowance of eight feet nine inches had been increased by some nine inches to accommodate the Churchill on a restricted selection of railway lines, and the tank's weight had increased to some 40 tons, its dimensions were still governed by the railway restrictions. The A34 Comet, which arrived in service in late 1944, was the first British tank to benefit from the abandonment of the gauge limitation.[85]

The impact of this restriction on the width of rail transportable AFVs was, therefore, a potentially limiting factor in the armour protection afforded to British tanks, and a possible explanation for their inability to mount new, larger armament as their turret diameters, restricted by the width of the tank, were too narrow.[86] The new Vickers HV 75 mm gun could not be fitted to the A27 Cromwell, for example, and the 40-ton A22 Churchill could not take the 17-pdr, because of the narrow diameters of the respective turret rings. In both cases contemporary and competing German tanks could upgrade or carry larger weapons, gaining a critical advantage. As Allied tanks were principally outperformed in firepower in Normandy, it has been argued that this was a serious and crucial consequence of the railway loading gauge policy imposed on British tank designers.[87]

However, this is an incomplete and misleading view of the situation. The notion that German tank armament was continually upgraded whilst British tanks did not follow suit, and that this was caused by narrow turret rings, is not entirely supported by the evidence. It is the case that the Panzer III had its armament upped from a 37 mm to a 50 mm, while the Panzer IV increased from a low-velocity 75 mm gun to a HV longer-barrelled 75 mm weapon, but in comparison the British tanks deployed in Normandy had had their armaments increased since 1942 from a 2-pdr, through the 6-pdr and up to the 75 mm in the case of the Churchill, and from the 6-pdr to the 75 mm in the case of the Cromwell. Moreover, the Germans mounted 75 mm guns on the Panzer III chassis only by stripping out the turret and replacing it with a non-traversable armoured compartment, creating the Sturmgeschütz assault gun.

Nevertheless, although British tanks did receive upgrades to their armament, it was also the case that the limitations on their capacity to be upgraded were greater than their similarly sized German contemporaries. Ultimately, the Panzer IV was able to mount a HV weapon, the L/48 l75 mm gun, which was some 153.6 inches long, whereas the Cromwell's limitation was a gun somewhat shorter than 136 inches, the length of the HV 75 mm gun which could not be fitted to the said tank. The Sherman, however, was able to take the 17-pdr, some 180 inches in length, from a similar-sized hull as the Panzer IV and the Cromwell.[88] Clearly, although the width of a tank would ultimately prove a limiting factor on the size of the gun capable of being mounted, it was not the obvious cause in the cases of the Cromwell and Churchill, both of which were wide enough to carry larger armament, certainly to the level of the HV 75 mm or 77 mm gun.

The limitation placed on the size of armament carried by British-designed tanks was connected to the narrow width of the turret ring, but the restricted diameter was a product of a self-imposed design feature, not a consequence of the width limitations imposed by adhering to railway loading gauges. British tanks carried their hulls and turrets between their tracks, to enhance their ability to traverse obstacles and difficult terrain, whereas German, American and Soviet designed tanks supported their turrets with a superstructure, which to a degree overhung the tracks. This could make the tank higher, as in the case of the M4 Sherman, but not necessarily so, as in the cases of the Panzer IV and the T-34. In essence, the Cromwell and the Churchill could not be up-gunned to the same degree as the Panzer IV because of a simple design principle, one that produced tanks such as the Churchill, which had

Plate 1 M4 Sherman. Plentiful and reliable, but weak in firepower and prone to 'brew-up' when penetrated. (IWM B6130)

Plate 2 A30 Challenger. A flawed and compromised tank which attempted to mount a 17-pdr in an elongated Cromwell chassis. It was effectively superseded by the Firefly, and saw only limited service in 1944–45. (IWM 9331)

Plate 3 A22/42 Churchill. Carrying heavier armour than the feared German Tiger, the Churchill was the epitome of the infantry support tank. (IWM 8568)

Plate 4 M10 17-pdr. The British boosted the hitting power of their M10 tank destroyers by equipping a proportion with the potent 17-pdr gun. (IWM 8303)

Plate 5 M3/5 Stuart (Honey). With a near worthless 37 mm gun, in Normandy the Stuart acted as little more than a tracked reconnaissance vehicle. (IWM 5608)

Plate 6 A Cromwell crew prepares a meal. Tank crew usually lived in and around their vehicle, often forming closer working relationships than in other sections of the army. (IWM 5681)

Plate 7 Tank crews endured the added burden of constant maintenance of their vehicles, often at the end of the day. (IWM 9043)

Plate 8 Panther. Manoeuvrable, with a hard hitting 75 mm gun and tough frontal armour, the Panther was a formidable opponent. (IWM 5769)

Plate 9 Percy Hobart (l), GOC 79th Armoured Division, and Pip Roberts, GOC 11th Armoured Division, with Monty in 1945. (IWM BU 10669)

Plate 10 Allan Adair (l), GOC Guards Armoured Division, with Second British Army Commander, Miles Dempsey. Dempsey and Monty had attempted to have Adair replaced prior to *Overlord*, but Adair performed well enough in northwest Europe. (IWM B13027)

Plate 11 Monty with Bobby Erskine, GOC 7th Armoured Division. Erskine was sacked in August during *Operation Bluecoat*, along with many other officers in the division and at corps level. (IWM H36006)

Plate 12 Pip Roberts, GOC 11th Armoured Division, considered to be the best armoured divisional commander in 21st Army Group. (IWM B9183)

Plate 13 Tiger. Heavily armoured and equipped with an 88 mm gun, the Tiger was much feared by Allied tank crews. Yet, only some 120 served in Normandy and the tank was notoriously unreliable. (BOV 438/H3)

Plate 14 Stug III. Unsophisticated and workmanlike, the increasing numbers of self-propelled weapons, such as the Stug, nevertheless caused tactical difficulties for the Allies in Normandy. (BOV 2175/D5)

Plate 15 A27M Cromwell. Fast and manoeuvrable, the Cromwell was superior to the Sherman, but still lacked sufficient firepower to tackle heavy German armour. (BOV 4751/E3)

Plate 16 Armour protection on most Allied tanks offered little defence against German anti-tank weaponry in Normandy. (BOV 2876/66)

a lower centre of gravity and could traverse more difficult terrain, but which simultaneously sacrificed turret width and armament-carrying capability as a consequence. Further, it should be noted that the HV 75 mm gun was a particularly short weapon, some 30 per cent shorter than the 17-pdr, and would have fitted easily into the Panzer IV. In essence, the inability of British-designed tanks to pack more punch was a product of a chosen design parameter, not one directly imposed by transportation limitations. By the time it was apparent that this choice of design feature was proving too restrictive, it was too late to modify the tank programmes already under way.

Options and decisions: finalising the plans for 1944

During the spring and summer of 1943 the various influences shaping British tank development precipitated a series of meetings and discussions at the highest level aimed at finalising the requirements for 1944. Many factors had played upon the design and procurement process prior to the spring of 1943, but it was at this stage that firm decisions and final arrangements had to be made to equip the tank arm for the Normandy campaign. Only a limited amount could be achieved during the time left as the major programmes were in place and the fundamental decisions regarding the types and nature of the tanks required for the northwest European campaign had already been made. The basis of the British armoured forces in Normandy was to be centred on four key models: the A22 Churchill for infantry support; the A27 Cromwell and the M4 Sherman for the cruiser role; and the M3/5 Honey in small numbers for reconnaissance duties. However, lines of development were still ongoing in 1943, and further work was to be completed in arming the tanks.

Debate over the role and need for a heavy infantry support tank continued. Although 4,000 Churchills were to be completed by Vauxhalls by the end of 1943, the tank's hitherto poor reliability and Montgomery's misgivings seemed to leave the A22's future looking somewhat bleak. However, the Prime Minister's enthusiasm for heavy armour, in conjunction with improved reports from Alexander in the Mediterranean, brightened the Churchill's prospects. As the Prime Minister noted, 'The warthog must play his part as well as the gazelle.'[89] In a joint memorandum by Oliver Lyttelton (Minister of Production), Andrew Duncan (Minister of Supply) and James Grigg (Secretary of State for War) to the War Cabinet, it was proposed to extend the production run of the Churchill by 1,000 such that it would carry on throughout 1944.[90] At the War Cabinet Defence Committee's (Supply) meeting on 20 April the Prime Minister also enthused about a plan to add some 1.5 inches of armour to the existing Churchill tank, and urged that effort on the project be stepped up. He claimed that too much attention was being paid to the experience of North Africa and that in northwest Europe a heavily armoured tank capable of surviving hits from all but the heaviest enemy anti-tank guns would be immensely desirable: 'What would be unpleasant would be to find ourselves up against the need for heavy tanks and to have none in our armoury. It would be too late to rectify matters.'[91] Although Churchill's further argument that a heavy tank should sacrifice armament as well as speed in order to carry more armour proved to be unsound, the notion of a heavily armoured tank for close support was validated in the close terrain of northwest Europe, and the A22 Churchill proved its worth, despite Montgomery's reservations.

Further plans to develop even heavier tanks, however, came to nought. A programme to fit the Churchill with a 17-pdr was not developed fully, and the efforts of Sir Albert Stern's team of semi-independent tank designers resulted in prototypes that were enormous, unwieldy and surprisingly weak in armour protection, offering no more than current production A22s, despite weighing in at over 60 tons. Lord Cherwell, the Prime Minister's scientific advisor, was despatched to check on Stern's progress, but he reported unfavourably in May 1943, as did Andrew Duncan and James Grigg, and the programme bothered the Defence Committee little from then on.[92]

Of greater concern, however, was the continuing issue of tank armament. Despite the influence of the desert campaign and the apparent acceptance in February 1943 of the 75 mm MV dual-purpose gun as the weapon to be fitted to some two-thirds of British tanks in Normandy, few were satisfied, and further debate ensued. In January 1943, Maj-Gen Edward Clarke, Director General of Artillery (DGA), had pointed out the shortcomings of adopting this policy, arguing that the requirements of a HV anti-armour weapon were incompatible with the lower-velocity type guns required to deliver HE shells. Consequently, he argued against the widespread adoption of the 75 mm dual-purpose gun.[93]

The Ministry of Production warmed to the debate. In a discussion paper on tank policy in March 1943, it was argued that the 6-pdr was currently only just about capable of dealing with the armour of the Tiger, and that as the MV 75 mm dual-purpose gun was inferior to the 6-pdr in armour penetration, it would be virtually inadequate in forthcoming campaigns in anti-armour duties. The situation would be made much worse as the Germans began to introduce new heavily armoured medium tanks, such as the Panther, in late 1943 and 1944.

The paper also questioned the popularity of the 75 mm gun in the Mediterranean theatre. It was claimed that the 75 mm gun was little better than the 6-pdr when firing HE, but in North Africa only the 75 mm gun had been supplied with HE rounds, thus making it appear much superior to the 6-pdr. Moreover, reports from the Middle East had not so much sung the virtues of the 75 mm gun as identified the crucial value of a weapon capable of firing HE, which by 1943 the 6-pdr could do. The paper strongly maintained that the widespread adoption of the MV 75 mm was an error:

> It would seem, therefore, that by adopting the 75 mm gun as the standard weapon for the majority of our tanks, we should be gratuitously

reproducing in 1943 and 1944 the state of weapon inferiority for which we had to pay so dearly in 1941 and 1942.[94]

Furthermore, the General Staff policy involved the maintenance of three types of gun in the field – the MV 75 mm (60 per cent), the 6-pdr (30 per cent) and the 95 mm close-support howitzer (10 per cent) and this would create a logistical headache. Consequently, the paper concluded, the 75 mm should be eliminated and replaced by the 6-pdr or better HV weapon and the 95 mm close-support howitzer in a roughly two-thirds to one-third proportion.

These points were submitted for discussion at the Defence Committee meeting of 20 April 1943, though greatest emphasis was placed on increasing the proportion of 95 mm howitzers. It was also pointed out that the Americans themselves were seriously considering replacing the 75 mm gun with a new 76 mm HV weapon, so the British decision to adopt the 75 mm and begin producing it in the UK was beginning to seem questionable in the extreme, especially as the British would be reliant on US supplies of 75 mm ammunition.[95]

Lord Cherwell concurred with Lyttelton's paper on tank armament circulated for the meeting and extolled the virtues of the 95 mm howitzer still further. Although this was a low-velocity weapon, with a shaped hollow charge, he argued it was likely to have armour penetration capability at least as potent as the 75 mm gun, while retaining better HE capacity.[96]

He maintained this position at the Defence Committee meeting of 20 April, where Churchill, unsurprisingly, backed Cherwell's view. Grigg disagreed and presented the War Office's judgment, based on available evidence from the Mediterranean theatre, that the 75 mm gun represented a reasonable compromise of anti-armour and HE firepower.[97] General Harold Alexander, CinC Middle East, had forwarded to the War Office a slight revision of the late 1942 policy backing the MV 75 mm. He claimed that if intelligence reports indicated that the 75 mm was going to be sadly lacking in AP capability by 1944, then a HV weapon would be required, and if this meant proportions of tanks in northwest Europe each carrying different weapons, then so be it. However, he rejected the 95 mm for anything other than employment in small numbers.[98] The Defence Committee concluded that the subject required further consideration and that a final decision on the proportions of weaponry to be fitted to British tanks in Normandy must be postponed.

Churchill wanted greater information to be provided before any verdict could be passed. He claimed that he had never been convinced by the adoption of the MV 75 mm gun in the first place, and that the Mediterranean forces had not witnessed any real alternatives to the 75 mm gun in action. Moreover, he was particularly conscious that if wrong decisions were made, the army for Normandy might find itself equipped with obsolescent weaponry, and the government held most blameworthy.[99]

On 3 May further discussion on tank armament took place in the Defence Committee. The two views were yet again expressed, with the War Office represented by James Grigg supporting the widespread adoption of the 75 mm, while the Ministry of Production, in the form of Oliver Lyttelton argued that the 6-pdr with the new HE round could do the job of both, with a proportion of 95 mm howitzers for specialist engagements. Maj-Gen Clarke, DGA, confirmed that the 75 mm was not up to the task of dealing with heavy German armour in any shape or form and he dismissed the notion that an effective dual-purpose weapon was viable without overly compromising either task. Gen Alan Brooke, however, added his weight to the War Office/ army's view gleaned from action in the Mediterranean, which continued to back the more potent explosive capacity of the 75 mm HE shell compared to the 6-pdr (15lbs. to 6.25lbs.). As engagement of soft targets was now the principal duty carried out by armour, it would be foolish, he argued, to weaken in any way this capability. Anti-armour firepower could be increased by retaining some 6-pdrs or better weapons, as current policy dictated. Cherwell disagreed, arguing that the 75 mm gun fell between two stools and that it made more sense to increase the proportions of 6-pdrs and 95 mms and dispense with the 75 mm completely. Still further disagreement ensued over the likelihood of spaced armour defeating hollow-charge rounds, thus rendering the 95 mm weapon impotent against enemy armoured vehicles.[100]

Churchill yet again put off a final definitive judgment, claiming to the meeting that the debate was evenly balanced and further consideration was required. Over the next two days Churchill exchanged correspondence with Cherwell on the matter, before provisionally concluding that the proportions of tank armaments be adjusted. The total of MV 75 mm guns was to be reduced to 30 per cent, 95 mms increased to 20 per cent, while the remaining 50 per cent should comprise of 6-pdrs. Both the MV 75 mm and the 6-pdr would be replaced by the new HV 75 mm gun when it appeared.[101] However, the Prime Minister called for further discussions of the Defence Committee under the tutelage of Andrew Duncan, Minister of Supply, to find a measure of agreement.

By June the situation had begun to clarify. Although further consideration was still being given to the proportions of MV 75 mms to 6-pdrs, the production plans agreed in February were in such an advanced state that reorienting them significantly would prove inordinately difficult. In addition, the situation concerning the HV 75 mm gun was now clear and it could not be produced in sufficient quantities nor fitted into a cruiser tank until well into the latter half of 1944. However, the Deputy Chief of the Imperial General Staff (DCIGS), Lt-Gen Ronald Weeks, reported to the Defence Committee on 16 June that a survey of armoured brigade and army tank brigade commanders in the Mediterranean provided overwhelming endorsement of the MV 75 mm gun over the 6-pdr, though in the long term they looked forward to the arrival of the HV 75 mm gun. There was little support for the widespread introduction of the 95 mm howitzer, while army tank brigades, employing heavier infantry support tanks, requested a higher proportion of superior anti-tank weapons. Thus, the policy agreed back in February 1943 was still valid. Moreover, the Defence Committee also considered the view that although the MV 75 mm gun was likely to struggle to deal with the armour on the Tiger tank, such opponents were unlikely to appear in great numbers, and would in any case prove less valuable in mobile warfare.[102]

The debate over the armament to be provided for British tanks the following year proved largely circular and the fundamental problem rested on the inability of the Allies to design and develop a dual-purpose gun similar to the German L/48 75 mm type early enough. As the summer of 1943 dragged on, moreover, the plans to get higher-powered weapons into tanks ran into difficulties. The HV 75 mm gun would not be in place for over a year and the chances of introducing a practical 17-pdr-equipped tank were receding, that is, until the Firefly programme emerged from Lulworth and Chobham in the autumn of 1943.

Ultimately, the decision either to adopt the 6-pdr or the MV 75 mm for Normandy was won by those who recognised that greater capacity for dealing with soft targets was the priority for Allied armour in 1943, and that the 6-pdr was inferior in this respect. In northwest Europe in 1944, however, the logic underpinning this view was jeopardised by the increased need to engage relatively well-armoured tanks and SP guns in very close terrain, where out-manoeuvring such opponents was much less of an option. In this case, the 6-pdr, especially when employing the new sabot round would have been much more effective, and the shortcomings of its HE shell may have been a price worth paying, though this is by no means certain.

Could this have been foreseen in the summer of 1943? The fact that the Germans were developing some heavily armoured tanks, such that they would defeat the MV 75 mm almost completely, was recognised, and the urgency of the Firefly conversion programme was evidence of this foresight. However, that there would be a reorientation back towards dealing with enemy armour of all kinds in 1944, and that the fighting would be static for two months in Normandy in dense terrain as a result of flawed German strategy, places an impressive expectation and burden of perspicacity upon those making the key decisions in 1943. Moreover, by that stage it is unclear what more might have been achieved prior to *Overlord*.

Conclusion

Although it is the case that the methods and structure of tank design and development were not firmly established until mid-1942, it is unclear whether this, or the continuing confusion and discontinuity throughout 1943, had any significantly detrimental effects on the provision of armoured equipment in 1944. If there was a great tank scandal in Britain, it centred on the failings and inadequacies of the tanks produced and delivered up to 1943, whereas the Churchills and Cromwells provided for *Operation Overlord*, although fulfilments of specifications laid down in the midst of the chaos in British tank production in 1940 and 1941, proved to be reasonable successes. It was hardly the fault of the designers that they were tasked with developing tanks that would be obsolescent by 1944; it was the function of the War Office to determine what would be required and they based their assumptions on the experience of 1940 and the western desert. Their adoption of the M4 Sherman and the MV 75 mm gun in 1942 was clear evidence of their views. Moreover, it was by no means apparent until late 1942/early 1943, though there were earlier indications, that the Germans were intent on upping the ante to such an extent as led to the emergence of the Tiger and later the Panther. In effect the British lagged a year to 18 months behind the Germans, but the tanks they eventually produced, the A34 Comet and the A41 Centurion would have met the requirements of 21st Army Group, though the extent to which they would have radically altered the success with which armour was employed in the Normandy campaign is by no means certain. Moreover, the British showed a good deal more prescience and flexibility than their American cousins in the crash programme to mount 17-pdrs on the M4 Sherman and the M10, and in pushing through the development of sabot ammunition.

However, criticism can be levelled in two cases, both of which impacted on the firepower capability of 21st Army Group armour. First, there was little ambition about tank design in the 1941–42 period. Although, the 6-pdr was considered adequate, and there were problems enough in getting this weapon into tanks until 1942, there was little pressure to link the new 17-pdr gun to a new tank. The A30 Challenger programme was only ever likely to be a stop-gap, and the British were locked into producing the A22 Churchill and the A27 Cromwell, neither of which were ever intended to carry a weapon as large as the 17-pdr. The explanation as to why the British settled for the 6-pdr as their gun of choice in 1941 is understandable, and the notion that both of those tanks could be abandoned in order to develop something new is unsustainable in the circumstances of the 1941–42 era. However, that such low priority was given to developing a high-quality 17-pdr tank, while explicable, is still somewhat questionable.

The second crucial error centred not just on the British but on the Americans as well, in succumbing to the belief that the MV 75 mm gun would suffice as a frontline weapon much beyond 1942. It was already only at best competitive with the Panzer IV Special's armament, yet it was intended that well over half of the tanks deployed in northwest Europe in 1944 would still be equipped with the MV 75 mm gun. This decision, made in December 1942, and ratified in February 1943, represented a significant error in judgement, and while the War Cabinet Defence Committee debated and bickered, the British tank programme coasted for six months or so. It took until the summer of 1943 before it was widely appreciated that in the following year armoured formations might have to go into combat with inadequate armament against heavily armoured German tanks and increasing numbers of SP guns. The 6-pdr versus MV 75 mm debate was in any case of limited importance by this stage as both weapons had shortcomings, and the degree to which these failings might be more starkly exposed in Normandy could hardly be foreseen in the summer of 1943.

The firepower problem was compounded when it became clear that the HV 75 mm gun was unlikely to be deployed until late 1944 and that the A30 Challenger was going to be a profound disappointment. This chain of events and decisions largely precipitated the weakness in Allied armoured firepower in June 1944, a shortcoming of which the senior commanders of 21st Army Group were well aware prior to D-Day.

Whether or not much more might have been achieved in closing this fire-power gap if greater urgency had been pressed from late 1942 is by no means clear, but there is no reason to believe it would have made matters worse. Nevertheless, the only notable enhancement to 21st Army Group firepower came with the development of the Sherman Firefly, an improvised stop-gap with some not inconsiderable deficiencies, such that even if more had been available, their impact on the Normandy campaign would have been strictly limited.

7

PRODUCTION AND SUPPLY

The inability of the British to produce an advanced and truly competitive battle tank for Normandy has been blamed to a significant extent on a weak industrial and production base. Beale, Jarymowycz and Barnett all subscribe to this view, claiming that the technical effort invested in the design and production of tanks in Britain was much lower than that placed in other areas, and that consequently, by 1944 British armour was not up to the task of competing with the latest German models.[1] In addition, Barnett and Jarymowycz are more critical of British industry generally and indeed argue that infrastructural deficiencies and weaknesses led to the failure of tank production, even as late as 1944.[2]

Particular criticism has been focused on the 1940–42 War Office policy known as ordering off the drawing board, in effect, by-passing pre-production tests in order to expedite output. This, it is argued, resulted in the manufacture of tanks of dubious worth. It is certainly the case that in the 1940–42 era a high percentage of British-built tanks were undermined by a series of flaws and faults. Some were even delivered with disclaimers from the manufacturers, apologising for shortcomings, a measure hardly likely to instil confidence in crews.[3] Ultimately, it seems that during this period, quantity was considered more important than quality.

The crisis of 1940, when much of the BEF's equipment was lost in the Dunkirk evacuation, hindered the design of new, competitive tanks for the best part of two years, as has been discussed in the previous chapter. This may have been a worthwhile price to pay if the tanks being delivered in the 1940–42 period were at least sound and reliable. However, they were not. The War Office and the Ministry of Production had believed that the competitiveness of some British equipment in 1940, such as the Matilda II infantry tank and the 2-pdr gun, allowed a breathing space in which all effort could be focused upon production of existing models. Once the quantitative gap had been closed, effort could then be directed towards the production of new designs.

This approach was flawed in two ways. First, as has been noted, the Germans leapt ahead in tank design after Dunkirk, leaving the British too great a deficit to close by *Overlord*, while second, the premise that the tanks being delivered by British industry in 1940 and 1941 were adequate foundered on problems of mechanical reliability, as well as declining relative capability. Indeed, prior to the emergence of the A27 Cromwell and the later versions of the A22 Churchill in 1944, most British-built tanks were hopelessly unreliable. This in turn made the M4 Sherman with its 75 mm gun appear to be a godsend in 1942, masking the fact that it was little, if any better than the Panzer Mark IV Special. The unreliability of home-built tanks tempted the British into embracing the reliable Sherman and other American designs, and came very close to causing the War Cabinet to abandon British manufactured tanks almost entirely, even when the A27 Cromwell and the A34 Comet appeared on paper superior to US models. Indeed, initial suspicion of the Comet programme was largely a consequence of the miserable performance of previous British cruiser tanks.

Nevertheless, the difficulties experienced in the early years of the war were on the face of it overcome by the time of Normandy. Emphasis had been placed squarely on tank production in the aftermath of Dunkirk, and this challenge was successfully met, for by May 1943 the British had produced 3,000 more tanks than Germany since the outbreak of war.[4] British industry also reacted commendably by significantly reducing the time taken to develop and produce new tanks, which was cut to less than two years by the midpoint of the war, compared to over four hitherto.[5]

Moreover, the models delivered in 1944 for use by 21st Army Group broadly met the requirements made of British manufacturers. The A27 Cromwell was a fast, manoeuvrable and reliable cruiser, while the A22 Churchill fulfilled the need for a heavily armoured infantry support tank. By the end of 1944, the A34 Comet was arriving in frontline units, and this proved to be an excellent tank, superior to anything the Americans could then provide.

Nevertheless, the British cut back on planned tank production from 1943, and thus such designs as the Cromwell and Churchill were only available in limited numbers in Normandy. Consequently, the tank most heavily employed by British units in the summer of 1944 was the American-designed and produced M4 Sherman, and it was this vehicle more than British models that provoked consternation, particularly over its tendency to incinerate its crew when penetrated. Did the British therefore err in selecting US armour in place of British designs, which then left them at the mercy of American concepts of armoured warfare and equipped with the M4 Sherman?

Although too much has been made of the technical shortcomings of Allied tanks in Normandy, it is the case that in 1944 the armour available to 21st Army Group was deficient in the level and force of the firepower it could deliver, and for this some investigation is required into the vicissitudes of the production process. Indeed, the most pressing problem in the months leading up to D-Day was the shortfall in top-class anti-armour weaponry. Essentially, why did the British fail to deploy the HV 75 mm gun (until the A34 Comet which did not enter service until late 1944) and why were there inadequate supplies of 17-pdr-equipped tanks in Normandy? In addition, despite ground-breaking work on ammunition types, there were still delays in the intro-duction of new types of round, while the 17-pdr was without a suitable HE shell throughout the campaign, a factor that somewhat undermines the call of some that the Sherman Firefly alone would have been a panacea in the summer of 1944.

Therefore, the degree to which quantitative and qualitative production issues shaped the tank arm in the months and years leading up to *Overlord* is crucial to any understanding of the armoured forces deployed in Normandy. Furthermore, it is necessary to analyse the factors and decisions that directed the development of armour supply to 21st Army Group and caused Montgomery's forces to deploy in the summer of 1944 with the equipment that they did.

The process of British armour production

In the period 1940–42 four key factors shaped and hindered the development of tank production. First, the tank design and manufacturing base in Britain was undoubtedly weak. In the interwar era few orders had been made, and even in the years leading up to the outbreak of war there was little financial return for engineering companies in tank design and production. Unlike the aero-industry, where a profitable civilian market existed for military-related equipment, tank technology was seriously limited by its very nature. Indeed, for most of the interwar era only Vickers had been interested in tank design, and there was no significant attempt to mirror the expansion of the aero-industry in the field of tank production in the late 1930s. When the crisis came in 1940, it proved inordinately difficult to expand the design and production base quickly while simultaneously maintaining quality and innovation.[6]

Second, the defeat in France placed absolute priority on straightforward quantity production of tanks. The British Army had been left with few armoured vehicles following the catastrophe in northwest Europe, and the requirements of producing any type of potentially viable and useful tank took precedence over the development of new designs. Britain was already short of tanks before the collapse in France and quantity ruled quality, but the demands of home defence and other theatres took control in the summer of 1940 and drove tank production through 1941 and into 1942.[7]

Such pressures led to the adoption of the policy of ordering tank designs straight from the drawing board and generally rushing into production inad-equately tested models. The measure was intended to reduce the time between drawing up the general specification and the production of the pilot for manufacturing, effectively negating the need to build prototypes.[8] The policy was not widely employed and in the army it was only adopted for the production of AFVs, meeting with mixed success. Indeed, in 1942 it was reported in the House of Commons that 'we were not avoiding the manufacture of prototypes, we were manufacturing nothing else'.[9] A whole series of problems arose from this drive for quantity, one being the heavy investment made in the A13 Covenanter, a tank rushed into production that never saw combat due to its shortcomings and general unreliability. Moreover, although the A22 Churchill, another product of 'off the drawing board' ordering, was ultimately to become an effective and useful addition to the Allied inventory, when first introduced it suffered from all manner of niggling problems and deficiencies.[10]

The third factor driving the production of tanks in Britain in the early stages of the war was the imprecision over the types of tanks required. The relative value placed on cruiser and infantry support designs fluctuated and was further shaped by information and experience from the battlefront, initially northwest Europe, and then North Africa.[11] Indeed, it took until September 1942 for the War Office to issue a coherent policy on tank design, by which time the basic tank chassis ultimately deployed in Normandy were in production.

However, concern and discussion over the armament to be fitted to British tanks continued, with the dual-purpose MV 75 mm gun being adopted in preference to the 6-pdr in late 1942 as a direct consequence of experience from North Africa. By the summer of 1943, however, the War Office, the Ministries of Production and of Supply and the RAC were beginning to seek measures to stiffen the anti-tank capability of their armour when more complete intelligence on the Tiger and Panther began to filter back to Britain. With around 12 months to D-Day, only a limited amount could be achieved, and it was as late as the autumn of 1943 that the conversion of M4 Shermans to carry 17-pdrs was authorised.

Yet criticism is still levelled at the production process for not providing sufficient tanks with HV weapons, even though neither the A22 Churchill nor the A27 Cromwell was ever intended to carry any weapon larger than the 6-pdr.[12] In reality, the headlong drive to deploy as many 17-pdr or HV 75 mm-gun-equipped AFVs as possible in Normandy did not accelerate sufficiently until it was already too late to affect significantly the make-up of the armoured force structure in June 1944.[13]

However, failures can be noted in two significant cases of consequence: the disappointing fruits of the A30 Challenger programme and the inability to match the A27 Cromwell to the HV 75 mm gun. In both cases the inadequacy of the design and production procedure served to undermine British armour in Normandy, for it was the weakness in firepower that created the most difficulty and both of these issues contributed directly to this failing. In the case of the A30 Challenger a clear specification had been laid down in early 1942 to mount the new 17-pdr gun in a tank but the resulting equipment was heavily delayed and only just survived attempts to junk it completely. It subsequently made little impact on the campaign in northwest Europe when eventually introduced in July 1944.

Finally, the structural make-up of the design and production process created inherent problems at various stages in the first three-to-four years of the war.

From 1940 onwards, the Ministry of Supply was responsible for issuing specifications to the firms likely to design and produce the tanks, and the DTD within the Ministry was in place to scrutinise such designs and offer advice, though not become directly involved with the design process itself. However, as the war progressed a greater degree of expertise began to reside in the DTD and this team became more closely involved in the actual design of tanks. However, such changes did not impact on the Normandy campaign because the first product of the DTD's direct involvement in design work came in meeting the General Staff specification for a heavy cruiser, the A41 Centurion, an excellent tank but a model which did not enter service until mid-1945.[14]

One of the key criticisms levelled at the production process was the separation of weaponry from vehicle design.[15] Armament during the Second World War was the responsibility of Maj-Gen Edward Clarke, the Director of Artillery (1938–42) and then DGA (1942–45), but the level of communication between the bodies responsible for vehicle and weapon design has been described as weak and inadequate.[16] However, it should be noted that Clarke pre-empted the requests of the General Staff in certain cases, preparing the 6-pdr before being asked, and acting on the 17-pdr in response to an enquiry from the Tank Division of the Ministry of Supply, not in response to a General Staff specification.[17] Indeed, in September 1940, in response to the earliest indications that the Germans might be developing tanks with 100–150 mm of armour, Clarke set in motion the development of a weapon to meet such a threat, which became the 17-pdr, a pilot of which was constructed by August 1941.[18] The 17-pdr programme was thus under way in advance of any official calls for such a weapon. Consequently, the design and production process was not entirely without merit, even if it acted at times in a seemingly ad hoc manner. It should also be noted that Clarke argued against the adoption of the MV 75 mm gun in December 1942, arguing that it was an 'unsatisfactory compromise'.[19]

Moreover, it is also unclear as to what direct impact the division of armament and vehicle design actually had on the ability of the British to construct a high-quality battle tank. Indeed, the inadequacies of firepower in Normandy were by no means the result of a breakdown in the relationship between the work of the Director (later Director-General) of Artillery and the DTD; the tanks designed to take the 17-pdr could mount them, and the failure to fit the HV 75 mm into the Cromwell could hardly be blamed on a structural or institutional failure, when the weapon was designed and produced externally by Vickers, not at the behest of the Director of Artillery.

However, perhaps the body most associated with the production of tanks during the Second World War was the Tank Board, a creation that went through a number of manifestations at different points between 1940 and 1945. It was first established in May 1940 in response to criticism of the Ministry of Supply, and was initially intended to act merely as a temporary advisory body.[20] It consisted of representatives from industry, the War Office and the Ministry of Supply, and its initial findings were all largely sensible, for example, calling for simplified procedures and a single channel of communication between the army and the forces of production.[21] However, the Tank Board lacked executive powers, its membership became frustrated, and it was effectively abolished in November, only to be reconstituted in January 1941. The representatives from industry were eventually dropped, with the place of the War Office and Ministry of Supply increasingly emphasised.[22] However, the Tank Board went through yet more change and transformation, and in the space of a little over two years the Board's terms of reference changed four times, and it had four different chairmen and 27 various members.[23] It took until September 1942 for the structure of the Tank Board to become settled, with greater emphasis being placed on the quality rather than just quantity of production. However, differences of opinion between the War Office and the Ministry of Supply remained within the Tank Board, and as late as 1943 the two factions refused to provide a single view to the Select Committee on National Expenditure.[24]

British armour supply for Normandy

With the recovery of British tank production, the influx of American designs and a plethora of reports and intelligence, principally from the Mediterranean, guiding and shaping tank production in 1943 and early 1944, key decisions had to be made as to the sources of supply for selected designs. During the winter of 1943 and spring of 1944 considerable pressure was brought to bear on the War Office, the Ministry of Production, the Ministry of Supply and the War Cabinet Defence Committee to revise their policy regarding tank supply and British production. Within these discussions, it was even proposed and debated that the British temporarily abandon home production, standardise on the M4 Sherman and concentrate on the long-term development of the A41 Centurion.

Mid-war plans for the production of British armour had already been curtailed in 1943 following discussions with the United States. It was concluded that British industry was best suited to supporting the Alliance with particular forms of heavy engineering and production, while the United States was better able to provide mass output of end use equipment.[25] Therefore, Britain should concentrate its production resources in certain key areas, to include aircraft design and supply which had hitherto proved highly successful. Tank production had not proved so useful nor effective by 1942, and as the British Army was enthusing about the new American M4 Sherman, it seemed logical to cut back British armour output and buy in US designs.

In January 1943 British tank output for 1944 was planned to be 10,000–11,000, though by April discussions were under way to reduce this figure to some 7,000, to focus British effort on other key areas of heavy engineering.[26] However, the production of British tanks was also shaped by the likely output of suitable engines. The best and most powerful engine then available to the British tank industry was the 600 hp Meteor design, derived from the famous Rolls-Royce Merlin aero-engine. When fitted to the A27, designated the Cromwell, top speeds of 40 mph were considered possible. However, supplies of this type of engine were strictly limited as priority was given to the needs of the aircraft industry, and thus the tank manufacturers had to rely on the older and less effective Liberty engine, rated at 340 hp. This, in contrast, when fitted to the A27, this time named the Centaur, could reach speeds of only 24 mph, and this did not meet the General Staff's minimum requirement for a cruiser tank.[27] Even with amendments, supply of Meteor engines was only ever likely barely to meet the requirements of A27 Cromwell output.

Clearly, top-grade British cruiser tank production was to be curtailed in deference to the priority given to aircraft output. With tank capacity already allocated to such programmes as the A22 Churchill, there was little likelihood of Britain being able to meet its cruiser needs without calling substantially upon American sources. To the General Staff, then contrasting the M4 Sherman with inadequate British-designed and produced cruisers, this seemed no bad thing. Indeed, the War Office estimated that the 1943 Tank Programme would yield only some 2,500 effective units in 1944, out of a total production figure in excess of 10,000.[28] Nevertheless, Churchill, Oliver Lyttelton (Minister of Production) and James Grigg (Secretary of State for War) claimed that they were unwilling to become fully reliant on US sources of tank supply, and in any case American designs did not meet the needs of the General Staff in all cases.

Pressure was also brought to bear on the British by American interests. General Somervell, US army, had already suggested earlier in 1943 that the UK take extra American tanks in place of British designs, though this was rejected.[29] Nevertheless, US representatives were persistent. Averell Harriman wrote to Churchill in May again requesting that the British take more M4 Shermans and cut back their own tank production. He pointed out that in the previous year Max Beaverbrook, then Minister of War Production, and Lyttelton had both called for ever greater numbers of medium tanks from the United States, and that tremendous efforts had been given over to boosting production facilities in America to meet the burgeoning demand. By the late spring of 1943, the Soviets had dropped out of the market for tanks, thus allowing the Americans to meet the needs of the British, though it now seemed as though a change of mind had taken place in Britain also, with a cut in the estimated requirement from 14,000. Harriman recognised that the British did not want to give up tank production, but argued that the Americans had responded quickly and helpfully to urgent requests made by the British for tanks in 1941 and 1942. Such requests for help in the future might not receive the same favourable treatment if the United States was left with excess Shermans when attempting to meet a British initiative. Having developed the plant and capacity, it would in any case be both wasteful and foolish for the Allies not to take up Sherman production.[30]

At the Defence Committee meeting on 15 June, Harriman's memo was discussed in some detail, with most representatives rejecting the American proposal. Lyttelton accepted that a request had been made of the Americans in the previous year for up to 14,000 tanks, but this had never been ratified. Moreover, in the interim the British had informed the Americans that they had revised their needs and that the United States was going to produce too many Shermans. Furthermore, it would be unwise to cut home tank production to such an extent that the British became wholly reliant on US imports. Churchill demurred and asked for consideration to be given to the repercussions of taking some 1,000–2,000 extra Shermans for 1944.[31] In recognition of a variety of constraints and pressures placed upon them, the Defence Committee lowered the 1944 figure for British tank output to 6,200 in July 1943, though imports of American 'cruisers' in 1944 would remain fixed at 8,500.[32]

British production was sluggish in a number of cases and design faults and delayed output frustrated and irked Churchill. In August 1943 he quizzed Lyttelton over the shortfalls in tank production, particularly the latest cruisers, to which the Minister of Production replied that this was due to workers taking holidays. If annual leave was taken into account, he argued, targets were being met. Churchill fumed, and berated Lyttelton for not taking this into account in the first place. Moreover, he again asked whether more Shermans would be required.[33] Although most difficulties with the Cromwell and Churchill were overcome, others did suffer and the A30 Challenger and the Valentine 17-pdr (or Archer) programmes fell behind schedule and saw estimates cut.[34]

By January 1944, however, a more pressing concern faced the War Cabinet. Lyttelton informed them on 12 January that because of the import situation, the estimated output of British tanks in 1944 would have to be revised down still further to 5,280. Although the A22 Churchill target would be exceeded, A27 Cromwell supply would fall short by some 500, and this was in spite of squeezing Centaur (the A27 with a lower-power Liberty engine) production to focus effort on the Cromwell. Nevertheless, Lyttelton claimed that he believed the Cromwell would be a success, though he admitted in January 1944 there were still a few teething troubles. He certainly advocated that the Cromwell would be superior to the Sherman, and that the A34 Comet, to succeed the Cromwell by the end of 1944, was likely to be better than the 76 mm-gun-equipped M4, lined up to phase out the 75 mm Sherman in the same year. It was in any case uncertain when, or indeed if, the British would secure a supply of 76 mm-gun-wielding tanks.

Consequently, a decision would have to be made by the Defence Committee regarding future supply for the British tank arm. Should they persist with the Cromwell–Comet series, or should they abandon the line, employ Shermans alone, and focus on designing and producing the A41 Centurion heavy cruiser? The former risked British tank units in Normandy being equipped with an unreliable model in too small a quantity to be useful, the latter placed the British squarely in the hands of the Americans. In addition, if the

Cromwell performed as imagined, it would be superior to the Sherman, and the Comet would certainly better anything likely to emerge from the United States before the spring of 1945. Yet if it failed, considerable industrial effort would have been expended fruitlessly at a time of great need. Despite the risk inherent in backing a British design, especially with their track record prior to 1944, Lyttelton favoured keeping the Cromwell and developing the Comet. Furthermore, he intended to concentrate 1944 production on Sherman 17-pdrs, heavy Churchills and the Comet.[35]

Churchill was unsure about the consequences of making such a decision and called upon Cherwell, his chief scientific advisor, to offer his comments. Cherwell largely agreed with Lyttelton, though he questioned the need to continue production of the underpowered A27 Centaur, destined for a run of 800 outputs in 1944. He also emphasised that the new tanks for *Overlord* would only be arriving in April and it was thus crucial that they were quickly distributed to units.[36]

Despite Cherwell's support for Lyttelton's policy, Churchill preferred scrapping the Cromwell–Comet chain of development and using American tanks, partly based on previous experience and partly because such a choice would release valuable labour to other needs. Nevertheless, he would accept Lyttelton's recommendations provided the Centaur was dropped.[37] Lyttelton was able to cut Centaur production by 15 per cent but most were already allocated to 21st Army Group as anti-aircraft tanks and were thus required.

Nevertheless, the possibility that Britain could suspend cruiser tank production in 1944 was discussed seriously at the highest level and indeed Churchill was of the opinion that such a policy was desirable. That the previous chequered history of British-supplied tanks in action informed this view is not in doubt, though nor is the fact that the final decision to continue with the Cromwell–Comet development was the correct one. Despite the shortcomings of the Cromwell, it was a superior tank to the Sherman, and without it, it is unlikely that the excellent Comet would have appeared in British units in late 1944.

The firepower crisis

Nevertheless, although delivery of reliable and relatively effective tanks was achieved for 21st Army Group, the key problem remained one of deploying effective firepower. The 1942–43 requirement for 25–30 per cent of British tanks to carry the best HV anti-tank weapon available was supposed to be met in a number of ways. Initially, this was to be fulfilled by the 6-pdr, potentially supplied with new types of ammunition. Subsequently, it was hoped that this weapon would eventually be superseded by the Vickers-designed HV 75 mm gun, along with a dedicated cruiser designed to mount the 17-pdr. In addition, the 17-pdr would be employed in a SP role to strengthen anti-armour capability in northwest Europe.

If the production and design process failed the British Army prior to Normandy it was in its failure to build a competitive tank mounting the 17-pdr in adequate quantities. The Tank Board, rather undermining the view that the British always settled for second best in tank design, first examined the possibility of fitting the 17-pdr to a tank in December 1941, long before the spectre of heavy German tanks fully emerged.[38] However, the proposed vehicle was not to place extra stress on the creaking British tank design base, and consequently, the new tank was to make use of existing technology by being based on the new A27 Cromwell. Indeed, the 17-pdr tank, named A30 Challenger, was at best a hybrid, being in effect an elongated Cromwell hull with a large high-profile turret. The turret, almost certainly adapted from an experimental heavy tank programme, had to be specially designed with a 70-inch ring to mount the 17-pdr and to carry a four-man turret crew as it was considered that, because of the weight of the 17-pdr round, it would be necessary to have two loaders as one would quickly tire.[39] A further significant design failure may have followed as a consequence of retaining the railway loading gauge restrictions on width. Indeed, the Challenger, although six feet longer than the Cromwell, was no wider and would thus encounter steering difficulties. Crucially, this increased stress on the suspension and prompted a reduction in weight, gleaned by reducing armour protection from 75 mm on the turret front to 63 mm and from 65 mm on the sides to just 40 mm.[40]

When the first pilots were examined in late 1942 and early 1943, they came in for some criticism, and in one case the A30 was described as a white elephant. The Chief Inspector, Gunnery, at the Armoured Fighting School, Lulworth, pointed out that the A30 was obviously primarily intended to duel with enemy tanks, yet had weaker armour than the A27 Cromwell, which was not. He called for the project to be abandoned in January 1943, but was ignored, and in February the General Staff claimed that the Challenger would prove acceptable in the cruiser role.[41] However, only some 200 A30s were ordered implying misgivings on the part of the War Office over the design, and its production was not without problems, with a number of ensuing delays.[42] Indeed, it was to take until May 1945 for the full order of 200 to be fulfilled.[43] Ultimately, because the A30 was not ready in time for D-Day, Cromwell regiments were equipped with a proportion of Sherman Fireflies instead.[44] Even when eventually deployed in Normandy in late July 1944, the Challenger proved faulty and the first batch had to be withdrawn for modification.[45] By this stage longer-term plans to investigate the possibility of up-armouring the A30 had been abandoned and it is clear that the vehicle was considered to be no more than a stopgap, being described as unsuitable for mass production and too thin skinned.[46] Certainly, compared to the A34 Comet it was a pale shadow, despite the confidence felt by crews in its firepower. However, the failure of the A30 should not be unduly emphasised, for its impact was never going to be great, being so limited in its planned production run.

Moreover, by the time of Normandy the introduction of Sherman Fireflies rendered the missing Challengers of less importance.[47]

A second measure to boost British firepower was the intention to fit the Vickers designed HV 75 mm gun into the latest modern cruiser tank. Vickers had begun design work on the gun in 1942, and the intention was to mount it on the A27 Cromwell, then under development.[48] The gun would be capable of firing an effective AP round, not so powerful as the 17-pdr, but still significantly better than the MV 75 mm, and a potent HE round. Initial development continued apace and there was an enthusiastic support for the combination of a reliable, mobile cruiser with a hard-hitting, but still dual-purpose main armament. As late as April 1943, in a joint memorandum from the Secretary of State for War and the Minister of Supply to the Defence Committee, all appeared well for the HV 75 mm gun and its mounting on the Cromwell. Indeed, it was planned that following successful testing of six pilot weapons by July, mass production could begin with a peak of 600–700 units per month from spring 1944 onwards.[49] There is little doubt that a cruiser force deployed in Normandy equipped with HV 75 mm guns would have allayed many of the fears beginning to emerge from mid-1943 onwards over heavy German tanks.

However, the whole plan collapsed in acrimony when the War Office discovered that the HV 75 mm would not in fact fit into the A27 Cromwell's turret, as the ring was too narrow to accommodate the 50-calibre long gun.[50] Indeed, a new tank, the A34 Comet, would be required to carry the new weapon, and this would not be ready until late 1944. The War Office vented its wrath on the Ministry of Supply at this point, arguing strongly that cruiser design in Britain had failed miserably. Lt-Gen John Fullerton Evetts, ACIGS, even claimed that there was little point in developing the A34 at all, as by the time it arrived, US 76 mm-equipped Shermans would be available and these were a safer purchase.[51] It would be better, he pointed out, to invest home effort in the A41 Centurion programme. In view of the poor reception given to the US 76 mm when it eventually arrived, the decision to persist with the A34 Comet's development was validated, for when it entered service and saw action in 1945, it was clearly superior to anything in the Allied inventory.

Nevertheless, the Ministry of Supply's failure to be aware of, or to communicate, the incompatibility of the HV 75 mm and the Cromwell is perplexing and had more significance than the weakness of the A30 Challenger. The latter was never more than a stopgap, even if it had been viewed more favourably, but the Cromwell fitted with the HV 75 mm appeared to be a design of great potential. Indeed, the A34 Comet differed very little in concept from the Cromwell, having a very similar suspension system and an identical power plant, the Meteor engine. The significant advance was in the turret design, which was built around the HV 75 mm gun, renamed in late 1943 the 77 mm gun to avoid confusion.[52] Most notable of all was the development and production time of around 18 months from specification to entry into service. In the final assessment, however, the A34 Comet came too late for Normandy and its delay must be considered a failure.

A further method by which the British intended to stiffen the anti-tank capability of their forces for Normandy was the introduction of SP equipment. There were a number of plans combining the development of home-designed AFVs and the purchase, and then conversion, of American tank destroyers. In essence though, the British did not accept the US view that enemy tanks could be neutralised by the so-called tank destroyer alone, and deployed their SP equipment as little more than mobile anti-tank guns.[53] Indeed, the SP equipment used by the British in Normandy came under the direction of RA units, which combined towed guns as well as the SP variety. The British believed that for AFVs to be of value in offence, they required reasonable armour protection in addition to HV weapons, speed and manoeuvrability. In view of this, only a limited and defensive role was envisaged for SP equipment in operations in northwest Europe.

Nevertheless, the British had been examining the possibility of mounting a 17-pdr on a chassis for some time prior to June 1944. A specification had been issued in September 1942 for a low-silhouette vehicle, mounting a 17-pdr anti-tank gun, preferably in a 360-degree traversing closed-in turret. Armour protection was to resist the German 50 mm at 800 yards.[54] However, it was also intended that a standard chassis could be used as the basis for SP equipment as well as tanks, and the British gravitated towards ordering the US M10 tank destroyer, a vehicle similar in many ways to the M4 Sherman. An initial order for 700 such vehicles equipped with the American three-inch gun was placed, though consideration at this stage of fitting the 17-pdr into the M10 was governed by the degree of difficulty likely to be involved.[55] However, the US designers had simplified the gun mounting to facilitate the adaptation of the three-inch mounting to take the 17-pdr.[56] The British took delivery of some 845 vehicles in 1943, but of the second version of the M10 which began to arrive later in that year, only the T71 mark could carry the 17-pdr, the T70 being specifically designed only to mount a lighter 76 mm gun, a weapon which had only similar capability to the three-inch gun it replaced.[57] The British planned to convert 1,000 of their M10s to mount 17-pdrs for Normandy, occasionally referring to such hybrids as Achilles, but by May 1944 it was estimated that less than 100 would be available for *Overlord*.[58] Unfortunately, the armour protection for the M10 was more limited than the Shermans, Churchills and Cromwells it was intended to support, rendering it vulnerable to smaller-calibre German weapons and its open-topped turret placed both crew and vehicle at a serious disadvantage when operating in a close-support role. However, there was little doubt that the SP 17-pdr had significant advantages in mobility and manoeuvre over the towed variety.[59] Indeed, despite the misgivings of some RA crews, they were also used to pep up the anti-tank firepower of Churchill regiments, for no Fireflies were allocated to such formations.[60]

What of the British intention to mount the 17-pdr on a home-designed chassis? There is no evidence of plans to mount the gun on an A27, either the Meteor-powered models (the Cromwell) or the under-powered Centaurs fitted with the Liberty engine, despite the modification of a number of the latter into a variety of other support roles.[61] The British for the most part stuck to the policy that true tanks with fully revolving turrets were necessary for offensive operations and by late 1943 the 17-pdr-equipped SP vehicle was being superseded by the development of the Sherman Firefly.

One curiosity that emerged from this chain of development was the Archer, a 17-pdr SP equipment based on the Valentine chassis. The Valentine, a hybrid cruiser–infantry tank designed by Vickers, went out of production in 1943, but a number were adapted to carry the 17-pdr gun in a rearward facing, limited traverse fighting compartment. Consequently, the vehicle reversed into position and this allowed it to scurry away more easily to avoid destruction once detected. Initially, the Archer's value rested on its ability to carry the 17-pdr, which at the time its rival, the M10, did not. Some 800 were ordered with 480 pencilled in for potential use as stopgaps in northwest Europe should the need arise, despite opposition from some sources who argued that the British would have enough SP equipment and that in any case, as the Archer was inferior to the M10 17-pdr, it was redundant.[62] None saw service in the Normandy campaign, but they were pressed into action in the autumn of 1944 and gained some popularity, though the M10 17-pdr remained the preferred vehicle.[63]

Therefore, it was becoming apparent by the early autumn of 1943 that with the failures of the A30 programme, the inability to fit the HV 75 mm gun into the A27 Cromwell, and the mixed abilities of the SP 17-pdr equipment likely to arrive in service by the summer of 1944, the British were faced with the prospect of invading Normandy with a tank force equipped almost entirely with MV 75 mm guns. Unsurprisingly concern grew that with new types of heavily armoured German tanks emerging, significant difficulties might be encountered. Two measures were to alleviate this situation, one ad hoc, the other a manifestation of innovative design and development. Neither proved to be a panacea, and neither was fully in place by the opening of the Normandy campaign, but both served to boost morale at a potentially difficult time for the armoured forces of 21st Army Group.

The first was the crash development of the Sherman Firefly. The option of fitting the 17-pdr into the M4 had initially been rejected by the Ministry of Supply's Tank Division as being impractical, but personal initiatives proved that this was not the case. Lt-Col George Witheridge, RTR, on arrival at Lulworth in 1943, became interested in mounting the 17-pdr in the Sherman after having seen the A30 Challenger and found it wanting.[64] Others at Lulworth, and possibly at Chobham's Fighting Vehicle Research and Development Establishment, were also investigating the possibility, with mixed outcomes, but despite warnings to abandon the project, Witheridge and his team, supported by the new DRAC, Maj-Gen Raymond Briggs and Claude Gibb of the Ministry of Supply, proved that the Sherman's turret could be modified without too much difficulty to accept the 17-pdr.[65] In October and November enthusiasm for the project began to grow and 21st Army Group was informed of the development in early October.[66] Even before the final testing had taken place in February, an order was placed for 2,100 M4 Shermans, named Fireflies, to be converted to carry the 17-pdr. Consequently, arguably the most effective tank employed by 21st Army Group in Normandy emerged in a semi-official manner. The programme was given 'highest priority' by Churchill and he commended the work of the Ministry of Supply in the rapid development and production of the 17-pdr Sherman.[67]

However, even had the Firefly been available in much larger numbers in Normandy, it would not have been the panacea some have claimed. There was a scarcity of 17-pdr HE ammunition, over which there were in any case question marks, and in order to load sufficient ammunition on to the Firefly, the hull machine gunner had been deleted. Consequently, the tank's value, other than in an anti-tank role, was small and it was still the case in Normandy that most of the tank's duties focused on overcoming soft targets. Nevertheless, the Firefly was very popular among tank crews in Normandy, and calls were made for an increase to two Fireflies per troop of four tanks, though no more than that until an effective HE round was provided.[68] Unfortunately, in spite of the speed with which the order was prosecuted and conversions were made, there simply were not enough to go around and the impact of the Firefly on the campaign was correspondingly limited. A month before D-Day it was estimated that only some 160 Fireflies would be delivered to 2nd British Army by the middle of May.[69] The target of 15 Fireflies per regiment was not met, with only 12 per regiment being available in June, a shortfall partly caused by the still missing A30 Challengers.[70]

The second measure employed to boost 21st Army Group's anti-tank firepower demonstrated innovative design and thinking on the part of the British. The traditional method of defeating armour protection on a vehicle was to fire a heavy chunk of metal at it and penetrate it by sheer kinetic energy. Once inside, the projectile would ricochet around destroying equipment, killing crew and potentially igniting ammunition and fuel. This most straightforward method was represented by the AP round. As the Second World War progressed, however, enhanced methods were introduced. First, the APC round was added to the British inventory in 1942.[71] In this case, in addition to the main penetrating body, the projectile was tipped with a softer cap of malleable metal which collapsed on impact and effectively glued the projectile for a fraction of a second to the target and thus helped to reduce the chance of it ricocheting away. This was particularly important against sloped armour. However, to work effectively the soft cap had to be blunt and thus, in order to reduce the air drag on the projectile created by the blunt cap, a thin aerodynamic ballistic cap was later added, creating the

APCBC (armour piercing capped, ballistic cap) round and these were available by 1943.

However, such rounds continued to rely on the basic premise that in order to develop hitting power still further, muzzle velocity had to be upped and/or the size and weight of the round increased. The Germans had amply demonstrated both methods, with the Panther's L/70 75 mm weapon increasing its muzzle velocity by lengthening the gun, and by the introduction of 88 mm guns, longer 88 mm guns and finally the monstrous and ultimately impractical and pointless 128 mm weapon. The problem of increased recoil caused by higher muzzle velocities was partly alleviated by the addition of muzzle brakes to German guns, a development soon copied by the Allies. Indeed, the muzzle brake on the Panther dispersed the recoil energy by some 70 per cent, and without it the gun could not be fired safely from the tank.[72]

In other ways, however, the British were less able to follow the German path as Allied tank designs often precluded mounting large guns, with the consequence that their main armaments remained of smaller calibre or shorter length. To solve this, two scientists, L. Perlmutter and S. W. Coppock, at the research unit of the Armaments Design Department at the Ministry of Supply, developed a round in which a narrow tungsten core was carried by light duralumin collars of bore diameter, the famous 'sabot' round. Earlier designs of similar principle (armour piercing, composite, rigid or APCR) had the collars or sleeve retained in flight, but this light and wide projectile rapidly lost velocity, and thus the effective range was short. Consequently, Perlmutter and Coppock designed an improved version in which the collars were engineered with weak spots such that they would begin to break up in the gun barrel after firing, but would remain in place until the round exited the muzzle. The collars would then be centrifugally discarded once the projectile was clear of the muzzle, facilitating more accurate flight and thus greater effective range. This round was named the APDS (armour piercing, discarding sabot) or 'sabot' round.[73] These designs allowed much greater muzzle velocity to be developed as the weight of the armour-piercing core was lower than that of a conventional round, but could still be fired from the same calibre weapon. Most importantly of all, this dramatically increased armour penetration capability. The APDS principle, now 'fin-stabilised', is still in use in modern anti-tank weaponry.[74]

Sabot rounds were developed for both the 6-pdr and the 17-pdr, and the former was in widespread use in Normandy, while the latter began to be introduced as the campaign unfolded. A sabot round could not be developed for the MV 75 mm gun but in contrast, the new ammunition development extended the useful life of the 6-pdr in an anti-tank role and rendered it competitive once more (see Chapter 5).[75] Moreover, it now easily surpassed the capability of the MV 75 mm gun in an anti-armour role. The 17-pdr sabot round was a revelation, with its muzzle velocity being increased by around 35 per cent and its AP capability by some 50 per cent at 1,000

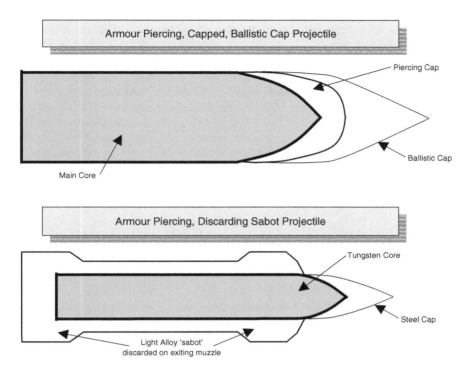

Figure 12. Principal Allied armour-piercing projectile types

yards.[76] Indeed, the standard APCBC type sometimes struggled to deal with the frontal armour of the Tiger and the Panther, but the 17-pdr sabot round cut through any German armour at likely battle ranges.

The drawbacks to the sabot round were its smaller projectile, which did less damage once it had penetrated its target, and its declining accuracy at long range.[77] The former was partly alleviated by using standard APCBC rounds at targets with less armour, up to and including the Panzer IV, and saving the sabot round for special heavily armoured targets. The fall off in accuracy proved to be a minor inconvenience in the close terrain of Normandy, as at likely battle ranges the sabot round was accurate enough.

However, there still remained the drawback of the weakness of the 6-pdr and the 17-pdr in a non-anti-tank role. The 6-pdr's HE charge remained too small, and nothing could be done to solve this, whereas the 17-pdr suffered from its high muzzle velocity, ideal for engaging armoured targets, but a severe hindrance for effective employment against soft targets. In essence, too high a muzzle velocity resulted in the HE content of the shell not having enough time to explode when it hit the target. Although an HE round was available for the 17-pdr, it had a low content to compensate for its high muzzle velocity, thus reducing its effectiveness, and it was not until a specially designed reduced charge version was introduced some months after Normandy that the problem was solved.[78]

Once again, although the British design and development process eventually produced the goods it proved to be some six to 12 months too late. Even in April 1945, SHAEF were still complaining that despite assurances given at the time of the decision to convert M4s into Fireflies that there would be sufficient quantities of both sabot and reduced charge HE ammunition, there were still shortages.[79] Despite the obvious advantages of the 17-pdr, even at the height of the crisis in July 1944, Montgomery passed over the idea of converting all tanks to mount the weapon until an effective HE round was available in sufficient quantity.[80]

Conclusion

The armour supplied to 21st Army Group for *Operation Overlord* represented both success and failure on the part of British industry. Following the disaster of 1940 and the urgent need for quantity output ahead of development, and in the light of the inherent weaknesses of the industrial base of tank production in Britain in the late 1930s and the early 1940s, the Cromwells and Churchills of 1944 marked a considerable recovery, to say nothing of the Comets and Centurions of 1945. Nevertheless, the recurring failures of 1940–43, when British tanks earned an unenviable reputation for poor reliability and qualitative deficiency, caused the adoption of solid and acceptable though flawed American designs. When the British tank industry appeared to have recovered by 1943 and was apparently capable of supplying more advanced models than contemporary US types, the lack of trust on the part of Churchill and the War Office was entirely understandable. The championing of the cause by the Ministries of Production and of Supply was only partially able to bridge the gap. The view persisted that British industry should concentrate on what it had thus far proved to be good at, and that did not include manufacturing first-class tanks. Indeed, the constant cuts in home-based tank production, down from an estimated figure of over 10,000 to less than 6,000 by 1944, and the unwillingness of the War Cabinet Defence Committee to interfere with aero-engine production was testament to this guiding principle. It took until 1945 for faith to be restored and when the equipment was being procured for Normandy in 1943, reliance was understandably placed on the M4 Sherman, available in large quantities and thoroughly dependable.

Nevertheless, there is no doubt that inadequacies existed in British armour by 1944. The lack of effective firepower was the most crippling deficiency, and for this the forces of production and supply must shoulder some responsibility with the relative failure of the A30 Challenger programme and the inability to co-ordinate the development of the A27 Cromwell and the HV 75 mm gun. In both cases the roots of the problem rested in the design process as well as failures of production, but the consequence was that whatever the shortcomings of the M4 Sherman, the British could produce little better for Normandy. Even in the case of the Churchill tank, which carried over 150 mm of armour and was by 1944 extremely reliable, its superiority over the Sherman in the close-support role was not so obvious that it could be considered an overwhelming vindication of the British tank industry.

However, the British production and supply process did achieve two considerable, though qualified successes in the months preceding *Overlord*, the Sherman Firefly and the sabot round. The former may have been a compromised hybrid, but it fulfilled a need and demonstrated considerable flexibility and ingenuity on the part of the British, while the new sabot round represented a substantial innovation, the basic concept of which still exists in modern armies. In both cases, however, the inability to provide either soon enough and in sufficient quantity was a limitation. Ultimately, the British tank industry and sources of overseas supply made good many of the deficiencies exposed in the 1940–42 period, but the design and production process was left with too much to accomplish prior to D-Day and only fully recovered by 1945. Indeed, although the technical shortcomings of Allied armour have been over-emphasised in explaining the difficulties faced by armoured forces in Normandy, it is indisputable that the inability to mount a top-grade weapon in a high-powered and relatively well-armoured tank did contribute partially to the predicament of British tank crews in 1944, and for this the forces of British armour production and supply must accept a degree of culpability.

8

MORALE AND MOTIVATION

'A louder crash sounds once, twice, thrice. A fan of fire shoots high into the sky, silhouetting a distant Sherman tank. Tiny figures of crewmen come squirming from its turret like maggots out of a ripe Camembert cheese. A new puff of fire lifts the turret into the air. Then there is only a Roman Candle of flame spurting the usual fireworks.'

Ken Tout, *Tank!*[1]

The morale and motivation of British troops in the Second World War has been under close scrutiny since the 1950s, when the view began to form that the British soldier lacked drive, determination and commitment, especially when compared to his German counterpart. It is further posited in many accounts and analyses that the supposedly moderate performance of 21st Army Group in Normandy was consequently, to a significant extent, explained by such weaknesses in morale. Ultimately, therefore, victory was attained through massive materiel superiority and that this compensated for the weaker morale and spirit of British fighting troops.[2] This view of moderate morale in 21st Army Group was in part shared by Allied high command in the Second World War. They contended that 21st Army Group's soldiers were, in comparison with their German counterparts, especially the Waffen SS, distinctly less well motivated and unwilling to conduct a high tempo of operations in trying circumstances. Consequently, Montgomery, who viewed good morale as fundamental to success in war, worked hard to sustain such levels as existed in his armies in order to facilitate the type of battlefield success he considered achievable. Alas, the exigencies of the nature of the fighting, his operational methods and the unfolding campaign served to weaken his efforts.

However, the assumption that reluctance to engage energetically and repeatedly in high-casualty close-quarter fighting was born of weak morale remains unproven and any direct link between fluctuating morale and battlefield performance is also both tenuous and circumstantial. Moreover, the accuracy of the general view, that Allied morale and motivation was significantly lower than that of German forces, is in itself doubtful. Indeed the sources

178

upon which these assumptions are predicated are vague and problematic and David French has recently called into question the soundness of the general perception that morale in 2nd British Army was unduly fragile.[3]

Armoured troops mirrored 21st Army Group as a whole and criticism was and has been levelled at the willingness of armoured formations to prosecute attacks as vigorously as they might. Liddell Hart argued in 1952 that all too often armoured units ground to a halt 'after suffering only "trifling casualties"', while Brig. James Hargest, the New Zealand army observer attached to XXX Corps, recorded in June 1944 that the Allies were suffering in part because of the Armoured Corps' lack of will to fight.[4] Kurt Meyer, GOC 12th SS during the latter part of the Normandy campaign, was scathing about the timidity of Allied tank crews, and in August 1944 German intelligence reports concluded that British armour was often halted when confronted by the most limited of opposition.[5]

It should be noted, however, that during the summer of 1944, British crews and commanders, often lacking battle experience, were confronted by a variety of issues and problems, many of them new, and had to deal with them whilst simultaneously prosecuting a campaign in which inflated expectations had been placed on the capabilities of armoured forces. As with the other ground troops deployed by the Allies, tank crews began *Operation Overlord* with high hopes, soon boosted by the apparent success of 6 June. However, difficulties quickly emerged. Tactical concerns, difficult terrain, a redoubtable enemy, 'Tiger-phobia', and declining faith in Allied equipment all supposedly served to weaken the resolve of tank crews.[6] Some units even developed a reputation for canniness and lack of drive, most famously in the case of the 7th Armoured Division. Soundly thrashed at Villers Bocage, criticised for lack of drive at *Goodwood* and sluggish during *Bluecoat* to the point that senior commanders were culled in an effort to reinvigorate the division, the famed Desert Rats are viewed as the prime example of an Allied armoured unit whose initially questionable morale slumped still further during the campaign. An obvious link is drawn between the formation's morale and its battlefield effectiveness and it is widely perceived that the experience of the fighting fused with latent resentment at having been used at the sharp end of yet another campaign, and that this resulted in the division's poor performance. Conversely, inexperienced units such as 11th Armoured acquitted themselves much better and ended the Normandy campaign with enhanced reputations.

This relationship between weak morale and operational shortcomings is by no means secure, however, for it is quite problematical to define morale, to ascertain how it was founded and fashioned, and indeed to what extent it determined battlefield success. Whatever may be gleaned from personal testimony, for example, notwithstanding all the inherent flaws and imperfections of such evidence, can rarely if at all, be quantified and can form only one part of a putative answer. Indeed, such evidence may support the contention that success on the battlefield was crucial to the sustenance and nurturing of morale and that troops were willing to endure greater suffering and loss if objectives were being achieved and the enemy being obviously defeated.[7] Yet it is difficult to quantify this evidence and offer an irrefutable case to support the contention. Moreover, although historians are drawn to combat as the true test of individual or unit morale, the great part of a soldier's time was, and is, spent in waiting. Maintaining morale through such periods of boredom and frustration while simultaneously carrying out mundane but essential tasks was crucial. An analysis of memoirs and oral evidence rapidly reveals the vital importance of hot food, tea and other basic essentials to fortifying the long-term resolve of soldiers.

Additionally, any study of morale in armoured units must take into account the factors that marked out the experience of fighting in a tank from the work of other military personnel. That armoured troops were different would seem obvious, but how did this manifest itself and what impact did it have on morale? Still further, as the experience of the Normandy campaign was distinct for tank crews, both in terms of how they existed and survived, and indeed in how they bore the burden of expectation placed upon them by fellow soldiers and senior officers, it is necessary to compare, where possible, respective levels of morale in armoured and non-armoured units. Consequently the aims of this chapter are to examine and analyse the experiences and detectable levels of morale in British armoured formations in Normandy, to highlight the distinctiveness of armoured troops, to ascertain any link between morale and battlefield performance, and to place armoured units within an overarching view of any morale problem in 21st Army Group and the manner in which this shaped the employment of armoured forces.

Montgomery, morale and 21st Army Group

The bolstering of morale was a key aspect of Montgomery's view on how 21st Army Group would conduct the campaign in northwest Europe in 1944. Indeed, he viewed morale as being the most important ingredient in determining the success or otherwise of *Operation Overlord* and the war generally.[8] To the commander of 21st Army Group, the fighting man was still the 'first weapon of war', and without good morale he contended that 'no success can be achieved in battle'.[9] Nevertheless, Montgomery almost certainly recognised the particular weaknesses of his command. While in public, he talked up the abilities of his forces and claimed that the British soldier, when led effectively, was the finest in the world, in private, it is more than likely that he took a more pragmatic view, one that recognised the shortcomings of his men in the same manner that Brooke and Wavell had discussed in 1942 (see Chapter 3).[10] As Stephen Hart has argued, however, this does not mean that Montgomery was not rightly proud of the progress the British Army had made in the years since 1940, but was evidence that he understood that 21st Army Group would not be battle hardened and brutalised in the way that the elite German units facing them in Normandy would be.[11] Consequently, Montgomery worked hard to boost morale where and whenever possible in an effort to encourage and support his troops. His tours of units prior to D-Day appear to have worked to some degree in raising spirits, and soldiers came away from such events with the view that here was a no-nonsense commander who, as in the Mediterranean theatre, was unlikely to fritter his men's lives away needlessly.[12] He was not, however, universally popular and his apparent craving of attention and publicity irritated some of the troops of his command, while others openly voiced their dismay to him at being deployed at the sharp end for *Operation Overlord*.[13] Nevertheless, there appears to have been at the very least grudging respect for Montgomery from most parts of 21st Army Group.[14]

Complicating matters still further was the manner in which command was exercised by 1944. Montgomery, in part influenced by his own Great War experiences, was acutely aware of the fact that the relationship between commanders and soldiers had changed by the Second World War. Troops could not be asked simply to obey orders when the likelihood of survival was low, while middle-ranking and junior officers were equally unwilling to issue such orders. As Gary Sheffield has argued, by the 1939–45 war command in the British Army was based partly on negotiation, and officers had to work harder to earn respect and trust before soldiers would follow orders instinctively.[15] For example, 19-year-old subaltern Robin Lemon, on joining 3RTR in the spring of 1944, was most conscious that his highly experienced desert veteran charges viewed him with great suspicion, and that until he had earned their trust he would have to tread carefully.[16] Sydney Jary, a junior officer in 4th Battalion Somerset Light Infantry, was also initially viewed most sceptically and had to prove himself capable before the soldiers, especially the NCOs, accepted his leadership.[17] It is apparent that broad concerns over the motivation and morale of the British soldier provided the backdrop to the nature of command in the summer of 1944. The effect of such qualms was the influence brought to bear on the methods with which operations would be conducted during the Normandy campaign.

Twenty-First Army Group was therefore a formation in which the commanding officer, in recognition of his concerns over his troops, endeavoured to limit the pressure placed on his forces, and thus sought to maintain adequate levels of morale in order to prosecute the campaign successfully. This was achieved in two particular ways. First, as has been previously argued, great weight was placed on firepower, to blast units on to objectives and thus limit casualties. Considerable preparation and planning was to precede each operation to enhance and focus such firepower to the utmost, and this included air power and naval gunnery as well as conventional artillery.[18] Second, armour was to play a vital role in supporting infantry and spearheading penetrations in an effort to provide mobile close-fire support and to maintain mobility and manoeuvre on the battlefield. In this way personnel losses would be held at acceptable levels and the strengths of 21st Army Group, firepower and mobility, would be employed to maximum effect.

The role of armour, therefore, in supporting morale was crucial. Tanks, like heavy artillery and air support, would demonstrate to ground troops the level of materiel superiority enjoyed by the Allies, and the commitment of commanders to defeat the enemy with metal rather than flesh, to paraphrase one contemporary observer.[19] Indeed, such was to be the impact of this measure that in time infantry became uneasy in the assault phase of operations when armour, sometimes for quite legitimate reasons, did not provide an obvious and comforting close presence.[20]

This role and importance placed a great burden of expectation on armoured formations in 21st Army Group, expectation that was at times out of proportion to the realities of armoured forces in Normandy in 1944. Inflated views of what might be achieved with armour and the consequent frustration that developed when such hopes were not realised created two problems. First, armoured formations were at times inappropriately employed by senior commanders. During *Operation Epsom*, Lt-Gen Richard O'Connor, GOC VIII Corps, prematurely launched 11th Armoured Division in the hope that it would be able to batter its way through to Hill 112, a task that should have been completed by other units, and which represented a misuse of an armoured division.[21] Most infamously, Lt-Gen Miles Dempsey's *Goodwood* plan called on three armoured divisions to spearhead the assault on the Bourguébus Ridge, a role for which they were clearly not structured or trained.[22] The losses incurred in such actions and, perhaps more importantly, the frustration and disappointment bred in units by operational failure served potentially to weaken morale and lessen determination in armoured formations.[23] Indeed, in the weeks following *Goodwood*, convictions in the three armoured divisions for desertion, going 'absent without leave' (AWOL), insubordination and drunkenness grew, while battle exhaustion rates likewise increased over the period of the operation.[24]

The second consequence of the undue expectations placed on armoured capabilities was the impact on other troops when it became clear that tanks and firepower could not solve the problems of confronting the stubborn German forces in Normandy. As the campaign slipped into a more attritional phase with the Allies hammering away repeatedly on German positions, and in mid-June to late July seemingly making little headway, the faith previously invested in artillery and armour began to be questioned. This was particularly so in infantry formations. Infantry shouldered a much greater burden during the campaign than had been expected or catered for, and the pressure increased when initially armour proved capable of offering only limited support during the all too often stymied break-in phases of battles. The difficulties faced by infantry were not salved by the patchy doctrine employed by armoured units. Great hopes had been built upon the employment of armour as a means of easing the pain of the infantry, which remained the job with the lowest survival rate on the Second World War battlefield. However, armoured forces were simply not capable of meeting such expectations in the operating environment and terrain of Normandy in 1944 with the result that the infantry were forced to fight at the sharp end more than had been imagined. Casualties mounted and morale in infantry formations slumped, more acutely and worryingly than in armoured formations.[25]

It is apparent that the operational methods developed by Montgomery and 21st Army Group, whilst generally serving the needs of the army, demonstrated a narrow understanding of what tanks could accomplish on the 1944 battlefield against an experienced and determined enemy. The problems were considerably exacerbated when the campaign bogged down, which further exposed the weaknesses in the thinking that underpinned the employment of armour in 21st Army Group. As will be discussed below, the impact of this on troops fighting at the sharp end was marked.

The experience of war

Soldiers in armoured units in Normandy endured a bloody and hard-fought campaign, suffering extreme hardship, for too long unmitigated by obvious success and progress on the battlefield. Not only did they have to cope with difficult and unexpected operating conditions, many also had to begin to learn the art of soldiering in its broadest sense as most had little if any experience of combat. Confronted with a recalcitrant and often more experienced foe, deployed in greater depth than encountered hitherto, and with heightening levels of frustration and desperation setting in, it is little wonder that morale began to slump as the summer dragged on. As it seems that morale and combat motivation never dipped to overly alarming levels, this should not be overstated, but it was with great relief that senior commanders welcomed the breakout in the closing days of July and early August.

Any examination of the morale of a body of troops exposed to campaigning can be effectively divided into two. First, soldiers' combat experience was essential in defining their continuing willingness to carry on putting themselves into the firing line. This was determined by perceptions of life expectancy in battle, confidence in command structures and recognition of progress and success. Second, soldiers required the basics of life to sustain them, and the quality of this support should not be dismissed as peripheral. The nature of most soldiering, even in an active campaign situation, is not of actual combat – this tends to occur in short, often clearly defined bursts – but of basic living, and recorded experiences of troops in Normandy support this view. Pre-*Overlord* discussions of how best to fortify resolve in soldiers focused on the comforts of life that could be afforded to those who were demonstrating signs of battle exhaustion.[26] Soldiers placed great emphasis on good food, shelter and relaxation time underpinning the maxim that an army marches on its stomach. Indeed, contrary to one recent view that a soldier's experience of war is defined by killing, the recurring theme of British troops' testimonies of Normandy is that of getting the job done and surviving.[27]

Moreover, tank crews had a series of morale and motivation issues peculiar to armoured forces. Unlike infantry or artillery units, where an obvious and open command structure existed, and where a clear division existed between officers and men, armoured units and most obviously individual crews, enjoyed a different and more intimate relationship. Whereas infantry units would work as a section or platoon with shifting and flexible group dynamics, and in which co-operating groups of soldiers could and often were fluid and interchangeable on the battlefield, tank crews acted as a single unit of four or usually five men in an enclosed and obviously defined space. They worked together closely, operating as a single fighting entity, with part of the crew often unaware of their battlefield situation or indeed predicament. They were often confined to their tanks for hours and sometimes days on end, forced into a situation where coping with differing personalities in an inescapable environment became of pressing importance. Ultimately, however, crews became acclimatised to such conditions and simply 'got on with it'.[28]

In most tanks in 21st Army Group, each crew consisted of five members fulfilling distinct roles. Although official policy dictated that individual crew members focused on their own task and supposedly learned to excel in this role, some crews took it upon themselves to cover two or three positions in the tank as insurance against injury and incapacitation in battle.[29] Churchills, Shermans and Cromwells conformed, as with most Second World War tanks, to a crew consisting of commander, gunner, loader/radio operator, driver, co-driver/hull machine gunner. The first three of these tasks were performed in the even more cramped turret, while the driving duties were conducted in the hull of the tank.

The commander, an officer or NCO, dictated the role of the tank in action, issuing tactical instructions from the turret hatch where much depended on visibility. Tanks were supposed to go into action 'buttoned up' with all hatches closed, but this rendered crews virtually blind in battle and commanders often operated with their upper turret hatch open to facilitate better situation awareness. However, the act of standing up for hours on end in extremely tense situations caused considerable fatigue and swollen ankles.[30] Moreover, this exposed them to small arms fire, shrapnel and snipers, and consequently commanders suffered the highest casualty rates within tank crews.[31] In some cases they were encouraged to wear steel helmets to reduce such head wounds, but this created problems with radio headsets and in the case of the Churchill, the commander could not simultaneously use the periscope and wear a standard issue British Army helmet.[32] The loss rate of commanders did at times become an issue, and between D-Day and 11 July the Nottinghamshire Sherwood Rangers Yeomanry, a highly experienced formation, suffered the loss of 40 tank commanders, including senior officers such as squadron commanders.[33] Of 3RTR's 39 officers, predominantly tank commanders, in situ at the commencement of the campaign in northwest Europe, only eight survived unscathed by May 1945, ten having being killed.[34] Despite such losses, however, commanders still considered it preferable to operating blind, one claiming that 'dangerous as it was for the commander to keep his head out, it was not so dangerous as shutting himself in'.[35]

The gunner was principally responsible for targeting and firing the main armament and operating the turret traverse mechanism, electrically powered in Allied tanks. Visibility again remained the greatest obstacle to fulfilling this role effectively, and to make matters worse there were complaints from gunners that ranging and optical devices were often inadequate, though comparisons with supposedly superior German equipment were largely based on hearsay and anecdotal evidence.[36]

The loader/radio operator fulfilled two duties. First, he would have to react to the communicated requirements of the commander for particular types of ammunition to be loaded, for which loaders sometimes wore asbestos mittens.[37] Rounds would be AP or HE, but could also be smoke and from the summer of 1944 special sabot AP rounds to combat heavily armoured German vehicles. This might be accomplished by the commander signalling to the loader, for example, one gesture or tap for HE, two for AP.[38] During battle, the loader would be 'too busy to be scared', locating appropriate rounds, pulling down the ejection lever, loading the gun sufficiently to close the breech and signalling to the gunner, only to repeat the operation seconds later.[39] The second role centred on the operation of the radio mostly for communication with troop or squadron commanders, as internal communication via the intercom was restricted largely to directions for the driver from the commander. Efficient radio operators were essential to the work of the commander, and a bad operator could increase the fatigue of the commander considerably.[40]

The driver, based in the hull of the tank, focused on the direction and speed of the tank, in action relying heavily on the commander's orders, as the hatches on the front of the tank, open in other situations, were obviously buttoned down in combat zones. Again visibility was poor and drivers had to traverse the tank across awkward terrain, perhaps under fire, using thick-glass vision blocks of limited value. Moreover, in the case of the Sherman, driving was a great physical effort, more so than forgiving British designs such as the Cromwell. Fatigue was the most significant problem facing a tank driver, coupled with concern over escape routes.[41] For the commander, the driver was considered the most important member of his crew, and the latter's ability to respond quickly and efficiently to commands was essential for successful battlefield operations.[42] Certainly a good driver increased the efficiency of those around him, as a balanced ride allowed others to carry out their tasks more effectively, without being thrown around inside the moving vehicle.[43]

The co-driver/hull machine gunner provided close anti-infantry support in action and aided the driver in other tasks. Perhaps equally importantly, the co-driver often doubled as the crew's cook, though in the Firefly, the hull machine gunner had to be removed to create space for the large 17-pdr rounds. In all cases, crews also had many other tasks to perform when not in action, centred on maintenance of the tank itself. Daily routines focused on the engine, armaments, radio and replenishing ammunition and fuel before basic human needs could be attended to. Consequently, excessive fatigue was a problem in armoured units as daily routines lasted longer than for many other arms.

Quite aside from the basic physical constraints and the problems therein, the psychological impact of prolonged confinement, often in highly dangerous situations, with a flow of radio information telling of fellow crews suffering casualties and deaths, heightened stress and neuroses to extreme levels. It was one thing to be told that life expectancy inside a tank was greater than that outside in a combat zone, but it was quite another to endure the long hours of stifling confinement with the horror of being incinerated inside your tank hanging over you.

Combat survivability was of critical concern to tank crews in Normandy and, as has been discussed in Chapter 4, there were stark problems confronting tank crews during the campaign. Testimony is replete with references to the fear of being caught inside a burning tank and was an obvious anxiety.[44] Troops were soon aware of the consequences of being trapped inside a vehicle in the process of 'brewing up', a view often informed by inspecting examples of such. Les Taylor, Northamptonshire Yeomanry:

> I climbed up to have a look inside the turret. The stench was indescribable. I saw the loader-operator, his hands frozen in the act of feeding a belt of ammo into his machine-gun, his head resting sideways on his arm. [T]he appalling thing was, the body was as black as coal. The gunner was just a shapeless mass of decomposition on the turret floor, but the most horrific sight of all was the crew commander... the projectile on entry had decapitated the poor man. [O]vercome with nausea, I scrambled down from that chamber of death and corruption and lit a cigarette... and vowed never again to look inside a k.o.'d tank.[45]

Maj. John Leytham, 82 Assault RE Squadron, ordered his men not to look inside destroyed tanks:

> Once an armoured piercing shell enters the turret of a tank, it acts in a manner similar to a domestic incinerator. The occupants of the turret are quickly smeared around the walls of the turret. I had given orders... that none of my men should look inside. A number were foolish enough to disobey my orders. It did not improve their morale. Vehicles like this should be taken back to the rear workshops where the experts spray the inside with creosote.

After a suitable interval they scrape off the remains from the walls of the turret.[46]

Studying the enemy's burned-out vehicles did little to ease the concern as a shared grisly fate confronted all tank crews:

> It was only curiosity which induced us to explore the burned-out German tank near Creully. We did not expect to intrude on the privacy of the crew still seated inside, charred to the size of wizened monkeys and to the consistency of burned sausages. The roasting of human flesh and the combustion of ammunition and the defecation of a million voracious flies created an aura of such sense-assaulting horror that we recoiled from it.[47]

Even the troops assigned to clear up the detritus of war after the action had moved on found the experience of investigating 'brewed up' tanks stressful and nauseating.[48]

Crews were well aware of the likelihood of their tanks, especially Shermans, 'brewing up' once penetrated, and that when hit or under fire, survival could be measured in seconds. To increase their chances of surviving being hit in combat, tank crews paid great attention to the task of bailing out, some even going as far as entering combat with all hatches open to expedite escape.[49] Brian Marchant, 9RTR, had specifically asked to join a Churchill unit partly because the Churchill tank had more escape hatches, while all crews considered it essential to ensure that prior to battle all hatches worked properly.[50] Moreover, although tank crews were drilled not to bail out until the commander had issued such an order, most learned to abandon the tank as soon as it had been hit or had struck a mine. Indeed, commanders often bailed out as fast as possible, without giving the order to abandon, for the turret crew might require them to get out first, there being insufficient turret hatches in some tanks.[51] However, it was not unusual in battle for hatches to be damaged or blocked. Indeed, hull crew could be trapped by the turret jamming and the main gun obstructing a hatch, while turret crew might be hindered by a body, most likely the commander, blocking the escape route.[52]

In hindsight, nicknaming the Sherman the Ronson or the Tommy Cooker seems sardonically humorous, but it represented clear and obvious contemporary anxieties. Senior officers discouraged the use of these terms, but to little avail.[53] Operational research reports confirmed the views of Sherman crews, as evidence suggested that around two-thirds to three-quarters of Shermans 'brewed up' when penetrated.[54] The tank crew would have a few seconds to bail out before the Sherman burst into flames, most often as a result of cordite flash, though petrol-fuelled fires also caused concern.[55] Any crew caught inside would meet a horrifying death. Indeed, the longer the period units spent equipped with Shermans the greater the fear of being burnt, one post-war report concluded, even though such worries were out of proportion to the likelihood of incineration. The report continued that crews often abandoned their tank as soon as their vehicle was hit for fear of being burned alive, even though it had not been penetrated, and that in all probability this tactic saved lives.[56]

Crews were also vexed by the apparent inadequacies of their own tanks, especially when compared to German opposition, and the weakness of armour protection sported by Allied tanks became of increasing concern as the campaign unfolded.[57] Although, in reality, armour protection was of little value against modern, heavy anti-tank weaponry at usual battle ranges, crews believed that their tanks were inadequately armoured. This was partly a result of the manner in which Allied tank armament proved to be inadequate against German Tigers and Panthers, and the lack of hitting power against the former in particular inflated the real value of the Tiger greatly. Allied crews in Panthers and Tigers would have encountered significant and similar problems if they had to maintain the burden of offence and if confronted by first-rate anti-tank weaponry, such as 88 mm or 17-pdr guns. Nevertheless, Allied tank crews understandably wanted the same level of apparent protection as offered by the superior German tanks. Indeed, when crews saw the mighty Tiger at close hand for the first time they were suitably impressed:

> A formidable monster, it looked much larger than our Churchills and half as heavy again. It was a real Tiger, the real McCoy.
> There was no doubt now, as we gazed up at its huge long gun . . . that here was the object of our nightmares.[58]

However, armour protection offered little resistance to HV 75 mm and 88 mm anti-tank guns, and although the Churchill tank carried heavier armour protection than almost any German tank in Normandy, it was still vulnerable, as crews found out to their chagrin.

It should be noted that crews claim not to have been fully informed of their predicament prior to D-Day, despite the dissemination of material to senior officers outlining the difficulties likely to be encountered.[59] Indeed, although less than a third of the tanks confronting 21st Army Group were clearly superior to Allied types, the discomfort felt by crews at the possibility of confronting a Tiger tank, even though so few were actually deployed by the Germans, fused with the growing frustration over slow progress to challenge morale.[60]

Tank crews attempted to increase their survival chances in whatever way they could. Many stacked track links, spare wheels, sandbags and discarded armour plate on their tanks in an effort to enhance protection, though technical investigation demonstrated that such measures did not increase the tank's survivability.[61] In an effort to assuage crew fears, appliqué armour was fitted to the hull sides of Shermans to provide extra protection for the ammunition bins. Again, operational research reports concluded that such additional defence made little if any difference, and may indeed have served as aiming points for German gunners.[62] In such cases, however, the operational research teams advised that, as crews seemed to believe that these measures were in some way beneficial, it was best to allow them to continue. Loading tanks with extra 'protection', however pointless in a physical sense, bolstered morale and increased the willingness of crews to expose themselves to combat.

Montgomery's views on sustaining morale were such that, expressly for the purposes of boosting the resolve of tank crews, he stamped very quickly and publicly on reports that began to circulate in June 1944 which claimed that Allied tanks were quite outclassed.[63] The reports were of an alarmist nature, as he put it, and he openly stated that the Allies had no difficulties dealing with Tigers and Panthers.[64] He was particularly scathing about reports being circulated from XXX Corps HQ, recently shaken by the debacle at Villers Bocage. He wrote to 21st Army Group HQ in London on 24 June arguing that:

If the sentiments expressed therein [XXX Corps report] get down to the troops, they may have a very great effect upon their fighting.

If we are not careful, there will be a danger of the troops developing a 'Tiger' and 'Panther' complex — when every tank becomes one of these types.[65]

Montgomery and his senior staff were well aware of the reality, however, and at the same time as downplaying the crisis, they were pushing hard for ever greater numbers of 17-pdr-equipped tanks and sabot ammunition to be introduced to alleviate the difficulties.[66] It is apparent that in an effort to maintain morale in armoured units during a difficult phase of the campaign, Montgomery claimed in public that which he knew in private to be untrue, that there was no problem with Allied equipment.

However, this policy may well have been counter-productive. In June 1944 few crews would have had experience of combating Tigers, fewer still, if any, had encountered the Panther, and in any case, most British and Canadian tank crews in 21st Army Group were green. Thus, as the intelligence passed on to senior commanders seems not to have filtered down to the sharp-end troops, it came as a serious and potentially disheartening shock when difficulties against the heavy German tanks were experienced. The policy of sustaining morale by inflating the capabilities and qualities of Allied tanks in pep talks and training therefore served only to breed frustration and resentment in tank crews when they discovered during the fighting in Normandy that all was not well. Jack Woods, 9RTR: 'What shook us all was the fact that we had been encouraged to believe that our Churchill tanks were practically invincible and the truth was very sobering indeed.'[67] Faith in Shermans and Cromwells was equally punctured, and in some cases crews also believed that information about the Panther had been concealed.[68] The dismay over lack of progress in June and July fused with this decline in faith in Allied equipment, and testimony and increasing exhaustion rates indicate that morale slumped. Post-war investigation argued that a more open and candid approach might have been beneficial. An ORS report claimed that morale was appreciably high in one regiment in which the CO had made a clear statement that Allied tanks were inferior. The report concluded: 'It is certain that high level statements to the effect that our armour was the "best in the world" were much resented by the men who fought in it as they considered the statement to be clearly untrue.'[69]

Whether a policy of openness and candour was realistic prior to D-Day in the prevailing optimistic climate is doubtful, and indeed it is also true that senior commanders did not expect the problems encountered by armoured units to be as severe as they subsequently proved to be. Nevertheless, the decline in confidence in their equipment felt by Allied tank crews was evident. One may question the extent to which this decline was actually caused by a 'tank gap', because it is almost certain that other factors were fundamental in creating the difficulties, but the perception in the minds of tank crews was real and formed an important part of the experience of armour personnel in the Normandy campaign. Allied tanks were more often than not being knocked out by Panzer IVs and Stugs, but the possibility existed that it might be a Tiger, and this created caution and reservation or what was known as Tiger-phobia.

However, although personnel losses to direct anti-tank fire were most prevalent, many casualties occurred when crews were outside their tanks. Later analysis demonstrated that while some 50 per cent of losses occurred to crewmen inside their vehicles, another 13 per cent became casualties when they were partially exposed, usually tank commanders directing actions from turret hatches. This accounted for the much higher proportion of officer casualties in this category (around 35 per cent). The remaining 37 per cent of casualties were inflicted on tank crews fully outside their vehicles.[70]

Bailing out of a damaged tank was dangerous enough, but when searching for cover, tank crews became dangerously exposed and vulnerable to small arms fire. Moreover, tanks were often sent forward into positions which would be considered too dangerous for infantry, but without their tank, this was effectively what tank crew became. Often in a dazed state after escaping a damaged vehicle, they fell easy prey to German infantry and vehicle-mounted machine guns. While in the North African campaigns opposing tank crews had often allowed bailed-out tank crews to run for cover, in Normandy less quarter was given, especially by the SS, and crews often became legitimate targets.[71] During fighting on Hill 112 in *Operation Jupiter*, a crew of 7 Troop,

B Squadron, 9RTR, were pinned down alongside their burning tank by enemy machine gun fire. The loader-operator, John Powell commented: 'Tankies [an RTR term for crew members] without their vehicles are a bit like shell-less tortoises on the battlefield and we felt strangely vulnerable.'[72] Moreover, the proportion of deaths to casualties when bailing out was much higher than in other categories and the chance of survival was rated at no better than 35 per cent in one report.[73]

In addition to casualties being suffered when bailing out, seeking cover or when partially exposed, many losses were endured when crews were caught outside their tanks during artillery bombardment. Artillery, and mortars in particular, caused the great majority of casualties on both sides during the war as a whole, and more emphatically so in Normandy where the often static nature of the campaign lent itself to heavy and sustained shelling and mortaring of enemy positions.[74] Tank crews repeatedly suffered casualties when caught outside their tanks during bombardments. Lt. Stuart Hills, Nottinghamshire Sherwood Rangers Yeomanry, 8th Armoured Brigade, noted the loss of the 'A' Squadron commander during a 'stonk', as well as other occasions when valuable crewmen were so lost. Indeed, he believed that most casualties in his unit were inflicted by mortar fire.[75] Robert Boscawen, Coldstream Guards, recorded the death of a fellow crew's radio operator from a mortar bomb which left the commander standing next to him unscathed.[76] During fighting on Hill 112 in mid-July, Stephen Dyson, 34th Tank Brigade, and his comrades endured the first of many casualties from flying shrapnel and quickly learnt that the safest place on the battlefield was inside their tanks:

> We dared not move outside the tank for more than a few minutes, as we were constantly subjected to mortar bomb attacks and shelling without warning. One corporal, caught outside his tank, didn't move quickly enough and was injured badly on the first day of our defensive vigil. He was the first of many such casualties.[77]

Officers would often dismount from their tanks in order to co-ordinate efforts with other units and commanders, usually infantry, but in so doing exposed themselves to artillery and mortar fire. For example, Maj. Douglas Ballantine, 'A' Squadron commander, 9RTR, was so lost at a critical moment of *Operation Jupiter*.[78]

Analysis indicated that at least 18 per cent of all armoured unit casualties were suffered when crewmen were on or off duty outside their tanks, while 12 per cent occurred when bailing out or seeking cover after being disabled. In addition a further 7 per cent were lost in unknown or non-identifiable circumstances when beyond the confines of their vehicles. Moreover, although the best statistical guide available, these figures cover the period subsequent to the crossing of the Rhine in 1945, and losses to artillery fire would almost certainly have been higher in the confined space of Normandy.[79] It is therefore likely that around a quarter of casualties in tank units occurred when away from actual sharp-end action and that while crews were encouraged to remain in their tanks when possible, even if in waiting areas or when leaguered, a variety of factors and basic needs drove crews into taking risks outside the protection of their armour plate.

This was quite understandable, however, as living inside a tank for long periods of time was not a pleasant experience:

> Five men in close proximity, three in the turret and two below in the driving compartment, all in a thick metal oven, soon produced a foul smell, humanity . . . cordite and heat.[80]

Another account implies a very similar life:

> As well as feeling the effects of claustrophobia, we found that the stench in the tank was almost unbearable at times during the hot summer days. The foul smell from the carcasses of dead cattle nearby added to the stink of decay emanating from half-buried corpses, disturbed in their last resting places by shelling. Apart from this, unburied human excreta and rotting leftovers of meals were littered all over the place, combining to create a flies' paradise. The masses of writhing maggots produced millions of huge bluebottles which plagued us constantly . . . [81]

Crews could be confined to their tanks for hours or even days on end, fearful of going outside and constantly on alert. Natural human functions had to be accommodated and crewmen made use of spent shell cases for urinating, though defecation forced tankers to run the gauntlet of the outside world, armed with a shovel. Such jaunts could be terminated by shelling or small arms fire and crewmen would have to make an undignified retreat back to their tank. Moreover, the tense atmosphere could easily fuse with the unpleasant smells inside the tank to provoke vomiting, which naturally made matters still worse.

In such confined circumstances, most crews were forced to live on tea and biscuits, sometimes smeared thickly with jam, and sustenance of this kind could be taken in the midst of battles, as crews awaited the call to move from one position to another.[82] A few more adventurous souls developed the skills to offer a greater variety of food to their comrades whilst confined, but most lived on simple fare, and the type of diet contributed to the ongoing problem of constipation, already rife because crew would put off the need to exit the tank as long as possible.

Action could often be a relief from the waiting and would actually act as a release for tension and fear. Many confided that it was the thinking time that most undermined their spirit and that when in combat, fears were forced to the back of the mind:

> It's only before battle (or after it) that the turmoil takes place and one has to conquer that all-important emotion of fear, which every single man inevitably experiences. Battle is pretty grim, but it's the after-effects and the realisation of losses and dangers encountered that is the other half of it.[83]

Moreover, if crews were confined to their tanks following intensive action, tensions could grow significantly, sometimes to breaking point:

> We saw a troop sergeant...being carried away unconscious in a scout-car having deliberately inhaled the exhaust fumes of a petrol-driven portable battery charger and suffered carbon monoxide poisoning. We heard later that he recovered, but we never saw him again.[84]

Breakdown could manifest itself in a number of ways:

> Our gunner...was carted off in an ambulance. Nobody quite knew what had happened, but for some reason he would not come out of the tank. He slept in it, ate in it, refused the opportunity even of a game of football, which he loved. Sam speculated that he had become 'armour-conscious', needing to feel he had the security of being inside the tank all the time. Or perhaps he had drawn too deeply on his own particular well of endurance, had seen too many terrible sights, suffered too many vivid nightmares.[85]

Tank crews had little sympathy for the cases of cowardice or self-inflicted wounds, and also believed that they could determine when a fellow was faking it or not:

> We couldn't do the same [give the benefit of the doubt] for a corporal, and a tank commander at that, who suddenly rushed away from his tank and crouched in a ditch, trembling as though shell-shocked.[86]

Some contrived to break a foot by trapping it whilst jumping out of their tank, though others thought this more courageous than facing the enemy. By the later stages of the campaign, anyone injured in a similar manner, even when genuine, was forced to endure the considerable embarrassment of being the subject of a special report.[87] Nevertheless, the incidence of self-inflicted wounds was probably low (such examples as were investigated tended to occur in infantry units), and in any case the issue was not considered a problem by the authorities during the campaign.[88]

Dealing with loss of colleagues and friends was, understandably, particularly difficult. Many became hardened to the realities of war and developed personal methods for dealing with the death of comrades. For Bill Close, 3RTR, 'it did not pay to make special pals. Too many friendships were cut short.'[89] Robert Boscawen thought similarly: 'In action where one sees so many of one's friends being killed and wounded, it seems to become a natural thing and one treats it with calm indifference, knowing I suppose one is so close to it oneself.'[90]

Combat was by necessity a desensitising experience for many soldiers, but tank crew endured a particular tension in battle, that of being detached from their surroundings. Unlike infantrymen, most tank crew were rarely aware of the ebb and flow of battle, and confusion and bewilderment could breed frustration and tension, adding to the pressures already being endured. Even commanders could feel confused and swept up in the chaos of the battlefield, unsure as to who was who, and crewmen inside had only a vague notion of how the battle was progressing, gleaning snippets of information from the radio or by deciphering the battle noises around them.[91]

Despite all these many stresses and pressures, breakdown due to battle exhaustion occurred less frequently in armoured units than infantry, though psychiatrists attached to 2nd British Army estimated that for every case recorded there were three or four ineffective men remaining with their unit.[92] When troops cracked they were sent to Battle Exhaustion Centres where treatment consisted of five to seven days of rest and recuperation, with drug-induced sleep, hot food, clean clothes, quiet, games and discussions.[93] Fatigue was viewed as the greatest contributor to battle exhaustion, and in many cases relaxation and rest was enough to allow some 30–40 per cent of such troops to return to their frontline units, though the rate at which these returned soldiers subsequently broke down was not recorded.[94]

Non-combat environment

Although the most stressful period of a soldier's life, combat constituted only a small percentage of his time. Even when close to frontline action, most tank crews were largely concerned with the humdrum necessities of life. Indeed, the basics provided the firm foundations upon which steady morale was based and testimony supports the view that decent food and shelter, links with home, and *esprit de corps* were critical in sustaining motivation and determination.[95]

Quality of food played an important part in bolstering morale. After a period in action troops recorded that the supply of hot food, tea and cigarettes was most definitely welcomed. The ration packs issued to tank crews were considered by veterans to be quite good and a distinct improvement on the staple diet of bully beef and biscuits endured in the desert. Indeed, three-day packs for a tank crew of five could consist of soups, stews, steak and dessert puddings, chocolate, sweets and so on with enough variety to tempt even the Americans.[96] The biscuits, used to replace bread in the troops' diet were not so popular, especially with new crews recently used to fresh bread.[97] When out of the line, mess facilities might be improved, but generally crews were forced to use their initiative. Supplements to the diet were gratefully accepted and trades with, and theft from, the civilian population could provide a feast of fresh food. Trevor Greenwood of 9RTR recorded:

> Most of the crews now seem to have a dead chicken hanging on their tanks. There are many more running wild in nearby village, also many tame rabbits. Know of at least one crew, in B [squadron], who have shot a young calf...and have veal.[98]

Crews could often trade cigarettes, sweets and chocolate for eggs, bread and sausages, all of which increased the range of culinary offerings in a manner that was never possible for those who had experienced the campaign in North Africa.

Tea was a key concern, unsurprisingly, for British tank crews and even in the midst of actions, if it were possible, crewmen would brew some tea to complement the jam and biscuits. Often during periods close to the frontline this might be the only means of sustenance. According to one rifleman, Roland Jefferson, 8th Rifle Brigade:

> The best way of making a cup of tea was to put some sandy soil in one biscuit tin and pour in liberal quantities of petrol. Then fill another tin with water, place one on top of the other and put a lighted match to the petrol.[99]

This was the desert method carried forward into northwest Europe. The ration pack tea, however, caused a little consternation to some, as remembered by John Stone, 9RTR:

> A tin contained pre-mixed powdered tea, powdered milk and powdered sugar. The question was, how to brew it? The tea needed infusing and the milk simmering, and a proper compromise seemed unattainable. We tried all sorts of ways, but our favourite was to brew it for thirty minutes, and then add three spoonfuls of sugar per cup. The original Sergeant-Major's tea![100]

Nevertheless, tea was an essential tool for providing crews with an occasional sense of normality. Keeping clean was likewise valued highly, but was difficult in the conditions.[101] Troops could go for days without proper cleaning, and this added to the problems of being confined to tanks for long periods of time.

Alcohol, identified by John Keegan as a key factor in fortifying the resolve of soldiers on the battlefield, certainly played a role in Normandy, though only in limited ways.[102] It was undoubtedly used to steady nerves at particular moments, and Robert Boscawen carried a bottle of whisky around to boost morale among fellows when required, while the 9RTR CO employed brandy in a similar vein.[103] Official rum rations, given in one-ounce tots per man, were also on occasion supplied to troops prior to going into action, but this does not seem to have been standard practice and was only supposed to be issued if considered 'essential for safeguarding the health of the troops under their [senior medical officer's] charge'. Hot soup, tea or cocoa was considered preferable to alcohol for reviving spirits.[104] Indeed, the acquisition by troops of Calvados, an apple brandy widespread in Normandy, whilst useful in some respects in providing a lift, caused difficulties in other ways, often being of poor quality. It was described as 'gut-rot' or 'awfully nasty stuff' by some, and commanders on occasion had to issue orders that it was not to be consumed. Not only did it cause minor discipline problems, but poor Calvados also induced stomach cramps, and in some cases supposedly affected sight.[105] Ultimately, in armoured units, alcohol was often eschewed as troops required all their faculties both in action and in maintaining their vehicles and alcohol was contrary to such efficiency.[106]

Links with the outside world, and families in particular, were considered essential for the maintenance of morale and soldiers were actively encouraged to read newspapers and write letters. Many recorded that it was a useful exercise in unburdening themselves, and though officers were supposed to vet such letters, they did so grudgingly and tried not to be seen to interfere with this link with normality.[107] Music and sing-a-longs were also widespread and helped to sustain identity and morale, especially when all became involved.[108] The use of entertainment units provided by ENSA was appreciated and in the wake of *Bluecoat*, 7th Armoured Division was treated to shows starring George Formby, which, coupled with glorious weather, did a good deal to strengthen morale.[109]

What does seem to be the case is that the notion of the war being a great crusade against Nazism was no more pronounced in armoured formations than in any others. Despite efforts by the British Army to inculcate into its recruits some view of what the war was about, that is, in terms of defending liberal democracy and freedom, most soldiers saw the war in narrower terms.[110] Political speeches and discussions with officers were viewed with suspicion and some amusement by the ranks, and appear to have had little impact.[111] There is evidence of a hazy view of the war being necessary and that Hitler had to be stopped, but a soldier's life in an active unit centred upon survival and mundane matters, such as food and shelter, and some form of recreation, usually beer (in too short supply in Normandy, according to some), football and women.[112] Ultimately, troops wanted to get the job done as quickly and efficiently as possible so that they could get home and resume their civilian lives.

However, there were other factors, peculiar to armoured troops, that proved important in maintaining spirits, and most notable of these was small group identity. Tankers spent most of their time in very close proximity with the other members of their crew, and daily routines involved close co-operation. Crews slept together under tarpaulins attached to the sides of their tanks, inside their vehicles, or in some cases under their tanks, though rumours spread that in soft ground tanks had been known to sink and smother their crews as they slept.[113] Moreover, although the relationship between officers and other ranks in the British Army was clearly defined in training philosophy as being one in which obedience was met with paternal leadership, in armoured units this dichotomy was less distinct.[114] Unlike the infantry or artillery, officers lived closely with the men, there being no easy or obvious way to remain separate. Indeed, within tank crews, though less so outside, officers and men occasionally referred to each other by first names, and this appears to have had no deleterious effect on discipline or command.[115] Consequently, a closer identity may have been formed in tank formations, aided in some units by the keen attention of officers to the well-being of their men. Maj. Bill Close, 'A' Squadron Commander, 3RTR, made strenuous efforts to get to know the first names of all the men in his squadron, believing that such links created a closer identity, enhanced the resilience of his unit in battle, and allowed them to deal with adversity more effectively.[116] Other officers attempted to support morale in a similar manner.[117]

There is little doubt that small unit identity, more pronounced in armoured units, was important, therefore, in sustaining morale, though with high casualty rates and rapid changes in crew members this should not be unduly overstated. It is also a valid proposition that NCOs and junior officers played a more important role in maintaining the thrust of an armoured force in battle, as they had much greater control over the manner in which their tanks and troops fought any given action. Unlike infantry leaders, whose men could seek opportunities to go to ground or hide more easily, individual tank crew were placed in a situation where they were under the direct and inescapable command of their leader. As motivation of NCOs and officers was more pronounced and ingrained, armoured formations usually displayed greater *elan* in battle than British infantry, as occasionally conceded in some, though not all, German sources.[118] It should also be noted that tank commanders suffered proportionately higher casualties than any other position in armoured units, but though this could have had the effect of depressing drive and commitment in action, there is no obvious evidence to support this possibility.[119] Indeed, replacement tank commanders tended to be well trained and competent, and any initial lack of experience was mitigated by ignorance and optimism.[120]

Officers and senior NCOs were also identified in pre-*Overlord* reports as being crucial to maintaining tactical effectiveness and supporting morale within units, as they were uniquely in a position to identify those troops who appeared to be on the verge of breakdown, whence appropriate action could be taken. They themselves were also open to scrutiny by fellow officers and commanders, and if it seemed that rest was required they too could and should, according to Medical Corps directives, be withdrawn for a short time to recuperate, aided by drug-induced sleep.[121] In armoured units, the role of the officer and NCO tank commanders was therefore fundamental to the well-being of their charges and fellows. They had a direct and pivotal role in driving units tactically, more so than in infantry formations, and in monitoring and detecting levels of battle exhaustion. Theoretically, this could create weaknesses, as the unit's effectiveness was markedly more vulnerable to the excessive pressures placed upon commanders. Ultimately, any crumbling of morale within the tank commanders would inevitably lead to lower battle-field effectiveness. However, such problems never manifested themselves in any serious manner, even, as will be explored below, in the much-maligned 7th Armoured Division.

The impact of war

Analysing the experience of war and its impact on morale and effectiveness in armoured units in Normandy is fraught with difficulties. Morale in its widest sense is notoriously difficult to define, despite many attempts, and thus interpreting incomplete evidence against a backdrop of vague and indeterminate concepts creates great problems. Conventional methods of gauging levels of morale have relied heavily on oral testimony, battle performance and reputation, and a limited number of observational reports, in some cases produced by German intelligence and units.[122] Those pieces of testimony relating to British and Canadian armour are likewise scant and on close examination potentially misleading, especially considering some of their authors.[123] As David French has argued, reliance on such sources and overviews can and has led to distorted assessments of the level and nature of morale in 21st Army Group, and 2nd British Army in particular.[124]

Nevertheless, alternative and additional sources are available which, while still suffering from flaws and discrepancies, allow a more complete view of morale in British units, and importantly differences between types of units and formations to be developed. Statistics covering convictions for desertion, going AWOL, insubordination and drunkenness, along with battle exhaustion rates in British 2nd Army offer a clearer though still not perfect view of the impact of war on armoured units' morale. In using such material a number of caveats should be accepted. Trends within the battle exhaustion rates are detectable, but are prone to influence from shifting initiatives imposed by higher authorities as they responded to the increasing numbers of cases being referred to the exhaustion centres established shortly after D-Day itself. It is more than likely that the figures for the campaign to mid-July exaggerated the numbers of cases, as soldiers suffering from a variety of problems were too freely categorised as exhaustion cases and returned to the newly established Corps Exhaustion Centres, and this in spite of instructions prior to *Overlord* that only clearly defined cases of battle exhaustion should be so referred.[125] The surge in exhaustion cases, doubling from c. 10 to 20 per cent as a proportion of all non-fatal battle casualties over the course of the first month's fighting, and which threatened to overwhelm the exhaustion centres, nevertheless remained within the predicted range, though a number of examples emerged of troops being evacuated to Britain when guidelines indicated that they should not have been.[126] Subsequent measures to bring the problem under control caused a reduction from mid-July onwards, back down towards 10 per cent, after RMOs were instructed to be much more precise in diagnosing battle exhaustion, which probably then led to an underestimation of exhaustion cases.[127] The establishment of divisional exhaustion centres also played a role by adding an extra filtering layer.[128] Nevertheless, the exhaustion figures are illuminating and an important source for understanding the ebb and flow of morale within all units in Normandy. Indeed, it was considered by the senior psychiatrist attached to 2nd British Army that the battle exhaustion rate provided an 'index of that unit's quality of men and of its well being and morale'.[129]

The figures covering convictions for desertion, AWOL, insubordination and drunkeness can also only be a guide as they are both incomplete and prone to unevenness. Indeed, some units and commanders dealt with potential convictions in quite different ways and at different times. Some proceeded with cases quickly, while others tended to allow a cooling off period.[130] Consequently, figures in some formations demonstrate a lag effect, and in all cases convictions listed in July may well have applied to incidents occurring in June and early July, while those in August may refer to cases from the latter half of July and early August, and so on. Moreover, pressure was certainly applied at one stage of the campaign by the Judge Advocate General's department in an effort to stiffen the resolve of commanders in the face of trying circumstances.[131] Nevertheless, certain interpretations can be derived from the conviction and exhaustion rates, painting a more complete picture of morale in armoured formations in 21st Army Group.

The conviction rates in Table 1 raise a number of issues. First, from a low starting point in June, numbers of convictions increased during the campaign's attritional phase, peaking in August, though at no time could they be considered excessive. Armoured formations mirror this trend, and though conviction figures are never high, they do increase in August following the heavy fighting in the difficult and frustrating terrain encountered in the *Bluecoat* battles, in

Table 1. Convictions for AWOL, desertion, insubordination and drunkenness in 2nd British
Army, June–September 1944

	Armoured brigades			
	June	July	Aug	Sept
Veteran				
22nd (*7th Armoured Divison*)	4	4	24	5
4th		3		4
Mixed veteran and green				
8th	1	1	1	
27th	1	0		
29th (*11th Armoured Division*)	1	0	8	5
Green				
5th Guards (*Guards Armoured Div*)	2	1	8	5
6th Guards Tank	0	2	6	3
33rd		0	0	1
31st Tank	2	1		
30th	2	2	0	
1st Tank			12	0
1st Assault		3		
Totals	13	17	59	23
Averages	1.6	1.5	7.4	3.8

	Infantry brigades			
	June	July	Aug	Sept
Veterans				
131st (7th Armoured Division)	1	11	7	38
185th (3rd Inf Division)	7	0	26	30
9th (3rd Inf Division)		0		2
8th (3rd Inf Division)		0	10	16
153rd (51st Highland Division)	1	3	6	14
152nd (51st Highland Division)		4	5	37
154th (51st Highland Division)	4	0		5
69th (50th Tyne and Tees Division)	3	26	82	24
151st (50th Tyne and Tees Division)		11	36	12
231st (50th Tyne and Tees Division)		51	59	1
Totals	16	106	231	179
Averages	3.2	10.6	28.9	17.9
Averages not including 50th	3.3	2.6	10.8	20.3
Green				
159th (11th Armoured Division)	2	1	0	10
32nd Guards (Guards Arm Division)	1	3	10	0
44th (15th Scottish Inf Division)		4	20	8
46th (15th Scottish Inf Division)	2	13	25	11
227th (15th Scottish Inf Division)	3	4	27	17

129th (43rd Wessex Inf Division)	3	0	6	11
130th (43rd Wessex Inf Division)		0	20	6
214th (43rd Wessex Inf Division)		0	1	3
70th (49th Inf Division)		5	9	
146th (49th Inf Division)		0	2	11
147th (49th Inf Division)		5	17	6
71st (53rd Inf Division)	3	1	3	5
158th (53rd Inf Division)	3	9	8	5
160th (53rd Inf Division)	2	0	9	3
177th (59th Inf Division)	1		15	
197th (59th Inf Division)			1	
176th (59th Inf Division)	2	1	30	
Totals	22	46	203	96
Averages	2.2	3.1	11.9	7.4

No figures for 34th Tank Brigade

Source: WO 171/182, War Diary, Deputy Judge Advocate General, 21st Army Group, April–December 1944.

which all three British armoured divisions were substantially involved. Second, infantry brigades as a whole suffered from higher numbers of convictions than armoured brigades. In the light of the excessive losses suffered by infantry units when attacking this again is understandable. Third, average figures imply that veteran infantry brigades may have suffered from larger numbers of convictions than inexperienced units. In part this is the product of the high numbers of convictions coming from 50th Northumbrian Division. Rates are consistently higher, implying that either morale was distinctly weaker in that formation, or that methods of dealing with potential miscreants were more robust or perhaps harsh. Finally, there is considerable unevenness in the figures between certain brigades, but also between divisions, perhaps again demonstrating that approaches to possible convictions varied.

The most comprehensive exhaustion figures available (see Table 2), largely drawn from VIII Corps medical diary returns, also allow certain tentative points to be raised. Rates for infantry formations again tend to be higher than for armoured units, even allowing for relative sizes of forces engaged. The 15th (Scottish) Infantry Division, considered by many to be one of the best formations in Normandy, still suffered a weekly exhaustion rate per thousand men double that of the two armoured divisions under VIII Corps command during a similar period and engaged in similar operations. Moreover, it can be seen that units deployed at the sharp end, such as 11th Armoured at *Goodwood*, witnessed a significant increase in exhaustion rates. Many crews in 3RTR considered that *Goodwood* was the worst battle they endured in the war, even more so than the disastrous *Knightsbridge* in the desert campaign. Indeed, after *Goodwood*, one highly experienced squadron commander was confronted by three of his surviving troop sergeants asking

Table 2. Battle exhaustion rates – VIII Corps units

Units	Days involved	Battle exhaustion			Total casualties			Average daily strength			Weekly exhaust rate per 1,000 men
		Offrs	Rnks	Total	Offrs	Rnks	Total	Offrs	Rnks	Total	
Involved in Operations Epsom *and* Jupiter											
4th Armoured Brig	16	0	21	21	28	229	257	260	4800	5060	1.82
31st Tank Brigade	16	0	5	5	21	208	229	150	2600	2750	0.80
43rd Inf Div	15	4	382	386	120	2800	2920	820	16000	16820	10.71
53rd Inf Div	11	5	90	95	45	659	704	830	16000	16830	3.59
Involved in Operation Goodwood 18–27 July 1944											
7th Armoured	10	0	26	26	44	473	517	780	14600	15380	1.18
11th Armoured	8	1	82	83	72	905	977	710	13500	14210	5.11
Guards Armoured	10	2	68	70	37	500	537	740	14000	14740	3.32
Involved in Operation Bluecoat *and subsequent actions, 30 July–15 August 1944*											
6th Guards Tank Brig	16	3	10	13	27	173	200	180	3400	3580	1.59
Guards Armoured Div	14	2	50	52	83	1311	1394	690	13000	13690	1.90
11th Armoured Div	14	4	144	148	76	1380	1456	730	14600	15330	4.83
15th (S) Inf Div	14	4	282	286	88	1742	1830	810	16100	16910	8.46
In action for extended period in VIII Corps											
11th Armoured Div	58	8	296	304	215	3106	3321	680	13000	13680	2.68
Guards Armoured Div	49	6	165	171	134	2096	2230	570	10800	11370	2.15
4th Armoured Brig	33	0	31	31	34	276	310	250	4700	4950	1.33
31st Tank Brig	36	0	5	5	29	253	282	14	2600	2740	0.35
15th (S) Inf Div	40	6	502	508	244	4645	4889	780	15000	15780	5.63

Source: WO 177/343, VIII Corps Medical War Diaries.

to be taken off frontline duties.[132] Figures are again higher following the grim fighting during *Operation Bluecoat*. It could also be inferred from the figures in VIII Corps that, as the independent armoured brigades suffered fewer exhaustion casualties than the armoured divisions, that the divisional casualties were disproportionately higher within infantry battalions than armoured regiments. This is partly supported by the figures from *Operation Epsom*, where regimental returns are available and indicate that the armoured regiments endured exhaustion rates at something around half the rate of the infantry battalions within 11th Armoured Division.[133]

The much higher exhaustion and conviction rates in infantry formations are entirely understandable when it is noted that although constituting only some 16 per cent of 2nd British Army's order of battle, they suffered 71 per cent of the casualties.[134] For units in action for extended periods, and which often acted as the point formation, it was also unsurprising that morale may have started to dip. It was certainly the case that survival rates in armoured formations remained notably higher than infantry units, and this fused with the greater grip that could be placed by officers and senior NCOs upon their tank crews to ensure that armour displayed greater aggression on the battlefield than infantry. It is worth noting that exhaustion rates among officers were appreciably lower than amongst the other ranks, despite the casualty rate being higher. Even critical German reports, primarily designed to boost their own troops' morale, accepted that, while Tommy was no soldier, the tank crews displayed greater *elan* than their infantry counterparts.

However, this has not been the uniform view of armoured units in 21st Army Group expressed by historians and commentators. The most famous case to the contrary is that of the 7th Armoured Division, the Desert Rats, which highlights an enduring claim that veteran units were dismayed that Montgomery had called for their return to Britain to play a leading role in *Operation Overlord*. This disgruntlement then manifested itself in weak battlefield performance resulting to a significant degree from poor or depressed morale. This was particularly apparent in the 7th Armoured and ultimately resulted in the sardonically titled 'night of the long knives' in early August, when a cull of commanders in the division was employed to pep up the performance. Maj-Gen Bobby Erskine, the GOC, and Brig. Robert 'Loony' Hinde, the armoured brigade commander, were the notable victims from the division, but in all some 100 officers were shipped out in an effort to reinvigorate the formation. However, Erskine's replacement, Maj-Gen Gerald Verney, previously the 6th Guards Tank Brigade commander, still found the 7th Armoured a sluggish and unimpressive division, and roundly criticised the fighting men. He claimed that the troops were war weary and unwilling to take chances and that this created great difficulties for senior commanders:

> The commander who finds his men getting canny soon loses confidence and becomes nervy himself. If he also happens to have done a lot

of fighting, and especially if he has been brewed up in his tank once or twice, he gets slow and deliberate and is quite unable to take advantage of a situation that requires dash and enterprise, two elements particularly important in an armoured division, which exists to quickly exploit [*sic*] a favourable situation.[135]

Verney's view was perhaps shaped by his own inability to stiffen the resolve of the division and his subsequent replacement, but it has since been accepted that the veteran formations in 2nd British Army, 7th Armoured and 51st Highlanders in particular, displayed signs of battle fatigue and weariness to such an extent that it appreciably influenced their battlefield performance. Maj-Gen Pip Roberts, GOC 11th Armoured, also commented after the war on the lower fighting morale of 'veteran' units:

I think there can be no doubt whatsoever that Monty's principle of including experienced formations and units in the invasion force was unsound ... I noticed on ... several occasions the differences in dash between formations which had been fighting a long time and those who were fresh.[136]

Lt-Gen Brian Horrocks, who replaced Bucknall as XXX Corps commander in early August, simultaneous with the 7th Armoured cull, also supported the view that experienced units lacked drive:

After a longish period of fighting, the soldiers, though capable of looking after themselves, begin to see all the difficulties and lack the *elan* of fresh troops. They begin to feel it is time that they had a rest and someone else did some fighting. No doubt this is what happened in Normandy to these veteran divisions from the Middle East.[137]

Historians have reiterated this view of the effects of 'over-experience' on the fighting abilities of veteran units in Normandy. D'Este (1983), Hastings (1984) and Hart (2001) have all subscribed to the argument that war weariness impacted upon the fighting ability of such units.[138] David French (1997), though with more circumspection, has also written that veteran troops in 2nd British Army were more likely to fall foul of battle exhaustion, and that this was a problem which most obviously affected 50th and 51st Infantry and 7th Armoured divisions.[139] However, this view, though not entirely without foundation, is not as secure as has been imagined and the link between veteran status and weak battlefield performance within armoured formations can be challenged on two counts.

First, great emphasis has been placed on the experience of 7th Armoured Division, implying that this armoured formation alone carried veteran status into Normandy. In fact, the pattern of battle experience varied between formations. In addition to 7th Armoured Division, 4th Armoured Brigade, deployed from the beginning of the Normandy campaign, and involved in some of the heaviest fighting, chiefly on and around Hill 112 during *Operations Epsom* and *Jupiter*, was also a vastly experienced unit, with its regiments having seen action in North Africa and Sicily. Yet there are no accounts of this brigade suffering poor morale or weaker battlefield performance than contemporary 'green' or inexperienced formations. Still further, on its return from the Mediterranean, the greatly experienced 8th Armoured Brigade saw two of its regiments (the Staffordshire Yeomanry and 3rd Battalion Royal Tank Regiment [3RTR]) despatched into other armoured brigades in order to instil some experience into otherwise green formations. The Staffordshire Yeomanry was placed in 27th Armoured Brigade whilst 3RTR went to 29th Armoured Brigade in 11th Armoured Division. The Sherwood Rangers remained in 8th Armoured Brigade to be joined by two green regiments, 4/7th Royal Dragoons and 24th Lancers. Eighth Armoured Brigade, therefore, despite being described in some sources as a veteran unit, was in fact little more experienced than 29th Armoured Brigade, for example, usually described as a green unit. This latter formation fought as part of 11th Armoured Division, considered to be the best armoured division in 21st Army Group, and the brigade's leading armoured regiment was 3RTR, probably the most experienced armoured regiment in the British Army. It had fought in northwest Europe in 1940, eventually being evacuated from Dunkirk, and was then transferred to the Mediterranean, fighting throughout the North African campaign, in the midst of which the formation endured another evacuation following a transfer to Greece in 1941. Yet, in northwest Europe in 1944–45, 3RTR displayed no obvious symptoms of war weariness, despite being heavily involved in *Epsom*, leading from the front at *Goodwood* where the great majority of its tanks were written off, and playing a key role in the successes of 11th Armoured during *Bluecoat*. Eighth and 27th Armoured Brigades were similarly constituted with one veteran regiment and two green, and there are no particular accounts concerning lack of drive in these formations, either.

A second challenge to the link between veteran units and low levels of motivation and morale can be derived from the conviction and exhaustion rates. The battle exhaustion figures for VIII Corps units show no correlation between levels of experience prior to Normandy and the weekly exhaustion rates (see Table 2). Indeed, the veteran 4th Armoured Brigade's weekly exhaustion rate was lower than that of the two divisions considered 'green' that were operating under VIII Corps command. However, it can be surmised that the higher levels occurring in the armoured divisions were a product of the exhaustion cases being generated in the divisional infantry brigades – one conclusion that can be drawn safely from the Corps figures is that infantry exhaustion rates were generally higher than rates in armoured units. Finally, the conviction rates in Table 1, though incomplete, show no obvious and consistent correlation between veteran armoured units and increased levels.

Nevertheless, two pieces of evidence seem to support the contention that all was not well within 7th Armoured Division. First, the conviction numbers for 22nd Armoured Brigade (7th Armoured Division) do show a definite and marked increase in August alone, followed by a significant peak in the division's infantry brigade in September. In the latter case these numbers are not greatly in excess of other infantry brigades, but the armoured brigade's figure is out of the ordinary. Second, in the days following its establishment on 14 June, XXX Corps exhaustion centre received a disproportionate number of cases from 7th Armoured Division, some 63 out of 153 admitted.[140] Both examples would seem to indicate that morale and discipline were poorer than might have been expected and add credence to post-war reflections on the canniness being displayed by the division's troops.

However, the figures require closer attention before any conclusions may be drawn. The division's battle exhaustion figures in early June are high, but it should be noted that 57 of these cases occurred in the infantry brigade, while the other six emerged from the 65th Anti-Tank Regiment, Royal Artillery. Indeed, there were no recorded examples from the 22nd Armoured Brigade, despite its mauling at Villers Bocage immediately prior to the XXX Corps exhaustion centre being opened. This casts some doubt on the reliability of the figures, but at the very least implies once again that, while infantry formations were suffering heavier casualties, both physical and exhaustion, armoured formations were not affected to the same degree. Moreover, although the figures are high, it should be noted that 7th Armoured was involved in heavy fighting throughout this period, initially during the advance on Tilly-sur-Seulles, then at Villers Bocage, and finally in beating off a German counter-attack, all in the space of a week. Additionally, cases which probably should not have been classed as exhaustion were at this stage being packed off to the Corps Exhaustion Centre rather than being properly vetted in their units, a practice which, as has been noted above, was stamped upon a few weeks later.

The second piece of evidence, the convictions for desertion, AWOL, insubordination and drunkenness in 22nd Armoured Brigade, only rise sharply during August, covering offences committed in late July and early August. Therefore, it is probable that it was the heavy fighting and sluggish advance during *Bluecoat* that caused the nerves in 7th Armoured to fray a little, and it should also be noted that by mid-August the division had been in action or in contact with the enemy for 40 days, a length of time comparable to opposing German units.[141] Indeed, from 18 July to the end of *Bluecoat*, the Queens' Brigade (131st Infantry Brigade) suffered over 1,000 casualties, close on one-third of its normal complement, and 1/6th Queens' four rifle companies had been reduced from a usual strength of 400 to just 108.[142] Even more significantly, the cull of the commanders undoubtedly had an initially damaging effect on morale and many in the division perceived the sackings as a slight on their capabilities.[143]

It should not be doubted that the 7th Armoured Division did perform moderately in Normandy, but the evidence does not substantially support the contention that this was in some way linked to war weariness and poor morale. Indeed, Michael Reynolds places considerable blame on the inadequacies not of the sharp-end troops, but on the senior commanders, interestingly those who later complained about the lack of drive in those they commanded.[144] The division was poorly handled at a tactical and operational level most obviously during *Operation Perch*, but also at *Goodwood* when Hinde, perhaps at this stage lacking confidence, hung back when arguably most urgently required on 18 July. In addition, though the division employed a flexible organisation in which armoured and infantry battalions would co-operate, Erskine and Verney did not mirror the brigade level reorganisation employed by 11th and Guards from *Bluecoat* onwards, in which two mixed infantry–armour brigade groups were established. These were clearly failures in command and displayed a certain lack of adaptability, especially as the division's initial structure, influenced by the arrival of the faster Cromwells in place of Shermans, presupposed a mobile role that was quite unsuited to the unfolding nature of the Normandy campaign. The comments by Verney that he inherited a division living on its past reputation, unable and unwilling to come to terms with the difficulties inherent in combating the Germans in northwest Europe, are to a degree valid therefore. However, it was this narrow and blinkered thinking that compromised their performances in Normandy, and any comment linking weak battlefield performance to lack of drive on the part of the troops is simply not sufficiently supported by the evidence.

Conclusion

Morale was a crucial factor in determining battlefield success in Normandy and the senior commanders of 21st Army Group were rightly concerned as to how their predominantly inexperienced charges would react to the exigencies of intense and bitter combat. Contrary to the received wisdom, however, there is little evidence that Allied troops suffered from lack of drive because of questionable determination and morale. In the light of the underestimation of the requirement for infantry in Normandy, and the subsequent heavy burden placed upon these units, it is little wonder that the greatest evidence of exhaustion occurred in infantry brigades. Nevertheless, armoured forces demonstrated great resilience in Normandy, and the lower incidence of breakdown illustrates that tank combat was, despite all the difficulties encountered, still appreciably safer than fighting as infantry.

This is not to underplay the problems confronting armour in Normandy. Concern over battlefield survivability grew as the campaign ruthlessly exposed the tactical advantages held by the defending Germans, the failings, though much overstated, of Allied tanks, and the consequent losses that would have to be endured. However, even in such slogging matches as *Blue-coat*, and on the spectacular scale of *Goodwood*, although equipment loss was high, personnel losses were not so heavy as to undermine seriously morale in armoured units. Furthermore, though 27th Armoured Brigade was broken up in late July to supply replacement regiments for other formations suffering losses, there is no indication that a crisis was brewing in the armoured elements of 21st Army Group in the manner that was developing in the infantry.

However, although casualty rates were lower in armoured forces, different factors can be identified as sustaining morale and motivation in ways that could not be matched in other types of formation. This may be explained in two ways. Perhaps most importantly, the very nature of armoured warfare forced tank crews to work more closely under the direction of junior commanders, and consequently 'stickiness' or lack of drive was much less of an issue in armoured formations. Indeed, a level of responsibility invested in the more able troops, and deployed in a way in which they could directly exercise greater influence on battlefield operations, imbued armoured formations with considerable control. Second, one could also point to small-group identity as providing stability to armoured units. This did not necessarily manifest itself as close and friendly relationships between tank crew, but more often as collective professionalism and a need to work together to get the job done as efficiently as possible.

Such drive could, however, be undone by poor tactical handling, governed by inexperience or inappropriate doctrine (see Chapter 4), or equally by the adept manner with which German forces exploited the advantages in defence provided by the operating environment of Normandy. Nonetheless, British armoured units, the much-derided 7th Armoured Division included, showed no significant signs of weak battlefield performance being shaped by questionable morale or motivation throughout the Normandy campaign. Indeed, there is much to support the view that the armoured formations displayed considerable determination and commitment in the face of difficult operating conditions and when confronted by a determined, skilful and at times brutal foe.

9

CONCLUSION

As British tanks swept across northern France and on into the Low Countries in 1944, it appeared self-evident to the crews that they had a played a full and vital part in the campaign in Normandy that preceded the pursuit. They had battled hard against canny and determined opponents, often through difficult and unhelpful terrain, and in less than three months helped to win a spectacular victory. Their achievement, considering the humiliating reverses of 1940 and the sometimes chaotic and embarrassing fighting in Egypt and Libya, appeared to them to be hugely impressive.

Yet history has not served them well. Critics of the nature of the victory point to the near two-month stalemate in June and July when, despite massive advantages in materiel and troops, the Allies could not break the deadlock. Implicated in this 'failure' was the armoured arm of 21st Army Group. It has been claimed that they signally failed in their efforts to deliver a *blitzkrieg* style blow to their enemy, suffered heavy equipment loss because of a poor grasp of tactics, laboured with inadequate equipment and had been exposed as lacking the determination and drive so obviously apparent in their much respected German opponents. Historians such as John Ellis, Carlo D'Este, Roman Jary-mowycz and of course Basil Liddell Hart have all favoured, to greater or lesser degrees, this interpretation.[1] Even the MP Richard Stokes, who had campaigned hard for the improvement of British tank equipment in the war years, served to focus attention on the negative aspects of armoured actions in northwest Europe in 1944–45 when he published his pamphlet *Some Amazing Tank Facts* in 1945.[2] In essence, the efforts of the British tank arm have been viewed harshly when compared with the successes of the German panzers during the halcyon days of 1940–41. Against limited numbers of defending troops in Normandy British tanks had too often come to grief, most spectacularly of all in *Operation Goodwood*, when over 400 tanks were knocked out in one action.

This book has demonstrated, however, that these views are incomplete, distorted and based largely on the assumption of certain writers that the Allies should have fought a campaign quite different to the one that they did. This has resulted in a search for the roots of the failure to break through the German defences before August, and an overemphasis on the supposedly poor performance

209

of the armoured divisions, the cutting edge of 21st Army Group. Such an approach has proved unsatisfying as it neglects to accommodate the politico-strategic context of the campaign, and does not allow for the possibility that the British and Canadians actually fought in the most appropriate style and with the most effective methods available to them. Moreover, with a starting point that the campaign was won in spite, not because of operational and tactical methods, a balanced and measured assessment of the role of the armoured forces and its contribution to Allied victory has not been forthcoming.

In order to establish a more effective analysis, therefore, it has been necessary to put aside any prejudgement over the nature of the Allied victory and the role of armour in the attainment of success during the summer of 1944. Consequently, this book has focused on three key themes – operational and tactical doctrine; design, supply and battlefield shortcomings of equipment; and morale – all central to any considered assessment of British armour in the Normandy campaign. Factors such as the terrain, the nature of the opposition and the political and strategic pressures playing on the high command all interacted with these three themes, further defining the role and employment of armour. By focusing on doctrine, equipment and morale against a backdrop of these other influences, however, a clearer understanding and analysis of the role and importance of armour to Allied victory can be established.

The methods with which Montgomery and 21st Army Group intended to defeat the Germans in Normandy are obviously fundamental to any analysis of the effectiveness of armour.[3] Armour was not an independent force and had to be integrated not only with other arms, but also into a whole operational approach, itself dictated by prevailing military and political strategy. It would be unwise to criticise the British armoured formations in Normandy for not adopting techniques similar to those employed by the Soviets or Germans if such methods did not fit to the overall strategic view and operational methods deemed appropriate by Montgomery and his staff for achieving victory. The techniques developed and employed by 21st Army Group were predicated upon the three principles of low casualties, bolstering morale and resource superiority. Montgomery's assessment that a careful low-risk strategy founded upon 21st Army Group's advantages in equipment, firepower and ordnance would deliver a victory to the Allies with tolerable casualties was to be justified by the Normandy campaign.

Operational methods supported this approach by adopting a strategy based upon carefully prepared set-piece battles, well supported by firepower. Armour was to play a major role in this technique by supporting infantry on to their objectives and then exploiting the breach in the enemy lines by unleashing an armoured division into the enemy's rearzone. Montgomery's operational methods had defeated Rommel and the Axis forces in North Africa and proved workable in Sicily and Italy, bringing success to the Commonwealth armies following a period of failure. Criticism that the method only worked because of the superiority in resources enjoyed by the Allies from 1942 onwards misses the crucial point that because of such superiority it was entirely logical for it to be so founded. British operational technique was different from that adopted by the Germans, but it was both a logical and entirely suitable response to the strategic environment in which Britain existed by 1944.

The operational methods employed by 21st Army Group did impact, however, on the conduct of armoured actions in the summer of 1944. The techniques of carefully controlled set-piece engagements did not always suit the force structure of British armoured units, most obviously the divisions. The requirement for heavy concentrations of firepower to support narrowly focused attacks could often hinder armoured formations by breaking up road networks, cratering the ground and allowing the enemy to reorient defensive forces into any given area quickly to stymie advancing Allied troops. Moreover, senior commanders did not always demonstrate a clear appreciation of what armour could and could not achieve on the European battlefield by 1944, most obviously exemplified by *Goodwood*, but also by *Epsom* and *Totalise*. There was therefore at times a mismatch between expectation and capability, and a failure to appreciate what the consequences of 21st Army Group's operational methods were for armoured forces. Matters were not aided by the initial force structure of British armoured divisions, which was intended to support a dynamic and exploitative role rather than one best suited to the more cautious and firepower reliant methods of Montgomery.

Nevertheless, these shortcomings and deficiencies were of much less importance than the impact of the strategy adopted by the Germans in their desperate defence of Normandy.[4] Allied planning expected the *Heer* and SS to adopt a logical and rational response to *Overlord*, once the Anglo-Canadians and Americans were firmly established in Normandy. Once Rommel's plan for defeating the Allies on the beaches and in the first few hours or days of an invasion had failed, the logical plan was for the Germans to fall back on to ground of their own choosing with properly prepared defences with a mobile armoured force in support. Hitler's decision to pin the Allies as close to the beaches in Normandy as possible had the benefit of frustrating the enemy, but conversely resulted in his commanders and troops being unable to fight flexibly, and caused newly arrived troops to be fed into the line piecemeal. Little co-ordination was possible and the frustration of the German troops and commanders was all too evident. Forced to operate in an ad hoc and splintered fashion and constantly under the guns of the Allied navies, it is little wonder they began to crumble as the summer progressed.

However, although German strategy ultimately contributed to the Allies' crushing victory, it also caused Montgomery, Bradley and Dempsey some headaches, and their troops no end of tactical difficulties. Most obviously the German forward defence in Normandy forced the Allies to batter their way through tortuous terrain that was completely unsuited to armoured warfare of the type preferred by the Germans, and that prepared for by British and Canadian armoured divisions and brigades. Twenty-First Army Group had planned to be beyond Caen, certainly after a few days' fighting. When they were not, they were forced to adapt to entirely new circumstances. The consequences of this impacted most on the close-combat elements of the British and Canadian forces – the infantry and the armour. Whilst the infantry began to suffer increasing casualties, however, it was the armoured contingent that faced the greatest need to adapt its tactics to the circumstances and the terrain over which it was now engaged.

In this, they were largely successful, which is little acknowledged in previous assessments. The armoured divisions quickly identified the greater need for closer infantry–tank co-operation and began to develop mixed brigade groups, while the independent brigades also adapted their tactical techniques to the environment. British armour demonstrated considerable flexibility and adaptability, shaping their operating methods and tactics to the conditions, whilst fully recognising the inherent difficulties in employing tanks in the Norman terrain against determined opposition. However, the view oft stated that the Germans would naturally have done a better job is open to question. When they attempted to attack, German units encountered as many, and arguably more difficulties than the British, and suffered often appalling casualties at the hands of Allied firepower. Senior German commanders, however, proved less willing to accept that a modification in tactics was required than their British counterparts and frontline German units began to disintegrate as a consequence.[5]

The much-maligned British Army's approach to the interpretation of official doctrine also proved beneficial in Normandy. Timothy Harrison Place has argued convincingly that the doctrine inculcated in training programmes in the UK prior to D-Day was often flawed and at times quite damaging.[6] The most notable example of this was the attempt by Montgomery to impose his view of infantry–tank co-operation tactics upon 21st Army Group following his appointment in 1943. However, although this did have an impact, it was less damaging than it might have been because commanders retained the freedom to interpret doctrine as they saw fit, although direct contradiction of official teachings was unacceptable.

British armoured units benefited from this flexibility in two ways in Normandy. First, the non-rigid enforcement of doctrine allowed units to adapt to new circumstances and formulate solutions as and when necessary. When the British then became bogged down around Caen, fighting in terrain for which they had not prepared, they were able to identify the problem and devise new methods for dealing with it. By developing much closer infantry–armour co-operation in theatre and during the most intensive campaign they had yet encountered, they demonstrated considerable doctrinal adaptability. At times it was a painful and difficult learning curve, but by the end of the campaign it was obvious that good progress had been made. A second benefit of the British approach to doctrine was the willingness to jettison doctrine when it proved inappropriate. The 8th Army method of integrating tanks and infantry, for example, was soon seen to be unworkable and was quickly replaced by other tactics, often methods developed in Normandy between armour and infantry commanders following experience in battle. However, even from the earliest actions there is evidence that commanders were interpreting doctrine in quite different ways, in spite of Montgomery's dissemination of his experience from the Mediterranean. Clearly, the non-rigid enforcement of official doctrine allowed British armoured units to develop their own methods when the original tactics were proved to be inappropriate.

There were, however, two obvious deficiencies with the system. First, although a flexible approach allowed units to escape their doctrine when it was wrong, it also meant that it was not as uniformly practised as it should have been when it was right. The tank–infantry doctrine being developed in 21st Army Group prior to Montgomery's arrival, although more demanding, was much closer to that which would be implemented and developed in Normandy a year later. In Normandy, however, units employed a whole host of different methods for infantry–tank co-operation, ranging from the 8th Army approach, to pre-Montgomery 21st Army Group theories, and even SP artillery tactics. Clearly, therefore, even when the correct tactical methods were identified, there was little likelihood of getting all units to sing from the same hymn sheet. However, as has been seen, the British Army had a chequered history in developing the appropriate methods of employing armour, so a flexible approach was ultimately more appropriate and less risky. To have rigidly enforced the preferred official doctrine in the summer of 1944 would undoubtedly have created even greater difficulties.

The second shortcoming, particularly for infantry–tank co-operation was the lack of a uniform set of practices. Infantry battalions and armoured or tank regiments did not have a clear and standard set of co-operating procedures because of the willingness of senior commanders to allow subordinates some leeway in interpreting doctrine. Developing methods in theatre would have been best served by battalions and regiments co-operating together regularly such that they could devise closely integrated operating practices known to all. However, all too often units were moved around and infantry units would find themselves being supported by different tank formations that may well have devised slightly different methods of co-operation. Valuable time was lost on each occasion new units had to become acquainted with each other. Indeed, it seems to have been the case that familiarity with working practices and personnel was more important to harmonious co-operation than standardised employment of official doctrine. During preparation in Britain, 15th Scottish Infantry Division trained with 6th Guards Tank Brigade, and when paired during *Bluecoat* worked effectively with each other. During *Epsom*, however, 15th Scottish were supported by 31st Tank Brigade and unfamiliarity caused difficulties.

Clearly there were problems in the operational and tactical employment of armour in Normandy, particularly in the early stages of the campaign. The terrain and German strategy caused considerable difficulties, complicated by less than perfect doctrine and training, while 21st Army Group did not always match the needs and capabilities of armoured units to operational objectives and methods. Nevertheless, British armoured formations proved flexible enough to adapt and learn as the summer progressed and ultimately played a full role in the defeat of the Germans.

Undoubtedly the most enduring and popular image of armoured combat in Normandy is of thinly skinned and combustible Shermans facing heavily armed and armoured Tigers, against which they had little chance other than to swamp them with numbers. It is a compelling image, and one supported by the testimony of many British veterans, who became increasingly concerned as the campaign progressed that behind every hedge there could lie a Tiger in wait for them. It is a view supported by historians such as Max Hastings, Roman Jarymowycz and Russell Hart, who have all explained to a significant extent the 'failure' of Allied armour in Normandy as one of technical short-comings.[7] In essence the Shermans, Cromwells and Churchills were not up to the task in 1944 and the British Army was badly let down by the tank design and supply process.

This, however, is a partial explanation. As has been seen, the great majority of German tanks in Normandy were little if any better than the Allied types facing them. Even the mighty Tigers were notoriously unreliable and in the close confined spaces of Normandy the superiority of the Panther was mitigated by its vulnerability to flanking attacks. In the *bocage*, some German commanders even preferred the Mark IV to the Panther because of its compact shape and non-overhanging gun.[8] Moreover, many Germans units were equipped with outdated vehicles and some had to make do with hybrids and lash-ups. Most, however, at least carried good-quality armament and it was this, rather than increases in armour, that proved most useful in Normandy. Indeed, by 1944, and particularly at short ranges, armour protection on tanks offered little defence against the latest anti-tank weaponry, and operational research reports clearly stated that increasing armour protection on Allied tanks was pointless. German 88 mm and long 75 mm guns would cut through virtually anything that could conceivably be fielded, as illustrated by the vulnerability of even the heavy Churchill with over 150 mm of frontal armour.

Thus the main shortcoming in British tanks in Normandy was not inadequate armour but their weak firepower.[9] Indeed, the experience of the campaign demonstrated that although tanks in both the German and Allied corners suffered from weaknesses, the most pressing failing of Allied tanks was their reliance on the MV 75 mm gun. This weapon was not sufficiently capable of duelling with armour by 1944, and with the increasing use of SP guns by the Germans and the density of the defences, this was precisely what British tanks were being forced to do. Nevertheless, although the 75 mm gun was almost redundant against the heavy armour of the Tiger, it could cope with the Panther from the flanks, and, at the average ranges over which tank-to-tank actions were fought in Normandy, it could disable a Panzer IV or a Stug. Although the tactical environment and the urgency of their need to retain the initiative were much greater problems facing British tank Crews in the Summer of 1944, it was nonetheless understandable that the cries for more 17-pdrs were loud, clear and vociferous.[10]

The key to enhancing Allied tanks was therefore to increase firepower, and the inability of the British design and supply process to provide superior levels of anti-armour weaponry remains its one serious failing of the 1942–44 period. The decisions made concerning the armament of tanks in British units in Normandy dated back to late 1942 when the experience of the desert campaign seemed to indicate that the dual-purpose MV 75 mm gun would suffice for the short-to-medium term. This fallacy was not recognised until the late spring of 1943 by which time it was too late to rectify the shortcoming other than by the crash conversion programme of Shermans into Fireflies.

However, in other ways the design and production process so heavily criticised since the Second World War in fact made good progress between 1942 and 1944, resolving many shortcomings and developing a new generation of tanks. The programmes of 1940–42 aimed at producing any tank just to plug the gap left by the loss of equipment in 1940, had been superseded by schemes that attempted to meet the needs defined by the War Office and the General Staff following the disaster of the French campaign. The A27M Cromwell effectively fulfilled the specification laid down for it, accepted later enhancement, and by 1944 was a fast, mobile and reliable cruiser, surpassing the Sherman in capability. The A22/42 Churchill again provided the reliable, heavily armoured infantry support tank specified and had proved capable of being both upgunned and uparmoured since 1941. Moreover, British designers and manufacturers had adapted in short order to the need for the Firefly conversion, and had introduced the discarding sabot round to enhance armour penetration capability. By late 1944 the A34 Comet was arriving in service and a few months later the A41 Centurion emerged. They may have been unavailable for Normandy, but the design and production of these tanks indicated that the process was functioning effectively and had recovered from the crisis of 1940–41.

Nevertheless, despite these successes, the design and supply process can be said to have failed by not developing a tank with a hard-hitting anti-armour gun as desired by the General Staff. The A30 Challenger proved to be a disappointment and the inability to link the new HV 75 mm gun (later renamed the 77 mm gun) with the Cromwell, when for a time it appeared as though it could be, caused consternation and resentment. Indeed, these errors merely compounded with the disasters of 1940–42 in British tank development, to undermine the faith of the army and the prime minister in the ability of British industry to supply good-quality tanks. The position was only retrieved by the advent of the Firefly, and the confidence expressed over the A34 Comet.[11]

That there were shortcomings in the tanks provided to 21st Army Group in 1944 is not in doubt, but the scale of such deficiencies has been overstated and the degree to which they impacted significantly on the conduct of armoured operations greatly exaggerated. It is clear that the flaws in British tanks were underscored by the tactical environment and by the type of campaign they were forced to fight, especially as neither the Sherman nor the Cromwell was well suited to close infantry support. It is worth conjecturing, however, that if the Germans had fallen back and conducted a fluid and flexible defence of France, the shortcomings of the M4 and the A27 would have merely been minor irritants, while the failings of the Tiger may well have been even more ruthlessly exposed.

The post-war predilection for emphasising the superiority of German methods and tactics in the Second World War, partly to legitimise and underpin the doctrine being developed by NATO, also served to highlight the supposed disparity in the morale and fortitude of Allied and German troops.[12] This, it was claimed, became most obvious in the later stages of the war when, despite being in a quite hopeless position, German troops fought on with resolve and determination. In contrast, Allied troops proved cautious and 'sticky', unwilling to take risks, and were uninspired, though perhaps doughty. The element of 21st Army Group most requiring high morale to be successful was the armoured arm, and for many historians this was often not the case in practice. The high degree of caution and lack of desire for close combat in the Allied forces, so much based on the interpretation of Liddell Hart, Wilmot and limited contemporary sources of questionable worth, has become the orthodoxy in the post-war era.[13] It is an interpretation that emphasises the link between low morale and low-tempo operations in 21st Army Group, and moreover questions the resolve of veteran formations most severely. For the tank arm in particular, it has been contended that 7th Armoured Division demonstrated most clearly the symptoms of war weariness and resentment at being deployed at the sharp end of a campaign yet again, and that this partly resulted in the division's poor showing in Normandy.

Yet as has been seen, the evidence does not support this interpretation. German troops displayed great determination and resolution, but this was enhanced by the tactical nature of the campaign, which supported tough defence above determined offence, and the harsh and brutal conditions in which the German troops operated. Fearful of retreat lest it show weakness, resulting in scrutiny and punishment, especially after 20 July, German soldiers dug in and hoped for the best. Coupled with elements of ideological fanaticism and the consequences of the brutal campaign against the Soviet Union, many German troops fought on to the bitter end with grim and sardonic fatalism. Desperation, however, should not necessarily be equated with high morale, and, moreover, one might question whether the British or Canadian states would want their armies to aspire to such attitudes and methods.

What mattered more in 1944 was devising a means of defeating the German forces without resorting to brutalising Allied troops, and with acceptable casualties. As has been argued, the techniques employed, whilst acknowledging that British troops could and should not fight in the manner of the Germans, were successful. Yet because Allied forces did not mirror the risky and aggressive attitudes of the Germans, this has been explained by poor morale on the part of the British, rather than the adoption of specific techniques reflective of the operational and tactical environment in 1944, and of the qualities and superiority of 21st Army Group in key areas. British armoured units in Normandy fought within particular parameters and to a set of principles quite different to those imbued in their opponents. There was little merit in risking lives when a more measured approach supported success more effectively and with fewer casualties. It should also be noted that the determination and morale of British armour formations was clearly demonstrated in particular during *Goodwood* and *Bluecoat*, when units pressed on despite heavy losses and when the tactical conditions and terrain created a dreadful operating environment.

What then of the view that veteran units suffered from lower morale than other fresh units? Again, there is little evidence to provide a convincing case to support this contention. As has been seen, there is no obvious, consistent and clear correlation between degree of experience and measurable levels of battle exhaustion and convictions. More telling still, there is no apparent link between veteran status and weak battlefield performance, supposedly the measure of this line of reasoning. Although 7th Armoured Division did not enhance its reputation in Normandy, and arguably struggled to adapt, other veteran units performed well, notably 4th Armoured Brigade, 3RTR, the Staffordshire Yeomanry and the Sherwood Rangers, and there is no measurable evidence that any of these units suffered from poor morale.[14]

What is clear is the lower level of battle exhaustion casualties and convictions in armoured formations than their infantry counterparts. Whatever difficulties were encountered by tank crews in Normandy, and there were many, the nature of tank warfare and life, underpinned by the closer levels of teamwork and small group identity, demonstrated that low morale was not a serious problem in tank units in 1944. For this, the support structure and logistical network plus continuing, if at times fluctuating, faith in the command structure right up to Montgomery proved highly effective. It should of course be remembered that the British armoured units deployed in Normandy were for the most part new to war, and many of the troops inexperienced in combat. In conjunction with the many and varied problems and difficulties thrown up by the campaign, it is testament to the morale and resolve of British tankers that they coped as well as they did.

Ultimately, British armour played a full and crucial role in the Allied victory in Normandy in 1944. Far from contributing little, or being disappointing, Anglo-Canadian tank units and crews adapted well to the new tactical and operational environment thrust upon them, and demonstrated considerable flexibility and determination. Moreover, it was the strategic, operational and tactical nature of the campaign far more than German superiority, doctrinal shortcomings and failings in equipment that presented the most serious challenge to British armour. In spite of such difficulties and problems, nevertheless, British crews and commanders prevailed and from June onwards transformed themselves from a largely inexperienced and at times naïve force into an increasingly potent and resourceful arm well suited to supporting the operations of 21st Army Group.

NOTES

1. INTRODUCTION

1 L. F. Ellis, *Victory in the West*, vol. I (London: Her Majesty's Stationery Office, 1962), p. 223.

2 Ellis, *Victory in the West*, vol. I, pp. 217, 504–7.

3 H. H. Arnold, *Second Report of the Commanding General of the United States Army Air Forces* (Washington, DC: US Government Printing Office, 1945), p. 36; Air Ministry, *The Rise and Fall of the German Air Force* (London: His Majesty's Stationery Office, 1983 [1947]), pp. 323–32.

4 Martin Blumenson, 'General Bradley's Decision at Argentan (13 August 1944)', in *Command Decisions*, online edn, Center of Military History, Department of the Army, Washington, 2000 (originally published in 1959), www.army.mil/cmh-pg/books.

5 David Irving, *The War between the Generals* (London: Allen Lane, 1981), and Russell Weigley, *Eisenhower's Lieutenants: The Campaign of France and Germany 1944–5* (London: Sidgwick & Jackson, 1981) as the most obvious examples.

6 Correspondence in *Journal of Military History*, vol. 66, no. 3, pp. 965–7; vol. 67, no. 1, pp. 335–6; vol. 67, no. 2, pp. 663–5.

7 Robin Neillands, *The Battle of Normandy 1944* (London: Cassell, 2002), pp. 17–24.

8 Russell Hart, *Clash of Arms: How the Allies Won in Normandy* (Boulder, CO: Rienner, 2001); Williamson Murray and Allan R. Millett, *A War to Be Won: Fighting the Second World War* (Cambridge, MA: Harvard University Press, 2000), pp. 417–29.

9 John Ellis, *Brute Force: Allied Strategy and Tactics in the Second World War* (London: Andre Deutsch, 1990), pp. 373–88.

10 John Gooch, preface to Timothy Harrison Place, *Military Training in the British Army, 1940–1944: From Dunkirk to D-Day* (London: Cass, 2000).

11 Comments by Lt-Gen Martel following a lecture at the Royal United Services Institute on tank design. *Journal of the Royal United Services Institute*, vol. 96 (1951), p. 62.

12 Terry Copp, introduction to *Fields of Fire: The Canadians in Normandy* (Toronto: University of Toronto Press, 2003), pp. 5–15. By June 1944, Germans had executed some 7,000 of their soldiers for desertion and subversion: Manfred Messerschmidt, *Nazi Political Aims and German Military Law in World War Two* (Kingston, Ontario: Royal Military College of Canada, 1981), pp. 8–10.

13 Basil Liddell Hart, *The Other Side of the Hill: Germany's Generals – Their Rise and Fall, with their Own Account of Military Events, 1939–1945* (London: Cassell, rev. edin 1951 [1948], pp. 120–1; see also J. P. Harris, 'The Myth of Blitzkrieg', *War in History*, vol. 2, no. 3 (1995), pp. 339–40; and John Mearsheimer, *Liddell Hart and the Weight of History* (London: Cornell University Press, 1988), pp. 182–217.

14 LHCMA, Liddell Hart, 9/28/84, 'Tanks in Normandy', Liddell Hart to C. S. Forester, 18 February 1952; Liddell Hart, 11/1944/43-52, Basil Liddell Hart, notes on Normandy, 1952.

15 Copp, *Fields of Fire*, pp. 6–7.

16 Roman Jarymowycz, *Tank Tactics: From Normandy to Lorraine* (Boulder, CO: Rienner, 2001), pp. 83–4.

17 Comments by veteran officers who appeared on these tours, Major Bill Close, 3RTR, and Captain Robin Lemon, 3RTR, interviews with author, September and December 2002.

18 Ellis, *Brute Force*, pp. 373–88; John English, *The Canadian Army and the Normandy Campaign: A Study in the Failure of High Command* (Westport, CT: Praeger, 1991), p. 312.

19 R. A. Hart, *Clash of Arms*, p. 309.

20 Carlo D'Este, *Decision in Normandy* (London: HarperCollins, 1983), introduction and 'Price of Caution' chapter; Jarymowycz, *Tank Tactics*.

21 LHCMA, Liddell Hart, 9/28/84, Tanks in Normandy, Liddell Hart to C. S. Forrester, 18 February 1952; LHCMA, Liddell Hart correspondence with Field Marshal Lord Carver, 8 May 1952; CAB 106/1060, report by Brig. James Hargest, XXX Corps observer, covering the period 6 June to 10 July 1944.

22 Stephen A. Hart, *Montgomery and Colossal Cracks: The 21st Army Group in northwest Europe, 1944–5* (Westport, CT: Praeger, 2000).

23 Hansard, vol. 398, pp. 861–3, 22 March 1944; vol. 399, pp. 23–4, 18 April 1944; vol. 402, pp. 567, 1469–71, 1533–8, 2 August 1944; see also 'Was There a Tank Scandal?' *Picture Post*, 23 February 1946, pp. 12–13.

24 Hansard, vol. 402, p. 1533, 2 August 1944.

25 BOV, Richard R. Stokes MP, *Some Amazing Tank Facts* (1945), p. 3.

26 Max Hastings, *Overlord: D-Day and the Battle for Normandy 1944* (London: Michael Joseph, 1984), p. 229; see also Jarymowycz, *Tank Tactics*, p. 255, Hart, *Clash of Arms*, p. 309, and Peter Beale, *Death by Design: British Tank Development in the Second World War* (Stroud: Sutton, 1998); Kenneth Macksey, *Tank Force: Allied Armour in the Second World War* (London: Pan, 1970), pp. 138–41.

27 Tim Ripley, *The Wehrmacht: The German Army in World War Two 1939–45* (London: Fitzroy Dearborn, 2003), p. 305.

28 Chester Wilmot, *The Struggle for Europe* (London: Collins, 1952), pp. 130–1, 427–8, 463–5.

29 LHCMA, Alanbrooke, 6/2/6, Wavell to Brooke, 31 May 1942 and Brooke to Wavell, 5 July 1942; 14/61/9, Montgomery to Brooke, 27 November 1942 are all examples of this view. Maj-Gen Gerald Verney, who commanded 7th Armoured Division and Lt-Gen Brian Horrocks, GOC XXX Corps, also both recorded their belief that veteran soldiers lacked drive.

30 LHCMA, Liddell Hart, 11/1944/43-52, Liddell Hart, 'Lessons of Normandy' (1952); Liddell Hart 9/28/84, Tanks in Normandy, Liddell Hart to C. S. Forester, 18 February 1952; see also Kurt Meyer, *Grenadiers* (Winnipeg, Manitoba: J. J. Federowicz, 1994), pp. 280–98; WO 219/1908, SHAEF G-2 records, Operational Intelligence Sectionnotes, no. 21, 3 August 1944.

31 See David French, '"Tommy is no soldier": The Morale of the Second British Army in Normandy, June–August 1944', in Brian Holden Reid, *Military Power: Land Warfare in Theory and Practice* (London: Frank Cass, 1997).

32 Maj-Gen Gerald Verney, quoted in Robin Neillands, *The Desert Rats: 7th Armoured Division 1940–45* (London: Weidenfeld and Nicolson, 1991), p. 231.

33 John Ellis, *The Sharp End of War* (London: Windrow & Greene, 1990 edn), p. 158; Gary Sheffield, 'The Shadow of the Somme: The Influence of the First World War on British

Soldiers' Perceptions and Behaviour in the Second World War', in Paul Addison and Angus Calder (eds), *Time to Kill: The Soldier's Experience of War in the West 1939–1945* (London: Pimlico, 1997), pp. 35–6; see also Terry Copp, '"If this war isn't over, and pretty damn soon, there'll be nobody left, in this old platoon..."' First Canadian Army, February–March 1945', also in Addison and Calder.

34 A point well made by John English, *The Canadian Army and the Normandy Campaign*, p. 311.

2. FIGHTING THE CAMPAIGN

1 Hart, *Clash of Arms*, p. 309; English, *The Canadian Army and the Normandy Campaign*, p. 12.

2 CAB 106/1121, War Cabinet historical section narrative, p. 25.

3 There have been many divisional histories of 7th, 11th and Guards Armoured Divisions, but until recently the armoured brigades had not received anything approaching the same amount of discussion.

4 Hart, *Clash of Arms*, ch. 8.

5 WO 106/4469, *79th Armoured Division Final Report* (War Office, July 1945), p. 6; US NAII RG331/210A/1, Lt-Col John Routh, HQ 12th Army Group, to Colonel Wright, notes on use of Churchill Crocodiles at Brest on 20 September 1944, report dated 3 October 1944.

6 See David Fletcher, *Vanguard of Victory – 79th Armoured Division* (London: Her Majesty's Stationery Office, 1984).

7 See Jarymowycz, *Tank Tactics*, as a very recent example.

8 Ellis, *Victory in the West*, vol. I, appendix IV.

9 This was the case in *Operations Epsom* and *Goodwood*.

10 Place, *Military Training in the British Army*, pp. 153–4.

11 Ibid., pp. 166–7.

12 WO 291/1331, *Tank Casualties during the Exploitation Phase after Crossing the Seine*, no. 2 ORS, report no. 18.

13 G. L. Weinberg, *A World at Arms: A Global History of World War Two* (Cambridge: University Press, 1994), p. 127.

14 J. Baynes, *The Forgotten Victor: General Sir Richard O'Connor* (London: Brassey's, 1989), pp. 213–14.

15 G. P. B. Roberts, *From the Desert to the Baltic* (London: William Kimber, 1987), pp. 184–5.

16 Allan Adair, *A Guards' General: The Memoirs of Major General Sir Allan Adair* (London: Hamish Hamilton, 1986), pp. 147–52; Jarymowycz, *Tank Tactics*, pp. 191–7.

17 Anon, *The Story of the 79th Armoured Division* (British Army of the Rhine, 1945), chs 1 and 2.

18 Anon, *The Story of the 79th Armoured Division*, chs 3 and 4; English, *The Canadian Army and the Normandy Campaign*, pp. 263–71.

19 IWM, Montgomery Papers, BLM 117/2, Montgomery to Archie Nye (VCIGS), 28 August 1943.

20 IWM, Montgomery Papers, BLM 129/2, *Future Design of the Capital Tank*, 24 October 1944.

21 David Fletcher, *Mr Churchill's Tank – The British Infantry Tank Mark IV* (Atglen, PA: Schiffer, 1999), pp. 142–54.

22 BOV, RAC Half-Yearly Reports, no. 9 – Military Mission no. 222 Report no. 1, Visit by Maj-Gen A. C. Richardson DRAC to North Africa and Italy, 9 March 1944; WO 171/1, *The Co-operation of Tanks with Infantry Divisions in Offensive Operations*, 21st Army Group (1943).

23 WO 205/57, Memorandum by J. Napier (BGS), 7 July 1943.

24 WO 205/57, Lt-Gen Morgan, GOC 21st Army Group, to War Office, 4 November 1943.

25 WO 205/57, Memoranda by Lt-Gen Charles Norrie (War Office RAC adviser), 29 October and 4 November 1943 and Memorandum by Gen William Morgan (21st Army Group Chief of Staff prior to Montgomery's appointment 6 November 1943).

26 US NAII RG337/26/40, Lt-Gen G. C. Patton to Maj-Gen G. R. Cook, HQ Army Ground Forces, Washington, 23 April 1945.

27 WO 205/57, Lt-Gen Anderson, GOC 2nd Army to 21st Army Group and RAC, 18 December 1943; Lt-Col N. M. H. Wall for Norrie to Anderson, 20 December 1943.

28 Ellis, *Victory in the West*, vol. I, pp. 169–74; Anon, *The Story of the 79th Armoured Division*, pp. 27–32.

29 WO 106/4469, *79th Armoured Division Final Report*, p. 64.

30 Anon, *The Story of the 79th Armoured Division*, ch. 2.

31 Ellis, *Victory in the West*, vol. I, pp. 194–5.

32 WO 106/4469, *79th Armoured Division Final Report*, p. 65.

33 Stephen Badsey, 'Terrain as a Factor in the Battle of Normandy, 1944', in Peter Doyle and Matthew R. Bennett (eds), *Fields of Battle: Terrain in Military History* (London: Kluwer, 2002), p. 356.

34 LHCMA, Alanbrooke, 6/2/24, Montgomery to Dempsey and Bradley, 15 April 1944.

35 WO 171/258, I Corps Operational War Diary, notes, April 1944.

36 Alexander McKee, *Caen: Anvil of Victory* (London: Souvenir, 1964), p. 43.

37 Maj-Gen N. Tapp, letter to Carlo D'Este, 22 March 1982, cited in *Decision in Normandy*, p. 129.

38 WO 171/863, Staffordshire Yeomanry War Diary, June 1944.

39 WO 171/1325, 2nd Battalion KSLI War Diary, 6 June 1944.

40 McKee, *Caen*, p. 61.

41 WO 171/1325, 2nd Battalion KSLI War Diary, 6 June 1944.

42 Badsey, 'Terrain as a Factor', pp. 355–6.

43 Brig. K. Pearce Smith, letter to Carlo D'Este 27/8/82, cited in *Decision in Normandy*, p. 129.

44 WO 219/1919, SHAEF Weekly Intelligence Reports, no. 9, 20 May 1944.

45 D'Este, *Decision in Normandy*, p. 139.

46 LHCMA, Interrogation of Lt Gen E. Feuchtinger, GOC 21st Panzers.

47 McKee, *Caen*, pp. 68–9; Ellis, *Victory in the West*, vol. I, pp. 208–12.

48 CCA RLEW 7/7, Dempsey to Ronald Lewin, 15 November 1968.

49 Patrick Delaforce, *Monty's Marauders: Black Rat 4th Armoured Brigade and Red Fox 8th Armoured Brigade* (Stroud: Sutton, 1993), pp. 145–8.

50 Ellis, *Victory in the West*, vol. I, pp. 252, 261; Delaforce, *Monty's Marauders*, pp. 149–52; CAB 106/963, Immediate Report no. 6, 'Capture of Cristot by One Battalion Supported by One Squadron of Tanks on 16 June 1944', 17 June 1944.

51 Delaforce, *Monty's Marauders*, pp. 152–3.

52 McKee, *Caen*, pp. 86–7.

53 D'Este falls into this trap, see *Decision in Normandy*, pp. 178–83, but for the complete German propaganda treatment see Gary L. Simpson, *Tiger Ace: The Life Story of Panzer Commander Michael Wittman* (Atglen, PA: Schiffer, 1994), pp. 275–98.

54 Hart, *Clash of Arms*, p. 308.

55 WO 285/1, Dempsey Papers, May 1944.

56 The best background narratives to this complex tale are D'Este, *Decision in Normandy*, pp. 168–75; Daniel Taylor, *Villers Bocage through the Lens* (London: Battle of Britain

International, 1999), pp. 9–11; and Michael Reynolds, *Steel Inferno: I SS Panzer Corps in Normandy* (London: Spellmount, 1997), pp. 99–101.

57 Letters from Maj-Gen G. T. A. Armitage to D'Este, 29 April 1982 and 16 June 1982, quoted in D'Este, *Decision in Normandy*, p. 174.

58 LHCMA, Liddell Hart, 15/4/85, Notes on 22nd Armoured Brigade Operations, 6–15 June 1944, compiled by Brig. Robert Hinde, 15 June 1944.

59 From an unpublished account of *Villers Bocage, 13 June 1944*, compiled by Maj. W. H. J. Sale in 1980, quoted in D'Este, *Decision in Normandy*, pp. 176–7.

60 WO 171/439, 7th Armoured Division's War Diary, 13 June 1944.

61 Gerald L. Verney, *The Desert Rats: The 7th Armoured Division in World War Two* (London: Greenhill, 1996 [1954]), pp. 197–9.

62 LHCMA, Liddell Hart, 9/28/84, Chester Wilmot interview with Dempsey.

63 LHCMA, Liddell Hart, 15/4/85, Notes on 22nd Armoured Brigade Operations 6–15 June 1944, compiled by Brig. Robert Hinde, 15 June 1944.

64 Letter from Maj-Gen G. P. Gregson to D'Este, 8/8/82, quoted in D'Este, *Decision in Normandy*, p. 189.

65 Hastings, *Overlord*, pp. 153–64; D'Este, *Decision in Normandy*, ch. 11; Reynolds, *Steel Inferno*, ch. 11.

66 The manner in which the German tanks blundered through the British-occupied town with little infantry support demonstrates this point.

67 See Taylor, *Villers Bocage through the Lens*, for the most detailed investigation and analysis of the events of 13 June.

68 LHCMA, Alanbrooke, 6/2/25, Montgomery to Brooke, 13–14 June 1944.

69 WO 171/439, 7th Armoured Division War Diary, 13 June 1944; WO 171/619, 22nd Armoured Brigade War Diary, 13–14 June 1944.

70 LHMCA, Liddell Hart, 15/4/85, O'Connor's notes on *Operation Epsom*, 5 September 1944; Baynes, *The Forgotten Victor*, pp. 190–5.

71 Hart, *Clash of Arms*, p. 312.

72 Reynolds, *Steel Inferno*, pp. 118–23; see also Kevin Baverstock, *Breaking the Panzers: The Bloody Battle for Rauray, Normandy, 1 July 1944* (Stroud: Sutton, 2002).

73 J. J. How, *Hill 112: Cornerstone of the Normandy Campaign* (London: William Kimber, 1984), p. 46; LHCMA, Liddell Hart, 9/28/84, Roberts to Liddell Hart, 30 January 1952.

74 Anon (Captain Edgar Pallamountain), *Taurus Pursuant: A History of 11th Armoured Division* (privately published, 1945), p. 20.

75 N. Thornburn, *The 4th King's Shropshire Light Infantry in Normandy* (Shrewsbury: King's Shropshire Light Infantry, Museum Trust, 1990), pp. 42–50.

76 LHCMA, O'Connor, 5/3/37, O'Connor to Lt Gen Allan Harding, 19 August 1944; LHCMA, Liddell Hart 9/28/84, Roberts to Liddell Hart, 30 January 1952.

77 LHCMA, Liddell Hart, 15/4/85, O'Connor's notes on *Operation Epsom*, 5 September 1944.

78 LHCMA, Liddell Hart, 9/28/84, Roberts to Liddell Hart, 30 January 1952.

79 M. Carver, *Out of Step: The Memoirs of Field Marshal Lord Carver* (London: Hutchinson, 1989), pp. 191–2

80 Ellis, *Victory in the West*, vol. I, p. 309.

81 NAC RG24, Winnipeg Rifles War Diary, 4 July 1944.

82 NAC RG24, Fort Garry Horse War Diary, 4 July 1944.

83 Copp, *Fields of Fire*, pp. 98–100.

84 Crocker to Dempsey, cited in Reynolds, *Steel Inferno*, p. 149.

85 Copp, *Fields of Fire*, p. 101.

86 Hubert Meyer, *The History of the 12th SS Panzer Division Hitlerjugend* (Winnipeg, Manitoba: Fedorowicz, 1994), p. 141.

87 Meyer, *Grenadiers*, p. 145.

88 C. P. Stacey, *The Official History of the Canadian Army in the Second World War*, vol. III (Ottawa: Queen's printer, 1960), p. 163; Reynolds, *Steel Inferno*, p. 156.

89 Ellis, *Victory in the West*, vol. I, p. 316.

90 Stacey, *Official History*, pp. 163–4; Reynolds, *Steel Inferno*, p. 155.

91 Stacey, *Canadian Army*, p. 161.

92 Copp, *Fields of Fire*, p. 104.

93 Meyer, *Grenadiers*, p. 146.

94 How, *Hill 112*, pp. 155–62.

95 WO 171/868 7th RTR War Diary, 10 July 1944; WO 171/1372, 4th Somerset Light Infantry War Diary, 10 July 1944.

96 Carver, *Out of Step*, pp. 193–4.

97 WO 171/633, 31st Tank Brigade War Diary, 10 July 1944.

98 Delaforce, *Monty's Marauders*, p. 78.

99 How, *Hill 112*, p. 166.

100 How, *Hill 112*, p. 167; Delaforce, *Monty's Marauders*, p. 78.

101 LHCMA, Liddell Hart, 15/4/85, Dempsey's notes on *Goodwood* revised 28 March 1952.

102 Ibid. Dempsey met with the Adjutant General, Sir Ronald 'Bill' Adam, who informed him of the coming replacement crisis. Dempsey was also probably influenced by Montgomery, who had confided to Brooke on 10 July that armour was plentiful, but infantry casualties were alarmingly high, LHCMA, Alanbrooke 6/2/27, General Operational Policy, Montgomery to Brooke, 10 July 1944.

103 WO 285/9, Dempsey's Diary, 12 July 1944.

104 LHCMA, Alanbrooke, 6/2/27, Operational objectives for *Goodwood* given to Dempsey and then to O'Connor, 15 July 1944.

105 Ibid.

106 Nigel Hamilton, *Monty: Master of the Battlefield* (London: Hamish Hamilton, 1983), ch. 12.

107 CAB 106/1037, Notes from 21st Army Group conference, 13 January 1944.

108 LHCMA, Liddell Hart, 15/4/85, Notes by Ronald Lewin on discussions with O'Connor concerning *Goodwood*, 11 July 1968.

109 Interview with O'Connor (13 August 1979) quoted in D'Este, *Decision in Normandy*, p. 389.

110 LHCMA, Liddell Hart, 9/28/84, Roberts to Liddell Hart, 30 January 1952; Roberts, *From the Desert to the Baltic*, pp. 169–71.

111 Interview with Roberts, 9 January 1980, in D'Este, *Decision in Normandy*, p. 373; Roberts, *From the Desert to the Baltic*, p. 171.

112 Maj. Bill Close, 3RTR, interview with author, September 2002.

113 Roberts's last view on the deployment of his division in Goodwood came in 1987 in his autobiography, *From the Desert to the Baltic*; LHCMA, 9/28/84, Roberts's notes on the aims of *Operation Goodwood* to Liddell Hart, 30 January 1952; LHCMA, Roberts, Roberts/Belchem correspondence, 23 November 1978.

114 William Moore, *Panzer Bait: With the 3rd Royal Tank Regiment 1940–1944* (London: Leo Cooper, 1991), p. 148.

115 Interview with Chester Wilmot, cited in D'Este, *Decision in Normandy*, p. 372.

116 Roberts, *From the Desert to the Baltic*, pp. 176–7.

117 Wilmot, *The Struggle for Europe*, p. 399.

118 WO 171/139, War Diary 21st Army Group. *Goodwood* losses from 0600 18 July to 0600 22 July.

119 WO 205/637, AFV States 30 July 1944 and Second Army Summaries; WO 205/638, AFV-RA Equipment States, August 1944; WO 205/631, WD Armd Replacement Group IV, July 1944; WO 171/196, Notes of RAC Conference at VIII Corps, 29 July 1944; WO 205/360, TFAG Ops (B), RAC Reinforcements, 7 August 1944.

120 WO 171/182, War Diary 21st Army Group, Deputy Judge Advocate General, April–December 1944. Figures for desertion and AWOL convictions increased markedly in the three armoured divisions in the weeks after *Goodwood* and *Bluecoat*.

121 Letter from Tony Sargeaunt to Terry Copp, 22 June 1990, and paper 'The Evolution of Tank Tactics during the Second World War'. I am indebted to Terry Copp for this information. See also Copp, *Fields of Fire*, pp. 129–30; WO 291/1331, 'Bombing in *Operation Goodwood*', Operational Research Report no. 6, no. 2 ORS, 21st Army Group.

122 Interview with Dempsey by Chester Wilmot, quoted in D'Este, *Decision in Normandy*, p. 387.

123 Reynolds, *Steel Inferno*, p. 191.

124 LHCMA, O'Connor, 5/3/22, O'Connor to Adair, 24 July 1944.

125 Jarymowycz, *Tank Tactics*, pp. 130–9.

126 WO 171/865, 1RTR War Diary and WO 171/856, 3/4CLY War Diary; Jarymowycz, *Tank Tactics*, pp. 133–4; Copp, *Fields of Fire*, p. 177.

127 Stacey, *Official History*, vol. III, p. 190.

128 Letters of instruction, M515, 27 July 1944, Heiberg Papers, Patton Museum Library, USA, quoted in Jarymowycz, *Tank Tactics*, p. 139.

129 LHCMA, Liddell Hart, 15/4/85, O'Connor's notes on Operation *Bluecoat*, undated, but probably September 1944; for an excellent narrative of *Bluecoat* see Major J. J. How's *Normandy: The British Breakout* (London: William Kimber, 1981).

130 LHCMA, Alanbrooke, 6/2/28, Montgomery to War Office and CIGS, 2 August 1944; Carver, *Out of Step*, p. 196; Wilmot, *The Struggle for Europe*, p. 398.

131 LHCMA, Liddell Hart, 9/28/84, Harold 'Peter' Pyman interview with Liddell Hart, 13 February 1952.

132 LHCMA, Verney I/i/3, O'Connor to Verney, 3 August 1944; Liddell Hart, 9/28/84, Pyman interview with Liddell Hart, 13 February 1952.

133 LHCMA, Verney I/i/3, 'Account of part played by 6th Guards Tank Brigade in Operation *Bluecoat*, 30 July 1944'.

134 Adair, *A Guards' General*, pp. 147, 152; Roberts, *From the Desert to the Baltic*, pp. 184–5, 202, 214.

135 LHCMA, O'Connor, 5/3/37, O'Connor to Lt-Gen Sir Allan Harding, CoS, HQ Allied Forces in Italy, 19 August 1944.

136 How, *Normandy*, pp. 43–85; Bryan Perrett, *Seize and Hold: Master Strokes on the Battlefield* (London: Arms and Armour Press, 1994).

137 G. Kitching, *Mud and Green Fields: The Memoirs of Major General George Kitching* (St. Catherine's, Ontario: Vanwell, 1993), p. 193.

138 NAC RG24, Second Canadian Corps HQ War Diary, 8 August 1944.

139 NAC RG24, Fourth Canadian Armoured Division War Diary, 8–9 August 1944.

140 Dominick Graham, *The Price of Command: A Biography of General Guy Simonds* (Toronto: Stoddart, 1993), p. 154; LHCMA, Liddell Hart, S/IS/130, queries for Gen Simonds, undated; Copp, *Fields of Fire*, pp. 210–11.

141 LHCMA, O'Connor, 5/4/1, O'Connor to Montgomery, 24 August 1944.

142 Jody Perrun, 'Best Laid Plans: Guy Simonds and Operation Totalize 7–10 August 1944', *Journal of Military History*, vol. 67, no. 1, January 2003, pp. 170–3.
143 C. P. Stacey, *The Victory Campaign: The Operations in Northwest Europe 1944–1945* (Ottawa: Queen's printer, 1962), pp. 238–40.
144 NAC RG24, 2nd Canadian Armoured Brigade War Diary, August 1944.
145 NAC RG24, II Can Corps War Diary, August 1944.
146 For an excellent account of this action see Jarymowcyz, *Tank Tactics*, pp. 191–7.
147 G. Kitching, *Mud and Green Fields*, pp. 205; Stanislaw Maczek, *Avec mes Blindés* (Paris: Presses de la Cité, 1967), p. 219; Copp, *Fields of Fire*, pp. 248–50.

3. OPERATIONAL TECHNIQUE

1 LHMCA, Liddell Hart, 9/28/84, Tanks in Normandy, Liddell Hart to C. S. Forester, 18 February 1952; English, *The Canadian Army and the Normandy Campaign*, p. 312; Hart, *Clash of Arms*, p. 309.
2 D'Este, *Decision in Normandy* and Ellis, *Brute Force*, pp. 373–88.
3 LHMCA, Alanbrooke, 6/2/24, Memo titled 'Some Army Problems' by Montgomery, 2 March 1944, and Montgomery to Dempsey and Bradley 15 April 1944; Hamilton, *Monty*, pp. 596, 631; J. Ellis, *Brute Force*, pp. 374–6.
4 Taylor, *Villers Bocage through the Lens*; Reynolds, *Steel Inferno*, ch. XI.
5 D'Este, *Decision in Normandy*, chs 20–2.
6 Hastings, *Overlord*, is the most popular example while E. Blandford's *Two Sides of the Beach – The Invasion and Defence of Europe 1944* (London: Airlife, 1999), is a good recent example.
7 Wilmot, *The Struggle for Europe*, p. 477, is an excellent example as is the general tone of Hastings, *Overlord*.
8 See David French, *Raising Churchill's Army: The British Army and the War against Germany 1919–1945* (Oxford: Oxford University Press, 2000), and Hart, *Montgomery and Colossal Cracks*.
9 D'Este, *Decision in Normandy*, was the first historian to develop this issue in 1983 (ch. 15), but the emphasis of his thesis has been criticised more recently by John Peaty, 'Myth, Reality and Carlo D'Este', *War Studies Journal*, vol. 1, no. 2, 1996, and by Hart, *Montgomery and Colossal Cracks*.
10 H. M. D. Parker, *Manpower: A Study in Wartime Policy and Administration* (London: Her Majesty's Stationery Office, 1957), pp. 226–8; WO 216/101, Army Manpower Requirement Estimates, 1943–44; WO 193/224, Alexander to Brooke, 3 December 1943.
11 CAB 78/184, Conference of Ministers, 5 November 1943; WO 199/1334, Maj-Gen Watson to CinC Home Forces, 28 December 1943.
12 LHCMA, Alanbrooke, 6/2/24, Montgomery to Brooke, 19 May 1944; DMT to Brooke, 23 May 1944; Brooke to Montgomery, 25 May 1944.
13 WO 285/2, Montgomery to Lt-Gen Ronald Weeks, DCIGS, 19 March 1944, is a clear example; CAB 106/313, Montgomery to Weeks, 19 March 1944.
14 LHCMA, Liddell Hart, 9/28/84, interview with Chester Wilmot, 18 May 1946.
15 WO 162/116, Battle Casualties, Northwest Europe, 1944.
16 Bernard L. Montgomery, *The Memoirs of Field Marshal the Viscount Montgomery of Alamein* (London: Collins, 1958), p. 332.
17 LHCMA, Alanbrooke, 6/2/6, Wavell to Brooke, 31 May 1942.
18 LHCMA, Alanbrooke, 6/2/6, Brooke to Wavell, 5 July 1942.
19 LHMCA, Alanbrooke, 14/61/9, Montgomery to Brooke, 27 November 1942.
20 LHCMA, Allfrey, 4/6, Lessons Learnt by 4th Armoured Brigade in Italy September to December 1943.

21 LHCMA, Alanbrooke, 7/3/12, War Office Exercise 'Evolution', August 1946, p. 7.

22 Hart, *Montgomery and Colossal Cracks*, pp. 61–2.

23 Sheffield, 'The Shadow of the Somme'.

24 CAB 106/1060, Reports on Normandy by Brig. James Hargest, XXX Corps, 25 June 1944.

25 LHMCA, Alanbrooke, 6/2/24, Memo titled 'Some Army Problems' by Montgomery, 2 March 1944, and Montgomery to Dempsey and Bradley, 15 April 1944.

26 LHCMA, Allfrey, 3/1, Diary 17/1/43; French, *Raising Churchill's Army*, p. 243.

27 Interview with Williams in Hastings, *Overlord*, p. 180 n.30; see also Roberts, *From the Desert to the Baltic*, p. 240.

28 F. Howe, *Seizing the Initiative in the West (the US Army in World War Two)* (Washington: OCMH, 1957), p.521.

29 Hart, *Montgomery and Colossal Cracks*, pp. 3–4; French, *Raising Churchill's Army*, pp. 2–7.

30 IWM, Montgomery Papers 126/35, Montgomery to Brooke, 17 November 1944.

31 NAC RG24, vol. 10797, 'Operational Policy – 2nd Canadian Corps, 17 February 1944'; plus letters from Dempsey and Montgomery, quoted in Copp, *Fields of Fire*, pp. 26–7.

32 Hart, *Montgomery and Colossal Cracks*, ch. 4.

33 IWM, Montgomery Papers, 126/35, Montgomery to Brooke, 17 November 1944.

34 WO 179/2579, Headley, 31 January 1944. Montgomery argued that divisions should attack one or two brigades up with one echeloned in the rear.

35 LHCMA, Liddell Hart, 15/4/85, Notes on VIII Corps operations by Lt-Gen R. O'Connor, 5 September 1944. This was an objective of *Operations Perch* and *Epsom*, though by later efforts such as *Goodwood* greater realism was displayed.

36 WO 171/1, 21st Army Group War Diary, August 1943, 'Lessons of Tunisian Campaign'.

37 WO 205/1021, Interrogation of Brigadeführer Wisch, 25 August 1945, in *Interrogation Reports of German Generals*, vol. I.

38 LHCMA, Liddell Hart, 15/15, Second Panzer Division operations 17 June to 7 July 1944.

39 Ian Gooderson, *Air Power at the Battlefront: Allied Close Air Support in Europe 1943–45* (London: Frank Cass, 1998).

40 Ellis, *Sharp End of War*, pp. 118–20; D'Este, *Decision in Normandy*, p. 235; English, *The Canadian Army and the Normandy Campaign*, p. 214; McKee, *Caen*, p. 254.

41 Hart, *Montgomery and Colossal Cracks*, p. 95.

42 Anon (Pallamountain), *Taurus Pursuant*, p. 119.

43 Copp, *Fields of Fire*, p. 129.

44 LHCMA, Liddell Hart, 15/8/206, *Infantry Training – Part One: The Infantry Battalion* (London, 1944), p. 24; WO 291/1370, Operational Research memo no. 5: *The Comparative Accuracy and Range and Line of British 3-inch and German 81 mm mortars under Field Conditions*.

45 WO 205/404, Royal Artillery notes on recent operations, 25 June 1944.

46 WO 291/1169, AORG Report no. 17/52, *Analysis of Infantry Rates of Advance in Battle*.

47 Baynes, *The Forgotten Victor*, p. 191.

48 WO 223/38, Military Training Pamphlet (MTP) no. 63, *The Co-operation of Tanks with Infantry Divisions*; WO 232/21, *Report on Operations I, 19 July 1944*.

49 IWM, MTP (no. 41), *The Tactical Handling of the Armoured Division and its Components –Part Two: The Armoured Regiment* (February 1943), ch. V, section 29; WO 166/10733, War Diary of 5th Guards Armoured Brigade, 17 July 1943.

50 WO 171/862, 1st East Riding Yeomanry War Diary, 9 April 1944.

51 Ibid., 8 July 1944.

52 English, *The Canadian First Army in the Normandy Campaign*, pp. 290–1.

53 Meyer, *Grenadiers*, pp. 275, 288; Perrun, 'Best Laid Plans', pp. 170–3.

54 J. F. C. Fuller, *Thunderbolts* (London: Skeffington, 1946), p. 72.

55 Maj. Bill Close, 3RTR, interview with author, September 2002; Moore, *Panzer Bait*, p. 148.

56 WO 171/456, 11th Armoured Division War Diary, 26–28 June 1944; Ellis, *Brute Force*, p. 383; How, *Hill 112*, pp. 60, 100–1.

57 D'Este, *Decision in Normandy*, pp. 240–1.

58 IWM, Bucknall, 80/33/1 – folder 12, Bucknall to Dempsey, 3 August 1944.

59 LHCMA, Liddell Hart, 15/4/85, Ronald Lewin's notes on discussion with O'Connor, 11 July 1978; LHCMA, Roberts, Box 2, Draft of first chapter for *Goodwood* book by J. J. How, written c. 1985/86.

60 Maj. Bill Close, 3RTR, interview with author, September 2002; Moore, *Panzer Bait*, p. 142.

61 WO 291/262, AORG Report no. 282, *Study of Casualties and Damage to Personnel and Equipment Caused by Some Air and Artillery Bombardments in European Operations*; Perrun, 'Best Laid Plans', pp. 144–5.

62 Ian V. Hogg, *British and American Artillery of World War Two* (London: Arms & Armour, 1978), pp. 26–8.

63 WO 277/5, Pemberton, *Artillery Tactics*, p. 12.

64 WO 163/183, Policy on Field, Medium and Heavy Artillery, 1 July 1942.

65 WO 291/1330, Army Operational Research Group no. 7, reports July–August 1944.

66 WO 291/1318, *Effects of Artillery Fire in Mountainous Country*, no.1 Operational Research Group, Italy, autumn 1944.

67 WO 163/183, Policy on Field, Medium and Heavy Artillery, 21 July 1942; WO 291/1330, Army Operational Research Group no. 7, reports July–August 1944; WO 277/5, Pemberton, *Artillery Tactics*, p. 170.

68 WO 171/3957, Second British Army Intelligence Summary no. 257, 15 February 1945.

69 See WO 277/5, Pemberton, *Artillery Tactics*, for more complete details; French, *Raising Churchill's Army*, pp. 256–8.

70 French, *Raising Churchill's Army*, p. 268.

71 WO 232/25, German Views of the Normandy Landing, 28 November 1944, Special Tactical Study no. 30.

72 English, *First Canadian Army and the Normandy Campaign*, p. 269.

73 LHCMA, Liddell Hart, 15/4/85, Notes by Dempsey on *Operation Goodwood*, February/March 1952.

74 Gooderson, *Air Power at the Battlefront*, ch. 5.

75 LHCMA, Liddell Hart, 1/153, Gen Carver to Liddell Hart, 8 May 1952.

76 CAB 106/959, Notes by O'Connor on VIII Corps operations, 9 September 1944. Accounts by advancing troops are testimony to the early success of the Allied fireplan, followed by its weakness.

77 LHCMA, Liddell Hart, 15/4/85, O'Connor's notes on *Operation Bluecoat*, undated, but c. September 1944.

78 LHCMA, Liddell Hart, 1/153, Gen Carver to Liddell Hart, 8 May 1952; English, *First Canadian Army and the Normandy Campaign*, pp. 290–1.

79 WO 171/291, VIII Corps War Diary, 2 July 1944.

80 Ellis, *Victory in the West*, vol. I, p. 278.

81 Michael Howard in Richard H. Kohn, 'The Scholarship on World War Two: Its Present Condition and Future Possibilities', *Journal of Military History*, vol. 55, July 1991, p. 379.

82 LHMCA, Alanbrooke, 6/2/12, Auchinleck to Brooke, 6 January 1942.

83 Montgomery, *Memoirs*, pp. 80–2.

84 Ibid.

85 LHCMA, Alanbrooke, 6/2/26, Montgomery to Brooke, 7 July 1944.

86 LHMCA, Alanbrooke, 6/2/22, Montgomery to Brooke, 28 February 1943; 6/2/23, Montgomery to Brooke, 28 December 1943; 6/2/26, Alanbrooke, Montgomery to Brooke, 7 July 1944.

87 Hart, *Montgomery and Colossal Cracks*, p. 136; Stephen Badsey, 'Faction in the British Army: Its Impact on 21st Army Group Operations in Autumn 1944', *War Studies Journal*, vol. 1, no. 1, 1995, pp. 13–28.

88 LHCMA, Alanbrooke, 6/2/23, Montgomery to Brooke, 28 December 1943.

89 Baynes, *The Forgotten Victor*, p. 186; LHCMA, Alanbrooke, 6/2/28, Montgomery to Brooke, and Simonds, 8 August 1944.

90 Roberts, *From the Desert to the Baltic*, ch. 8.

91 Baynes, *The Forgotten Victor*, pp. 186–7; LHCMA, Liddell Hart, 15/15, Notes on Dempsey's diary, 27 June 1946.

92 LHCMA, Liddell Hart, 9/28/84, Roberts to Liddell Hart, 5 March 1952.

93 LHCMA, O'Connor, 5/3/37, O'Connor to Lt-Gen Allan Harding, 19 August 1944; English, *The First Canadian Army and the Normandy Campaign*, pp. 306–7, 313.

94 CAB 106/1037, Staff Conference notes, 13 January 1944.

95 LHCMA, Verney, IV/2, *Some Notes on the Conduct of War and the Infantry Division in Battle*, November 1944; IV/3, *The Armoured Division in Battle*, December 1944.

96 CCA RLEW 7/7, Dempsey to Ronald Lewin, 15 November 1968.

97 WO 232/21, Theatre Notes, report by Capt. C. L. Coleman, 3 October 1944.

98 Adair, *A Guards' General*, p. 148.

99 Roberts, *From the Desert to the Baltic*, p. 94; LHCMA, Liddell Hart, 1/553, Lewin to Liddell Hart, 29 August 1968.

100 Ellis, *Victory in the West*, vol. I, pp. 271–7.

101 LHCMA, Liddell Hart, 15/4/85, Brigadier's notes on 22nd Armoured Brigade Operations 6–15 June 1944.

102 Anon (Pallamontain), *Taurus Pursuant*, p. 20; LHCMA, Liddell Hart, 15/4/85, O'Connor's notes on *Operation Epsom*, 5 September 1944; Basil Liddell Hart, *The Tanks*, vol. II (London: Cassell, 1959), p. 35.

103 Baynes, *The Forgotten Victor*, pp. 211–12.

104 Ibid., pp. 198–200.

105 Ellis, *Victory in the West*, vol. I, pp. 329–30. Notes by Lt-Col Dawnay on meeting with Montgomery prior to *Goodwood*.

106 Baynes, *The Forgotten Victor*, p. 220.

107 LHCMA, Liddell Hart, LH15/4/85, 'Some light on the missed opportunity in the Caumont offensive (*Operation Bluecoat*) following the break-through that the 8th Corps made on the right wing', by Chester Wilmot, from conversations with Roberts, 1 August 1944, and O'Connor, 3 August 1944.

108 Reynolds, *Steel Inferno*, is the best source on this effort along with Taylor, *Villers Bocage through the Lens*,

109 D'Este, *Decision in Normandy*, pp. 425–6; LHCMA, Liddell Hart, 15/4/85, O'Connor's notes on *Operation Bluecoat*, September 1944.

110 Perrun, 'Best-Laid Plans', pp. 137–73; English, *The First Canadian Army in Normandy*.

111 Hart, *Montgomery and Colossal Cracks*, pp. 88–9.

112 LHCMA, Liddell Hart, 15/4/85, O'Connor's notes on *Operation Epsom*, 5 September 1944; WO 277/5, Pemberton, *Artillery Tactics*, p. 225.

113 Robin Prior and Trevor Wilson, *Command on the Western Front: The Career of Sir Henry Rawlinson* (Oxford: Oxford University Press, 1992), pp. 318, 375.
114 WO 179/2579, War Diary Canadian Planning Staff, Headley, 31 January 1944.
115 LHCMA, Liddell Hart, 15/4/85, O'Connor's notes on *Operation Epsom*, 5 September 1944; Roberts, *From the Desert to the Baltic*, pp. 170–1.
116 IWM, Montgomery Papers 78/1, notes on Northwest European Campaign.
117 LHCMA, Liddell Hart, 9/28/84, Liddell Hart interview with Brig. Harold 'Peter' Pyman, 13 February 1952.
118 LHCMA, Liddell Hart, 15/4/85, O'Connor's notes on *Operation Epsom*, 5 September 1944.
119 How, *Hill 112*, provides a good example of this; Roberts, *From the Desert to the Baltic*, pp. 163–4.
120 R. H. W. Dunn, 'Reminiscences of a Regimental Soldier: SP Guns in Normandy', *Journal of the Royal Artillery*, vol. 75, April 1948, p. 93.
121 LHCMA, Liddell Hart, 15/4/85, O'Connor's notes on *Operation Epsom*, September 1944; see Baverstock, *Breaking the Panzers*.
122 IWM, Bucknall Papers, Lt-Gen Bucknall to Col. M. Browne, 17 August 1944.
123 LHCMA, Liddell Hart, 15/4/85, notes by Brig. Hinde on 22nd Armoured Brigade operations 6–15 June 1944.
124 Delaforce, *Monty's Marauders*, p. 78.
125 Roberts, *From the Desert to the Baltic*, p. 177.
126 Wilmot, *The Struggle for Europe*, p. 399.
127 English, *The First Canadian Army and the Normandy Campaign*, p. 271.
128 D'Este, *Decision in Normandy*, ch. 14.
129 Ellis, *Victory in Normandy*, vol. I, pp. 315–18.
130 WO 231/10, W. E. Clutterbuck, 1st Division, Lessons of the North African Campaign, 29 May 1943.
131 BOV, RAC Half Yearly Reports no. 9 – Military Mission no. 222 Report no. 1, Visit by Maj-Gen A. C. Richardson, DRAC, to North Africa and Italy, 9 March 1944.
132 LHCMA, Alanbrooke, *Some Army Problems*, Montgomery, 20 March 1944.
133 LHCMA, Alanbrooke, Montgomery to Dempsey and Bradley, 15 April 1944.
134 Ibid.
135 WO 171/258, I Corps Operational Notes.
136 David Belchem, *Victory in Normandy* (London: Chatto & Windus, 1981), pp. 49–55.
137 LHCMA, Alanbrooke, Montgomery to Brooke, 17 April 1944.
138 CCA RLEW 7/7, notes on discussions between Dempsey and Ronald Lewin, 1968.
139 LHCMA, Maturin-Baird, Alexander to Maturin-Baird, 29 January 1942; CAB 146/15, Enemy Documents Section, no. 9, appendix 9.
140 WO 205/1021, Interrogation of General Diestel, Interrogation of German Generals, reports volume I.
141 Ellis, *Brute Force*, pp. 374–7; McKee, *Caen*, pp. 61–2.
142 CCA RLEW 7/7, notes on discussions between Dempsey and Ronald Lewin 1968; Hastings, *Overlord*, pp. 132–45.
143 LHCMA, Liddell Hart, 15/4/85, Dempsey's comments and notes on *Goodwood*, 18 and 28 March 1952.

4. FIGHTING THE BATTLE

1 LHCMA, Liddell Hart, 9/28/84, correspondence with C. S. Forester, 18 February 1952.
2 LHCMA, Liddell Hart, 9/28/84, correspondence with Field Marshal Carver, 8 May 1952.

3 CAB 106/1060, report by Brigadier James Hargest, XXX Corps observer, covering the period 6 June–10 July 1944.

4 LHCMA, Liddell Hart, 9/28/84, Roberts to Liddell Hart, 5 March 1952.

5 LHCMA, Liddell Hart, 15/4/85, notes by Brig. Robert 'Loony' Hinde on 22nd Armoured Brigade operations, 6–15 June 1944.

6 WO 106/1775, Report of the Bartholomew Committee, 2 July 1940; See also French, *Raising Churchill's Army*, pp. 189–92.

7 IWM MTP (Military Training Pamphlet) no. 41, *The Armoured Regiment* (July 1940); MTP no. 51, *Troop Training for Cruiser Tanks Troops* (September 1941).

8 H. F. Joslen, *Orders of Battle, volume I: UK and Colonial Formations and Units in the Second World War 1939–45* (London: Her Majesty's Stationery Office, 1960), pp. 4–9.

9 Michael Carver, *Dilemmas of the Desert War: A New Look at the Libyan Campaign* (London: Batsford, 1986), for a detailed discussion.

10 Jarymowycz, *Tank Tactics*, pp. 87–9.

11 Joslen, *Orders of Battle*, pp. 5–6.

12 IWM MTP. no. 41, *The Tactical Handling of the Armoured Division and Its Components* (July 1943), part 1.

13 WO 166/8576, 2nd Armoured Irish Guards, War Diary, 19 October 1942; WO 166/12687, 8th Rifle Brigade, War Diary, 6 May 1943; IWM NTW (Notes from Theatres of War) no. 14, *Western Desert and Cyrenaica, August to December 1942* (June 1943) and NTW no.16, *North Africa, November 1942 to May 1943* (October 1943).

14 Maj. John Langdon, 3RTR, interview with author, October 2002.

15 See Chapter 6, *Design and Development*.

16 IWM NTW no.10 (October 1942), *Cyrenaica and the Western Desert, January to June 1942*, section 3. The consequences of this can be clearly seen in armoured actions in Normandy, for example, Villers Bocage.

17 WO 166/860, 11th Armoured Division Training Instruction no. 3, appendix L to divisional G branch War Diary, May 1941.

18 Place, *Military Training in the British Army*, pp. 118–26.

19 Examples being 40 minutes during *Blackbull* Exercise, WO 166/11080, War Diary 2nd Fife and Forfar Yeomanry, May 1943, and three hours during *Moon* Exercise, WO 166/12460, War Diary 1st Coldstream Guards, November 1943.

20 WO 166/11080, War Diary 2nd Fife and Forfar Yeomanry, June 1943.

21 WO 166/10521, War Diary 11th Armoured Division, Maj-Gen G. P. B. Roberts, 'Notes on Armoured Divisional Tactics', December 1943.

22 Maj. Bill Close, 3RTR, interview with author, September 2002.

23 WO 32/10390, Letter from DMV to AFV School, Bovington, 2 March 1944; ATM (Army Training Memorandum) no. 48 (May 1944) and no. 49 (June 1944).

24 WO 205/57, memos circulated by Maj-Gen C. W. M. Norrie, RAC, and Lt-Gen W. D. Morgan, 21AG CoS, 29 October, 4 November and 6 November 1943.

25 LHCMA, Alanbrooke, 6/2/22, Montgomery to Brooke, 12 January 1943.

26 IWM, Montgomery Papers, BLM 117/2, Montgomery to Lt-Gen Archie Nye (VCIGS), 28 August 1943; BLM 129/2, *Future Design of the Capital Tank*, 24 October 1944, summarised his views formed since 1942.

27 CAB 106/1037, notes from staff conference held by Montgomery, 13 January 1944.

28 See Place, *Military Training in the British Army*, ch. 9, pp. 160–7.

29 IWM MTP no. 22, *Tactical Handling of Army Tank Battalions* (1939).

30 IWM ATI no. 2, *The Employment of Army Tanks in Co-operation with Infantry* (March 1941).

31 IWM NTW (Notes from Theatres of War) no. 2, *Cyrenaica: November–December 1941* (March 1942).

32 PREM 3/440/2. There were certainly some reservations stated by Lt-Gen Kenneth Anderson, GOC 1st Army, in his despatch, *Operations by First Army in North Africa: November 1942 to May 1943*.

33 WO 166/10747, *34th Tank Brigade Training Directive Tank/Infantry Co-operation* (September 1943), 34th Tank Brigade War Diary, September 1943.

34 WO 231/10, 'Lessons of the Tunisian Campaign 1942–43', reports from commanding officers of 21st and 25th Tank Brigades and Responses by 1st Division to British Military Training Directorate (North Africa) questionnaire, undated but prior to July 1943.

35 IWM CRO (Current Reports from Overseas) no. 17 (25 September 1943).

36 IWM ATI no. 2 (May 1943), *The Co-operation of Infantry and Tanks*.

37 IWM 21st Army Group pamphlet, *The Co-operation of Tanks with Infantry Divisions in Offensive Operations* (November 1943).

38 WO 171/1, 21st Army Group HQ, War Diary, 30 December 1943.

39 IWM BLM 52/18, Montgomery's notes on the 21AG armour–infantry co-operation pamphlet.

40 LHCMA, Alanbrooke, 6/2/23, Montgomery to Nye (VCIGS), 7 December 1943.

41 LHCMA, Alanbrooke, 6/2/23, Nye to Montgomery, 21 December 1943.

42 LHCMA, Alanbrooke, 6/2/23, Nye's notes on Montgomery's comments concerning the Pyman pamphlet, 17 December 1943.

43 IWM BLM 52/17, *Eighth Army Notes on the Employment of Tanks in Support of Infantry in Battle* (November 1943).

44 LHCMA, de Guingand, *21st Army Group Notes on the Employment of Tanks in Support of Infantry in Battle* (February 1944).

45 Place, *Military Training in the British Army*, pp. 147–52.

46 Tpr Austin Baker, 4/7th Royal Dragoon Guards, Diary 1942–1947 and interview with author, April 2003.

47 Maj. Bill Close, 3RTR, interview with author, September 2002; Maj. John Langdon, 3RTR, interview with author, October 2002; Maj-Gen Roy Dixon, 5RTR, interview with author, November 2002.

48 Maj. Bill Close, 3RTR, interview with author, September 2002.

49 Jarymowycz, *Tank Tactics*, pp. 94–7; Capt. Robin Lemon, 3RTR, interview with author, December 2002; Maj-Gen Roy Dixon, 5RTR, interview with author, November 2002.

50 Comments by Montgomery in 1942, quoted in Jarymowycz, *Tank Tactics*, pp. 94, 103.

51 WO 285/1, 2nd British Army correspondence regarding the organisation of armoured regiments, squadrons and troops, March–April 1944.

52 Maj-Gen Roy Dixon, 5RTR; Maj. John Langdon, 3RTR; and Maj. Bill Close, 3RTR, interviews with author 2002. See also Mark Hayward, *The Sherman Firefly* (London: Barbarossa, 2001), ch. 3.

53 Maj. John Langdon, 3RTR, interview with author, October 2002; Place, *Military Training in the British Army*, p. 85.

54 Maj. Bill Close, 3RTR, interview with author, September 2002.

55 Tpr Austin Baker, 4/7th Royal Dragoon Guards, 8th Armoured Brigade, interview with author, March 2003, plus written memoir; WO 106/4469, *79th Armoured Division Final Report* (War Office, 1945); and Fletcher, *Vanguard of Victory*.

56 LHCMA, Alanbrooke, 6/2/25, *Overlord* planning maps and phase lines.

57 D'Este, *Decision in Normandy*, ch. 6.

58 LHCMA, Alanbrooke, 6/2/24, Montgomery, *Some Army Problems*, 20 March 1944; Montgomery to Brooke, 3 April 1944; Montgomery to Dempsey and Bradley, 15 April 1944.

59 For the best assessment of the terrain over which the Normandy campaign was conducted see Badsey, 'Terrain as a Factor'; WO 171/456, planning notes for *Operation Overlord* distributed to divisions, 11th Armoured Division War Diary, May 1944; Ellis, *Victory in the West*, vol. I pp. 79–81.

60 Liddell Hart, *The Other Side of the Hill*, pp. 409–11; Helmut Ritgen, *The Western Front 1944: Memoirs of a Panzer Lehr Officer* (Winnipeg, Manitoba: J. J. Federowicz, 1995), pp. 51, 62–3, 71, 75–6.

61 Ellis, *Victory in the West*, vol. I, pp. 259–69, 319–22.

62 Carver, *Out of Step*, p. 180.

63 Badsey, 'Terrain as a Factor', pp. 358–60.

64 German crews camouflaged their tanks particularly well. US NAII RG 331/210A/1, Lt-Col Sidney Brown, Armored Section, 12th Army Group, 'Notes on Separate Tank Battalions – no. 2', 13 August 1944.

65 This is referred to in many sources but in some detail in interviews with Maj. Bill Close, Maj-Gen Roy Dixon, Capt. Robin Lemon and Tpr Austin Baker.

66 Maj-Gen Roy Dixon, 5RTR, 7th Armoured Division, interview with author, November 2002.

67 Maj. Bill Close, 3RTR, 11th Armoured Division, interview with author, September 2002.

68 LHCMA, Liddell Hart, 9/28/84, interview with Lt-Gen Fritz Bayerlein, Panzer *Lehr*, in 1945.

69 WO 171/456, 2nd British Army intelligence summary no. 26, translation of Panzer *Lehr* document, 11th Armoured Division War Diary, 11 July 1944.

70 Montgomery, *Memoirs*, pp. 237–40.

71 *Die Panzerfaust (Pzf – 60 m: D560/3)*, German training document distributed in 1944.

72 WO 291/1331, AORG Report no. 33, The use of the *Panzerfaust* in the Northwest European Campaign, 1945; WO 205/1165, Capt. H. B. Wright RAMC and Capt. R. D. Harkness RAMC, *A Survey of Casualties amongst Armoured Units in Northwest Europe*, no. 2 ORS, 21AG, 1945.

73 LHCMA, Allfrey, 4/5. This trend had been identified in Italy in late 1943, Capt. T. P. Weaver, *History of the 4th Armoured Brigade – September to December 1943*.

74 WO 208/3577, summary of technical reports regarding weapons, war industry and transportation, issued by MI 10, no. 62, 20 January 1942; WO 219/810, SHAEF technical intelligence summary, no. 1, May 1944.

75 WO 291/1336, Self-propelled artillery in 21st Army Group – analysis of the opinions of users, November 1944; WO 277/5, Brig. A. L. Pemberton, *The Development of Artillery Tactics and Equipment* (War Office, 1950), p. 223.

76 Capt. Andrew Burn, 5RHA, 7th Armoured Division, interview with author, May 2002; WO 291/1336, Self-propelled artillery in 21st Army Group – analysis of the opinions of users, November 1944.

77 WO 219/3350, SHAEF intelligence report, interrogation of Kurt Arnoldt, Henschel chief technical engineer, 23 May 1945.

78 WO 219/810, SHAEF technical intelligence summary no. 1, 'Notes on German tanks', May 1944.

79 Maj. Bill Close, 3RTR, 11th Armoured Division, interview with author, September 2002; Ken Tout, *Roads to Falaise: Cobra and Goodwood Reassessed* (Stroud: Sutton, 2002), ch. five.

80 Some 44 per cent of German tanks were knocked out by direct gunfire: David C. Hardison, *Data on World War II Tank Engagements Involving the US Third and Fourth Armored Divisions* (1947), quoted in Jarymowycz, *Tank Tactics*, pp. 281–2. German tank losses in the eastern sector may well have been higher in view of the greater density of German armour around Caen.

81 US NAII RG 331/210A/1, Lt-Col Sidney Brown, Armored Section, 12th Army Group, 'Notes on Separate Tank Battalions – no. 2', 13 August 1944.

82 BOV, Mediterranean Technical Report no. 23, report on captured Tigers, 18 August 1944; NAC RG 24 14186, 'Who Killed Tiger?' written by 2nd New Zealand Division intelligence, July 1944. A New Zealand Army report from Italy in 1944 confirmed that Tigers were mechanically unreliable and the best way of dealing with a Tiger was to 'make him run'.

83 WO 208/3579, MI 10 report, 12 August 1943.

84 WO 171/456, 2nd British Army intelligence summary no. 1, appendix D, 'Expected Levels of Armoured Opposition', May 1944.

85 Maj. Bill Close, 3RTR, interview with author, September 2002.

86 WO 291/1331, 21st Army Group ORS report no. 12, *Analysis of 75 mm Sherman Tank Casualties Suffered between 6 June and 10 July 1944*.

87 BOV, 'Effects of Enemy Projectiles on Sherman and Churchill Tanks', 79th Armoured Division report for 21st Army Group, 26 August 1944. This stated that direct fire engagements in Normandy were usually under 400 yards. Even to the south of Caen the average range of anti-tank gunnery was considerably less than 1,000 yards, based on engagements involving the Canadians in August 1944 (Jarymowycz, p. 270), *Tank Tactics*, while First US Army figures offered an average figure of some 600 metres.

88 Many examples of this from oral testimony and printed primary sources but see Richard Holmes's *War Walks – Goodwood*, BBC television episode (1996) for interview with Normandy tank veteran and author Ken Tout.

89 English, *The Canadian Army and the Normandy Campaign*, p. 311.

90 WO 171/456, appendix A to British Second Army intelligence summary no. 26, translation of enemy document, 11th Armoured Division War Diary, 11 July 1944.

91 Liddell Hart, *The Other Side of the Hill*, p. 427.

92 LHCMA, Liddell Hart, 15/4/85, Notes from 22nd Armoured Brigade HQ on operations in Normandy, 6–15 June 1944.

93 WO 171/153, 21st Army Group Liaison letter no. 2, 6 September 1944, covering period June–August, RAC branch, HQ, 21AG.

94 BOV, minutes of conference on tactics, gunnery and administration, 34 Tank Brigade HQ, 25 August 1944. Similar lessons were drawn by 2nd Canadian Armoured Brigade, quoted in Copp, *Fields of Fire*, p. 128.

95 Capt. Robin Lemon, 3RTR reconnaissance troop commander, interview with author, December 2002.

96 Maj. John Langdon, 3RTR, interview with author, October 2002.

97 BOV, minutes of conference on tactics, gunnery and administration, 34 Tank Brigade HQ, 25 August 1944.

98 Roberts, *From the Desert to the Baltic*, pp. 184–5.

99 Maj. Bill Close, 3RTR, interview with author, September 2002.

100 LHCMA, Liddell, Hart 15/4/85, Notes from 22nd Armoured Brigade HQ on operations in Normandy, 6–15 June 1944.

101 Maj. John Langdon, 3RTR, interview with author, October 2002.

102 BOV, minutes of conference on tactics, gunnery and administration, 34 Tank Brigade HQ, 25 August 1944.

103 Maj-Gen Roy Dixon, 5RTR; Maj. Bill Close, 3RTR; and Maj. John Langdon, 3RTR, interviews with author, September–November, 2002.

104 WO 171/153, notes on close co-operation between tanks and infantry, RAC branch, 21AG, August 1944.

105 WO 171/456, 11th Armoured Division War Diary, Intelligence Summary, no. 11, 28 June 1944, and notes for August 1944; US NAII, RG 331/240E/17, 'Lessons from combat in Normandy', Armored Section Memo. no. 1, First US Army HQ, 19 June 1944.

106 WO 171/456, 11th Armoured Division War Diary, July 1944; Maj. Bill Close, 3RTR, interview with author, September 2002. Major Close commanded the lead squadron of the whole *Goodwood* advance.

107 WO 285/1, 2nd British Army correspondence concerning organisation of armoured regiments, squadrons and troops, March–April 1944.

108 Maj. John Langdon, 3RTR, interview with author, October 2002.

109 WO 171/456, 2nd British Army intelligence summary no. 26, translation of Panzer *Lehr* document.

110 BOV, minutes of conference at 34th Tank Brigade HQ on armour tactics, gunnery and administration, 26 August 1944.

111 Maj. Bill Close, 3RTR, interview with author, September 2002.

112 WO 291/1331, 'Bombing in *Operation Goodwood*', no. 2 ORS, 21AG, July 1944.

113 WO 171/456, report from HQ 159th Infantry Brigade, 'To describe the methods used to defeat German tactics and retain the initiative in the bridgehead over the Odon', 28 June–5 July 1944.

114 WO 171/153, notes on close co-operation between tanks and infantry, RAC branch 21AG, August 1944.

115 Maj. John Langdon, 3RTR; Maj-Gen Roy Dixon, 5RTR, interviews with author, October and November respectively, 2002.

116 US NAII RG 331/210A/1, Lt-Col Sidney Brown, Armored Section, 12th Army Group, 'Notes on Separate Tank Battalions – no. 2', 13 August 1944; Jarymowycz, *Tank Tactics*, p. 274.

117 WO 171/153, 21st Army Group Liaison letter no. 2, 6 September 1944.

118 LHCMA, Liddell Hart, 15/4/85, 22nd Armoured Brigade notes on operations, 6–15 June 1944.

119 WO 171/1257, 3rd Irish Guards War Diary, 13 July 1944; Earl of Rosse and E. R. H. Hill, *The Story of the Guards Armoured Division 1941–1945* (London: Geoffrey Bles, 1956), p. 190.

120 Geoffrey Bishop, *The Battle: A Tank Officer Remembers*, pp. 60–1, quoted in Ian Daglish, *Operation Bluecoat: Battleground Normandy* (Barnsley: Pen & Sword, 2003), p. 71.

121 US NAII, RG 337/26/40, Brig-Gen Bruce Clarke, Plans Section AGF to Major-General Cook, Assistant CoS, comments on 'Notes on Combat – The Infantry Division' by Gen George Patton, 16 November 1945. The comments by Patton also covered infantry in armoured divisions.

122 LHCMA, O'Connor, 5/3/37, O'Connor to Lt-Gen Sir Allan Harding, CoS, HQ Allied Forces in Italy, 19 August 1944; Baynes, *The Forgotten Victor*, pp. 213–14; Roberts, *From the Desert to the Baltic*, pp. 184–5; Adair, *A Guards' General*, pp. 147–52.

123 Daglish, *Operation Bluecoat*, pp. 68–72.

124 Robin Neillands, *The Desert Rats: 7th Armoured Division 1940–1945* (London: Orion, 1997 [1991]), pp. 236–8.
125 For 7th Armoured see CAB 106/963, 'Co-operation of armour and infantry' by GSO1(L), 7th Armoured Division, 12 June 1944.
126 US NAII RG 331/210A/1, Lt-Col J. B. Routh, Assistant Armored Officer, HQ 12th Army Group, to Colonel Wright, 'Employment of Armor at Brest', 21 September 1944.
127 Tpr Austin Baker, 4/7th Dragoons, 27th Armoured Brigade, interview with author, April 2003; Ellis, *Victory in the West*, vol. I, p. 252; LHCMA, Liddell Hart, 15/4/85, 22nd Armoured Brigade notes on operations, 6–15 June 1944.
128 Ellis, *Victory in the West*, vol. I, p. 252.
129 Delaforce, *Monty's Marauders*, pp. 149–50.
130 CAB 106/963, Immediate Report no. 6, 'Capture of Cristot by one battalion supported by one squadron of tanks on 16 June 1944', 17 June 1944; Ellis, *Victory in the West*, vol. I, p. 261; Delaforce, *Monty's Marauders*, p. 153.
131 Ellis, *Victory in the West*, vol. I, pp. 390–1; CAB 106/1029, Capt. H. W. Llewellyn Smith's account of 3rd Tank Battalion Scots Guards, 20 July 1944–8 May 1945.
132 LHCMA, Allfrey, 4/5, XIII Corps conference, 'Need for a common doctrine for infantry–tank co-operation', 8 April 1944.
133 WO 171/862, 1st East Riding Yeomanry War Diary, June–July 1944.
134 LHCMA, Allfrey, 4/5, XIII Corps conference, 'Need for a common doctrine for infantry–tank co-operation', 8 April 1944.
135 Daglish, *Operation Bluecoat*, p. 69.
136 BOV, minutes of conference held at 34 Tank Brigade HQ to discuss tactics, gunnery and administration, 25 August 1944; LHCMA, Allfrey, 4/5, XIII Corps conference, 'Need for a common doctrine for infantry–tank co-operation', 8 April 1944.
137 LHCMA, Allfrey, 4/5, XIII Corps conference, 'Need for a common doctrine for infantry–tank co-operation', 8 April 1944.
138 Maj-Gen Roy Dixon, 5RTR, interview with author, November 2002; Delaforce, *Monty's Marauders*, pp. 152–3.
139 Basil Liddell Hart, John Ellis and Roman Jarymowycz are quite vociferous about this, see introduction.
140 I am indebted to Dr Stephen Badsey for this Soviet view of *Operation Totalise*, gleaned in discussion with senior Red Army officers in the late 1980s.

5. THE TANK GAP

1 Hastings, *Overlord*, pp. 224–31, 280.
2 Ibid., p. 229.
3 Jarymowycz, *Tank Tactics*, p. 255.
4 Hart, *Clash of Arms*, p. 309.
5 French, *Raising Churchill's Army*, p. 102.
6 WO 205/5b, de Guingand to Montgomery, 24 June 1944; How, *Hill 112*, p. 14.
7 How, *Hill 112*, p. 48, offers a good example of this occurrence.
8 Wilson, *Flamethrower*, p. 54.
9 CAB 106/1060, Notes on Tanks, Brig. Hargest, 17 June 1944.
10 Meyer, *Grenadiers*, p. 108.
11 WO 219/791, SHAEF Army Group records, report filed to SHAEF, 16 June 1944.
12 Anon, *The Story of the 23rd Hussars* (British Army of the Rhine, 1945).

13 Moore, *Panzer Bait*, pp. 126–8; W. S. Brownlie, *The Proud Trooper: The History of the Ayrshire Yeomanry* (London: Collins, 1964), pp. 364–5.

14 WO 291/1331, *Analysis of German Tank Casualties in France 6 June 1944 to 31 August 1944*, Operational Research Group, report no. 17.

15 WO 205/1165, Capt. H. B. Wright RAMC and Capt. R. D. Harkness RAMC, *A Survey of Casualties amongst Armoured Units in Northwest Europe*, no. 2 ORS, 21AG, 1945.

16 WO 205/422, Dempsey to 21st Army Group HQ, 24 June 1944.

17 WO 205/422, 21st Army Group Combat Reports, Brig. H. E. Pyman (BGS) XXX Corps to Major General Erskine, 7th Armoured Division, 16 June 1944.

18 WO 205/422, Erskine to XXX Corps HQ, 17 June 1944.

19 Ibid.

20 WO 205/422, Lt-Col J. R. Bowring, Immediate Report IN20, 'Impressions on Fighting in Normandy', 17 June 1944.

21 WO 205/5b, Brig. Freddie de Guingand (21st Army Group CoS) to Montgomery, 24 June 1944.

22 WO 205/422, Maj-Gen G. W. Richards to 2nd Army and 21st Army Group HQ, 22 June 1944.

23 LHCMA, Alanbrooke, 6/2/25, Montgomery to Brooke (CIGS), 27 June 1944.

24 LHCMA, Alanbrooke, 6/2/25, Montgomery to Dempsey, 25 June 1944.

25 LHCMA, Alanbrooke, 6/2/25, Montgomery to Brooke (CIGS), 27 June 1944.

26 CCA, PJGG, 9/8/11, Papers of James Grigg, Montgomery to Grigg, 25 June 1944.

27 BOV, *Operation Overlord* – Reports on Equipment, box 623-438, CinC, 21st Army Group to RAC, Memo M506, received 6 July 1944. A report similar to M506 was despatched to Grigg along with the letter of 25 June 1944, CCA, PJGG, 9/8/11, Papers of James Grigg, Montgomery to Grigg.

28 WO 205/5b, de Guingand to Montgomery (TAC HQ 21AG), 24 June 1944; Hansard, vol. 398 – 22 March 1944, vol. 399 – 18, 19 and 25 April 1944, vol. 402 – 25 July 1944 and 2 August 1944.

29 BOV, *Operation Overlord* – Reports on Equipment, box 623-438, CinC, 21st Army Group to RAC, memo M506, 6 July 1944; LHCMA, Alanbrooke, 6/2/25, Montgomery to Dempsey, 25 June 1944; Montgomery to Brooke (CIGS), 27 June 1944.

30 R. P. Hunnicut, *Sherman: A History of the American Medium Tank* (Novato, CA: Presidio, 1994 edn), pp. 159–68.

31 Patrick Delaforce, *Monty's Marauders*, p. 73.

32 NAC White, Gen I. D., *US v German Equipment*, Brig-Gen J. H. Collier, Command CC A Exhibit no. 1, 1945, see Jarymowycz, *Tank Tactics*, p. 348.

33 WO 291/1299, Capt. D. H. Parkinson to Army Council Scientific Advisor, 15 July 1943; LHCMA, Alanbrooke, 6/2/22, Montgomery to Brooke, 25 March 1943; BOV, RAC Half Yearly Reports, no. 6, 1 July–31 December 1942, report by DAFV to WO following visit to Middle East, 30 July–27 August 1942.

34 WO 205/57, Organisation of armoured brigades, Lt-Gen K. Anderson, GOC 2nd British Army, to 21st Army Group RAC, 18 December 1943 and Lt-Col N. M. H. Wall to 21st Army Group, December 1943.

35 BOV, 693-438, XXX Corps to 21st Army Group, 18 June 1944; WO 194/309, Tank armament research report no. 29, 17 April 1945; and WO 194/646, Tank armament research report no. 40, 1 November 1945. Both reports examined the use of chemicals and different muzzle breaks to solve the problem that had been identified since Normandy.

36 BOV, 623-438, Report by Maj. H. R. Gray and Maj. C. Cashmore, 17–26 July 1944; WO 201/2852, camouflage techniques, Italian campaign, 1945.

37 Hayward, *The Sherman Firefly*, p. 54; Brownlie, *The Proud Trooper*, p. 33.

38 Material relating to the technical capabilities of the M4 Sherman drawn from Hunnicut, *Sherman*; Stephen Zaloga and Peter Sarson, *Sherman Medium Tank 1942–1945* (London: Osprey, 1978); J. Sandars, *The Sherman Tank in British Service 1942–45* (London: Osprey, 1982 [1980]); Hayward, *The Sherman Firefly*.

39 Hastings, *Overlord*, p. 226.

40 LHCMA, Liddell Hart, 9/28/84, interview in 1945 with Gen Fritz Bayerlein, GOC Panzer *Lehr*.

41 WO 205/57, Organisation of Armoured Brigades, Maj-Gen Norrie (RAC) to BGS (SD), 22 December 1943.

42 BOV, *Operation Overlord* – Reports on Equipment, box 623-438, 21AG Report, 16 June 1944; WO 205/404, Report on reliability of mechanical equipment, August 1944; Patrick Delaforce, *The Black Bull: From Normandy to the Baltic with the 11th Armoured Division* (Stroud: Sutton, 1993), p. 14.

43 BOV, Box 623 – *Operation Overlord* – Reports on Equipment, Maj-Gen Gerald Verney to Maj-Gen Raymond Briggs DRAC, September 1944.

44 LHCMA, Liddell Hart, 15/15/150, Liddell Hart's interviews with Bayerlein, August 1950; IWM Bucknall Papers, XXX Corps Intelligence Report, no. 452, 19 July 1944, appendix A.

45 BOV, Tank Situation report by Lt-Gen John Fullerton Evetts, ACIGS, 11 September 1943, annexure B.

46 David Fletcher, *The Universal Tank: British Armour in the Second World War – Part Two* (London: Her Majesty's Stationery Office, 1993), p. 100.

47 BOV, *Operation Overlord* – Reports on Equipment, box 623-438, CinC, 21st Army Group to RAC, memo M506, 6 July 1944.

48 BOV, RAC Half Yearly reports, no. 10, 1 July–31 December 1944.

49 BOV, 21st Army Group Technical Reports, Maj-Gen Dumphie's report on visit to 21AG, December 1944; Fletcher, *The Universal Tank*, pp. 100–1; Beale, *Death by Design*, p. 144.

50 WO 205/57, Memorandum by J. Napier (BGS), 7 July 1943.

51 IWM, Montgomery Papers, BLM 117/2, Montgomery to Archie Nye (VCIGS), 28 August 1943; BLM 129/2, *Future Design of the Capital Tank*, 24 October 1944.

52 Fletcher, *Mr Churchill's Tank*, p. 142.

53 Peter Beale, *Tank Tracks: 9th Battalion Royal Tank Regiment at War 1940–45* (Stroud: Sutton, 1995), p. 145; WO 171/9002, 9RTR War Diary.

54 WO 32/101365, Army Operational Research Group Middle East, memo no. 6, *The Distribution and Effect of AP and HE*, 25/8/43; Fletcher, *Mr Churchill's Tank*, p. 142.

55 LHCMA, Verney, I/i/3, 'Account of part played by 6th Guards Tank Brigade in *Operation Bluecoat*', 30 July 1944.

56 BOV, *Operation Overlord* – reports on equipment, Memo no. 506 Future Policy on Tanks, Montgomery, 6 July 1944.

57 BOV, *Operation Overlord* – reports on equipment, Memo no. 506 Future Policy on Tanks, Montgomery, 6 July 1944.

58 Niklas Zetterling, *Normandy 1944: German Military Organization, Combat Power and Organizational Effectiveness* (Winnipeg: J. J. Fedorowicz, 2000), pp. 59–64; David Fletcher, *Churchill Tank: Vehicle History and Specification* (London: Her Majesty's Stationery Office, 1983), p. 136.

59 Fletcher, *Mr Churchill's Tank*, p. 143.

60 US NAII RG331/240E/17, Brig-Gen R. E. Jenkins, GSC, Assistant Chief of Staff G-3, 'Increasing Fire of US Tank Battalions', 6 August 1944.

61 Capt. Robin Lemon, 3RTR reconnaissance troop commander, interview with author, December 2002; Jonathan Forty, *Tanks in Detail: M3–M3A1–M3A3–Stuart I to V* (Hersham: Ian Allan, 2002), pp. 6–9; US NAII RG331/240E/17, Jenkins, 'Increasing Fire of US Tank Battalions', 6 August 1944.

62 Peter Brown, 'What's in a Nomenclature?', *Tracklink: The Magazine of the Friends of the Tank Museum*, no. 58, May 2003, pp. 12–14.

63 WO 291/1336, Self-propelled artillery in 21st Army Group – analysis of the opinions of users, November 1944; WO 277/5, Brig. A. L. Pemberton, *The Development of Artillery Tactics and Equipment* (War Office, 1950), p. 223.

64 BOV, RAC 3 (O) 17/2, War Office memo, *Self-propelled anti-tank gun situation*, for the 38th meeting of the Tank Board, 14 February 1944; Jarymowycz, *Tank Tactics*, p. 277.

65 US NAII RG 337/28/378, HQ Tank Destroyer Center, Camp Hood Texas, *Combat Experiences of Tank Destroyer Employment*, 26 December 1944.

66 US NAII RG 331/240E/14, HQ 6th Army Group, GS, G-3 Armored Section, 11 and 16 February 1945; Hunnicut, *Sherman*, pp. 360–82.

67 WO 291/74, Army Operational Research Group memo no. 415, *Comparison of the performance of 75 mm and 76 mm tank gun ammunition*, 9 October 1944.

68 WO 219/3115, Maj. G. H. Pinckney, GSC, Assistant Secretary General Staff, SHAEF to Eisenhower, 11 July 1944; WO 219/2806, Tanks, HQ US 1st Army to Lt-Gen Smith, CoS SHAEF, 2 July 1944.

69 BOV, RAC 3 (O) 17/2, War Office memo, *Self-propelled anti-tank gun situation*, for the 38th meeting of the Tank Board, 14 February 1944; WO 205/151, Availability of vehicles and equipment in 21st Army Group, minutes of meeting held at G(SD) branch 21AG, 8 August 1944.

70 WO 291/74, Army Operational Research Group memo no. 415, *Comparison of the performance of 75 mm and 76 mm tank gun ammunition*, 9 October 1944; Zetterling, *Normandy*, pp. 62–4; Hunnicut, *Sherman*, p. 562.

71 WO 291/74, Army Operational Research Group memo no. 415, *Comparison of the performance of 75 mm and 76 mm tank gun ammunition*, 9 October 1944.

72 US NAII RG 331/210A/1, Lt-Col Sidney Brown, 'Visit to Armored Units', interview with prisoner of war, 13 February 1945.

73 US NAII RG 331/240E/15, 'Periodic Report – US Armor', no. 3, HQ 12th Army Group, translation of German document, 5 September 1944.

74 LHCMA, Liddell Hart, 9/28/84, Interview with General Fritz Bayerlein, 1945.

75 BOV, Col. Gordon Hall (DDAFV(T)), *AFVs in Mediterranean 1939–1945*, compiled from Mediterranean Area AFV technical reports nos. 1–27.

76 WO 171/1002, 9RTR War Diary, August 1944.

77 US NAII RG 331/210A/1, Lt-Col Sidney Brown, 'Visit to Armored Units', interview with prisoner of war, 13 February 1945.

78 Maj. Bill Close, 3RTR, interview with author, September 2002; Maj-Gen Roy Dixon, 5RTR, interview with author, November 2002.

79 LHCMA, Dempsey, box 1, Second Army intelligence summaries, no. 12, 17 June 1944.

80 Taylor, *Villers Bocage through the Lens*.

81 LHCMA, Dempsey, box 1, Second Army intelligence summaries, no. 20, 24 June 1944.

82 Only 12 Tiger IIs participated in the campaign.

83 Zetterling, *Normandy*, pp. 65–8; Eric Lefèvre, *Panzers in Normandy: Then and Now* (London: Battle of Britain Press, 1983), pp. 43–5.

84 LHCMA, Dempsey, box 1, Second Army intelligence summaries, no. 26, 30 June 1944.

85 US NAII RG 331/240E/14, 7th Army Interrogation Center, interviews with Generals Heinz Guderian, Leo Geyr von Schweppenburg, Sepp Dietrich and Paul Hausser, 18 May 1945.

86 L.Ellis, *Victory in the West*, vol. I (London: Her Majesty's Stationery Office, 1962), p. 492.

87 WO 219/792, SHAEF Reports, *Defensive Tendencies in German Weapon Design*, undated.

88 WO 205/212, *Foreign Armour, Equipment and Ammunition*, notes from 21AG HQ, 5 September 1944.

89 US NAII RG331/240E/14, notes submitted by 191, 753 and 756 Tank Battalions for period 5 October 1944–14 December 1944, Brig. R. E. Jenkins, G3 Armor 6th Army Group, 19 December 1944; WO 205/1165, Capt. H. B. Wright RAMC and Capt. R. D. Harkness RAMC, *A Survey of Casualties amongst Armoured Units in Northwest Europe*, no. 2 ORS, 21AG, 1945; WO 219/600, SHAEF Reports, Eisenhower to 6th AG and 12th AG, 12 December 1944.

90 BA/MA RH 19/IX/3, Anlage 3 zu HGr. B/Stoart Nr. 630/44 g.Kdos, Panzerabschußliste, 29 June 1944; WO 205/1165, Capt. H. B. Wright RAMC and Capt. R. D. Harkness RAMC, *A Survey of Casualties amongst Armoured Units in Northwest Europe*, no. 2 ORS, 21AG, 1945; WO 291/1331, AORG Report no. 33, The Use of the *Panzerfaust* in the NW European Campaign, 1945; US NAII 331/210A/1, 'Intelligence Report of Tanks Rendered Inoperative due to Enemy Action', June–August 1944, First US Army.

91 WO 291/1331, AORG report no. 12, Analysis of 75 mm Sherman Tank Casualties Suffered between 6 June and 10 July 1944; Jarymowycz, *Tank Tactics*, p. 270; WO 205/1165, Capt. H. B. Wright RAMC and Capt. R. D. Harkness RAMC, *A Survey of Casualties amongst Armoured Units in Northwest Europe*, no. 2 ORS, 21AG, 1945; US NAII 331/210A/1, 'Intelligence Report of Tanks Rendered Inoperative due to Enemy Action', June–August 1944, First US Army.

92 WO 291/1331, AORG report no. 12, Analysis of 75 mm Sherman Tank Casualties Suffered between 6 June and 10 July 1944; Jarymowycz, *Tank Tactics*, pp. 271–2; US NAII 331/210A/1, 'Intelligence Report of Tanks Rendered Inoperative Due to Enemy Action', June–August 1944, First US Army.

93 Zetterling, *Normandy*, p. 72.

94 WO 291/1331, AORG report no. 12, Analysis of 75 mm Sherman Tank Casualties Suffered between 6 June and 10 July 1944.

95 WO 171/456, 11th Armoured Division War Diary, pre-*Overlord* intelligence summary no. 1, appendix D; BA/MA RH 19/IX/3, Anlage 3 zu HGr. B/Stoart Nr. 630/44 g.Kdos, Panzerabschußliste, 29 June 1944.

96 WO 285/1, Dempsey Papers, Lt-Gen Richard O'Connor to Lt-Gen Miles Dempsey, 29 May 1944; BOV, *Operation Overlord* – reports on equipment, Memo no. 506 Future Policy on Tanks, Montgomery, 6 July 1944.

97 AGF Study no. 798, BRL MR-798, *Data on World War Two Tank Engagements Involving the US Third and Fourth Armored Divisions*, Ballistic Research Laboratories, Aberdeen Proving Ground, MD, 1 April 1947, quoted in Jarymowycz, *Tank Tactics*, p. 267.

98 Brownlie, *The Proud Trooper*, pp. 364–5.

99 Stuart Hamilton, *Armoured Odyssey: 8th Royal Tank Regiment in the Western Desert 1941–1942: Palestine, Syria, Egypt 1943–1944: Italy 1944–1945* (London: Tom Donovan, 1995), p. 46; A. Graham, *Sharpshooters at War* (London: Sharpshooters Regimental Association,

1964), p. 66; J. Sandars, *British Guards Armoured Division 1941–1945* (London: Osprey, 1979), p. 12.

100 Stephen Dyson, *Tank Twins: East End Brothers in Arms 1943–45* (London: Leo Cooper, 1994), pp. 46–7.

101 WO 219/600, SHAEF Records, HQ to 6th and 12th US Army Groups, 12 December 1944; WO 291/2384, 21st Army Group Operational Research Section, Examination of Tank Casualties; US NAII RG 331/210A/1, memo by Col. E. K. Wright, Armored Section, 12th Army Group, 7 December 1944; US NAII RG 331/240E/14, Maj. Millard Thompson, 1st Armored Group, report on 'Sand-bagging' M4 Tanks for added protection, 10 March 1945.

102 BOV, 21st Army Group Technical Reports, no. 16, 14 October 1944; US NAII RG 331/210A/1, memo by Col. E. K. Wright, Armored Section, 12th Army Group, 7 December 1944.

103 US NAII 331/210A/1, 'Intelligence Report of Tanks Rendered Inoperative due to Enemy Action', June to August 1944, First US Army; BRL MR-798, quoted in Jarymowycz, *Tank Tactics*, p. 270.

104 WO 205/1165, Capt. H. B. Wright RAMC and Capt. R. D. Harkness RAMC, *A Survey of casualties amongst armoured units in northwest Europe*, no. 2 ORS, HQ 21st Army Group.

105 WO 291/1331, 21st Army Group ORS Section, report no. 12, *Analysis of 75 mm Sherman tank casualties suffered between 6th June and 10th July 1944*.

106 US NAII 331/210A/1, 'Intelligence Report of Tanks Rendered Inoperative due to Enemy Action', June–August 1944, First US Army.

107 Beale, *Tank Tracks*, p. 145.

108 WO 205/1165, Capt. H. B. Wright RAMC and Capt. R. D. Harkness RAMC, *A Survey of casualties amongst armoured units in northwest Europe*, no. 2 ORS, HQ 21st Army Group.

109 BOV, 21st Army Group Technical Reports, WTS, FF Report D+6 to D+11, 21AG 19 June 1944; US NAII RG 331/210A/1, Notes on separate tank battalions, no. 2, 12th US Army Group, 13 August 1944; WO 291/1331, 21st Army Group ORS Section, report no. 12, *Analysis of 75 mm Sherman tank casualties suffered between 6th June and 10th July 1944*.

110 Delaforce, *The Black Bull*, p. 13.

111 WO 205/1165, Capt. H. B. Wright RAMC and Capt. R. D. Harkness RAMC, *A Survey of casualties amongst armoured units in northwest Europe*, no. 2 ORS, HQ 21st Army Group.

112 BOV, Box 623-438, *Operation Overlord* – Reports on Equipment, Majors Cashmore and Gray, 17–26 July 1944 report; Lt-Gen Ronald Weeks, Lt-Gen Ronald Weeks, DCIGS Report 324/5; Letter from ADAFV(T) 2nd Army to DDAFV(D); Major Matthew's report (RAC).

113 WO 291/1331, 21st Army Group ORS Section, report no. 12, *Analysis of 75 mm Sherman tank casualties suffered between 6 June and 10 July 1944*.

114 BOV, Box 623-438, *Operation Overlord* – Reports on Equipment, Letter from ADAFV(T) 2nd Army to DDAFV(D).

115 US NAII 331/210A/1, 'Intelligence Report of Tanks Rendered Inoperative due to Enemy Action', June–August 1944, First US Army.

116 WO 291/2384, no. 1 ORS, report no.1/21; WO 291/2386, Operational Research memo no. 6, *The distribution and effect of AP shot and HE in Churchill tank casualties*, August 1943; US NAII 331/210A/1, 'Intelligence Report of Tanks Rendered Inoperative due to Enemy Action', June to August 1944, First US Army.

117 BOV, Effects of Enemy Projectiles on Sherman and Churchill tanks, Maj-Gen Percy Hobart, 79th Armoured Division, 26 August 1944.

118 BOV, Mediterranean technical reports, no. 26, February/March 1945.

119 BOV, Box 623–438, *Operation Overlord* – Reports on Equipment, Lt-Gen Ronald Weeks, DCIGS Report 324/5, and report by Major Matthews (RAC); Delaforce, *Monty's Marauders*, p. 73.

120 US NAII RG 331/240E/15, Lt-Col Holmes Bevington, 894th T. D. Battalion, 'Report on T-70 Tank Destroyer', 18 June 1944.

121 BOV, Col. G. Hall, *AFVs in the Mediterranean 1939–45*, Fighting Vehicle Division, compiled from Mediterranean area AFV technical reports nos. 1–27, 1945.

122 BOV, Colonel Blayden AFV (Tech), report in *AFVs in Mediterranean*.

123 WO 291/1331, 21st Army Group ORS, report no. 12, *Analysis of 75 mm Sherman tank casualties suffered between 6 June and 10 July*.

124 WO 291/2384, no. 1 ORS report no. 1/21, Examination of Tank Casualties – causes of fires in Shermans.

125 Brownlie, *The Proud Trooper*, p. 153; BOV, Colonel Blayden AFV (Tech), report in *AFVs in Mediterranean*.

126 WO 291/2384, no. 1 ORS, report no. 1/21, Examination of Tank Casualties – causes of fires in Shermans.

127 BOV, RAC Half Yearly Report no. 9, 1 January 1944–30 June 1944.

128 WO 291/1331, 21st Army Group ORS, report no. 12, *Analysis of 75 mm Sherman tank casualties suffered between 6 June and 10 July*; BOV, RAC Half Yearly Report no. 9, 1 January–30 June 1944.

129 US NAII RG331/210A/1, operational information on M-4 medium tanks, HQ 26th Infantry Division to XII Corps, 1 December 1944; BOV, Effects of Enemy Projectiles on Sherman and Churchill tanks, Maj-Gen Percy Hobart, 79th Armoured Division, 26 August 1944.

130 Hart, *Clash of Arms*, p. 309.

131 WO 205/1165, Capt. H. B. Wright RAMC and Capt. R. D. Harkness RAMC, *A Survey of casualties amongst armoured units in Northwest Europe*, no. 2 ORS, HQ 21st Army Group.

132 Moore, *Panzer Bait*, pp. 126–8; Delaforce, *The Black Bull*, p. 13.

133 Delaforce, *The Black Bull*, pp. 13–14.

134 Dyson, *Tank Twins*, p. 47.

135 WO 291/1331, 21st Army Group no. 2 ORS, report no. 17, Analysis of German Tank Casualties in France, 1944.

136 BOV, RAC Half Yearly Reports, no. 10, 1 July–31 December 1944, Ammunition requirements; see notes 81–4.

137 WO 291/74, AORG memo no. 415, *Comparison of the Performance of 75 mm and 76 mm Tank Gun Ammunition*, 9 October 1944; Hunnicut, *Sherman*, p. 562.

138 WO 205/422, 21st Army Group combat reports, correspondence by Brig. H. E. Pyman, 16 June 1944; Maj-Gen G. W. Erskine, 17 June 1944; Lt-Col J. H. Gibbons, 6 July 1944.

139 BOV, RAC Half Yearly Report no. 10, 1 July–31 December 1944, memo no. 506, Gen B. L. Montgomery, 21st AG HQ, 6 July 1944.

140 WO 291/74, AORG memo no. 415, *Comparison of the Performance of 75 mm and 76 mm Tank Gun Ammunition*, 9 October 1944.

141 WO 219/2806, Tanks, Brig. H. B. Lewis (USA), 25 April 1944.

142 BOV, RAC Half Yearly Reports no. 10, 1/7/44 to 1/1/45, memo by the War Office in reply to Montgomery's M506, 8 July 1944.

143 WO 205/422, 21st Army Group Combat Reports, Lt-Gen Miles Dempsey, 24 June 1944.

144 WO 285/1, Dempsey Papers, pre-*Overlord* planning, O'Connor to Dempsey, 29 May 1944.

145 Delaforce, *Monty's Marauders*, p. 73.

146 WO 205/422, 21st Army Group Combat Reports, Lt-Gen K. Stuart, Canadian Military HQ, 12 July 1944.

147 BOV, Box 623-438, *Operation Overlord* – Reports on Equipment, Montgomery's memo M506, 6 July 1944; US NAII RG331/210A/1, Lt-Col Joel Stratton, Cav, Armored Section, 12th Army Group HQ, to Colonel Wright, 12 August 1944.

148 WO 291/213, 'The accuracy of anti-tank gunnery – trials carried out at the School of Artillery, Larkhill', by Col. O. M. Solandt and R. J. Whitney, AORG report no. 230, 21 November 1944.

149 BOV, *Operation Overlord* – Reports on Equipment, War Office responses to memo M506, 10 July 1944.

150 WO 291/770, AORG memo no. 448, 'Some jump and dispersion trials with the 17-pdr gun in Sherman Ic using APCBC and Discarding sabot'.

151 US NAII RG 331/210A/1, HQ 12th Army Group, 'Final report of board of officers appointed to determine comparative effectiveness of ammunition of 76 mm and 17-pdr gun', 30 August 1944.

152 WO 194/646, Tank Armament Research report no. 40, 1/11/45; BOV, *Operation Overlord* – Reports on Equipment, XXX Corps to 21AG, 18 June 1944; US NAII RG 331/210A/1, Lt-Col Sidney Brown, 'Visit to Armored Units', interview with prisoner of war, 13 February 1945.

153 WO 205/1165, 'A survey of tank casualties', July 1944.

154 WO 291/213, AORG report no. 230, 'The accuracy of tank gunnery' by R. J. Whitney, 21 November 1944.

155 WO 205/637, Daily AFV States, 2nd British Army, June–July 1944.

6. DESIGN AND PLANNING

1 BOV, Tank Situation memo, Lt-Gen John Fullerton Evetts, ACIGS, to James Grigg, Secretary of State, War Ministry, 11 September 1943.

2 Ellis, *Victory in the West*, vol. I, pp. 545–50; M. M. Postan, D. Hay and J. D. Scott, *Design and Development of Weapons: Studies in Government and Industrial Organisation* (London: HMSO, 1964), p. 321.

3 David Fletcher, *The Great Tank Scandal: British Armour in the Second World War – Part One* (London: Her Majesty's Stationery Office, 1989), and *The Universal Tank: British Armour in the Second World War – Part Two* (London: Her Majesty's Stationery Office, 1993).

4 Postan, Hay and Scott, *Design and Development*, ch. XIII.

5 See Chapter 5.

6 Peter Gudgin, *Armoured Firepower: The Development of Tank Armament 1939–1945* (Stroud: Sutton, 1997), p. 75.

7 Beale, *Death by Design*.

8 An argument used by Beale and Barnett.

9 WO 205/636 and WO 205/637, Tank and AFV states, 21st Army Group summaries; approximations derived from Ellis, *Victory in the West*, vol. I, appendix IV.

10 LHCMA, Liddell Hart, 15/8/81, General Staff, *Modern Formations (1931), Provisional*.

11 See the Tank Board minutes and RAC Half-Yearly Progress Reports held at Bovington or WO 165 for 1941–44 for the lack of direction in War Office policy regarding light tanks.

12 Postan, Hay and Scott, *Design and Development*, pp. 310–11; WO 219/5326, 21st Army Group (B. L. Montgomery), *The Armoured Division in Battle*, December 1944.

13 Cap. Robin Lemon, 3RTR, interview with author, December 2002.

14 Postan, Hay and Scott, *Design and Development*, pp. 309–10.

15 WO 32/4441, CIGS to Secretary of State, 9 October 1936.

16 J. P. Harris, *Men, Ideas and Tanks: British Military Thought and Armoured Forces 1903–1939* (Manchester: Manchester University Press, 1995), pp. 276–9.

17 BOV, RAC Half-Yearly Progress report no. 6, 1 July–31 December 1942, DAFV's paper for discussion at first meeting of reconstituted Tank Board, 17 July 1942.

18 LHCMA, Alanbrooke, 6/2/22, Montgomery to Brooke, notes on formations, 12 January 1943; IWM BLM 49/14, Montgomery to Brooke, notes on formations, 12 Jan 1943.

19 LHCMA, Alanbrooke, 6/2/22, Montgomery to Brooke, notes on AFV design, 10 April 1943; BOV, RAC Half-Yearly Progress report no. 7, 1 January 1943–30 June 1943, Montgomery to War Office tank armament policy, 10 April 1943.

20 BOV, RAC Half-Yearly Progress report no. 7, 1 January 1943–30 June 1943, General Staff Policy on Tanks, War Office to Tank Board 21st meeting, 19 February 1943; Development of AFV Equipment, appendix A.1, General Staff Policy on Tanks, 9 March 1943, and appendix A.36, General Staff Policy on Tanks, Organisation and Weapons Policy Committee, 24 September 1943; IWM BLM 117/3, Lt-Gen Archie Nye, VCIGS, to Montgomery, 12 January 1944.

21 BOV, RAC Half-Yearly Progress report no. 9, 1 January 1944–30 June 1944, Military Mission no. 222, report no. 1, visit to North Africa and Italy by Maj-Gen Alexander Richardson, CoS 15th Army Group, Italy, 9 March 1944.

22 LHCMA, Alanbrooke, 6/2/23. See exchange of correspondence between Montgomery and Nye, 7, 17 and 21 December 1943; BOV, Development of AFV Equipment, appendix A.36, General Staff Policy on Tanks, Organisation and Weapons Policy Committee, 24 September 1943.

23 BOV, minute 18/3 by Winston Churchill to Tank Board, minutes to meeting of 23 April 1943.

24 Beale, *Tank Tracks*, pp. 144–5.

25 US NAII RG337/26/40, notes by Brig-Gen Bruce Clarke, Plans Section, AGF, to Maj-Gen Cook, on memo by Gen George Patton, 'Notes on Combat', 16 November 1945; US NAII RG331/210A/1, 'Tank Requirements' by Lt-Col Sidney Brown, undated but based on experience in the European theatre of operations.

26 IWM BLM 129/2, Montgomery, *Future Design of the Capital Tank*, 24 October 1944.

27 BOV, RAC Half-Yearly Progress report no. 2, 1 May 1940–31 December 1940.

28 Ibid., and no. 3, 1 January–30 June 1941.

29 LHCMA, Alanbrooke, 6/2/22, Montgomery to Brooke, notes on formations, 12 January 1943; IWM BLM 117/2, Montgomery to Nye, 28 August 1943 (see Chapter 5).

30 WO 199/3186, 1st Armoured Division HQ to divisional brigadiers, 26 June 1940; LHCMA, Bridgeman, 2/6, *The Campaign of the BEF, May 1940*.

31 BOV, notes on spare parts, RAC Half-Yearly Progress report no. 2, 1 May 1940–31 December 1940; Postan, Hay and Scott, *Design and Development*, p. 316.

32 BOV, notes on spare parts, RAC Half-Yearly progress report no. 2, 1 May–31 December 1940.

33 WO 163/50/ACM(41)6, minutes of the Army Council, 1 May 1941; LHCMA, Alanbrooke, 6/2/12, Auchinleck to Brooke, 6 January 1942.

34 LHCMA, Alanbrooke, 6/2/12, Auchinleck to Churchill, 12 January 1942; WO 236/36, undated [probably late 1942] report by Maj-Gen AFV to DAFV.

35 Postan, Hay and Scott, *Design and Development*, p. 323.

36 WO 201/479, lessons from operations in Cyrenaica no. 8, 27 December 1941.

37 WO 201/2505, Wavell to CIGS [Dill], 2 January 1941.

38 BOV, Tank Board minutes, 8th meeting, December 1941, and Griggs's response to report by Lt-Gen G. le Q. Martel, 19 January 1942.

39 BOV, Development of AFV Equipment, 'General Staff Policy on Tanks', 10 September 1942; Postan, Hay and Scott, *Design and Development*, p. 324; BOV, Tank Board minutes, 9th meeting, 3 January 1942.

40 BOV, 7th meeting of reconstituted Tank Board, 17 August 1942.

41 WO 106/1775, Report of the Bartholomew Committee, July 1940; Gudgin, *Armoured Firepower*, pp. 75–7.

42 BOV, RAC Half-Yearly Progress report no. 2, 1 May–31 December 1940; French, *Raising Churchill's Army*, pp. 189–92.

43 BOV, RAC Half-Yearly Progress report no. 2, 1 May–31 December 1940.

44 WO 32/4684, Director of Artillery to Superintendent of Design, 13 and 25 April 1938.

45 Postan, Hay and Scott, *Design and Development*, p. 316.

46 WO 277/32, Lt-Col French, Rearmament, p. ii. 100 6-pdrs would have required the loss of 600 2-pdrs.

47 WO 106/2223, NTW no. 2, Cyrenaica, *November to December 1941*, 7 March 1942.

48 WO 32/101365, 'Accuracy of Fire from Anti-tank guns, Army Operational Research Group, Middle East, 30 March 1942.

49 BOV, Development of AFV Equipment, appendix A.1 General Staff Policy on Tanks, 10 September 1942.

50 BOV, RAC Half Yearly report no. 6, 1 July–31 December 1942, DAFV's paper for discussion at first meeting of reconstituted Tank Board, 17 July 1942.

51 LHCMA, Alanbrooke, 6/2/21, Montgomery to Brooke, 28 December 1942; 6/2/22, Montgomery to Brooke, 12 January 1943; Postan, Hay and Scott, *Design and Development*, pp. 325–6; Fletcher, *The Universal Tank*, pp. 13–15.

52 PREM 3/427/1, Memo by Secretary of State for War (Grigg), Minister of Supply (Duncan) and Minister of Production (Lyttelton) for War Cabinet Defence Committee (Supply), 16 April 1943.

53 BOV, RAC Half-Yearly Progress report no. 7, 1 January 1943–30 June 1943, Montgomery to War Office, 16 April 1943.

54 PREM 3/427/1, Appendix C in Tank Policy memorandum by Grigg and Duncan for Defence Committee (Supply) meeting, 30 April 1943.

55 BOV, Development of AFV Equipment, Tank Situation, Lt-Gen John Fullerton Evetts, ACIGS, 11 September 1943, annexure B, 75 mm medium and HV guns.

56 BOV, Tank Board Minutes, 4th meeting, 6 July 1940.

57 WO 208/3577, War Office summaries based on MI 10 technical reports: nos 40 (April 1941); 53 (8 September 1941); 54 (20 September 1941); 58 (8 November 1941); and 64 (11 February 1942); WO 208/3578, War Office summaries based on MI 10 technical reports, no. 75 (4 June 1942).

58 Gudgin, *Armoured Firepower*, pp. 85–7.

59 WO 208/3578, MI 10 technical summaries, no. 84, 15 August 1942; WO 219/1983, 'Summary of German Tanks' from operational subdivision, November 1944.

60 WO 208/2287, 'Development of German tank and anti-tank guns', MI 10 and War Office, 26 January 1943.

61 WO 208/3578, MI 10 technical summaries, no. 84, 15 August 1942.

62 Ibid.

63 WO 208/3577, summary of technical reports regarding weapons, war industry and transportation, issued by MI 10, no. 62, 20 January 1942.

64 WO 219/810, SHAEF technical intelligence summary no. 1, May 1944.

65 WO 219/792, SHAEF reports, 'Defensive tendencies in German weapon design' by Brig-Gen R. A. Osmun, Chief, Military Intelligence Service, undated but probably July/August 1944.

66 WO 208/3578, MI 10 technical summaries, no. 77, 20 June 1942; WO 208/3579, MI 10 report on German Tank and Anti-tank Armaments, 12 August 1943.

67 WO 219/810, SHAEF technical intelligence summary no. 2, 23 June 1944.

68 WO 208/2290, MI 10 technical summaries nos. 131 (23 June 1944); 140 (23 August 1944); 142 (6 September 1944); and 146 (4 October 1944).

69 WO 219/792, SHAEF reports, 'Defensive tendencies in German weapon design' by Brig-Gen R. A. Osmun, Chief, Military Intelligence Service, undated but probably July/August 1944.

70 WO 208/2287, MI 10 technical summaries, no. 94, 5 December 1942; David Fletcher, *Tiger! The Tiger Tank: A British View* (London: Her Majesty's Stationery Office, 1986), pp. 5–9.

71 WO 208/2287, 'Development of the German Tank and Anti-tank Guns', War Office and MI 10, 26 January 1943.

72 WO 208/3579, MI 10 technical intelligence summary no. 99, 20 February 1943.

73 Fletcher, *Tiger!*, pp. 50–6.

74 WO 208/3579, MI 10 Report, 12 August 1943.

75 BOV, RAC Half-Yearly Progress report no. 8, 1 July–31 December 1943, report by Maj-Gen Raymond Briggs, DRAC, on future tank policy.

76 BOV, RAC Half-Yearly Progress report no. 8, 1 July–31 December 1943, memo on tank policy for 29th meeting of *Organisation and Weapons Policy Committee*, DRAC, 10 August 1943.

77 BOV, RAC Half-Yearly Progress report no. 8, 1 July–31 December 1943, 29th and 30th meetings of *Organisation and Weapons Policy Committee*, 14 August and 4 September 1943.

78 WO 208/2288, MI 10 technical summary no. 106, 9 June 1943.

79 WO 208/3579, MI 10 report, 12 August 1943.

80 WO 208/2288, MI 10 technical intelligence summaries, no. 114, 10 October 1943.

81 WO 219/3115, preliminary report on captured Panther tank by DRAC, 3 June 1944.

82 BOV, Minutes of meeting held at War Office 19 April 1944 to discuss the general policy regarding AFVs.

83 Fletcher, *Mr Churchill's Tank*, p. 11.

84 Postan, Hay and Scott, *Design and Development*, pp. 335–6; Brig. O. E. Chapman, 'The Influence of the Late War on Tank Design', *Journal of the Royal United Services Institute*, vol. 96, 1951, p. 51.

85 Chapman, 'The Influence of the Late War on Tank Design', p. 51.

86 An explanation offered by David French, for example, in *Raising Churchill's Army*, p. 99.

87 Ibid., p. 99; Fletcher, *Mr Churchill's Tank*, p. 11; Gudgin, *Armoured Firepower*, p. 75.

88 Figures drawn from Gudgin, *Armoured Firepower*, pp. 223–35, and Hunnicut, *Sherman*, pp. 527–71.

89 PREM 3/427/1, Churchill to Ministers of Production and Supply and to the Paymaster-General (Cherwell), 23 April 1943.

90 PREM 3/427/1, memo by Grigg, Lyttelton and Duncan for War Cabinet Defence Committee (Supply), 16 April 1943.

91 PREM 3/427/1, Minutes of War Cabinet Defence Committee Meeting, 20 April 1943.

92 PREM 3/427/1, Cherwell to PM, 3 May 1943, and Joint Memorandum on Tank Policy from Grigg and Duncan for War Cabinet Defence Committee (Supply), 30 April 1943.

93 BOV, RAC Half-Yearly Progress report no. 6, 1 July–31 December 1942, notes of meeting on tank armament, 23 December 1942.

94 PREM 3/427/1, Tank Policy discussion paper, 24 March 1943.

95 PREM 3/427/1, Tank Supply Policy, paper no. DC(S) (43) 22, 16 April 1943.

96 PREM 3/427/1, Cherwell to Churchill, 20 April 1943.

97 PREM 3/427/1, Minutes of Defence Committee (Supply) meeting, 20 April 1943.

98 PREM 3/427/1, Alexander to War Office, 17 April 1943.

99 PREM 3/427/1, Churchill to Duncan, Grigg, Lyttelton and Cherwell, 23 April 1943.

100 PREM 3/427/1, Minutes of Defence Committee (Supply) meeting, 3 May 1943.

101 PREM 3/427/1, Cherwell to Churchill, 3 May 1943; Churchill to E. Bridges, Secretary to the War Cabinet, 5 May 1943.

102 PREM 3/427/1, Minutes of Defence Committee (Supply) meeting, 15 June 1943.

7. PRODUCTION AND SUPPLY

1 Beale, *Death by Design*, chs 4 and 6; Jarymowycz, *Tank Tactics*, pp. 257–9; Correlli Barnett, *The Audit of War: The Illusion and Reality of Britain as a Great Nation* (London: Macmillan, 1986), pp. 161–5.

2 Jarymowycz, *Tank Tactics*, pp. 257–60; Barnett, *The Audit of War*, pp. 161–5.

3 Vauxhall delivered the first A22 Churchills with such disclaimers. Beale, *Tank Tracks*, pp. 4–6.

4 Ellis, *Victory in the West*, vol. I, pp. 545–6.

5 Postan, Hay and Scott, *Design and Development*, ch. XIV, and pp. 356–8 in particular.

6 Beale, *Death by Design*, pp. 36–82; Postan, Hay and Scott, *Design and Development*, pp. 302–21.

7 Postan, Hay and Scott, *Design and Development*, pp. 321–3.

8 Ibid. pp. 353–6.

9 *Hansard*, House of Commons debates, vol. 381, cols 224–476, 1 July 1942, and cols 527–610, 2 July 1942.

10 Fletcher, *Mr Churchill's Tank*, pp. 82–101; Beale, *Tank Tracks*, pp. 4–7.

11 BOV, Tank Board minutes, 1 February 1941.

12 BOV, A22 and A27 specifications were drawn up in July 1940 and January 1941 respectively, with the A22s being altered to take the 6-pdr in March 1941, Tank board minutes, 9 December 1941.

13 WO 205/637, Daily AFV States, 2nd British Army, June–July 1944.

14 Beale, *Death by Design*, pp. 152–4.

15 BOV, Tank Situation memo, ACIGS Lt-Gen John Fullerton Evetts to Secretary of State James Grigg, War Ministry, 11 September 1944.

16 BOV, 'Report on the Tank Situation', Lt-Gen John Fullerton Evetts, ACIGS, September 1943; Beale, *Death by Design*, p. 160.

17 BOV, *Development of AFV Equipment*, note by Ministry of Supply on 6-pdr production to Tank Board, 19 March 1942; Postan, Hay and Scott, *Design and Production*, p. 365.

18 BOV, RAC Half-Yearly Progress report no. 5, 1 January 1942–30 June 1942, note on the situation of armoured forces, 25 June 1942.

19 BOV, Tank Board minutes, meeting on tank armament, 23 December 1942.

20 Postan, Hay and Scott, *Design and Development*, p. 331.

21 BOV, Development of AFV Equipment, part V, War Cabinet, 'Formation of Tank Board'.

22 Postan, Hay and Scott, *Design and Development*, p. 332.
23 BOV, Tank Board minutes and constitution; Beale, *Death by Design*, p. 165.
24 Cmd. 6865, *Wartime Tank Production* (London: His Majesty's Stationery Office, July 1946).
25 PREM 3/427/1, War Cabinet Defence Committee (Supply), Tank Supply Policy, 16 April 1943.
26 PREM 3/427/1, United States Medium Tank Assignments, War Cabinet Defence Committee (Supply), Tank Supply Policy, 16 April 1943.
27 PREM 3/427/1, Future Policy, War Cabinet Defence Committee (Supply), Tank Supply Policy, 16 April 1943.
28 PREM 3/427/1, Tank Policy document, Ministry of Production, 24 March 1943.
29 PREM 3/427/1, United States Medium Tank Assignments, War Cabinet Defence Committee (Supply), Tank Supply Policy, 16 April 1943.
30 PREM 3/427/1, Harriman to Churchill, 25 May 1943.
31 PREM 3/427/1, minutes of War Cabinet Defence Committee (Supply) meeting, 16 June 1943.
32 PREM 3/427/7, 'Tank Policy' note by Oliver Lyttelton, Minister of Production, 12 January 1944.
33 PREM 3/427/9, correspondence between Churchill and Lyttelton, 11 August–1 September 1943.
34 PREM 3/427/7, 'Tank Policy' note by Oliver Lyttelton, Minister of Production, 12 January 1944.
35 PREM 3/427/7, Lyttelton to Churchill, 12 January 1944; Memo to War Cabinet Defence Committee from Minister of Supply and Secretary of State for War, January 1944.
36 PREM 3/427/7, Cherwell to Churchill, 28 January 1944.
37 PREM 3/427/7, Churchill to Lyttelton, 12 February 1944.
38 BOV, Tank Board Minutes, 9 December 1941; Fletcher, *The Universal Tank*, p. 82.
39 BOV, Paper circulated by H. H. Burness, 14th meeting of Tank Board, May 1942.
40 BOV, Memo by Lt-Gen Ronald Weeks, DCIGS, to Montgomery, 5 August 1944, appendix D.
41 WO 232/36, Memo on the tank situation by DRAC Maj-Gen Alexander Richardson, War Office, 7 February 1943; Fletcher, *The Universal Tank*, pp. 83–4.
42 BOV, Tank Board minutes, 26th meeting, 10 February 1943.
43 BOV, RAC Half-Yearly Progress report no. 11, 1 January–30 June 1945.
44 BOV, Maj-Gen Raymond Briggs, DRAC, report no. 9, Tank Armament situation, 27 June 1944.
45 BOV, 21st Army Group equipment reports, Lt-Gen Ronald Weeks, DCIGS, to Montgomery, CinC, 21st Army Group, 10 July 1944; reiterated in a report by Weeks on 5 August 1944 to Montgomery.
46 BOV, Tank Board minutes, short-term policy, 35th meeting of the Tank Board, 1 October 1943.
47 There were six regiments of Cromwells in the three British armoured divisions deployed in Normandy, requiring some 100 Challengers. These were replaced by Fireflies.
48 Fletcher, *The Universal Tank*, p. 39.
49 BOV, AFV Liaison Committee meetings, 9 March, 13 April, 11 May and 25 May 1943, Appendix to 'The Tank Situation', memo from Lt-Gen John Fullerton Evetts, ACIGS, to James Grigg, Secretary of State, 11 September 1943.
50 Fletcher, *The Universal Tank*, p. 82.
51 BOV, 'The Tank Situation', Memo from Evetts to Grigg, 11 September 1943.

52 BOV, War Office memo to CinC 21st Army Group, 10 July 1944, Maj-Gen Raymond Briggs, DRAC, report no.10; Fletcher, *The Universal Tank*, pp. 112–13.

53 BOV, Report of meeting of Joint Military Sub-committee held at US Ordnance, Washington, DC, 17 March 1942, in RAC Half-Yearly reports, no. 5, 1 January 1942–30 June 1942.

54 BOV, Tank Board minutes, GS specification for SP anti-tank gun, September 1942.

55 BOV, Tank Board minutes, AFV and Self-propelling artillery group meeting, September 1942.

56 Hunnicut, *Sherman*, p. 365.

57 BOV, Tank Board memos, note circulated by the War Office on SP anti-tank gun situation for 38th meeting of the Tank Board, 14 February 1944.

58 WO 205/151, Availability of Vehicles and Equipment, War Office note based on Ministry of Supply figures.

59 WO 291/1336, 'Self-propelled artillery in 21st Army Group', report issued in November 1944; BOV, Tank Board memos, 'Weapons and ammunition for AFVs and SP vehicles', circulated for 39th meeting of the Tank Board, 1 May 1944.

60 BOV, Minutes of conference held at 34th Tank Brigade HQ, 25 August 1944; 21AG technical reports, no. 20, January 1945.

61 The shortages of the Meteor aero-engine had rendered a number of A27 hulls without engines, and the older Liberty had been pressed into service to plug the gap.

62 BOV, Tank Board memos, 'Weapons and ammunition for AFVs and SP vehicles', circulated for 39th meeting of the Tank Board, 1 May 1944; BOV, Tank Board meetings, AFV Liaison Meeting paper, 26 April 1944.

63 WO 219/3353, SHAEF reports, 21st Army Group AFV technical report no. 25, May 1945; BOV, Box 623-438, 21AG technical report no. 21, February 1945; BOV, Mediterranean AFV Technical Report no. 25, 16 December 1944.

64 BOV, Letter from George Witheridge on the emergence of the Firefly, 3 February 1972.

65 BOV, Article on W. G. K. Kilbourn and his involvement in fitting the 17-pdr to the Sherman by Howard Johnson, *Surrey Herald*, 26 July 1979; Fletcher, *The Universal Tank*, pp. 84–5; Postan, Scott and Hay, *Design and Development*, p. 346; Hunnicut, *Sherman*, p. 303; Hayward, *Sherman Firefly*, pp. 13–15.

66 Hayward, *Sherman Firefly*, p. 13.

67 PREM 3/427/7, Supply Policy; WO 165/110, Warlike Stores, June 1941–March 1946.

68 WO 165/137, RAC Half-Yearly Progress report no. 11, Maj-Gen Raymond Briggs, DRAC, 1 January–30 June 1945.

69 WO 205/151, Availability of vehicles and equipment, 5 May 1944.

70 BOV, Maj-Gen Raymond Briggs, DRAC, Report no. 9, Tank Armament situation, 27 June 1944.

71 Postan, Scott and Hay, *Design and Development*, p. 347.

72 US NAII RG331/210A/1, Lt-Col Sidney Brown, 'Visit to Armored Units', interview with prisoner of war, 13 February 1945.

73 Ian Hogg, *Tank Killing: Anti-tank Warfare by Men and Machines* (London: Sidgwick and Jackson, 1996), pp. 18–20; John Weeks, *Men against Tanks: A History of Anti-tank Warfare* (London: David and Charles, 1975), pp. 12–15; Anthony G. Williams, 'The Search for High Velocity', *Guns Review International*, May–September 1996, www.quarry.nildram. co.uk/highvel.htm.

74 The 17-pdr sabot projectile was 7.9 lbs, compared to the APCBC's 17 lbs.

75 WO 171/456, Intelligence Summary no. 6, 11th Armoured Division War Diary, 19/20 June 1944.

76 Hunnicut, *Sherman*, pp. 558–71.

77 BOV, Mediterranean AFV Technical Reports, no. 25, 16 December 1944.

78 BOV, DCIGS Lt-Gen Ronald Weeks to CinC, 21AG, 5 August 1944.

79 WO 219/3353, G-4 records, SHAEF, tanks 21AG returns, 6 April 1944.

80 BOV, 21AG memo M506 on British Armour, 6 July 1944.

8. MORALE AND MOTIVATION

1 Quoted in Ken Tout, *A Fine Night for Tanks: The Road to Falaise* (Stroud: Sutton, 1998), p. 61.

2 The view was formed in particular by Wilmot, *The Struggle for Europe*, pp. 130–1, 427–8, 463–5; Liddell Hart, *The Other Side of the Hill* and Ellis, *Brute Force*, pp. 373–88.

3 David French, '"Tommy is no soldier"' Brian Holden Reid, *Military Power: Land Warfare Theory and Practice* (London: Frank Cass, 1997).

4 LHCMA, Liddell Hart, 11/1944/43-52, Basil Liddell Hart, notes on Normandy, 1952, and Liddell Hart, 9/28/84, 'Tanks in Normandy', Liddell Hart to C. S. Forester, 18 February 1952; CAB 106/1060, report by Brig. James Hargest, XXX Corps observer, covering the period 6 June–10 July 1944.

5 Meyer, *Grenadiers*, pp. 280–98; WO 219/1908, SHAEF G-2 records, Operational Intelligence Section notes, no. 21, 3 August 1944.

6 WO 177/321, Maj. D. J. Watterson, report by psychiatrist attached 2nd Army for month of July, 5 August 1944.

7 CAB 106/1060, report by Brig. James Hargest, XXX Corps observer, covering the period 6 June to 10 July 1944.

8 IWM, BLM Papers, unnumbered, comments to Middle East Staff College, Haifa, 21 September 1942. For a general discussion of Montgomery's views on morale in 21st Army Group see Hart, *Montgomery and Colossal Cracks*, pp. 24–7.

9 LHCMA, Alanbrooke, 7/3/12, War Office exercise *Evolution*, August 1946, p. 7.

10 Michael Howard, 'Monty and the Price of Victory', *The Sunday Times*, 16 October 1983.

11 Hart, *Montgomery and Colossal Cracks*, p. 26.

12 Capt. Andrew Burn, 5RHA, 7th Armoured Division, interview with author, May 2002; S. Dyson, *Tank Twins*, p. 18.

13 D. Houldsworth, *One Day I'll Tell You* (Marlborough: Heraldry Today, 1994), p. 12.

14 Peter Carrington, *Reflect on Things Past: The Memoirs of Lord Carrington* (London: Fontana, 1989), pp. 35–6.

15 Sheffield, 'The Shadow of the Somme', pp. 32–4.

16 Capt. Robin Lemon, 3RTR, 11th Armoured Division, interview with author, December 2002.

17 Sydney Jary, *18 Platoon* (Bristol: Sydney Jary, 1987), p. 4.

18 See Chapter 3, 'Firepower'.

19 LHCMA, Allfrey, 3/1, diary 17 January 1943.

20 Beale, *Tank Tracks*, p. 77.

21 LCHMA, Liddell Hart, 15/4/85, Lt-Gen Richard O'Connor's notes on *Operation Epsom*, 5 September 1944; LHCMA, Liddell Hart, 9/28/84, Maj-Gen G. P. B. Roberts to Liddell Hart, 30 January 1952; see also J. J. How, *Hill 112*, p. 46.

22 See Chapter 2, *Goodwood*.

23 Maj. Bill Close, 3RTR, interview with author, September 2002.

24 WO 177/343, VIII Corps Medical War Diaries; WO 171/182, War Diary 21st Army Group, Deputy Judge Advocate General, April–December 1944.

25 WO 177/343, VIII Corps Medical War Diaries; WO 171/182, War Diary 21st Army Group, Deputy Judge Advocate General, April–December 1944

26 WO 177/335, I Corps Medical War Diary, operational instruction no. 1, 15 May 1944.

27 See Joanna Bourke, *An Intimate History of Killing: Face to Face Killing in 20th Century Warfare* (London: Granta, 1999).

28 Maj. John Langdon, 3RTR, interview with author, October 2002.

29 WO 166/8576, War Diary of 2nd Armoured Irish Guards, 31 October 1942; see also Place, *Military Training in the British Army*, pp. 82–3; on multi-roles of crew see Robert Boscawen, *Armoured Guardsmen: A War Diary June 1944–April 1945* (London: Leo Cooper, 2001), p. 75.

30 WO 291/2384, AORG report no. 1/21, *Examination of tank casualties* by no. 1 ORS, autumn 1943; Rea Leakey with George Forty, *Leakey's Luck: A Tank Commander with Nine Lives* (Stroud: Sutton, 1999), pp. 127–8.

31 Boscawen, *Armoured Guardsmen*, p. 34.

32 Stuart Hills, *By Tank into Normandy: A Memoir of the Campaign in Northwest Europe from D-Day to VE Day* (London: Cassell, 2002), p. 72; WO 291/2384, AORG report no. 1/21, *Examination of Tank Casualties* by no. 1 ORS, autumn 1943.

33 Hills, *By Tank*, p. 114.

34 Correspondence with Capt. Robin Lemon, 3RTR, 11th Armoured Division, December 2002.

35 P. Elstob, *Warriors for the Working Day* (London: Jonathan Cape, 1960), p. 23.

36 WO 291/92, AORG report no. 99, *The Accuracy of Central Laying in Tank Gunnery with Different Types of Central Aiming Marks* by B. J. Schonland, 20 April 1943.

37 Lt Michael Trasenster, 'A' Squadron, 4/7th Royal Dragoon Guards, quoted in Patrick Delaforce, *Marching to the Sound of Gunfire: Northwest Europe 1944–45* (Stroud: Sutton, 1996), p. 31.

38 See, for example, Ken Tout interviewed by Richard Holmes on the television series *War Walks* (BBC, 1996).

39 Robert Crisp, *Brazen Chariots – An Account of Tank warfare in the Western Desert* (London: Frederick Muller, 1959), p. 57.

40 Boscawen, *Armoured Guardsmen*, p. 66.

41 PREM 3/427/6, correspondence on escape hatches in Cromwell tanks, April–May 1944; Hills, *By Tank*, p. 123; Ellis, *The Sharp End of War*, p. 149.

42 Maj. John Langdon, 3RTR, interview with author, October 2002.

43 Norman Smith, Cromwell tank driver, 5RTR, quoted in Delaforce, *Marching to the Sound of Gunfire*, p. 103.

44 Dyson, *Tank Twins*, p. 57; Ellis, *The Sharp End of War*, pp. 152–3.

45 Les Taylor, unpublished manuscript, quoted in Tout, *A Fine Night for Tanks*, pp. 7–8.

46 J. Leytham, quoted in Delaforce, *Marching to the Sound of Gunfire*, p. 38.

47 Ken Tout, *Tanks Advance! Normandy to the Netherlands* (London: Hale, 1987), p. 56.

48 WO 177/362, 'Removal of Dead Bodies from AFVs', report by Maj. Peter Duke RAMC, Guards Armoured Division, Medical War Diary, 10 August 1944.

49 WO 205/1165, Survey of casualties amongst armoured units in northwest Europe, by Capt. H. B. Wright RAMC and Capt. R. D. Harkness RAMC, no. 2 ORS 21st Army Group, 1945.

50 Beale, *Tank Tracks*, p. 18.

51 Dyson, *Tank Twins*, pp. 58–9.

52 Sgt Bob Anderson, C Squadron, 9RTR, quoted in Beale, *Tank Tracks*, p. 61; Maj. John Langdon, 3RTR, interview with author, October 1944.

NOTES

53 Boscawen, *Armoured Guardsmen*, p. 41.

54 WO 291/1331, 21st Army Group ORS report no. 12, *Analysis of 75 mm Sherman tank casualties suffered between 6 June and 10 July 1944*; BOV, Box 623-438, *Operation Overlord* – reports on equipment, letter from ADAFV(T) 2nd Army to DDAFV(D).

55 Delaforce, *Monty's Marauders*, p. 73; Boscawen, *Armoured Guardsmen*, p. 7.

56 WO 205/1165, Capt. H. B. Wright RAMC and Capt. R. D. Harkness RAMC, *A survey of casualties amongst armoured units in Northwest Europe*, no. 2 ORS, 21st Army Group, 1945.

57 Boscawen *Armoured Guardsmen*, pp. 40, 48; W. S. Brownlie, *The Proud Trooper*, pp. 364–5; Dyson, *Tank Twins*, pp. 46–7.

58 Dyson, *Tank Twins*, p. 55.

59 WO 205/422, Maj-Gen George Richards, RAC 21AG, to 2nd Army, 22 June 1944.

60 Fewer than 130 Tigers were used against the Allies in Normandy.

61 WO 219/600, SHAEF records, HQ to 6th and 12th US Army Groups, 12 December 1944; WO 291/2384, 21st Army Group ORS, examination of tank casualties.

62 WO 291/1331 21st Army Group ORS report no. 12, *Analysis of 75 mm Sherman tank casualties suffered between 6 June and 10 July*; WO 291/2384, no. 1 ORS report no. 1/21, *Examination of Tank Casualties – causes of fires in Shermans*; Brownlie, *The Proud Trooper*, p. 153.

63 LHCMA, Alanbrooke, 6/2/25, Montgomery to Brooke, 27 June 1944.

64 CCA, PJGG, 9/8/11, papers of Sir James Grigg, Montgomery to Grigg, 25 June 1944.

65 WO 205/5b, Montgomery to 21st Army Group HQ, London, 24 June 1944.

66 LHCMA, Alanbrooke, 6/2/25, Montgomery to Dempsey, 25 June 1944; Montgomery to Brooke, 27 June 1944.

67 Jack Woods, 'C' Squadron, 9RTR, quoted in Beale, *Tank Tracks*, p. 49.

68 Keith Jones, *Sixty Four Days of a Normandy Summer: With a Tank Unit after D-Day* (London: Hale, 1990), pp. 16–17; Boscawen, *Armoured Guardsmen*, p. 18.

69 WO 205/1165, Capt. H. B. Wright RAMC and Capt. R. D. Harkness RAMC, *A survey of casualties amongst armoured units in Northwest Europe*, no. 2 ORS 21st Army Group, 1945.

70 Ibid.

71 Maj. Bill Close, 3RTR, interview with author, September 2002.

72 John Powell, 'B' Squadron, 9RTR, quoted in Beale, *Tank Tracks*, p. 71.

73 WO 205/1165, Capt. H. B. Wright RAMC and Capt. R. D. Harkness RAMC, *A survey of casualties amongst armoured units in Northwest Europe*, no. 2 ORS 21st Army Group, 1945.

74 WO 291/1331, Operational Research in Northwest Europe: The work of no. 2 ORS and 21st Army Group, June 1944–July 1945, AORG 1945, edited by M. M. Swann, p. 217.

75 Lt Stuart Hills, quoted in Delaforce, *Marching to the Sound of Gunfire*, p. 40; Hills, *By Tank*, pp. 94, 114.

76 Boscawen, *Armoured Guardsmen*, p. 82.

77 Dyson, *Tank Twins*, pp. 55, 64.

78 Beale, *Tank Tracks*, p. 65.

79 WO 205/1165, Capt. H. B. Wright RAMC and Capt. R. D. Harkness RAMC, *A survey of casualties amongst armoured units in Northwest Europe*, no. 2 ORS 21st Army Group, 1945.

80 D. Erskine, *The Scots Guards 1919–1945* (Edinburgh: W. Clowes, 1956), pp. 366–7.

81 Dyson, *Tank Twins*, p. 65.

82 Maj. John Langdon, 3RTR, interview with author, October 2002.

83 Hills, *By Tank*, p. 116.

84 Dyson, *Tank Twins*, p. 65.

85 Hills, *By Tank*, p. 130.

86 Dyson, *Tank Twins*, p. 67.

87 How, *Hill 112*, p. 141.
88 IWM, Browne 86/41/1, Lt-Col A. T. A. Browne, *Destiny: Portrait of a Man in Two World Wars*; French, '"Tommy is no soldier"'.
89 Bill Close, *A View from the Turret* (Bredon: Dell & Bredon, 1998), p. 68.
90 Boscawen, *Armoured Guardsmen*, p. 94.
91 Beale, *Tank Tracks*, p. 51; Boscawen, *Armoured Guardsmen*, p. 32.
92 WO 177/321, Report by Maj. D. J. Watterson RAMC, psychiatrist attached to 2nd Army, 5 August 1944.
93 WO 177/335, I Corps Medical War Diary, Operation Instruction no. 1, 15 May 1944.
94 R. H. Ahrenfeldt, *Psychiatry in the British Army in the Second World War* (London: Routledge and Kegan Paul, 1958), p. 175; LHCMA, de Guingand, IV/4/3, *The Administrative History of the Operations of 21st Army Group on the Continent of Europe 6 June 1944 to 8 May 1945* (Germany, 1945), p. 27; the best discussion on battle exhaustion in 21st Army Group is Terry Copp and Bill McAndrew, *Battle Exhaustion: Soldiers and Psychiatrists in the Canadian Army 1939–1945* (London: McGill-Queen's University Press, 1990), especially pp. 109–27.
95 WO 177/335, I Corps Medical War Diary, Operational Instruction no. 1, 15 May 1944.
96 Maj. Bill Close, 3RTR, interview with author, September 2002; John Stone, 9RTR, quoted in Beale, *Tank Tracks*, p. 80.
97 Dyson, *Tank Twins*, pp. 43–3.
98 Trevor Greenwood, 9RTR, quoted in Beale, *Tank Tracks*, p. 81.
99 Pte Roland Jefferson, 8th Rifle Brigade, 11th Armoured Division, quoted in Delaforce, *Marching to the Sound of Gunfire*, p. 85.
100 John Stone, 9RTR, quoted in Beale, *Tank Tracks*, p. 80.
101 Boscawen, *Armoured Guardsmen*, pp. 60, 62.
102 John Keegan, 'Toward a Theory of Combat Motivation', in Paul Addison and Angus Calder (eds), *Time to Kill: The Soldier's Experience of War in the West 1939–1945* (London: Pimlico, 1997).
103 Les Arnold, 9RTR, quoted in Beale, *Tank Tracks*, pp. 31–2; Boscawen, *Armoured Guardsmen*, p. 80.
104 WO 177/371, 11th Armoured Division Medical War Diary, standing orders, 8 June 1944.
105 Capt. Andrew Burn, 5RHA, and Maj. Bill Close, 3RTR, interviews with author, May and September 2002.
106 Maj. John Langdon, 3RTR, interview with author, October 2002.
107 Hills, *By Tank*, pp. 116–17; Capt. Andrew Burn, 5RHA, and Maj. Bill Close, 3RTR, interviews with author, May and September 2002.
108 Dyson, *Tank Twins*, p. 48; Hills, *By Tank*, p. 142.
109 WO 171/440, 131st Infantry Brigade, 7th Armoured Division, War Diary, August 1944.
110 S. P. Mackenzie, *Politics and Military Morale: Current Affairs and Citizenship Education in the British Army 1914–1950* (Oxford: Oxford University Press, 1992), pp. 91–3.
111 Maj-Gen Roy Dixon, 5RTR, 7th Armoured Division, interview with author, November 2002.
112 Maj. Bill Close, 3RTR, interview with author, September 2002; J. Sims, *Arnhem Spearhead: A Private Soldier's Story* (London: Imperial War Museum; Seeley, 1978), p. 22.
113 Ellis, *The Sharp End of War*, pp. 151–2.
114 General Staff, WO, *Infantry Training, part one. Training*, (1932), p. 11.
115 Dyson, *Tank Twins*, p. 48.

116 Maj. Bill Close, 3RTR, interview with author, September 2002.

117 Capt. Robin Lemon, 3RTR, maintained a notebook with personal details of his charges, interview with author, December 2002; Maj. John Langdon, 3RTR, regarded this part of an officer's duties as crucial, interview with author, October 2002.

118 Maj-Gen Roy Dixon, 5RTR, 7th Armoured Division, interview with author, November 2002; LHCMA, Dempsey, British 2nd Army Intelligence Summary no. 46, translation of Panzer *Lehr* report, 20 July 1944.

119 WO 106/1024, Operational Research Unit, report no. 23, Battle Study, *Operation Goodwood*.

120 Maj. Bill Close, 3RTR, interview with author, September 2002.

121 WO 177/335, I Corps Medical War Diary, minutes of medical conference at Cobham, 27 April 1944.

122 LHCMA, Dempsey, 2nd Army Intelligence Summary, no. 46, translation of Panzer *Lehr* report, 20 July 1944; CAB 106/1060, reports from Normandy, 6 June–10 July 1944, by Brig. James Hargest, XXX Corps.

123 Kurt Meyer is an oft-quoted source. See *Grenadiers* on the Normandy campaign and his views on the determination and resolve of British and Canadian tank crews.

124 French, '"Tommy is no soldier"', pp. 154–78.

125 WO 177/335, I Corps Medical War Diary, minutes of medical conference, Cobham, 27 April 1944.

126 WO 177/335, I Corps medical war diary, operational instruction no. 4, 9 July 1944.

127 WO 177/343, VIII Corps medical war diary, appendix I, 17 July 1944.

128 WO 177/321, Maj. D. J. Watterson, RAMC, 21st Army Group psychiatrist, July report, 5 August 1944.

129 WO 177/321, Maj. D. J. Watterson, RAMC, 21st Army Group psychiatrist, June report, 11 July 1944.

130 Maj. Bill Close, 3RTR, interview with author, September 2002.

131 WO 177/321, Maj. D. J. Watterson, RAMC, 21st Army Group psychiatrist, July report, 5 August 1944.

132 Maj. John Langdon and Maj. Bill Close, 3RTR, both interviewed by author, October and September 2002.

133 WO 177/343, VIII Corps medical war diary, returns from corps exhaustion centres, 26–30 June 1944.

134 CAB 106/112, British 2nd Army composition, 30 June 1944; Ellis, *The Sharp End of War*, p. 158.

135 Maj-Gen G. L. Verney quoted in Neillands, *The Desert Rats*, p. 231.

136 LHCMA, Liddell Hart, 9/28/84, correspondence between Liddell Hart and Maj-Gen Pip Roberts, February and March 1952.

137 Brian Horrocks, *Corps Commander* (London: Sidgwick & Jackson, 1977), pp. 28–9.

138 D'Este, *Decision in Normandy*, ch. 16; Hastings, *Overlord*, pp. 162–3, 371; Hart, *Clash of Arms*, p. 308.

139 French, '"Tommy is no soldier"', p. 166.

140 WO 177/321, 2nd Army Medical war diary, Psychiatric Summary, week ending 18 June 1944, appendix C to SA/99/5, 21 June 1944.

141 Michael Reynolds, *Sons of the Reich: II SS Panzer Corps* (London: Spellmount, 2002), p. 77.

142 Neillands, *The Desert Rats*, pp. 238–9; Anon, *History of the 7th Armoured Division: June 1943–July 1945* (privately published, 1945), pp. 57–8.

143 Capt. Andrew Burn, 5RHA, 7th Armoured Division, interview with author, May 2002.

144 Reynolds, *Steel Inferno*, ch. XI.

9. CONCLUSION

1 Ellis, *Brute Force*, pp. 373–88; D'Este, *Decision in Normandy*, introduction and 'Price of Caution' chapter; Jarymowycz, *Tank Tactics*; Basil Liddell Hart, *The Other Side of the Hill*, ch. XXI, and *Idem, History of the Second World War* (London: Cassell, 1970), ch. 31.

2 Richard Rapier Stokes, *Some Amazing Tank Facts* (Dugdale Printing, 1945).

3 The best single volume analysing 21st Army Group's operational methods is Hart, *Montgomery and Colossal Cracks*.

4 Ellis, *Victory in the West*, vol. I (London: Her Majesty's Stationery Office, 1962), pp. 259–69.

5 Helmut Ritgen, *The Western Front 1944*, is a good example of this.

6 Place, *Military Training in the British Army*.

7 Hastings, *Overlord*; Jarymowycz, *Tank Tactics*; Hart, *Clash of Arms*.

8 LHCMA, Liddell Hart, 15/15/150, interview with General Fritz Bayerlein, GOC Panzer *Lehr*, August 1950.

9 WO 291/1331, 21st Army Group ORS report no. 12, *Analysis of 75 mm Sherman tank casualties suffered betweeen 6 June and 10 July 1944*.

10 BOV, Box 623-438, *Operation Overlord*, reports on equipment, Montgomery's memo M506, 6 July 1944.

11 PREM 3/427/7, Oliver Lyttelton to Churchill, 12 January 1944; memo to War Cabinet Defence Committee from Minister of Supply and Secretary of State for War, January 1944.

12 Copp, *Fields of Fire*, see introduction.

13 LHCMA, Liddell Hart, 11/1944/43-52, B. H. Liddell Hart, 'Lessons of Normandy' (1952); Wilmot, *The Struggle for Europe*, pp. 130–1, 427–8, 463–5.

14 WO 177/343, VIII Corps Medical War Diary, June–August 1944; WO 171/182, War Diary 21st Army Group, Deputy Judge Advocate General, April–December 1944.

BIBLIOGRAPHY

Public Record Office, Kew, London

Cabinet Office documents (CAB)

CAB 78, War Cabinet and Cabinet: Miscellaneous Committees: Minutes and Papers
CAB 106, Cabinet Office Historical Section Papers
CAB 146, Historical Section, Enemy Documents Section: Files and Papers

Prime Minister's Office documents (PREM)

PREM 3, Operations Papers

War Office documents (WO)

WO 32, General Series
WO 106, Directorate of Military Operations and Military Intelligence, Correspondence and Papers
WO 162, Papers of Adjutant General's Department
WO 163, Army Council Records
WO 165, War Diaries and Progress Reports of War Office Directorates
WO 166, War Diaries of Home Forces Formations and Units
WO 171, War Diaries of 21st Army Group Formations and Units
WO 177, Medical War Diaries
WO 179, War Diaries, Canadian, South African, New Zealand and Indian (United Kingdom) Forces (Dominion Forces)
WO 193, Directorate of Military Operations Records
WO 194, Military Vehicles and Engineering Establishment, Papers
WO 199, Military Headquarters Papers, Home Forces
WO 201, Military Headquarters Papers, Middle East Forces
WO 205, Military Headquarters Papers, 21st Army Group
WO 208, Directorate of Military Operations and Intelligence, and Directorate of Military Intelligence
WO 216, Papers of the Chief of the Imperial General Staff
WO 219, Supreme Headquarters Allied Expeditionary Force: Military Headquarters Papers
WO 223, Staff College Camberley, 1947 Course Notes on D-Day Landings and Ensuing Campaigns
WO 231, Directorate of Military Training Records

WO 232, Directorate of Tactical Investigation Records
WO 236, Papers of General Sir George 'Bobby' Erskine
WO 277, Historical Monographs
WO 285, Papers of General Sir Miles Dempsey
WO 291, Operational Research Papers

US National Archives II, Maryland

RG 165: Records of the War Department General and Special Staffs
RG 331: Records of Allied Operational and Occupation Headquarters, World War II
RG 337: Records of Headquarters Army Ground Forces
RG 407: Records of the Adjutant General's Office

National Archives of Canada, Ottawa, Ontario

RG 24, Department of National Defence Papers

Bundesarchiv-Militärarchiv, Freiburg

Kommandobehörden und Divisionen des Heeres

RH-19 Army Group B, War Diaries and Formation Statistics and Listings
RH-20 War Diaries

Royal Armoured Corps Tank Museum Archives, Bovington, Dorset

Half Yearly Progress Reports of the Royal Armoured Corps 1940–1945
Tank Board Minutes and Memoranda
Operation Overlord, reports on equipment
Colonel Gordon Hall, 'AFVs in the Mediterranean 1939–45'
Mediterranean AFV Technical Reports, nos. 1–27.
Papers relating to development of Sherman Firefly
'Development of AFV Equipment', War Cabinet Defence Committee (Supply) 1940–43

Liddell Hart Centre for Military Archives, King's College London

General Sir Ronald Adam, papers
Field Marshal Viscount Alanbrooke, papers
Lieutenant General Sir Charles Allfrey, papers
Major-General Robert Bridgeman, papers
Major-General Sir Francis de Guingand, papers
General Sir Miles Dempsey, papers/ 2nd British Army Intelligence Reports
Captain Sir Basil Liddell Hart, papers
General Sir Richard O'Connor, papers
General Sir Harold Pyman, papers

Major-General Sir Philip Roberts, papers
Major-General Sir Gerald Verney, papers

Churchill College Archives, Cambridge

Sir James Grigg, papers
Ronald Lewin, papers

Imperial War Museum, London

Department of Documents

Field Marshal the Viscount Montgomery of Alamein, papers
Major-General Sir Ronald Belchem, papers
Major-General Raymond Briggs, papers
Lieutenant General Sir Gerald Bucknall, papers
Major-General Sir Francis de Guingand, papers

Department of Printed Books

Army Training Instructions (ATI)
ATI No. 2 (March 1941) *The Employment of Army Tanks in Co-operation with Infantry*
ATI No. 2 (May 1943) *The Co-operation of Infantry and Tanks*
ATI No. 3 (May 1941) *Handling of an Armoured Division*

Military Training Pamphlets (MTP)
MTP No. 22 (August and September 1939) *Tactical Handling of Army Tank Battalions*
MTP No. 41 (July 1940) *The Armoured Regiment*
MTP No. 41 (July 1943) *The Tactical Handling of the Armoured Division and its Components – part 1: The Tactical Handling of Armoured Divisions*
MTP No. 41 (February 1943) *The Tactical Handling of the Armoured Division and its Components – part 2: The Armoured Regiment*
MTP No. 41 (June 1943) *The Tactical Handling of the Armoured Division and its Components – part 3: The Motor Battalion*
MTP No. 63 (May 1944) *The Co-operation of Tanks with Infantry Divisions*
Army Training Memoranda (ATM) 1939–1945
Notes from Theatres (NTW) 1942–1945
Current Reports from Overseas (CRO) 1942–1945

Official publications

Cmd 6865, *Wartime Tank Production* (London: His Majesty's Stationery Office, 1946)
Hansard

Internet sources

US Army Center of Military History: www.army.mil/cmh-pg/

Anthony Williams, *The Search for High Velocity*: www.quarry.nildram.co.uk/highvel.htm
British Generals of the Second World War: www.generals.dk/Great_Britain.htm

Unpublished papers and memoirs supplied by authors

Trooper Austin Baker, *C Squadron, 4/7th Royal Dragoon Guards, 1944–1945*
Captain Andrew Burn, *May the Fathers Tell their Children*, 2002
Captain Robin Lemon, notes on *Operation Goodwood*, correspondence with family, 1944–45, BAOR Battlefield Tour Guides and Notes.

Interviews conducted by the author

Captain Andrew Burn, May 2002
Major Bill Close, September 2002
Major John Langdon, October 2002
Major-General Roy Dixon, November 2002
Captain Robin Lemon, December 2002
Trooper Austin Baker, April 2003

Books

Adair, Allan, *A Guards' General: The Memoirs of Sir Allan Adair* (London: Hamish Hamilton, 1986)
Addison, Paul and Calder, Angus (eds), *Time to Kill: The Soldier's Experience of War in the West 1939–45* (London: Pimlico, 1997)
Ahrenfeldt, R. H., *Psychiatry in the British Army in the Second World War* (London: Routledge and Kegan Paul, 1958)
Air Ministry, *The Rise and Fall of the German Air Force* (London: His Majesty's Stationery Office, 1947)
Ambrose, Stephen E., *Citizen Soldier: The US Army from the Normandy Beaches to the Bulge to the Surrender of Germany* (London: Schuster & Schuster, 1997)
Anon. *History of the 7th Armoured Division June 1943–July 1945* (privately published, 1945)
—— *The Story of the 34th Armoured Brigade* (privately published, 1945)
—— *The Story of the 23rd Hussars* (British Army of the Rhine, 1945)
—— (Captain Edgar Pallamountain), *Taurus Pursuant: A History of 11th Armoured Division* (privately published, 1945)
—— *The Story of the 79th Armoured Division* (British Army of the Rhine, 1945)
Arnold, H. H., *Second Report of the Commanding General of the United States Army Air Forces* (Washington, DC: US Government Printing Office, 1945)
Badsey, Stephen, *Normandy 1944* (London: Osprey, 1990)
Bailey, Jonathan, *Field Artillery and Firepower* (Oxford: Military Press Oxford, 1989)
Baker, A. H. and Rust. B., *A Short History of the 50th Northumbrian Division* (Yarmouth: privately published, 1966)
Barbé, Dominique, *Charnwood: La Bataille de Buron-Saint-Contest* (Conde: Charles Corlet, 1994)
Barclay, C. N., *The History of the 53rd (Welsh) Division in the Second World War* (London: William Clowes, 1956)
Barnett, Correlli, *The Desert Generals* (London: Allen & Unwin, 1983 edn)
—— *The Audit of War: The Illusion and Reality of Britain as a Great Nation* (London: Macmillan, 1986)

Bartov, Omer, *Hitler's Army: Soldiers, Nazis and War in the Third Reich* (Oxford: Oxford University Press, 1991)

Baverstock, Kevin, *Breaking the Panzers* (Stroud: Sutton, 2002)

Baynes, J., *The Forgotten Victor: General Sir Richard O'Connor* (London: Brassey's, 1989)

Beale, Peter, *Tank Tracks: 9th Battalion Royal Tank Regiment at War 1940–45* (Stroud: Sutton, 1995)

—— *Death by Design: British Tank Development in the Second World War* (Stroud: Sutton, 1998)

Belchem, David, *Victory in Normandy* (London: Chatto and Windows)

Belfield, E. and Essame, H., *The Battle for Normandy* (London: Hutchinson, 1967)

Bellamy, Chris, *The Evolution of Modern Land Warfare: Theory and Practice* (London: Routledge, 1990)

Bennett, Ralph, *Ultra in the West: the Normandy Campaign 1944–45* (London: Hutchinson, 1979)

Bernage, Georges, *Album Mémorial Normandie* (Bayeux: Heimdal, 1983)

Bernage, Georges and Benamou, Jean-Pierre, *Goodwood: Bombardement Géant Anti-panzers* (Bayeux: Heimdal, 1994)

Bernage, George and McNair, Ronald, *Le Couloir de la Mort: Falaise–Argentan* (Bayeux: Heimdal, 1994)

Bidwell, Shelford, *Gunners at War: A Tactical Study of the Royal Artillery in the Twentieth Century* (London: Arms & Armour Press, 1970)

—— *Artillery Tactics 1939–1945* (New Malden: Almark, 1976)

Bidwell, Shelford and Graham, Dominick, *Firepower: British Army Weapons and Theories of War 1904–1945* (London: Allen & Unwin, 1985)

Blandford, Edmund, *Two Sides of the Beach – The Invasion and Defence of Europe 1944* (London: Airlife, 1999)

Blumenson, Martin, *Breakout and Pursuit* (Washington, DC: Center of Military History, 1961)

—— *The Duel for France: The Men and Battles that changed the Fate of Europe* (New York: Da Capo, 1963)

—— *The Battle of the Generals* (New York: Morrow, 1993)

Blumentritt, Gunther, *Von Rundstedt: The Soldier and the Man* (London: Odhams, 1952)

Bond, Brian, *Liddell Hart: A Study in his Military Thought* (London: Cassell, 1977)

—— *British Military Policy between the Two World Wars* (Oxford: Oxford University Press, 1980)

Boscawen, Robert, *Armoured Guardsmen: A War Diary June 1944–April 1945* (London: Leo Cooper, 2001)

Bourke, Joanna, *An Intimate History of Killing: Face to Face Killing in 20th Century Warfare* (London: Granta, 1999)

Bradley, Omar, *A Soldier's Story* (London: Eyre & Spottiswoode, 1951)

Bradley, Omar and Blair, Clay, *A General's Life: An Autobiography by General of the Army Omar N. Bradley* (London: Sidwick & Jackson, 1983)

Brisset, Jean, *The Charge of the Bull: A History of the 11th Armoured Division in Normandy 1944* (Norwich: Bates, 1989)

Brooks, S. (ed.), *Montgomery and the Eighth Army* (London: Bodley Head, 1991)

Brooks, Victor, *The Normandy Campaign: From D-Day to the Liberation of Paris* (New York: Da Capo, 2002)

Brown, Gordon and Copp, Terry, *Look to Your Front, Regina Rifles: A Regiment at War, 1944–45* (Waterloo, Ontario: Laurier Centre for Military Strategic and Disarmament Studies, 2001)

Brownlie, W. S., *The Proud Trooper: The History of the Ayrshire Yeomanry* (London: Collins, 1964)

Bruce, Colin, *War on the Ground, 1939–45* (London: Constable, 1995)

Carafano, James J., *After D-Day: Operation Cobra and the Normandy Breakout* (Boulder, CO: Rienner, 2000)

Carrell, Paul, *Invasion: They're Coming: The German Account of the D-Day Landings and the 80 Days' Battle for France* (Atglen, PA: Schiffer, 1995 [1964])

Carrington, Peter, *Reflect on Things Past: The Memoirs of Lord Carrington* (London: Fontana, 1989)

Carver, Michael, *El Alamein* (London: Batsford, 1962)

—— *Tobruk* (London, Batsford, 1964)

—— *Dilemmas of the Desert War: A New Look at the Libyan Campaign* (London: Batsford, 1986)

—— *Out of Step: The Memoirs of Field Marshal Lord Carver* (London: Hutchinson, 1989)

Chalfont, Alun, *Montgomery of Alamein* (London: Methuen, 1977)

Churchill, Winston S., *The Second World War*, 6 vols (London: Cassell, 1950–56)

Clark, Ronald W., *Montgomery of Alamein* (London: Phoenix House, 1960)

Clay, Ewart W. (ed.), *The Path of the 50th: The Story of the 50th (Northumbrian Division) in the Second World War* (Aldershot: Gale & Polden, 1950)

Close, Bill, *A View from the Turret* (Bredon: Dell & Bredon, 1998)

Connell, John, *Wavell: Soldier and Scholar* (London: Collins, 1964)

Cooling, B. F. (ed.), *Case Studies in the Development of Close Air Support* (Washington, DC: Office of Air Force History, 1990)

Cooper, Matthew, *The German Army 1933–45: Its Political and Military Failure* (London: Macdonald & Jane's, 1978)

Copp, Terry, *Fields of Fire: The Canadians in Normandy* (Toronto: Toronto University Press, 2003)

Copp, Terry (ed.), *Montgomery's Scientists: Operational Research in Northwest Europe – The work of No. 2 Operational Research Section with 21st Army Group, June 1944 to July 1945* (Waterloo, Ontario: Laurier Centre for Military Strategic and Disarmament Studies, 2000)

Copp, Terry and McAndrew, Bill, *Battle Exhaustion: Soldiers and Psychiatrists in the Canadian Army 1939–1945* (Montreal: McGill-Queen's University Press, 1990)

Copp, Terry and Vogel, Robert, *Maple Leaf Route: Caen* (Alma, Ontario: Maple Leaf Route, 1983)

Crang, Jeremy, *The British Army and the People's War 1939–45* (Manchester: Manchester University Press, 2000)

Creveld, Martin van, *Fighting Power: German and US Army Performances 1939–45* (London: Arms & Armour Press, 1983)

Crisp, Robert, *Brazen Chariots – An Account of Tank Warfare in the Western Desert* (London: Frederick Muller, 1959)

Daglish, Ian, *Operation Bluecoat: Battleground Normandy* (Barnsley: Pen & Sword, 2003)

Danchev, Alex (ed.), *War Diaries, 1939–45: Field Marshal Lord Alanbrooke* (London: Weidenfeld & Nicolson, 2001)

Darby, H. and Cunliffe, M., *A Short History of 21st Army Group* (London: Gale & Polden, 1949)

Delaforce, Patrick, *Monty's Marauders: Black Rat 4th Armoured Brigade and Red Fox 8th Armoured Brigade* (Stroud: Sutton, 1990)

—— *The Black Bull: From Normandy to the Baltic with the 11th Armoured Division* (Stroud: Sutton, 1993)

—— *Churchill's Desert Rats: From Normandy to Berlin with the 7th Armoured Division* (Stroud: Sutton, 1994)

—— *The Fighting Wessex Wyverns: From Normandy to Bremerhaven with the 43rd Wessex Division* (Stroud, Gloucs: Sutton, 1994)

—— *Monty's Ironsides: From the Normandy Beaches to Bremen with 3rd Division* (Stroud: Sutton, 1995)

261

—— *Marching to the Sound of Gunfire: British Army Europe 1944–45* (Stroud: Sutton, 1996)

—— *The Polar Bears: From Normandy to the Relief of Holland with the 49th Division* (Stroud: Sutton, 1996)

D'Este, Carlo, *Decision in Normandy* (London: HarperCollins, 1983)

—— *Bitter Victory: The Battle for Sicily, July–August 1943* (London: Collins, 1988)

—— *Eisenhower: A Soldier's Life* (London: Weidenfeld & Nicolson, 2003)

Doubler, Michael, *Closing with the Enemy: How GIs Fought the War in Europe 1944–5* (Kansas: Kansas University Press, 1994)

Doyle, Peter and Bennett, Matthew R. (eds), *Fields of Battle: Terrain in Military History* (London: Kluwer, 2002)

Duncan, N. W., *79th Armoured Division – Hobo's Funnies* (Windsor: Profile, 1972)

Dyson, Stephen, *Tank Twins: East End Brothers in Arms 1943–1945* (London: Leo Cooper, 1995)

Ehrman, John, *Grand Strategy*, vols 5 and 6 (London: Her Majesty's Stationery Office, 1956)

Ellis, C. and Chamberlain, P. (eds), *Handbook on the British Army 1943* (London: Military Book Society, 1975)

Ellis, John, *Brute Force: Allied Strategy and Tactics in the Second World War* (London: Andre Deutsch, 1990)

—— *The Sharp End of War: The Fighting Man in World War Two* (London: Windrow & Greene, 1990 edn)

Ellis, L. F., *Victory in the West*, vol. I (London: Her Majesty's Stationery Office, 1962)

—— *Victory in the West*, vol. II (London: Her Majesty's Stationery Office, 1968)

Elstob, P., *Warriors for the Working Day* (London: Jonathan Cape, 1960)

English, John A., *The Canadian Army and the Normandy Campaign: A Study in the Failure in High Command* (Westport, CT: Praeger, 1991)

English, John A. and Gudmundsson, B., *On Infantry* (Westport, CT: Praeger, 1994)

Erskine, D., *The Scots Guards 1919–1945* (Edinburgh: W. Clowes, 1956)

Fitzgerald, D. J. L., *History of the Irish Guards in the Second World War* (Aldershot: Gale & Polden, 1952)

Fletcher, David, *Churchill Tank: Vehicle History and Specification* (London: Her Majesty's Stationery Office, 1983)

—— *Cromwell Tank: Vehicle History and Specification* (London: Her Majesty's Stationery Office, 1983)

—— *Vanguard of Victory – 79th Armoured Division* (London: Her Majesty's Stationery Office, 1984)

—— *Tiger! The Tiger Tank: A British View* (London, Her Majesty's Stationery Office, 1986)

—— *The Great Tank Scandal: British Armour in the Second World War – Part One* (London: Her Majesty's Stationery Office, 1989)

—— *The Universal Tank: British Armour in the Second World War – Part Two* (London: Her Majesty's Stationery Office, 1993)

—— *Mr Churchill's Tank – The British Infantry Tank Mark IV* (Atglen, PA: Schiffer, 1999)

Forbes, Patrick, *6th Guards Tank Brigade: The Story of the Guardsmen in Churchill Tanks* (London: Sampson Low, Marston, undated)

Ford, Roger, *The Sherman Tank* (London: Spellmount, 1999)

Forty, George, *Desert Rats at War* (London: Allan, 1975)

—— *M4 Sherman* (Poole, Dorset: Blandford, 1987)

—— *Tank Warfare in the Second World War: An Oral History* (London: Constable, 1988)

Forty, Jonathan, *Tanks in Detail: M3–M3A1–M3A3 – Stuart I to V* (Hersham: Ian Allan, 2002)

Fraser, D., *Alanbrooke* (London: Collins, 1982)

—— *And We Shall Shock Them* (London: Hodder & Stoughton, 1983)

French, David, *The British Way in Warfare 1688–2000* (London: Unwin Hyman, 1990)

—— *Raising Churchill's Army: The British Army and the War Against Germany 1919–1945* (Oxford: Oxford University Press, 2000)

Fuller, J. F. C., *Thunderbolts* (London: Skeffington, 1946)

Gelb, Norman, *Ike and Monty: Generals at War* (London: Constable, 1994)

Gill, R. and Groves, J. (eds), *Club Route in Europe: The Story of 30 Corps in the European Campaign* (Hanover: privately published, 1946)

Gooch, John, *Armies in Europe* (London: Routledge & Kegan Paul, 1980)

Gooch, John (ed.), *Decisive Campaigns of the Second World War* (London: Cass, 1990)

Gooderson, Ian, *Air Power at the Battlefront: Allied Close Air Support in Europe 1943–45* (London: Cass, 1998)

Graham, A., *Sharpshooters at War* (London: Sharpshooters Regimental Association, 1964)

Graham, Dominick, *The Price of Command: A Biography of General Guy Simonds* (Toronto: Stoddart, 1993)

Griffith, Paddy, *Forward into Battle: Fighting Tactics from Waterloo to Vietnam* (Chichester: Anthony Bird, 1981)

—— *Battle Tactics of the Western Front: The British Army's Art of Attack 1916–1918* (London: Yale University Press, 1994)

Grigg, P. James, *Prejudice and Judgement* (London: Jonathan Cape, 1948)

Grove, E., *World War Two Tanks* (London: Orbis, 1976)

Guderian, Heinz G., *From Normandy to the Ruhr with the 116th Panzer Division* (Bedford: Aberjona, 2001)

Gudgin, Peter, *Armoured Firepower: The Development of Tank Armament 1939–1945* (Stroud: Sutton, 1997)

Gudmundsson, B., *On Artillery* (Westport, CT: Praeger, 1993)

Guingand, Francis de, *Operation Victory* (London: Hodder & Stoughton, 1947)

—— *Generals at War* (London: Hodder & Stoughton, 1964)

Halle, A., and Demand, C., *Tanks: An Illustrated History of Fighting Vehicles* (London: Patrick Stephens, 1971)

Hamilton, Nigel, *Monty: Master of the Battlefield 1942–1944* (London: Hamish Hamilton, 1983)

—— *The Making of a General 1887–1942* (London: Hamish Hamilton, 1984)

—— *Monty: The Field Marshal* (London: Hamish Hamilton, 1986)

Hamilton, Stuart, *Armoured Odyssey: 8th Royal Tank Regiment in the Western Desert 1941–1942: Palestine, Syria, Egypt 1943–1944: Italy 1944–1945* (London: Tom Donovan, 1995),

Harris, J. P., *Men, Ideas and Tanks: British Military Thought and Armoured Forces 1903–1945* (Manchester: Manchester University Press, 1995)

Harris, J. P. and Toase, F. H. (eds), *Armoured Warfare* (London: Batsford, 1990)

Harrison, Gordon, *Cross Channel Attack* (Washington, DC: Center of Military History, 1951)

Hart, Russell A., *Clash of Arms: How the Allies Won in Normandy* (Boulder, CO: Rienner, 2001)

Hart, Stephen A., *Montgomery and Colossal Cracks: The 21st Army Group in Northwest Europe 1944–5* (Westport, CT: Praeger, 2000)

Hastings, Max, *Overlord: D-Day and the Battle for Normandy 1944* (London: Michael Joseph, 1984)

Hastings, R. H. W. S., *The Rifle Brigade in the Second World War* (Aldershot: Gale & Polden, 1950)

Hayward, Mark, *The Sherman Firefly* (Tiptree: Barbarossa Press, 2001)

Hills, Stuart, *By Tank into Normandy: A Memoir of the Campaign in Northwest Europe from D-Day to VE Day* (London: Cassell, 2002)

Hinsley, F. H., *British Intelligence in the Second World War*, vols 1–3 (London: Her Majesty's Stationery Office, 1979–90)

Hogg, Ian V., *British and American Artillery of World War Two* (London: Arms and Armour Press, 1978)

—— *Tank Killing: Anti-tank Warfare by Men and Machines* (London: Sidgwick & Jackson, 1996)

Holmes, Richard, *War Walks* (London: BBC, 1996)

—— *The Firing Line* (London: Jonathan Cape, 1985)

Horne, Alastair with David Montgomery, *The Lonely Leader: Monty 1944–1945* (London: Macmillan, 1994)

Horne, Alastair and Montgomery, Brian, *The Lonely Leader: Monty 1944–45* (London: Macmillan, 1994)

Horrocks, Brian, *A Full Life* (London: Collins, 1960)

—— *Corps Commander* (London: Sidgwick & Jackson, 1977)

Houldsworth, D., *One Day I'll Tell You* (Marlborough: Heraldry Today, 1994)

How, J. J., *Normandy: The British Breakout* (London: William Kimber, 1981)

—— *Hill 112: Cornerstone of the Normandy Campaign* (London: William Kimber, 1984)

Howe, F., *Seizing the Initiative in the West (the US Army in World War Two)* (Washington: Office of the Chief of Military History, 1957)

Hunnicut, R. P., *Sherman: A History of the American Medium Tank* (Novato, CA: Presidio, 1994 edn)

Irving, David, *The War between the Generals* (London: Allen Lane, 1981)

Isby, David C. (ed.), *Fighting the Invasion: The German Army at D-Day* (London: Greenhill, 2000)

—— *Fighting in Normandy: The German Army from D-Day to Villers Bocage* (London: Greenhill, 2001)

Jackson, G. S., *Operations of 8th Corps: Normandy to the River Rhine* (London: St Clements Press, 1948)

Jackson, W., *The Mediterranean and the Middle East – volume IV, parts II and III* (London: Her Majesty's Stationery Office, 1987–88)

Jamar, K., *With the Tanks of the 1st Polish* (Hengelo: H. L. Smith & Son, 1946)

Jary, Sydney, *18 Platoon* (Bristol: Sydney Jary, 1987)

Jarymowycz, Roman J., *Tank Tactics: From Normandy to Lorraine* (Boulder, CO: Rienner, 2001)

Johnson, David E., *Fast Tanks and Heavy Bombers: Innovation in the US Army 1917–1945* (London: Cornell University Press, 1998)

Jones, Keith, *Sixty Four Days of a Normandy Summer: With a Tank Unit after D-Day* (London: Hale, 1990)

Joslen, H. F., *Orders of Battle, volume I: UK and Colonial Formations and Units in the Second World War 1939–1945* (London: Her Majesty's Stationery Office, 1960)

Keegan, John, *Six Armies in Normandy: From D-Day to the Liberation of Paris* (Harmondsworth: Penguin, 1983)

Keegan, John (ed.), *Churchill's Generals* (London: Weidenfield & Nicolson, 1991)

Kitching, George, *Mud and Green Fields: The Memoirs of Major General George Kitching* (St Catherine's, Ontario: Vanwell, 1993)

Knight, Peter, *The 59th Division* (London: Frederick Muller, 1954)

Lamb, Richard, *Montgomery in Europe 1943–1945: Success or Failure?* (London: Buchan & Enright, 1983)

Larson, R. H., *The British Army and the Theory of Armoured Warfare 1918–1940* (London: Associated University Press, 1984)

Leakey, Rea with Forty George , *Leakey's Luck: A Tank Commander with Nine Lives* (Stroud: Sutton, 1999)

Lefèvre, Eric, *Panzers in Normandy: Then and Now* (London: Battle of Britain International, 1983)

Lehmann, Rudolf and Tiemann, Ralf, *The Leibstandarte IV/1* (Winnipeg: J. J. Federowicz, 1993)

Lewin, Ronald, *Montgomery as Military Commander* (London: Batsford, 1971)

—— *Man of Armour: A Study of Lt-General Vyvyan Pope and the Development of Armoured Warfare* (London: Leo Cooper, 1976)

—— *Ultra Goes to War: The Secret Story* (London: Hutchinson, 1978)

Liddell Hart, Basil, *The Other Side of the Hill: Germany's Generals – Their Rise and Fall with their Own Account of Military Events* (London: Cassell, rev. edn 1951 [1948])

—— *The Tanks: The History of the Royal Tank Regiment and its Predecessors Heavy Branch Machine Gun Corps and Royal Tank Corps*, 2 vols (London, Cassell, 1959)

—— *History of the Second World War* (London: Cassell, 1970)

Liddell Hart, Basil (ed.), *The Rommel Papers* (London: Collins, 1953)

Luck, Hans von, *Panzer Commander: The Memoirs of Colonel Hans von Luck* (London: Cassell, 1989)

Luther, Craig, *Blood and Honor: The History of the 12th SS Panzer Division 'Hitler Youth', 1943–1945* (San Jose, CA: Bender, 1987)

Mackenzie, J. J. G. and Reid, Brian Holden (eds), *The British Army and the Operational Level of War* (London: Triservice Press, 1989)

Mackenzie, S. P., *Politics and Military Morale: Current Affairs and Citizenship Education in the British Army 1914–1950* (Oxford: Oxford, University Press)

Macksey, Kenneth, *Armoured Crusader: A Biography of Major General Sir Percy Hobart* (London: Hutchinson, 1967)

—— *Tank Force: Allied Armour in the Second World War* (London: Pan, 1970)

—— *Tank Tactics, 1939–1945* (New Malden: Almark, 1976)

—— *The Tank Pioneers* (London: Jane's, 1981)

—— *A History of the Royal Armoured Corps and its Predecessors 1914–1970* (Beaminster: Newtown, 1983)

Macleod Ross, R., *The Business of Tanks 1933–1945* (Ilfracombe: Arthur H. Stockwell, 1945)

Maczek, Stanislaw, *Avec mes Blindés* (Paris: Presses de la Cité, 1967)

—— *La Premiere Division Blindée Polonaise au Combat – Journal de Marche du 7 Aout au 9 Septembre 1944* (privately published, contemporary document, Mont Ormel Museum)

Marie, Henri *et al.*, *Villers Bocage: Tigres au Combat – Le Champ de Bataille* (Bayeux: Heimdal, 1993)

Marshall, S. L. A., *Men against Fire* (New York: William Morrow, 1947)

Martel, Giffard Le Quesne, *Our Armoured Forces* (London: Faber & Faber, 1945)

Maule, Henry, *Caen: The Brutal Battle and the Breakout from Normandy* (London: Purnell, 1976)

McInnes, Colin and Sheffield, Gary (eds), *Warfare in the Twentieth Century: Theory and Practice* (London: Unwin Hyman, 1988)

McKee, Alexander, *Caen: Anvil of Victory* (London: Souvenir, 1964)

McNish, Robin, *Iron Division: The History of the 3rd Division* (London: Allan, 1978)

Mearsheimer, John, *Liddell Hart and the Weight of History* (London: Cornell University Press, 1988)

Mellenthin, F. W. von, *Panzer Battles* (London: Ballentine, 1985)

Messerschmidt, Manfred, *Nazi Political Aims and German Military Law in World War Two* (Kingston, Ontario: Royal Military College of Canada, 1981)

Meyer, Hubert, *The History of the 12th SS Panzer Division Hitlerjugend* (Winnipeg, Manitoba: J. J. Fedorowicz, 1994)

Meyer, Kurt, *Grenadiers* (Winnipeg, Manitoba: J. J. Federowicz, 1994)

Miller, Russell, *Nothing Less than Victory: The Oral History of D-Day* (London: Michael Joseph, 1993)

Millett, Allan and Murray, Williamson (eds), *Military Effectiveness, vol. III: The Second World War* (London: Unwin Hyman, 1988)

Molony, C. J. *et al.*, *The Mediterranean and the Middle East, vols V and VI, part 1* (London: Her Majesty's Stationery Office, 1973, 1984)

Montgomery, Bernard L., *Normandy to the Baltic* (London: Hutchinson, 1947)

—— *The Memoirs of Field Marshal the Viscount Montgomery of Alamein* (London: Collins, 1958)

Moore, William, *Panzer Bait: With the 3rd Royal Tank Regiment 1940–1944* (London: Leo Cooper, 1991)

Moorehead, Alan, *Montgomery: A Biography* (London: Hamish Hamilton, 1946)

Morgan, Frederick E., *Overture to Overlord* (London: Hodder & Stoughton, 1950)

Murray, G. E. Patrick, *Eisenhower versus Montgomery: The Continuing Debate* (Westport, CT: Praeger, 1996)

Murray, Williamson and Millett, Allan R., *A War to Be Won: Fighting the Second World War* (Cambridge, MT: Cambridge University Press, 2000)

Myatt, F., *The British Infantry 1660–1945: The Evolution of a Fighting Force* (Poole: Blandford, 1983)

Neillands, Robin, *The Desert Rats: 7th Armoured Division 1940–1945* (London: Weidenfeld & Nicolson, 1991)

—— *The Battle of Normandy 1944* (London: Cassell, 2002)

Nicolson, Nigel, *Alex: The Life of Field Marshal Earl Alexander of Tunis* (London: Weidenfeld & Nicolson, 1973)

North, John, *North-West Europe 1944–45* (London: Her Majesty's Stationery Office, 1953)

Ogorkiewicz, R. M., *Armoured Forces: A History of Armoured Forces and their Vehicles* (London: Arms & Armour Press, 1970)

Overy, Richard, *Why the Allies Won* (London: Jonathan Cape, 1995)

Parker, H. M. D., *Manpower: A Study in Wartime Policy and Administration* (London: Her Majesty's Stationery Office, 1957)

Pemberton, A. L., *The Development of Artillery Tactics and Equipment – The Second World War 1939–45* (London: War Office, 1951)

Perrett, Bryan, *Through Mud and Blood: Infantry – Tank Operations in World War Two* (London: Robert Hale, 1975)

—— *Churchill Infantry Tank 1941–51* (London: Osprey, 1993)

—— *Seize and Hold: Master Strokes on the Battlefield* (London: Arms & Armour Press, 1994)

Perry, F. W., *The Commonwealth Armies: Manpower and Organisation in Two World Wars* (Manchester: Manchester University Press, 1988)

Place, Timothy Harrison, *Military Training in the British Army 1940–44: From Dunkirk to D-Day* (London: Cass, 2000)

Playfair, I. S. O., *The Mediterranean and the Middle East*, vols I–IV (London: Her Majesty's Stationery Office, 1954–66)

Postan, M. M., Hay, D. and Scott, J. D., *Design and Development of Weapons: Studies in Government and Industrial Organisation* (London: Her Majesty's Stationery Office, 1964)

Prior, Robin and Wilson, Trevor, *Command on the Western Front: The Career of Sir Henry Rawlinson* (Oxford: Oxford University Press, 1992)

Pyman, Harold E., *Call to Arms* (London: Leo Cooper, 1971)

Reid, Brian Holden, *J. F. C. Fuller: Military Thinker* (London: Macmillan, 1987)

—— *Military Power: Land Warfare Theory and Practice* (London: Cass, 1997)

—— *Studies in British Military Thought: Debates with Fuller and Liddell Hart* (Lincoln, NE: University of Nebraska Press, 1998)

Reynolds, Michael, *Steel Inferno: I SS Panzer Corps in Normandy* (London: Spellmount, 1997)

—— *Sons of the Reich: II SS Panzer Corps* (London: Spellmount, 2002)

Richardson, C. M., *Send for Freddie: The Story of Monty's Chief of Staff* (London: William Kimber, 1987)

Richardson, F. M., *Fighting Spirit: A Study of Psychological Factors in War* (London: Leo Cooper, 1978)

Ripley, Tim, *The Wehrmacht: The German Army in World War Two 1939–45* (London: Fitzroy Dearborn, 2003)

Ritgen, Helmut, *The Western Front 1944: Memoirs of a Panzer Lehr Officer* (Winnipeg, Manitoba: J. J. Fedorowicz, 1995)

Roberts, G. P. B., *From the Desert to the Baltic* (London: William Kimber, 1987)

Rosse, Earl of, and Hill, E. R. H., *The Story of the Guards Armoured Division* (London: Geoffrey Bles, 1956)

Ryan, Cornelius, *The Longest Day* (London: Gollancz, 1960)

—— *A Bridge Too Far* (London: Hamish Hamilton, 1974)

Ryder, Rowland, *Oliver Leese* (London: Hamish Hamilton, 1987)

Salmond, J. M., *History of the 51st Highland Division 1939–1953* (Edinburgh: Pentland, 1953)

Sandars, J., *The Sherman Tank in British Service 1942–1945* (London: Osprey, 1982 [1980])

—— *British Guards Armoured Division 1941–1945* (London: Osprey, 1979)

Saunders, Tim, *Hill 112: Battles of the Odon, 1944* (Barnsley: Pen & Sword, 2001)

—— *Operation Epsom: Battleground Normandy* (Barnsley: Pen & Sword, 2003)

Schneider, Wolfgang, *Panzertaktik: German Small-Unit Armor Tactics* (Winnipeg, Manitoba: J. J. Fedorowicz, 2000)

Shulman, Milton, *Defeat in the West* (London: Secker & Warburg, 1947)

Simpson, Gary L., *Tiger Ace: The Life Story of Panzer Commander Michael Wittman* (Atglen, PA: Schiffer, 1994)

Sims, J., *Arnhem Spearhead: A Private Soldier's Story* (London: Imperial War Museum; Seeley, 1978)

Sixsmith, E. K. G., *British Generalship in the Twentieth Century* (London: Arms & Armour Press, 1970)

Snowie, J. Allan, *Bloody Buron: The Battle of Buron, Caen, 8 July 1944* (Erin: Boston Mills, 1984)

Speidel, Hans, *We Defended Normandy* (London: Herbert Jenkins, 1951)

Stacey, Charles C. P., *The Victory Campaign: The Operations in Northwest Europe 1944–1945* (Ottawa: Queen's Printer, 1962)

Stacey, C. P., *The Official History of the Canadian Army in the Second World War*, vol. III (Ottawa: Queen's Printer, 1960)

Stokes, Richard R., *Some Amazing Tank Facts* (Dugdale, 1945)

Stone, John, *The Tank Debate: Armour and the Anglo-American Tradition* (London: Harwood, 2000)

Taylor, Daniel, *Villers Bocage through the Lens* (London: Battle of Britain International, 1999)

Thompson, R. W., *Montgomery the Field Marshal* (London: Allen & Unwin, 1969)

Thornburn, Ned, *The 4th King's Shropshire Light Infantry* (King's Shropshire Light Infantry Museum Trust, 1990)

Tout, Ken, *Tank! 40 Hours of Combat, August 1944* (London: Robert Hale, 1985)

—— *Tanks Advance! Normandy to the Netherlands* (London: Hale, 1987)

—— *A Fine Night for Tanks: The Road to Falaise* (Stroud: Sutton, 1998)

—— *The Bloody Battle for Tilly* (Stroud: Sutton, 2000)

—— *Roads to Falaise: Cobra and Goodwood Reassessed* (Stroud: Sutton, 2002)

Tuker, Francis, *Approach to Battle – A Commentary: Eighth Army, November 1941 to May 1943* (London: Cassell, 1963)

Van Creveld, Martin, *Fighting Power: German and US Army Performance 1939–1945* (London: Arms & Armour Press, 1983)

Verney, Gerald L., *The Desert Rats: The 7th Armoured Division in World War II* (London: Hutchinson, 1954)

—— *The Guards Armoured Division: A Short History* (London: Hutchinson, 1955)

Walther, Herbert, *The 12th SS Armored Division* (Atglen, PA: Schiffer, 1989)

Warner, Philip, *Horrocks: The General Who Led from the Front* (London: Hamish Hamilton, 1984)

Weeks, John, *Men against Tanks: A History of Anti-tank Warfare* (London: David & Charles, 1975)

Weigley, Russell F., *Eisenhower's Lieutenants: The Campaigns of France and Germany 1944–5* (London: Sidgwick & Jackson, 1981)

Weinberg, G. L., *A World at Arms: A Global History of World War Two* (Cambridge: Cambridge University Press, 1994)

Whitaker, Denis, and Whitaker, Sheila with Copp, Terry, *Victory at Falaise: The Soldiers' Story* (Toronto, Ontario: HarperCollins, 2000)

White, B. T., *Tanks and Other Armoured Fighting Vehicles 1942–1945* (Poole: Blandford, 1975)

Whitelaw, W., *The Whitelaw Memoirs* (London: Headline, 1990)

Wilmot, Chester, *The Struggle for Europe* (London: Collins, 1952)

Wilson, A., *Flamethrower* (London: privately published, 1974)

Wright, Patrick, *Tank: The Progress of a Monstrous War Machine* (London: Faber & Faber, 2000)

Zaloga, Stephen, *Sherman Medium Tank 1942–1945* (London: Osprey, 1982)

—— *M3 and M5 Stuart Light Tank 1940–1945* (London: Osprey, 1999)

Zaloga, Stephen and Sarson, Peter, *Sherman Medium Tank 1942–1945* (London: Osprey, 1978)

Zetterling, Niklas, *Normandy 1944: German Military Organization, Combat Power and Organizational Effectiveness* (Winnipeg, Manitoba: J. J. Federowicz, 2000)

Articles and chapters

Badsey, Stephen, 'Faction in the British Army: Its Impact on 21st Army Group Operations in Autumn 1944', *The War Studies Journal*, vol. 1, no. 1, 1995

—— 'Terrain as a Factor in the Battle of Normandy', in Peter Doyle and Matthew R. Bennett (eds), *Fields of Battle: Terrain in Military History* (London: Kluwer, 2002)

Bartov, Omer, 'Indoctrination and Motivation in the Wehrmacht: The Importance of the Unquantifiable', *Journal of Strategic Studies*, vol. 9, no. 1, March 1986

Bechtold, Michael, 'The Development of an Unbeatable Combination: US Close Air Support in Normandy', *Canadian Military History*, vol. 8, no. 1, 1999

Blumenson, Martin, 'The Most Over-rated General of World War Two', *Armor*, May–June 1962

Brown, John S., 'Colonel Trevor N. Dupuy and the Mythos of Wehrmacht Superiority: A Reconsideration', *Military Affairs*, vol. 50, 1986

—— 'The Wehrmacht Myth Revisited: A Challenge to Colonel Trevor N. Dupuy', *Military Affairs*, vol. 51, 1987

Brown, Peter, 'What's in a Nomenclature?', *Tracklink: The Magazine of the Friends of the Tank Museum*, no. 58, May 2003

Chapman, O. E., 'The Influence of the Late War on Tank Design', *Journal of the Royal United Services Institute*, vol. 96, 1951

Copp, Terry, '"No Lack of Rational Speed": 1st Canadian Army Operations, September 1944', *Journal of Canadian Studies*, vol. 16, nos. 3 and 4, 1981

—— 'Scientists and the Art of War: Operational Research in 21 Army Group', *Journal of the Royal United Services Institute*, vol. 136, no. 4, 1991

—— Counter Mortar Operational Research in 21 Army Group', *Canadian Military History*, vol. 3, no. 2, 1994

—— '"If this war isn't over, and pretty damn soon, there'll be nobody left, in this old platoon..." First Canadian Army, February–March 1945', in Paul Addison and Angus Calder (eds), *Time to Kill: The Soldier's Experience of War in the West 1939–1945* (London: Pimlico, 1997)

Corkhill, W. G. R., 'The Effectiveness of Conventional Field Branch Artillery in General War in Northwest Europe', *Journal of the Royal Artillery*, vol. 94, no. 2, September 1967

Currie, David D., 'Story in his Own Words', *After the Battle: The Battle of the Falaise Pocket*, no. 8, 1982

Dick, C. J., 'The Goodwood Concept – Situating the Appreciation', *Journal of the Royal United Services Institute*, vol. 127, 1982

Dunn, R. H. W., 'Reminiscences of a Regimental Soldier: SP Guns in Normandy', *Journal of the Royal Artillery*, vol. 75, no. 2, April 1948

Dupuy, Trevor N., 'Mythos or Verity? The Quantified Judgement Model and German Combat Effectiveness', *Military Affairs*, vol. 50, October 1986

Evans, Christopher, 'The Fighter-Bomber in the Normandy Campaign: The Role of 83 Group', *Canadian Military History*, vol. 8, no. 1, 1999

Foulds, Tony, 'In Support of the Canadians: A British Anti-tank Regiment's First Five Weeks in Normandy', *Canadian Military History*, vol. 7, no. 2 1998

French, David, 'Colonel Blimp and the British Army: British Divisional Commanders in the War against Germany 1939–1945', *English Historical Review*, vol. CXI, November 1996

—— '"Tommy is no soldier": The Morale of Second in Normandy, June–August 1944', in Brian Holden Reid, *Military Power: Land Warfare Theory and Practice* (London: Cass, 1997)

Fuller, J. F. C., 'Training for Armoured Warfare', *Harper's Magazine*, March 1943

Gat, Azar, 'Liddell Hart's Theory of Armoured Warfare: Revising the Revisionists', *Journal of Strategic Studies*, vol. 19, no. 1, March 1996

Gooderson, Ian, 'Heavy and Medium Bombers: How Successful Were They in the Close Air Support Role during World War Two?', *Journal of Strategic Studies*, vol. 15, no. 3, September 1993

Grodzinski, John, 'Kangaroos at War', *Canadian Military History*, vol. 4, no. 3, 1995

Harris, J. P., 'The Myth of Blitzkrieg – Debate', *War in History*, vol. 2, no. 3, 1995

Hart, Russell A., 'Feeding Mars: The Role of Logistics in the German Defeat in Normandy 1944', *War in History*, vol. 3, no. 4, November 1996

Hart, Stephen A., 'Montgomery, Morale, Casualty Conservation and "Colossal Cracks": 21st Army Group's Operational Technique in Northwest Europe 1944–1945', *Journal of Strategic Studies*, vol. 19, no. 4, December 1996

Jarymowycz, Roman J., 'Der Gegenangriff vor Verrières: German Counterattacks during *Operation Spring*, 25–6 July 1944', *Canadian Military History*, vol. 2, no. 1, 1993

—— 'Canadian Armour in Normandy: *Operation Totalize* and the Quest for Operational Manoeuvre', *Canadian Military History*, vol. 7, no. 2, 1998

Keegan, John, 'Towards a Theory of Combat Motivation', in Paul Addison and Angus Calder (eds), *Time to Kill: The Soldier's Experience of War in the West 1939–1945* (London: Pimlico, 1997)

Kiszely, John, 'The British Army and Approaches to Warfare since 1945', *Journal of Strategic Studies*, vol. 19, no. 4, December 1996

Kohn, Richard H., 'The Scholarship on World War Two: Its Present Condition and Future Possibilities', *Journal of Military History*, vol. 55, no. 3, July 1991

Lossow, W. von, 'Mission Type Tactics versus Order Type Tactics', *Military Review*, vol. 57, June 1977

Luttwak, E. N., 'The Operational Level of War', *International Security*, vol. 5, no. 3, winter 1980–81

Martel, G. Le Q., 'Gun versus Armour', *Army Quarterly*, October 1944

McAndrew, William, 'Fire or Movement? Canadian Tactical Doctrine, Sicily – 1943', *Military Affairs*, vol. 51, no. 3, 1987

Montgomery, Bernard L., 'Twenty-First Army Group in the Campaign in North-West Europe 1944–45', *Journal of the Royal United Services Institute*, vol. 90, November 1945

Peaty, John, 'Myth, Reality and Carlo D'Este', *War Studies Journal*, vol. 1, no. 2, Spring 1996

Perrun, Jody, 'Best Laid Plans: Guy Simonds and Operation Totalize, 7–20 August 1944', *Journal of Military History*, vol. 67, no. 1, January 2003

Place, Timothy Harrison, 'British Perceptions of the Tactics of the German Army, 1938–40', *Intelligence and National Security*, vol. 9, no. 3, 1994

Powers, Stephen T., 'The Battle of Normandy: The Lingering Controversy', *Journal of Military History*, vol. 56, no. 3, July 1992

Rippe, S. T., 'Leadership, Firepower and Manoeuvre: The British and the Germans', *Military Review*, October 1985

Rockingham, J. M., 'The Royal Hamilton Light Infantry at Verrières Ridge', *Canadian Military History*, vol. 2, no. 1, 1993

Rose, E. P. F and Pareyn, C., 'British Applications of Military Geography for *Operation Overlord* and the Battle of Normandy, France 1944', in J. R. Underwood and P. L. Guth (eds), *Military Geology in War and Peace – Reviews in Engineering Geology*, vol. XIII (Boulder, CO: Geological Society of America, 1998)

'Sarkie', 'Anti-tank Artillery – Has It a future?', *Journal of Royal Artillery*, July 1944

Samuels, Martin, '*Operation Goodwood:* The Caen Carve-Up', *British Army Review*, vol. 96, December 1990

Scott, G. L., 'British and German Operational Styles in World War Two', *Military Review*, vol. 65, October 1985

Sheffield, Gary, 'The Shadow of the Somme: The Influence of the First World War on British Soldiers' Perceptions and Behaviour in the Second World War', in Paul Addison and Angus Calder (eds), *Time to Kill: The Soldier's Experience of War in the West 1939–45* (London: Collins, 1997)

Shills, E. and Janowitz, M., 'Cohesion and Disintegration in the Wehrmacht in World War Two', *Public Opinion Quarterly*, vol. 12, 1948

Spiller, Roger S., 'S. L. A. Marshall and the Ratio of Fire 1, no. 4', *Journal of the Royal United Services Institute*, 1988

Tuker, Major-General F. S., 'The Preparation of Infantry for Battle', *Army Quarterly*, October 1944

Vogel, Robert, 'Tactical Air Power in Normandy: Some Thoughts on the Interdiction Plan', *Canadian Military History*, vol. 3, no. 1, 1994

Wilson, T. N. F., 'The Role of Infantry', *Journal of the Royal United Services Institute*, vol. 89, February 1944

Young, Captain W. R., 'Artillery Support for Tanks', *Army Quarterly*, November 1942

INDEX

INDEX